D1000481

Language and Literacy from an Educational Perspective

Volume I
Language Studies

E815 central course team

L. John Chapman
Janet Maybin
Neil Mercer
Harold Rosen

Language and Literacy from an Educational Perspective

Volume I: Language Studies

A reader edited by Neil Mercer
at the Open University

OPEN UNIVERSITY PRESS
Milton Keynes · Philadelphia

Open University Press
Open University Educational Enterprises Limited
12 Cofferidge Close
Stony Stratford
Milton Keynes MK11 1BY, England

and
242 Cherry
Street
Philadelphia, PA 19106, USA

First Published 1988

British Library Cataloguing in Publication Data
Language and literacy from an educational
perspective.
Vol. 1, Language studies : a reader
1. Language acquisition
I. Mercer, Neil
401′.9 P118

ISBN 0–335–10275–1

ISBN 0–335–15553–7 Pbk

Library of Congress Cataloging-in-Publication Data

Language and literacy from an educational perspective.
Contents: v. 1. Language studies.
Complied by the E815 Course Team.
1. Language and languages. 2. Literacy.
3. Language and education. I. Mercer, Neil.
II. Open University. E815 Course Team.
P106.L314 1987 400 87–22046

ISBN 0–335–10275–1 (v. 1)

ISBN 0–335–15553–7 (pbk. : v. 1)

Project management: Clarke Williams
Printed in Great Britain

Contents

Preface

The study of spoken and written language — its nature, use and development — is a field in which variety flourishes. It benefits from the involvement of linguists, psychologists, sociologists, anthropologists and philosophers, and there are different perspectives on language to be found within each of those disciplines. In this volume, I have tried to represent not only this variety, but also the healthy climate of conflict and controversy that has stimulated activity in this field in recent years.

The articles in this book, the first of two volumes of *Language and Literacy from an Educational Perspective*, have also been chosen because they represent research about spoken and written language that has implications for educational theory and practice. In the second volume, entitled *In Schools*, matters of educational practice are dealt with more directly. Both volumes are primarily designed to serve the needs of the Open University course *E815 Language and Literacy*, which is one module of the university's taught MA in Education. These books should therefore provide suitable reading for all postgraduate students of language in education, and especially those who are also practising teachers.

For the sake of brevity, most of the articles included are shorter forms of their originals (editorial cuts are indicated thus: [. . .]). I am very grateful for the help of Harold Rosen, John Chapman and Janet Maybin in preparing this collection of readings.

Neil Mercer

Acknowledgements

All possible care has been taken to trace ownership of the material included in this volume, and Open University Press would like to make grateful acknowledgement for permission to reproduce it here.

1.1 R. Williams (1977). 'Language', *Marxism and Literature* reprinted by permission of Oxford University Press, pp. 21–44.

1.2 J.P.B. Allen and H. G. Widdowson (1975). 'The Edinburgh Course in Applied Linguistics' by J.P.B. Allen and S. Pit Corder (Book 2 : *Papers in Applied Linguistics*) reprinted by permission of Oxford University Press, pp. 45–97.

1.3 J. Culler (1976). 'Saussure's Theory of Language', *Saussure* reprinted by permission of Peter Owen, pp. 18–52.

1.4 T.A. Van Dijk (1985). 'Introduction: Discourse Analysis as a New Cross-Discipline', *Handbook of Discourse Analysis* edited by T.A. Van Dijk, Volume 1, pp. 1–10. Copyright © 1985 by Academic Press, Inc. (London) Ltd.

1.5 M.M. Bakhtin (1981). 'Discourse in the Novel', *The Dialogic Imagination*, University of Texas Press, pp. 287–422.

1.6 R. Hasan (1985). 'A Framework for the Study of Verbal Art', *Linguistics, Language and Verbal Art*, Deakin University Press, Australia, pp. 90–119.

1.7 R. Hudson (1982). 'Some Issues over Which Linguistics Can Agree', *Linguistics and the Teacher* edited by R. Carter, Routledge and Kegan Paul PLC, pp. 54–64.

2.1 J. Bruner (1985). 'Vygotsky: A Historical and Conceptual Perspective', *Culture, Communication and Cognition: Vygotskyan Perspectives* edited by J.V. Wertsch, Cambridge University Press, pp. 21–34.

2.2 Reprinted by permission of the publishers from *Actual Minds, Possible Worlds* by Jerome S. Bruner, Cambridge, Mass.: Harvard University Press, Copyright © 1986 by The President and Fellows of Harvard College.

2.3 B. Mayor (1987). Commissioned for this collection.

3.1 J.J. Gumperze and J. Cook-Gumperze (1982). 'Introduction: Language and the Communication of Social Identity', *Language and Social Identity*, edited by J.J. Gumperze, Cambridge University Press, pp. 1–21.

3.2 W. Labov (1969). 'The Logic of Nonstandard English', Copyright © 1969 Georgetown University Press, Washington D.C.

3.3 J. Honey (1983). Excerpt from *The Language Trap : Race, Class and Standard English in British Schools*, National Council for Educational Standards.

3.4 J.R. Edwards (1983). 'A Review of the Language Trap', *Journal of Language and Social Psychology* Volume 2, No. 1, pp. 67–76.

3.5 J. French and P. French (1984). 'Sociolinguistics and Gender Divisions', *World Yearbook of Education 1984 : Women and Education*, Kogan Page, pp. 52–63.

4.1 G.A. Miller (1972). 'Reflections on the Conference', *Language by Ear and by Eye* edited by J.F. Kavanagh and I.G. Mattingly, MIT Press, Cambridge, Mass., pp. 373–381.

4.2 D.R. Olson (1984). ' "See! Jumping!" Some Oral Language Antecedents of Literacy', *Awakening to Literacy* edited by H. Goelman, A.A. Obert and F. Smith, Heinemann Educational Books, Portsmouth, U.S.A., pp. 185–192.

4.3 B. Street (1984). 'The Autonomous Model : I Literacy and Rationality', *Literacy in Theory and Practice*, Cambridge University Press, pp. 19–31.

4.4 S. Scribner and M. Cole (1981). 'Unpackaging Literacy', *Writing: The Nature, Development and Teaching of Written Communication* edited by M.F. Whiteman, Lawrence Erlbaum Associates, New Jersey, U.S.A., pp. 71–87.

4.5 W.H. Teale and E. Sulzby (1986). 'Introduction : Emergent Literacy as a Perspective for Examining How Young Children Become Writers and Readers', *Emergent Literacy : Writing and Reading*, Ablex, Norwood, New Jersey.

SECTION I

The Language System

Introduction

The Articles in this section have been chosen to provide a historical perspective on the formal study of language and also to reflect the breadth of this field of study. In the first, Raymond Williams shows how different conceptions of the nature of language have been associated with particular conceptions of human social existence. In the second, Allen and Widdowson concentrate on the study of *grammar*. They outline some of the most influential varieties of grammar, past and present, and point to the strengths and weaknesses of each in turn.

The article which follows, by Jonathan Culler, presents and explains major concepts from the theory of language of Ferdinand de Saussure (1857–1913), one of the founding fathers of linguistics whose influence is still felt strongly today. It is a remarkable thought that we might have missed the full benefit of Saussure's ideas but for the efforts of his former students, from whose lecture notes his *Cours de Linguistique Générale* was compiled and published three years after his death.

The fourth article, by Teun van Dijk, reviews the history and current state of a fast-developing field of language study, the 'new cross-discipline' of *discourse analysis*. This is followed by an essay by the Russian scholar M.M. Bakhtin, whose work (first published in the 1920s) has re-emerged as a powerful contemporary influence on the study of discourse. In it, he discusses the inherently diverse nature of language in use, which he refers to as *heteroglossia*.

Like Bakhtin, the author of the sixth article is engaged in a linguistic analysis of literary texts—the kind of language both writers call 'verbal art'. Ruqaiya Hasan is a linguist who has done much to advance the study of textual structures in recent years. In accord with Bakhtin, she offers a framework for the analysis of literary texts which is based on the principle that literature is no less amenable to linguistic analysis than any other form of language in use.

The final article brings us back to broader issues. In it, Richard Hudson uses the results of a survey of British linguists to show the extent of agreement on matters of principle and practice which exists in the contemporary field of language study.

1.1 Language

R. Williams

Source: Extracts from Williams, R. (1977) 'Language'. In *Marxism and Literature*. Oxford: Oxford University Press, pp. 21–44.

A definition of language is always, implicitly or explicitly, a definition of human beings in the world. The received major categories – 'world', 'reality', 'nature,' 'human' – may be counterposed or related to the category 'language', but it is now a commonplace to observe that all categories, including the category 'language', are themselves constructions in language, and can thus only with an effort, and within a particular system of thought, be separated from language for relational inquiry. [. . .]

[. . .] The major emphasis on language as activity began in the eighteenth century, in close relation to the idea of men having made their own society, which we have seen as a central element in the new concept of 'culture'. In the previously dominant tradition, through all its variations, 'language' and 'reality' had been decisively separated, so that philosophical inquiry was from the beginning an inquiry into the connections between these apparently separate orders. The pre-Socratic unity of the *logos*, in which language was seen as at one with the order of the world and of nature, with divine and human law, and with reason, had been decisively broken and in effect forgotten. The radical distinction between 'language' and 'reality', as between 'consciousness' and 'the material world', corresponding to actual and practical divisions between 'mental' and 'physical' activity, had become so habitual that serious attention seemed naturally concentrated on the exceptionally complicatedly consequent relations and connections. Plato's major inquiry into language (in the *Cratylus*) was centred on the problem of the correctness of *naming*, in which the interrelation of 'word' and 'thing' can be seen to originate either in 'nature' or in 'convention'. Plato's solution was in effect the foundation of idealist thought: there is an intermediate but constitutive realm, which is neither 'word' nor 'thing' but 'form', 'essence' or 'idea'. The investigation of either 'language' or 'reality' was then always, at root, an investigation of these constitutive (metaphysical) forms.

Yet, given this basic assumption, far-reaching inquiries into the uses of language could be undertaken in particular and specialized ways. Language as a way of indicating reality could be studied as *logic*. Language as an accessible segment of reality, especially in its fixed forms in writing, could be studied as *grammar*, in the sense of its formal and 'external' shape. Finally, within the distinction between language and reality, language could be conceived as an *instrument* used by men for specific and distinguishable purposes, and these could be studied in *rhetoric* and in the associated *poetics*. Through prolonged academic and scholastic development, these three great branches of language study — *logic*, *grammar* and *rhetoric* — though formally associated in the medieval *trivium*, became specific and eventually separated disciplines. Thus, though they made major practical advances, they either foreclosed examination of the form of the basic distinction between 'language' and 'reality', or determined the grounds, and especially the terms, in which such an examination might be made.

This is notably the case with the important medieval concept of *sign*, which has been so remarkably readopted in modern linguistic thought. 'Sign', from Latin *signum*, a mark or token, is intrinsically a concept based on a distinction between 'language' and 'reality'. It is an interposition between 'word' and 'thing' that repeats the Platonic interposition of 'form', 'essence' or 'idea', but now in accessible linguistic terms. Thus in Buridan[1] 'natural signs' are the universal mental counterparts of reality and these are matched, by convention, with the 'artificial signs', which are physical sounds or letters. Given this starting-point, important investigations of the activity of language (but not of language as an activity) could be undertaken: for example, the remarkable speculative grammars of medieval thought, in which the power of sentences and of the modes of construction which underlay and complicated simple empirical notions of 'naming' was described and investigated. Meanwhile, however, the *trivium* itself, and especially grammar and rhetoric, moved into relatively formal, though immensely learned, demonstrations of the properties of a given body of 'classical' written material. What was later to be known as 'literary study' and from the early seventeenth century as 'criticism', developed from this powerful, prestigious and limited mode.

Yet the whole question of the distinctions between 'language' and 'reality' was eventually forced into consciousness, initially in a surprising way. Descartes, in reinforcing the distinction and making it more precise, and in demanding that the criterion of connection should be not metaphysical or conventional but grounded in scientific knowledge, provoked new questions by the very force of his scepticism about the old answers. It was in response to Descartes that Vico proposed his criterion that we can have full knowledge only of what we can ourselves make or do. In one decisive respect this response was reactionary. Since men have not in any obvious sense made the physical world, a powerful new conception of scientific knowledge was ruled out *a priori* and was, as before, reserved to God. Yet on the other hand, by insisting that we can understand society because we have made it, indeed that we understand it not abstractly but in the very process of making it, and that the activity of language is central in this process, Vico opened a whole new dimension. [. . .] Verbal language is then distinctively human; indeed, constitutively human. This was the point taken up by Herder, who opposed any notion of language being 'given' to man (as by God) and, in effect, the apparently alternative notion of language being 'added' to man, as a special kind of acquisition or tool. Language is then, positively, a distinctively human opening of and opening to the world: not a distinguishable or instrumental but a constitutive faculty.

Historically this emphasis on language as constitutive, like the closely related emphasis on human development as culture, must be seen as an attempt both to preserve some idea of the generally human, in face of the analytical and empirical procedures of a powerfully developing natural science, and to assert an idea of human creativity, in face of the increased understanding of the properties of the physical world, and of consequently causal explanations from them. As such this whole tendency was in constant danger of becoming simply a new kind of idealism — 'humanity' and 'creativity' being projected as essences — while the tendencies it opposed moved towards a new kind of objective materialism. This specific fission, so fateful in all subsequent thought, was in effect masked and ratified by a newly conventional distinction between 'art' (literature) — the sphere of 'humanity' and 'creativity' — and 'science' ('positive knowledge') — the knowable dimension of the physical world and of physical human beings within it. Each of the key terms — 'art', 'literature', and 'science', together with the associated 'culture' and with such a newly necessary specialization as 'aesthetic' and the radical distinction between 'experience' and 'experiment' — changed in meaning between the early eighteenth and early nineteenth centuries. The resulting conflicts and confusions were severe, but it is significant that in the new situation of the nineteenth century the issues were never really joined on the ground of language, at any radical level, though it was precisely in relation to language that the newly conventional distinctions most needed to be challenged.

What happened instead was an extraordinary advance in empirical knowledge of languages, and a wholly remarkable analysis and classification of this knowledge in terms which set some of the basic questions aside. It is impossible to separate this movement from its political history, within the dynamic development of Western societies in a period of extending colonialism. Older studies of language had been largely contained within the model of the dead 'classical' languages (which still effectively determined 'grammar' in both its syntactic and literary senses) and of the 'derived' modern vernaculars. European exploration and colonization, meanwhile, had been dramatically expanding the available range of linguistic material. The critical encounter was between the European and Indian civilizations: not only in available languages but in European contact with the highly developed methods of Indic grammatical scholars, with their alternative body of 'classical' texts. It was as an Englishman in India that William Jones learned Sanskrit and from an observation of its resemblances to Latin and Greek began the work which led to classification of the Indo-European (Aryan) and other 'families' of languages.

This work, based on comparative analysis and classification, was procedurally very close to the evolutionary biology with which it is contemporary. It is one of the major periods of all scholarly investigation, empirically founding not only the major classifications of language families, including schemes of their evolutionary development and relationships, but also, within these schemes, discovering certain 'laws' of change, notably of sound-change. In one area this movement was 'evolutionary' in a particular sense: in its postulate of a proto-language (Proto-Indo-European) from which the major 'family' had developed.

But in its later stages it was 'evolutionary' also in another sense. Increasing rigour in the study of sound-changes associated one branch of language study with natural science, so that a system of linguistic phonetics marched with physical studies of the language faculty and the evolutionary origins of speech. This tendency culminated in major work in the physiology of speech and in the field significantly designated within this area as experimental *psychology*.

This identification of language use as a problem in psychology was to have major effects on concepts of language. But meanwhile within general language studies there was a new phase which reinforced inherent tendencies to objectivism. What was characteristically studied in comparative philology was a body of *records* of language: in effect, centrally, the alien written word. This assumption of the defining material of study was already present, of course, in the earlier phase of 'classical' language studies: Greek, Latin, Hebrew. But then the modes of access to a wider range of languages repeated this earlier stance: that of the privileged (scientific) observer of a body of alien written material. Methodological decisions, substantially similar to those being developed in the closely related new science of anthropology, followed from this effective situation. On the one hand there was the highly productive application of modes of systematic observation, classification and analysis. On the other hand there was the largely unnoticed consequence of the privileged situation of the observer: that he was observing (of course scientifically) within a differential mode of contact with alien material: in texts, the records of a *past* history; in speech, the activity of an alien people in subordinate (colonialist) relations to the whole activity of the dominant people within which the observer gained his privilege. This defining situation inevitably reduced any sense of language as actively and presently constitutive. The consequent objectivism of fundamental procedure was intensely productive at the level of description, but necessarily any consequent definition of language had to be a definition of a (specialized) philological *system*. In a later phase of this contact between privileged observer and alien language material, in the special circumstances of North America where hundreds of native American (Amerindian) languages were in danger of dying out after the completion of European conquest and domination, the earlier philological procedures were indeed, characteristically, found to be not objective enough. Assimilation of these even more alien languages to the categories of Indo-European philology — the natural reflex of cultural imperialism — was scientifically resisted and checked by necessary procedures which, assuming only the presence of an alien system, found ways of studying it in its own (intrinsic and structural) terms. This approach was a further gain in scientific description, with its own remarkable results, but at the level of theory it was the final reinforcement of a concept of language as an (alien) objective system.

Paradoxically, this approach had even deeper effect through one of the necessary corrections of procedure which followed from the new phase of contact with languages without texts. Earlier procedures had been determined by the fact that a language almost invariably presented itself in specific past texts: finished monologic utterances. Actual speech, even when it was available, was seen as *derived*, either historically into vernaculars, or practically into speech acts which were instances of the fundamental (textual) forms of the language. Language use could then hardly ever be seen as itself active and constitutive. And this was reinforced by the political relations of the observer–observed, where the 'language habits' studied, over a range from the speech of conquered and dominated peoples to the 'dialects' of outlying or socially inferior groups, theoretically matched against the observer's 'standard', were regarded as at most 'behaviour', rather than independent, creative, self-directing life. North American empirical linguistics reversed one part of this tendency, restoring the primacy of speech in the literal absence of 'standard' or 'classical' texts. Yet the objectivist character of the underlying general theory came to limit even this, by converting speech itself to a 'text' — the characteristically persistent word in orthodox structural linguistics. Language came to be seen as a fixed, objective and in these senses 'given' system, which had theoretical and practical priority over what were described as 'utterances' (later as 'performance'). Thus the living speech of human beings in their specific social relationships in the world was theoretically reduced to instances and examples of a system which lay beyond them.

The major theoretical expression of this reified understanding of language came in the twentieth century, in the work of Saussure, which has close affinities to the objectivist sociology of Durkheim. In Saussure the social nature of language is expressed as a system (*langue*), which is at once stable and autonomous and founded in normatively identical forms; its 'utterances' (*paroles*) are then seen as 'individual' (in abstract distinction from 'social') uses of 'a particular language code' through an enabling 'psycho-physical mechanism'. The practical results of this profound theoretical development, in all its phases, have been exceptionally productive and striking. The great body of philological scholarship has been complemented by a remarkable body of linguistic studies, in which the controlling concept of language as a formal system has opened the way to penetrating descriptions of actual language operations and many of their underlying 'laws'.

This achievement has an ironic relation with Marxism. On the one hand it repeats an important and often dominant tendency within Marxism itself, over a range from the comparative analysis and classification of stages of a society, through the discovery of certain fundamental laws of change within these systematic stages, to the assertion of a controlling 'social' system which is *a priori* inaccessible to 'individual' acts of will and intelligence. This apparent affinity explains the attempted synthesis of Marxism and structural linguistics, which has been so influential a phenomenon of the mid-twentieth century. But Marxists have then to notice, first, that history, in its most specific, active and connecting senses, has disappeared (in one tendency has been theoretically excluded) from this account of so central a social activity as language; and second, that the categories in which this version of system has been developed are the familiar bourgeois categories in which an abstract separation and distinction between the 'individual' and the 'social' have become so habitual that they are taken as 'natural' starting-points. [. . .]

[. . .]

Any constitutive theory of practice, and especially a materialist theory, has important effects beyond the question of origins, in restating the problem of the active process of language at any time: a restatement which goes beyond the separated categories of 'language' and 'reality'. Yet orthodox Marxism remained stuck in reflection theory, because this was the only plausible materialist connection between the received abstract categories. Reflection theory, in its first period, was itself specialized to crude stimulus-and-response models, adapted from positivist physiology. In its second period, in the later work of Pavlov, it added, as a way of dealing with the special properties of language, the concept of the 'second signal system', the first being the simple physical system of sensations and responses. This was better than nothing, but it assimilated language to the characteristics of a 'signal system', in relatively mechanistic ways, and was in practice unequal to problems of meaning beyond simple models of the associative. Setting out from this point, L. S. Vygotsky (*Thought and Language*, Moscow, 1934) proposed a new social theory, still named the 'second signal system', in which language and consciousness are freed from simple analogies with physical perception. His work on the development of language in children, and on the crucial problem of 'inner speech', provided a new starting-point, within a historical-materialist perspective. But for a generation, in orthodox Marxism, this was neglected. [. . .]

[. . .] A tragic element in this history is that such theories had been profoundly opposed in the 1920s in Leningrad, where the beginnings of a school of Marxist linguistics, of a significant kind, had in fact emerged. It is best represented by the work of V. N. Vološinov, whose *Marxism and the Philosophy of Language* appeared, in two editions, in 1929 and 1930; the second edition has been translated into English (Matejka and Titunik, New York and London, 1973). Vološinov had been associated with M. M. Bakhtin. [. . .] Sometime during the 1930s Vološinov disappeared. Nearly half a century was then lost, in real terms, in the development of his exceptionally important realigment of the argument.

Vološinov's decisive contribution was to find a way beyond the powerful but partial theories of expression and objective system. He found it in fundamentally Marxist terms, though he had to begin by saying that Marxist thinking about language was virtually non-existent. [. . .]

[. . .] Vološinov argued that meaning was necessarily a social action, dependent on a social relationship. But to understand this depended on recovering a full sense of 'social', as distinct both from the idealist reduction of the social to an inherited, ready-made product, an 'inert crust', beyond which all creativity was individual, and from the objectivist projection of the social into a formal system, now autonomous and governed only by its internal laws, within which, and solely according to which, meanings were produced. [. . .]

[. . .] Following Vološinov, we can see that just as all social process is activity between real individuals, so individuality, by the fully social fact of language (whether as 'outer' or 'inner' speech), is the active constitution, within distinct physical beings, of the social capacity which is the means of realization of any individual life. Consciousness, in this precise sense, is social being. It is the possession, through active and specific social development and relationships, of a precise social capacity, which is the 'sign-system'. Vološinov, even after these fundamental restatements, continues to speak of the 'sign-system': the formulation that had been decisively made in Saussurean linguistics. But if we follow his arguments we find how difficult and misleading this formulation can be. 'Sign' itself — the mark or token; the formal element — has to be revalued to emphasize its variability and internally active elements, indicating not only an internal structure but an internal dynamic. Similarly, 'system' has to be revalued to emphasize social process rather than fixed 'sociality' [. . .]

These changes will have to be made, in the continuing inquiry into language. But the last point indicates a final difficulty. Much of the social process of the creation of meanings was projected within objectivist linguistics to the formal relations — thus the systematic nature — of signs. What at the level of the sign had been abstractly and statically conceived was set into a kind of motion — albeit a frozen, determinate motion, a movement of ice-fields — in the relational 'laws' or 'structures' of the system as a whole. This extension to a relational system, including its formal aspect as grammar, is in any case inevitable. Isolation of 'the sign', whether in Saussure or Vološinov, is at best an analytical procedure, at worst an evasion. Much of the important work on relations within a whole system is therefore an evident advance, and the problem of the variability of the sign can appear to be contained within the variability of its formal relations. But while this kind of emphasis on the relational system is obviously necessary, it is limited by the consequence of the initial abstract definition of the sign. The highly complex relations of (theoretically) invariable units can never be substantive relationships; they must remain as formal relationships. The internal dynamics of the sign, including its social and material relationships as well as its formal structure, must be seen as necessarily connected with the social and material as well as the formal dynamics of the system as a whole. There have been some advances in this direction in recent work (Rossi-Landi, 1975).

But there has also been a move which seems to reopen the whole problem. In Chomskyan linguistics there has been a decisive step towards a conception of system which emphasizes the possibility and the fact of individual initiative and creative practice, which earlier objectivist systems had excluded. But at the same time this conception stresses deep structures of language formation which are certainly incompatible with ordinary social and historical accounts of the origin and development of language. An emphasis on deep constitutive structures, at an evolutionary rather than a historical level, can of course be reconciled with the view of language as a constitutive human faculty: exerting pressures and setting limits, in determinate ways, to human development itself. But while it is retained as an exclusively evolutionary process, it moves, necessarily, towards reified accounts of 'systemic evolution': development of constituted systems and structures (the constitution now at once permitting and limiting variations) rather than by actual human beings in a continuing social practice. Here Vygotsky's work on inner speech and consciousness is theoretically crucial:

> If we compare the early development of speech and of intellect — which, as we have seen, develop along separate lines both in animals and in very young children — with the development of inner speech and of verbal thought, we must conclude that the later stage is not a simple continuation of the earlier. *The nature of the development itself changes*, from biological to socio-historical. Verbal thought is not an innate, natural form of behaviour but is determined by a historical-cultural process and has specific properties and laws that cannot be found in the natural forms of thought and speech. (*Thought and Language*, 51)

Thus we can add to the necessary definition of the biological faculty of language as *constitutive* an equally necessary definition of language development — at once individual and social — as historically and socially *constituting*. What we can then define is a dialectical process: the *changing practical consciousness of human beings*, in which both the evolutionary and the historical processes can be given full weight, but also within which they can be distinguished, in the complex variations of actual language use. [. . .]

Note

1. Buridan, Jean (1295–1366), French philosopher and polymath. *Ed.*

References

Rossi-Landi, F., *Semiotica e Ideologia*, Milan, 1972.
Vico, G., *The New Science*, tr. Bergin, T., and Fisch, M., Ithaca, N.Y., 1948.
Vološinov, V.N., *Marxism and the Philosophy of Language*, New York, 1973.
Vygotsky, L.S., *Thought and Language*, Cambridge, Mass., 1862.

1.2 Grammar and Language Teaching

J.P.B. Allen and H.G. Widdowson

Source: Extracts from Allen, J.P.B. and Widdowson, H.G. (1975) 'Grammar and language teaching'. In Allen, J.P.B. and Pit Corder, S. (eds) *The Edinburgh Course in Applied Linguistics, Vol. 2: Papers in Applied Linguistics.* Oxford: Oxford University Press, pp. 45–97.

I Introduction

Let school masters puzzle their brain
With grammar and nonsense and learning;
Good liquor, I stoutly maintain,
Gives genius a better discerning.

Thus sings Tony Lumpkin in *She Stoops to Conquer*, reflecting the popular view that grammar is one of the most boring and obscure subjects in the school curriculum. It is perhaps not surprising that grammar should have acquired a reputation for dullness, since very often the way it is taught in the schools seems deliberately designed to kill all interest in the subject. Many of us retain from our schooldays memories of the repetitious, mechanical parsing of sentences, the rote-learning of paradigms, word-lists and artificial 'rules of diction', and old-fashioned handbooks which quoted abundantly from the classics of English literature but almost entirely ignored the living colloquial language that we hear around us every day.

For a time, in the late fifties and early sixties, it seemed possible that grammar teaching in the schools would be reinvigorated under the influence of important work being done in the field of linguistics. Unfortunately, however, the idea gained ground among teachers that there was a fundamental conflict between the traditional grammar they were accustomed to using in the classroom, and the 'new linguistics' which was being urged upon them. Soon many teachers found themselves in a serious dilemma. On the one hand, traditional grammar was supposed to be 'unscientific' and therefore unworthy of serious consideration, while linguistics seemed to be a highly esoteric subject beyond the comprehension of any but the most dedicated of university scholars. The situation was made more difficult by the fact that linguists were apparently unable to make up their minds about the nature of language and how it should be studied. Those teachers who attempted to inform themselves about recent developments in the subject found that a number of distinct schools of linguistics had emerged, each with its band of enthusiastic followers who strenuously urged the merits of their own particular approach to the study of language. Many language teachers were further confused by the increasing tendency of linguists to use a highly technical terminology, and a rapid increase in the number of books and articles which assumed a considerable amount of background knowledge and made little or no concession to the general reader. As a result many teachers became disillusioned, not only about modern linguistics, but about linguistics in general, including traditional grammar, and there was a widespread reaction against grammar teaching in the schools. [. . .]

We believe that there is basically no conflict between traditional grammar and modern linguistics. Some writers have referred to a 'revolution in grammar', thus implying a sharp break between the old and the new. The fact is, however, that the traditional parts of speech approach to grammar is still one of the most widely taught and studied systems of linguistic methodology. Modern grammarians have developed methods that are more concise and more theoretically consistent than the older methods. However, whereas the traditional handbooks provided descriptions of wide areas of surface structure, a typical paper or book written by a contemporary linguist discusses theoretical issues and presents only as much of the data as is necessary to support the hypotheses advanced. In filling out the details, we find ourselves drawing more and more upon the work of the scholarly traditional grammarians. It is particularly important for language teachers to maintain a balanced point of view and to avoid setting the new types of grammar too sharply in opposition to the old.

[. . .] Contemporary linguistic theory is very far from being a single monolithic system; rather, it is a combination of different approaches, all of which are subject to constant development and change. We have also emphasized, elsewhere [. . .] that a teacher must make his own choice from among the various models of grammar available in linguistics, and decide for himself what kind of grammatical statement is most likely to be suitable for the particular group of students he has in mind. At first sight it may appear that the teacher is faced with a formidable task of selection. Let us suppose that we are setting out to write a textbook for students of English as a second language. What facts should we select from among the vast amount of information available in books and journals, to use as a basis for our classroom presentation of English grammar? Fortunately we will find that, despite the volume of current work in English grammar, and the variety of views expressed, there is a remarkable consensus of opinion about what constitutes the fundamentals of the subject. Over the years linguists have succeeded in identifying a body of basic facts about the structure of English which have been tested and verified, and which can now be stated with a high degree of confidence. Where shortcomings existed in a particular grammar of English, these can be identified and the student advised to proceed with care. If we find failures of coverage in one linguist's description we can often supplement it by drawing upon the work of other linguists, but in order to do this with confidence we must know exactly the terms of reference of each grammar we use, and its characteristic strengths and limitations. In this chapter we hope to make the task of selection easier by outlining the various approaches to grammatical analysis which have been developed during the past fifty years, at the same time attempting to discover what each of these models of grammar can contribute to the practical study of languages.

2 Traditional grammar

Modern structural linguistics can be said to begin with the posthumous publication of Ferdinand de Saussure's lectures under the title of *Cours de Linguistique Générale* in 1916. Behind de Saussure, stretching back over 2000 years, lies the era of traditional grammar. To write an account of pre-Saussurean grammar with any hope of doing justice to this long, rich and varied tradition would be an immense task. Assuming that we limited our aim to tracing the development of linguistic studies in the West, we would have to go back to the Greek scholars of the fourth and fifth century BC to find the origins of the grammar that most of us learned at school.

The linguistic analysis carried out by the Greeks between the fourth century BC and the second century AD included most of the basic concepts which still constitute the layman's conception of 'grammar'. The classification of words according to gender (masculine, feminine and neuter) was carried out by Protagoras and the fifth-century Sophists. The Stoics classified the patterns of inflexion, established the distinction between the active and passive voices and between transitive and intransitive verbs, and defined the function of nominative and the 'oblique' cases. The Alexandrians classified all Greek words in terms of case, gender, number, tense, voice and mood. Dionysius Thrax classified the words of the Greek language into eight parts of speech — noun, verb, participle, article, pronoun, preposition, adverb and conjunction. The Greek model was largely followed by the later Roman grammarians. The grammars of Donatus (*c.* AD 400) and Priscian (*c.* AD 500) were used as teaching grammars through the Middle Ages and as late as the seventeenth century. The traditional categories were then taken over by prescriptive grammarians like John Wallis, Robert Lowth and Lindley Murray, thus helping to preserve an unbroken tradition of grammatical analysis which has lasted from the time of Aristotle to the present day.

A study of traditional grammar would not be complete without an account of the work of the medieval scholars who brought about many advances in the analysis of Latin. The scholastic philosophers, or modistae, were interested in grammar as a tool for analysing the structure of reality, and they deliberately attempted to relate the categories of grammar to those of logic epistemology and metaphysics. The ideals of medieval 'speculative' grammar — 'speculative' in the sense of providing a mirror of the world — were revived in seventeenth-century France by the teachers of Port Royal, who believed that the structure of language is a product of reason, and that all the languages of the world are varieties of the same underlying logical and rational system. These philosophical presuppositions, expressed in the famous Port Royal *Grammaire Générale et Raisonnée* of 1660, bear some resemblance to the theory of language currently being developed by Noam Chomsky.

Coming closer to our own time, a writer on the history of linguistics would have to devote many pages to an account of nineteenth-century comparative philology. Towards the end of the eighteenth century a number of scholars, including the British civil servant Sir William Jones, drew attention to the similarities between many words in Sanskrit and their equivalents in Latin, Greek, Celtic, Germanic and certain other European and Middle Eastern languages, and suggested that all these languages derived from a single source. As a result of this observation linguists became deeply interested in the Indo-European family of languages, and many attempts were made to reconstruct the forms of Proto-Indo-European, believed to be the common ancestor. Throughout the nineteenth century a long line of distinguished scholars studied the systematic correspondences between the sounds of equivalent words and patterns of inflexion in different languages, and as a result they succeeded in establishing a general theory of linguistic relationship and language change.

It will be apparent, then, that 'traditional grammar', although it can be criticized from the point of view of modern ideas of what constitutes scientific precision and objectivity, is far richer and far more diversified than one would suppose on the basis of the rather disparaging references which have been made to it by many modern linguists. Two types of traditional grammar, not always clearly distinguished in the literature, are usually taken as the point of departure for a discussion of modern theories: (a) the 'scholarly' or 'compendious' reference grammars of the late nineteenth and early twentieth centuries, for example those of Kruisinga, Poutsma, Sweet, Curme and Jespersen, and (b) the school grammars, by such writers as Nesfield and Lindley Murray, which were essentially a simplification of the work of the scholarly grammarians. The widespread criticism of traditional grammar voiced in recent years relates in part to the methods employed by the scholarly grammarians, but is mainly concerned with the shortcomings of the simplified versions of scholarly grammar intended for use in schools. A great deal of this criticism fails to take into account the special circumstances for which the simplified grammars were designed.

Both the scholarly and the pedagogic grammarians have been blamed for their too-ready acceptance of 'notional' and 'imprecise' definitions for the parts of speech and other grammatical categories. It should be realized that there is often more than one way of defining a category in linguistics; for example, the definition of a noun may be morphological, functional or notional. By a morphological definition we mean one which is based on the classification of the physical forms of a language. A functional definition is one based on the relation of words to other words in a sentence with reference to such concepts as 'subject', 'object', 'complement', etc., and a notional definition is one based on our understanding of the relationship of words to the actual, real-world phenomena which they denote. Thus, a noun may be defined morphologically as a word that fits into an inflexional series built on the contrast between singular and plural numbers (*boy, boys*) and between common and possessive cases (*boy, boy's, boys, boys'*), and on no other contrasts (Sledd, 1959). It may be defined functionally as a word that can serve as subject of a verb, and notionally as the name of a person, place or thing. None of these definitions is complete as it stands, but they all draw attention to different characteristics of nouns that are relevant at different points in the description of a language.

In many classroom grammars, nouns and verbs are defined notionally and the other parts of speech are defined functionally, on the basis of the definition of noun and verb: thus, we may say that an adjective is a word that modifies a noun; an adverb is a word that modifies a verb; a pronoun is a word that replaces a noun; a preposition is a word relating other parts of speech; an interjection stands alone with no relationship to other parts of speech. Formal definitions may then be added to the notional and functional definitions; for example, it might be stated that a large subclass of adjectives fits into an inflexional series like *tall, taller, tallest*, and that most verbs fit into a pattern *sing, sings, sang, sung, singing* or *play, plays, played, playing*. The triple basis of definition may appear complicated, but in the classroom it seems to work quite well. Most linguists now acknowledge that it is not possible to formulate simple water-tight definitions of basic categories like noun and verb, sentence, clause and word. It is perfectly feasible, however, to impart a knowledge of word classes by listing typical examples, and this in practice is how many students learn to identify nouns and verbs and other grammatical categories. For example, the teacher or textbook writer might give a partial definition followed by a list of examples. The learner studies the examples, discovers for himself what they have in common, and arrives inductively at an understanding of what a noun is, or a verb. He is not dependent for this knowledge on the 'definition', which in most cases simply serves as a useful reminder.

A more serious criticism concerns the excessively diffuse, 'atomistic' nature of many traditional reference grammars. Much of the work of the traditional scholarly grammarians suffered from the lack of a coherent theoretical framework, or model, which ideally should underlie the analysis and give unity and shape to the way in which the results are presented. Because in writing a grammar we normally progress from more general to more detailed statements — a process which involves an increasingly detailed subdivision of the word classes — there is a tendency for the broad patterns of the language to be obscured as the grammarian accumulates more and more facts. [. . .]

3 Taxonomic grammar

We have seen that a fundamental difficulty in traditional grammar is an over emphasis on the details of a language and a tendency to obscure the larger patterns. The view that language elements are related to one another in a system (or network of systems) rather than being mere collections of individual items is characteristic of what has come to be known as the structural approach to linguistic analysis. At the end of the nineteenth century linguistic science was still more or less equated with comparative linguistics, which in turn tended to mean the comparison of Indo-European languages and the reconstruction of Proto-Indo-European. The prevailing philosophical point of view was that of the *Junggrammatiker* or 'newgrammarians', whose work tended to result in the amassing of large amounts of data and the proliferation of rules to account for each individual phenomenon without establishing any very clear picture of the language as a whole. In the first two decades of the present century, however, fundamental change of direction in linguistic studies took place. This change can be characterized as a shift from an item-centred view of language to one that is structure-centred. According to the structuralists, individual sounds, words or parts of sentences have no linguistic significance in themselves; they have significance only as they contrast and combine with other items in the patterns of linguistic system.

At this point it should be made clear that the expression 'structuralism' has two distinct senses in current linguistic discussion. In its first and more general sense, structuralism is based on the belief that each language is a unique relational structure, and that the key to linguistic scholarship is to study the elements of a language not in isolation but as parts of a systemic whole. Structuralism in this sense of the term had its formal beginnings in the famous *Thèses* presented collectively by the members of the Prague Linguistic Circle to the First International Congress of Slavic Philologists held in Prague in 1929. The interpretation of structuralism associated with the Prague linguists has continued to be the basis of structural linguistics up to the present day. In its second and narrower sense, structuralism refers to the views and methodology of the dominant school of American linguists in the 1940s and 1950s. During this period an important group of linguists, including Bloch, Wells, Harris and Hockett, published a substantial body of work in the tradition which is known variously as 'structural', 'taxonomic' or 'Bloomfieldian' grammar. The term 'structural' in this context indicates a characteristic preoccupation with form rather than meaning, 'taxonomic' refers to the inductive classificatory procedures on which such grammars were mainly based, and 'Bloomfieldian' (or 'post-Bloomfieldian') refers to the influence of Bloomfield's ideas as embodied in his book *Language* (1933), where many of the basic assumptions of the group were set out in a definitive form. As so often in linguistics, the wealth of terminology associated with post-Bloomfieldian grammar can give rise to serious problems for the non-specialist. In this discussion we use the term 'taxonomic' to refer to that type of linguistic analysis which is concerned mainly with the segmentation and classification of utterances, without reference to the 'deeper', more abstract levels of linguistic organization. The term 'structural' is used more generally, with reference to all grammars which emphasize the phonological grammatical structure of language, in contrast with the semantic.

The procedures of taxonomic grammar were developed as a conscious revolt against traditional methods of analysis. The features of traditional grammar to which taxonomic linguists took particular exception were the establishment of grammatical categories on the basis of notional definitions and the assumption that there are universal categories (parts of speech, tense, mood, etc.) which hold for all languages. By contrast, taxonomic linguists based their work on the assumption that grammatical categories should be defined not in terms of meaning but in terms of distribution, and that the structure of each language should be described without reference to the alleged universality of such categories as tense, mood and parts of speech. Unlike the work of traditional grammarians, a taxonomic description is said to be formal, in the sense that the units of the analysis are defined internally in relation to each other, rather than externally in relation to psychological, logical or metaphysical categories which are not part of the language system as such [. . .]

The procedures of taxonomic linguistics are typically concerned with a formalization of surface structure. By 'surface structure' we mean a type of analysis which segments each sequence of elements of a sentence into its constituent parts, and further segments the constituents in such a way that all the elements in the analysis are directly related to the linearly arranged sequence of events in the original text or speech signal. Thus the surface structure of a sentence is a linearly arranged sequence of 'immediate constituents' which can be presented in the form of a hierarchical bracketing.

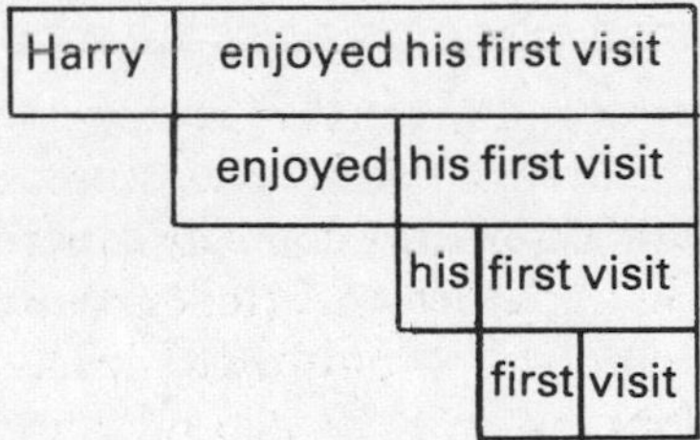

This type of representation is known as an immediate constituents, or IC analysis. It can be made more useful if the constituents are assigned to categories which are given appropriate names, or labels. Thus, *Harry* might be given the label 'noun phrase' and *enjoyed his first visit* the label 'verb phrase'; *enjoyed* might be labelled 'verb' and *his first visit* identified as another occurrence of the category 'noun phrase', and so on for all the constituents in the sentence. [. . .]

4 Phrase structure grammar[1]

In the two decades after the Second World War techniques of pattern practice and grading based on a combination of taxonomic linguistics and behavioural psychology were firmly established as a part of foreign language teaching methodology. Methods of mother-tongue instruction, on the other hand, either remained fairly traditional, with much time devoted to précis, the analysis of literary texts and the parsing of sentences on a largely intuitive, logico-semantic basis, or tended to emphasize creative self-expression with little attempt to provide any systematic instruction in the underlying principles of grammar. More recently, the interest of linguists and language teachers alike has centred on the development of various generative models in linguistics, of which Chomsky's transformational-generative grammar in particular has been very widely discussed. A generative grammar is one which aims to specify the nature of a speaker's knowledge about his language, but with such accuracy and in such detail that someone who does not know the language will be able to produce its forms simply by following the rules of the grammar, and without having to refer to any source of information outside the grammar. A transformational grammar is one which incorporates two aspects of syntactic description, a surface structure and a more abstract deep structure, together with a set of transformational rules relating deep and surface structure. Transformational-generative grammar as developed by Chomsky is potentially of great interest to language teachers since it provides deep and important insights into language structure, and in recent years a number of writers have attempted to show how these insights can be utilized in the development of teaching materials for first or second language learners.

The transformational grammar outlined by Chomsky in *Syntactic Structures* (1957) contains three components: phrase structure rules, transformational rules and morphophonemic rules. We will not discuss morphophonemic rules here except to say that they operate on the sequences of symbols generated by the phrase structure and transformational rules and assign a phonemic representation to them. Phrase structure and transformational rules must be discussed in some detail, however. As a simple example of phrase structure rules, consider the following:

1 (i) S → NP + VP
(ii) VP → Vb + NP
(iii) NP → Det + N
(iv) Vb → Aux + V
(v) Det → {the, a, this, that, . . .}
(vi) N → {man, boy, letter, car, policeman, thief . . .}
(vii) Aux → {will, can, might, would . . .}
(viii) V → {post, repair, bake, arrest, buy . . .}

Suppose we interpret each rule X → Y of 1 as the instruction 'rewrite X as Y'. In generating a sentence from these rules we start from the initial symbol S, which is rewritten as a string of symbols NP + VP. Rules (ii–iv) develop each of these constituents into further structures. In the last four rules each of the symbols Det, N, Aux and V is replaced by one of the words, or lexical items, in the braces on the right of the rule. The rules of 1 will generate such sentences as *This boy will post the letter, That man can repair the car, A policeman would arrest the thief*, and automatically assign to each sentence a phrase marker as follows:

2

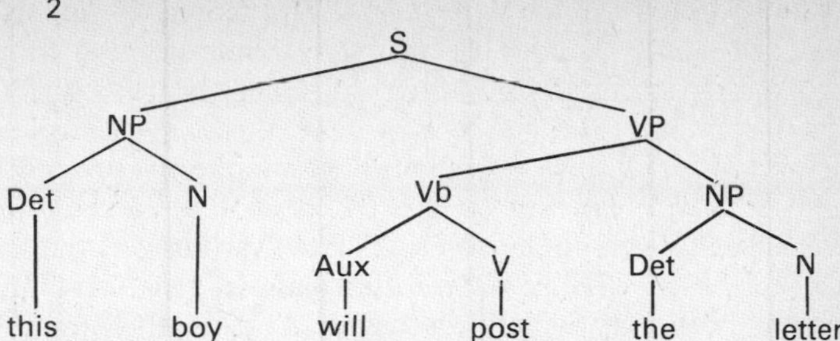

Clearly, we must assume some restriction on the co-occurrence of lexical items in order to prevent the grammar from generating such controversial sentences as *The letter will post will this boy, The policeman can repair that man.* We will return to this question presently; for the time being it is sufficient to see that a problem exists.

So far our rules will generate only a small number of rather simple sentences. We can extend the rules of the grammar and make it capable of generating different types of sentences in various ways. One method is to develop constituents like NP and VP in such a way that we are provided with a set of alternative choices. For example, we might want to include noun phrases consisting of a proper noun, or a pronoun, as well as those which consist of a determiner plus noun as in 1. To allow for such a possibility, rule (iii) would have to be amended as follows (the brackets indicate an alternative choice):

3

$$\text{NP} \rightarrow \left\{ \begin{array}{l} \text{Pronoun} \\ \text{Proper Noun} \\ \text{Det} + \text{N} \end{array} \right\}$$

We would now need additional rules at the end of the grammar:

4 Pronoun → {he, she, you . . .}
Proper Noun → {Robert, Helen, John Brown . . .}

Similarly, we can expand our description of the verb phrase to allow for different types of predicate constructions, for example *The baby should sleep* (intransitive verb); *Helen is happy* (copula verb plus adjective); *He puts the letter in the box* (locational verb + noun phrase + prepositional phrase). Rule (ii) will now look like this:

5

$$\text{VP} \rightarrow \left\{ \begin{array}{l} \text{Vb}_{\text{instrans}} \\ \text{Vb}_{\text{trans}} + \text{NP} \\ \text{Vb}_{\text{cop}} + \text{Adj} \\ \text{Vb}_{\text{loc}} + \text{NP} + \text{Prep Phrase} \end{array} \right\}$$

In a full grammar of English there would be a very large number of subclasses of verb, categorized in terms of the syntactic environment in which they occur. Again we would need additional lexical rules to introduce predicate adjectives and the appropriate subclasses of verb:

6 $Vb_{intrans}$ → (sleep, work, eat . . .)
Vb_{trans} → (repair, arrest, buy . . .)
Vb_{cop} → (be, become . . .)
Adj → (happy, busy, intelligent . . .)

Phrase structure grammar contains the same type of information as an immediate constituent diagram of the type discussed on p. 17 but presented in the form of rules which are subject to the requirement that every step in the derivation of sentences must be fully and accurately specified. In order to meet this requirement as economically as possible, linguists are constantly searching for new ways of designing the rules of the grammar, and this process may provide pedagogically useful insights into language data. For example, Jacobson (1966) claims that the learning of a number of apparently identical constructions in English can be simplified if the teaching is based on information drawn from a phrase structure grammar. Jacobson discusses three sentences which look alike:

7 (a) He asked me a question.
(b) He made me a suit.
(c) He gave me a book.

When paraphrased, the three sentences still look alike as far as surface structure is concerned:

8 (a) He asked a question of me.
(b) He made a suit for me.
(c) He gave a book to me.

However, a closer examination reveals that 8(a) and 8(b) belong to one sentence type while 8(c) belongs to another type. Thus we can have 9(a) and 9(b) but not 9(c):

9 (a) He asked a question.
(b) He made a suit.
(c) He gave a book.[2]

8(a) and (b) are different from (c) because *of me* and *for me* are independent prepositional phrases while *to me* is an integral part of the sentence. Jacobson calls the first type of sentence a direct object + complement construction and the second type an indirect object construction. The direct object + complement construction is divided into three subtypes as follows:

eleciting:	He asked a question of me.
benefactive:	He made a suit for me.
directional:	He said 'good morning' to me.

[. . .]

5 Transformational grammar

So far, in our discussion of phrase structure grammar, we have only considered rather simple active declarative sentences, but let us suppose we also want to include in our grammar passive sentences like:

10 The letter will be posted by this boy.

Clearly there is a close correspondence in meaning between 10 and the active sentence *This boy will post the letter*, but the two sentences are quite different in terms of the arrangement of their surface structure. It would be possible to write a phrase structure grammar which generated both active and passive forms, but as Chomsky points out, an attempt to extend phrase structure grammar in this way would simply serve to complicate the description without throwing any new light on to language structure. Instead, Chomsky suggests that the notion of phrase structure is adequate for only a small proportion of the sentences of a language, and that the rest should be derived by the application of rules of different type, called 'transformational' rules, to the structures given by the phrase structure grammar. To illustrate, the passive transformation is given in *Syntactic Structures* as follows:

11 $NP_1 - Aux - V - NP_2 \Rightarrow NP_2 - Aux + be + en - V - by + NP_1$

The sequence of elements to the left of the arrow is called the structural description and the operation indicated by the rule is called the structural change.[3] The passive transformation applies to all strings that can be analysed in terms of the elements referred to in the structural description. For example, the grammar in 1 will generate the phrase marker illustrated in 2. This structure can be analysed in terms of the left-hand side of rule 11, i.e. *this boy* is an NP; *will* is an Aux; *post* is a V; *the letter* is an NP. A sentence analysed as *this boy* — *will* — *post* — *the letter* (NP — Aux — V — NP) can be changed by the passive transformation 11 into *the letter* — *will* + *be* + *en* — *post* — *by this boy*[3]. This structure becomes *The letter will be posted by this boy* by the operation of further rules. It is necessary to specify the passive transformation in rather an abstract way in order to capture the fact that the rule applies to a wide range of sentences. For example, in the structural description of 11, NP_1 and NP_2 each function as a variable which may take as its value any noun phrase generated by the phrase structure rules including those which are ultimately realized as *Robert, the boy, his sister, the little old lady with the white cat and the boxer dog who lives across the road*, and others theoretically without limit. In the same way, Aux on the left-hand side of 11 does not refer to any one specific auxiliary, but to a wide range of possible choices, including those which are realized in the sentences *He can deliver the letter, He will be delivering the letter, He must have been delivering the letter*, and many more.

With respect to their formal properties transformational rules such as 11 are quite different from phrase structure rules like those in 2. Phrase structure rules develop a single symbol at a time. In the fragment of grammar on page 17, for example, the single symbol S is rewritten as NP + VP, the single symbol VP is rewritten as Vb + NP, and so on. Transformational rules are different in that each rule operates on a whole structure, provided it can be analysed in terms of the elements referred to on the left-hand side of the rule. Phrase structure rules are very restricted in terms of the way they can operate, but transformational rules can perform a number of complex operations. For example, rule 11 permutes two NPs and adds a number of elements. Transformational rules can also delete elements, as seen in the rule which changes the underlying structure of *The letter will be posted by NP* into *The letter will be posted.* Rule 11 is fundamentally different from the rules of phrase structure grammar in another important respect. The limitations on phrase structure grammar mean that each phrase structure rule applies or fails to apply to a given sequence of elements according to the symbols actually present in the sequence, without reference to any of the earlier rules in the grammar. In the case of 11, however, we must know not only that *this boy, will, post, the letter* are constituents, but also what kind of constituents they are. Unlike phrase structure grammar, 11 requires us to 'look back' to earlier stages of the derivation in order to determine whether the passive rule will apply.

A study of English reveals many sets of sentences which can be related by transformational rules. For example, Chomsky (1968) discusses the following interrogative sentences:

12 Who expected Bill to meet Tom?
13 Who(m) did John expect to meet Tom?
14 Who(m) did John expect Bill to meet?
15 What (books) did you order John to ask Bill to persuade his friends to stop reading?

As the above examples show, a noun phrase in any of the three italicized positions in a sentence such as '*John* expected *Bill* to meet *Tom*' can be questioned. The process can be stated informally:

16 (a) Assign the marker *wh-* to a noun phrase.
(b) Place the marked noun phrase at the beginning of the sentence.
(c) Move a part of the verbal auxiliary to the second position in the sentence.
(d) Replace the marked noun phrase by an appropriate interrogative form (*who, what*, etc.)

Sentence 13, for example, is formed by assigning the marked *wh-* to the noun phrase 'someone' in 'John expected someone to meet Tom'. The marked noun phrase is then placed at the beginning of the sentence, giving '*wh-*someone John expected to meet Tom'. The process of auxiliary attraction 16(c) gives '*wh-*someone did John expect to meet Tom' and, finally, the process of phonological interpretation 16(d) gives 13.

Sentence 15 shows that these processes can extract any noun phrase, subject to certain restrictions which we need not go into here, and place it at the beginning of the sentence, however complex the sentence structure may be.

Another important series of transformations form what are known traditionally as subordinate clauses and infinitival and gerundial phrases:

17 He said *that John went to the theatre.*
I stayed at home *while John went to the theatre.*
John, *who went to the theatre,* say 'Hamlet'.
John dined after *going to the theatre.*
John didn't want *to go to the theatre.*
We didn't like *John going to the theatre.*
John's going to the theatre surprised his friends.

In a transformational analysis it can be shown that the italicized portion of each of the above sentences derives from the structure underlying the sentence *John went to the theatre.* In other words, by using transformational rules we are able to state systematic relations between sentences, even though in terms of their superficial structure the sentences may be quite different from one another.

In *Aspects of the Theory of Syntax,* published in 1965, Chomsky suggested a number of important modifications to transformational theory. For example, he proposed an extension of phrase structure grammar to include rules of the following type:

18 (i) $$\text{VP} \rightarrow \text{Vb} \begin{Bmatrix} \text{(NP)} \quad \text{(Prep Phrase)} \\ \text{S} \end{Bmatrix}$$

(ii) NP → (Det)N(S)

In 18(i) the brace brackets indicate that VP may be rewritten either as verb followed by two optional elements, Noun phrase and prepositional phrase, or as verb followed by sentence. In 18(ii) Noun phrase is rewritten as Noun, preceded optionally by determiner and followed optionally by sentence. The new phrase structure rules contain two instances of the symbol S, which marks the position where an embedded sentence may be introduced. Rules 18(i) and 18(ii) are recursive in that the symbol S constitutes an instruction to return to the beginning and to run through the rules a second time, thus generating a 'sentence within a sentence'. The process of recursion can apply over and over again so that the phrase structure, or base, rules are capable of generating sentences in which clauses are embedded inside clauses in a series to which there is no definite limit.

We can now return to the question of how to impose restrictions on the co-occurrence of nouns and verbs so that the grammar will generate, for example, *This boy will post the letter* but not *This letter will post the boy.* The approach adopted in Aspects is to include rules like those of 19 in the grammar:

19 (i) N → [+ N, ± Common]
(ii) [+ Common] → [± Count]
(iii) [− Common] → [± Animate]
(iv) [+ Animate] → [± Human]
(v) [− Count] → [± Abstract]

The function of rules 19(i–v) is to develop the category 'noun' into a set of grammatical features. Rule (i) states that every member of the category 'noun' has the property, or feature, of being a noun and the property of being either 'common' (*boy, girl, table*) or 'non-common'. Rule (ii) states that all categories with the property 'common' must be either countable (*boy, table, chair*) or uncountable (*tea, bread, sugar*). Rule (iii) states that all categories with the property 'non-common' must be either animate (*Robert, Helen*) or non-animate (*Edinburgh, Egypt*), and so on. The grammar will now generate structures which contain complex symbols, e.g.: [+ N, + Common, + Count, + Animate, + Human] or [+ N, + Common, + Count, – Animate]. If we assume a lexicon, or word list, which has entries in the following form:

20 *boy* [+ , + Common, + Count, + Human]
letter [+ N, + Common, + Count, – Animate]

we can formulate a rule which allows us to insert a lexical item into a structure generated by the grammar whenever a certain type of symbol in that structure matches a similar symbol in the lexical entry. Since nouns are selected first in the *Aspects* model, verbs have to be specified according to the syntactic environment in which they occur. For example, the deviance of *This letter will post the boy* is accounted for by saying that the verb *post* occurs only with human nouns in the subject position and inanimate nouns in the object position. We can include a rule to this effect which will specify that the verb *post* is selected only in those cases where the subject noun is marked by the feature [+ Human] and the object noun is marked by the feature [– Animate]. Given this framework, we can remove rules like those in 5 and 6 from the grammar, and rephrase as in 18(i), where the brackets indicate optional constituents. We can now insert into any of the structures generated by the grammar any verb which is classified in the lexicon as belonging to the appropriate environment.

[. . .] Transformational linguists aim to specify the nature of language competence, seen as a highly abstract system of rules which underlie performance. Chomsky makes it quite clear that neither the *Syntactic Structures* nor the *Aspects* model is intended in any sense to be a model of performance, that is, a representation of the way language is used in actual communication. [. . .]

6 Case grammar

We have seen that a constituent structure analysis of *This boy will post the letter* runs as follows: it is a sentences (S) composed of a noun phrase (NP) and a verb phrase (VP), the noun phrase is composed of a determiner (Det) and a noun (N), and the verb phrase is composed of a verb (Vb) and a noun phrase (NP). In addition, traditional grammar provides information of the following sort: the NP *this boy* functions as the subject of the sentence, whereas the VP *will post the letter* functions as the predicate; the NP *the letter* functions as the object of the Vb, and the Vb *will post* as its main verb. Following Chomsky (1965), we call such terms as 'noun phrase', 'verb phrase' *categorial labels*, and such terms as 'subject', 'object' *functional labels*. Chomsky proposes that we define the notion 'subject of' as [NP, S] and say, with respect to 2, that *this boy* is the subject of the sentence *This boy will post the letter* by virtue of the fact that it is the NP which is directly dominated by S in the phrase marker associated with the sentence. Similarly, the following definitions are proposed:

'Predicate of' [VP, S]
'Direct Object of' [NP, VP]
'Main Verb of' [Vb, VP]

Grammatical relations of the sort that hold between *boy* and *post* and between *post* and *letter* are defined derivatively in terms of the functional relations already established. In principle, then, according to Chomsky, we extract information concerning grammatical functions directly from the rewriting rules of the base, so as to avoid having to elaborate the rules to provide specific mention of grammatical functions.

One reason why sentences with superficially different structures are felt to be related is because the functional relationships between the various noun phrases and the verb remain constant under transformation. For example, the subject noun of an active sentence and the head noun of the by-phrase in its passive transform bear the same functional relationship to the verb — both denote the agent of the action denoted by the verb. Returning to a pair of sentences mentioned earlier:

21 (a) This boy will post the letter.
(b) The letter will be posted by this boy.

we find that *this boy* in both sentences may be referred to as the 'logical subject', whereas it is the 'grammatical subject' of the first sentence only. If we suppose that both sentences derive from a common underlying structure similar to 2, then we can account for this sense of relatedness by saying that the 'logical subject' of a passive sentence is the NP directly dominated by S in the underlying phrase marker, and the 'grammatical subject' is the NP directly dominated by S in the derived phrase marker.

However, not all logical subjects are agents like *this boy* in 21(a). Consider for example the following sentences:

22 The boy received a letter.
The boy fell down the stairs.
The boy had a headache.
The boy owned a boxer dog.

The involvement of *the boy* in the event or situation described appears to be quite different in each case, and in none of the sentences can the subject be regarded as an 'agent' in the sense of 'agent' being the deliberate originator of an action.

It appears from the sentences in 22 and from many other examples that the functional relationships between noun phrases and verbs are a good deal more complex than would seem to be suggested by Chomsky's treatment of function. For this reason, Chomsky's conclusions have been challenged by a number of linguists who argue that the definition of 'subject' and 'object' should take precedence over categorial terms like 'noun phrase' and 'verb phrase'. Others have gone further and have suggested that functions like 'subject' and 'object' are relatively superficial, and that underlying them is a 'deep' syntactic specification in which such items as 'agentive', 'instrumental', 'locative', 'dative' are the determinant elements. In particular, Fillmore has argued that the semantic roles which noun phrases have with respect to their predicate verbs and the position of noun phrases in syntactic configurations are two different aspects of description, and that linguistic theory should provide some way of distinguishing between them.

In an attempt to account for the functional relations between noun phrases and the verb, Fillmore, in an article entitled 'The case for case', suggests that the underlying structure of a sentence contains a verb and one or more noun phrases, each noun phrase being associated with the verb in a particular case relationship. Among the cases he proposes are:

Agentive (A), the case of the typically animate perceived instigator of the action identified by the verb.
Instrumental (I), the case of the inanimate force or object causally involved in the action or state identified by the verb.
Dative (D), the case of the animate being affected by the state or action identified by the verb.
Locative (L), the case that identifies the location or spatial orientation of the state or action identified by the verb.
Objective (O) (or *Neutral*), the case of anything representable by a noun whose role in the action or state identified by the verb is identified by the semantic interpretation of the verb itself.

There is no one-to-one relationship between case categories in deep structure, and surface structure categories such as 'subject' or 'object'. Thus, *John* is Agentive in 23(a) and (b):

23 (a) John opened the door.
(b) The door was opened by John.

John is Dative in 24(a) and (b), but also in (c):

24 (a) We persuaded John that he would win.
(b) It was apparent to John that he would win.
(c) John believed that he would win.

In all of the following, *the key* is Instrumental:

25 (a) The key opened the door.
(b) John opened the door with the key.
(c) John used the key to open the door.

In 23, 24, or 25 the function of each noun phrase remains the same despite the different surface realizations of the sentences. If we want to describe the processes whereby a set of case categories in deep structure is realized in different ways in surface structure, we need to know the transformational properties of verbs, which include the selection of prepositions and complementizers (*that, -ing, to*, etc.) appearing in surface structure, and the choice of one noun phrase to become the surface subject. For example, 'unmarked' active sentences like 23(a) follow the rule suggested by Fillmore: 'if there is an A it becomes the subject; otherwise the subject is the O.' For passive sentences like 23(b) we need a rule which states that if there is an A and an O and the O is selected as subject, then the verb must be in the passive form and the A must be preceded by the preposition *by* and follow the verb.

The emphasis on predicates and role-types in Fillmore's grammar makes it possible to separate purely syntactic phenomena, having to do with the left-to-right positioning of elements in the flow of speech, from semantic interpretation. One advantage of this approach is that two phonologically distinct predicate verbs — *buy/sell, teach/learn, send/receive* — can be interpreted as being semantically identical in that they have the same number of elements in the same roles, but differ in the processes which arrange their elements into syntactic configurations. Thus, in the pair of sentences *John sold the house to Bill/Bill bought the house from John* the relationship of 'John' to 'sold' is the same as that of 'bought' to 'John', and the relationship of 'sold' to 'Bill' is the same as that of 'Bill' and 'bought'. Using case notions we are able to express the fact that in both sentences *John* is Agentive, *the house* is Objective and *Bill* is the 'receiver' (Benefactive). [. . .]

Notes

1. We would like to acknowledge the help of Keith Brown in Sections 4, 5 and 6.
2. He gave a book in the sense of 'He gave a book to someone' is questionable. The answer to *What did he give to Mary* is not *He gave a book* but *He gave her a book*. However, *He gave a book* does occur if 'give' has the meaning of 'donate'. Thus, *What did he give to the jumble sale — He gave a book.*
3. For the purpose of the present discussion the difference between plus-signs and dashes used as concatenation symbols can be disregarded.

References

Bloomfield, L. (1933) *Language*. New York: Holt, Rinehart, Winston. (1935) London: Allen & Unwin.

Chomsky, N. (1957) *Syntactic Structures*. The Hague: Mouton.

Chomsky, N. (1965) *Aspects of the Theory of Syntax*. Cambridge, Mass.: MIT Press.

Chomsky, N. (1968a) *Language and Mind*. New York: Harcourt Brace. New enlarged edition 1972.

Fillmore, C. J. (1968) 'The case for case'. In Bach E. and Harms R. T, (eds) *Universals in Linguistic Theory*. New York: Holt, Rinehart, Winston.

Jacobson, R. (1966) 'The role of deep structures in language teaching', *Language Learning*, Vol. 16, pp 153–60.

Saussure, Ferdinand de (1955) *Cours de Linguistique Générale*, 5th edition Paris: Payot (First edition 1916). English translation by Wade Baskin, (1959) *Course in General Linguistics*. New York: Philosophical Library.

Sledd, J. (1959) *A Short Introduction to English Grammar*. Chicago: Scott, Foresman.

1.3 Saussure's Theory of Language

J. Culler

Source: Extracts from Culler, J. (1976) *Saussure*. Sussex, Fontana/Harvester, pp. 18–52.

Saussure was unhappy with linguistics as he knew it because he thought that his predecessors had failed to think seriously or perceptively about what they were doing. Linguistics, he wrote, 'never attempted to determine the nature of the object it was studying, and without this elementary operation a science cannot develop an appropriate method' (*Course*, 3; *Cours*, 16).

This operation is all the more necessary because human language is an extremely complex and heterogeneous phenomenon. Even a single speech act involves an extraordinary range of factors and could be considered from many different, even conflicting points of view. One could study the way sounds are produced by the mouth, vocal cords and tongue; one could investigate the sound waves which are emitted and the way they affect the hearing mechanism. One could consider the signifying intention of the speaker, the aspects of the world to which this utterance refers, the immediate circumstances of the communicative context which might have led him to produce a particular series of noises. One might try to analyse the conventions which enable speaker and listeners to understand one another, working out the grammatical and semantic rules which they must have assimilated if they are to communicate in this way. Or again, one could trace the history of the language which makes available these particular forms at this time.

Confronted with all these phenomena and these different perspectives from which one might approach them, the linguist must ask himself what he is trying to describe. What in particular is he looking at? What is he looking for? What, in short, is language?

Saussure's answer to this question is unexceptionable but extremely important, since it serves to direct attention to essentials. Language is a system of signs. Noises count as language only when they serve to express or communicate ideas; otherwise they are just noise. And to communicate ideas they must be part of a system of conventions, part of a system of signs. The sign is the union of a form which signifies, which Saussure calls the *significant* or signifier, and an idea signified, the *signifié* or signified. Though we may speak of signifier and signified as if they were separate entities, they exist only as components of the sign. The sign is the central fact of language, and therefore in trying to separate what is essential from what is secondary or incidental we must start from the nature of the sign itself.

The arbitrary nature of the sign

The first principle of Saussure's theory of language concerns the essential quality of the sign. The linguistic sign is arbitrary. A particular combination of signifier and signified is an arbitrary entity. This is a central fact of language and linguistic method. 'No one', he writes,

> contests the principle of the arbitrary nature of the sign, but it is often easier to discover a truth than to assign it its rightful place. The above principle dominates the whole of linguistic analysis of a language. Its consequences are innumerable, though they are not all, it is true, equally evident straight away. It is after many detours that one discovers them, and with them the fundamental importance of this principle (*Course*, 68; *Cours*, 100)

What does Saussure mean by the arbitrary nature of the sign? In one sense the answer is quite simple. There is no natural or inevitable link between the signifier and the signified. Since I speak English I may use the signifier represented by *dog* to talk about an animal of a particular species, but this sequence of sounds is no better suited to that purpose than another sequence. *Lod, tet* or *bloop* would serve equally well if they were accepted by members of my speech community. There is no intrinsic reason why one of these signifiers rather than another should be linked with the concept of a 'dog'.[1]

Are there no exceptions to this basic principle? Certainly. There are two ways in which linguistic signs may be motivated, that is to say, made less arbitrary. First, there are cases of onomatopœia, where the sound of the signifier seems in some way mimetic or imitative, as in the English *bow-wow* or *arf-arf* (cf. French *ouâ-ouâ*, German *wau-wau*, Italian *bau-bau*). But there are few such cases, and the fact that we identify them as a separate class and special case only emphasizes more strongly that ordinary signs are arbitrary.

However, within a particular language signs may be partially motivated in a different way. The machine on which I am writing is called a *typewriter*. There is no intrinsic reason why it should not be called a *grue* or a *blimmel*, but within English *typewriter* is motivated because the meanings of the two sound sequences which compose its signifier, *type* and *writer*, are related to its signified, to the notion of a 'typewriter'. We might call this 'secondary motivation'. Notice, for example, that only in English is the relation between sound-sequence and concept motivated. If the French were to use the same form to speak of this machine, that would be a wholly arbitrary sign, since the primary constituent, *writer*, is not a sign in the French language. Moreover, for Saussure, as we shall see later, the process of combining *type* and *writer* to create a new motivated sign is fundamentally similar to the way in which we combine words to form phrases (whose meaning is related to the combined meanings of individual words). We can say, therefore, that all languages have as their basic elements arbitrary signs. They then have various processes for combining these signs, but that does not alter the essential nature of language and its elementary constituents.

The sign is arbitrary in that there is no intrinsic link between signifier and signified. This is how Saussure's principle is usually interpreted, but in this form it is a wholly traditional notion, a rather obvious fact about language. Interpreted in this limited way, it does not have the momentous consequences which, according to the students' notes, Saussure repeatedly claimed for it: 'the hierarchical place of this truth is at the very summit. It is only little by little that one recognizes how many different facts are but ramifications, hidden consequences of this truth' (Engler, 153). There is more to the arbitrary nature of the sign than the arbitrary relation between signifier and signified. We must push further.

From what I have said so far about signifier and signified, one might be tempted to think of language as a nomenclature: a series of names arbitrarily selected and attached to a set of objects or concepts. It is, Saussure says, all too easy to think of language as a set of names and to make the biblical story of Adam naming the beasts an account of the very nature of language. If one says that the concept 'dog' is rendered or expressed by *dog* in English, *chien* in French and *Hund* in German, one implies that each language has an arbitrary name for a concept which exists prior to and independently of any language.

If language were simply a nomenclature for a set of universal concepts, it would be easy to translate from one language to another. One would simply replace the French name for a concept with the English name. If language were like this the task of learning a new language would also be much easier than it is. But anyone who has attempted either of these tasks has acquired, alas, a vast amount of direct proof that languages are not nomenclatures, that the concepts or signifieds of one language may differ radically from those of another. The French 'aimer' does not go directly into English; one must choose between 'to like' and 'to love'. 'Démarrer' includes in a single idea the English signifieds of 'moving off' and 'accelerating'. English 'to know' covers the area of two French signifieds, 'connaître' and 'savoir'. The English concepts of a 'wicked' man or of a 'pet' have no real counterparts in French. Or again, what English calls 'light blue' and 'dark blue' and treats as two shades of a single colour are in Russian two distinct primary colours. Each language articulates or organizes the world differently. Languages do not simply name existing categories, they articulate their own.

Moreover, if language were a set of names applied to independently existing concepts, then in the historical evolution of a language the concepts should remain stable. Signifiers could evolve; the particular sequence of sounds associated with a given concept might be modified; and a given sequence of sounds could even be attached to a different concept. Occasionally, of course, a new sign would have to be introduced for a new concept which had been produced by changes in the world. But the concepts themselves, as language-independent entities, would not be subject to linguistic evolution.

In fact, though, the history of languages is full of examples of concepts shifting, changing their boundaries. The English word *cattle*, for example, at one point meant property in general, then gradually came to be restricted to four-footed property only (a new category), and finally attained its modern sense of domesticated bovines. Or again, a 'silly' person was once happy, blessed and pious. Gradually this particular concept altered; the old concept of 'silliness' transformed itself, and by the beginning of the sixteenth century a silly person was innocent, helpless, even deserving of pity. The alteration of the concept continued until eventually a silly person was simple, foolish, perhaps even stupid. [. . .]

What is the significance of this? What does it have to do with the arbitrary nature of the sign? Language is not a nomenclature and therefore its signifieds are not pre-existing concepts but changeable and contingent concepts which vary from one state of a language to another. And since the relation between signifier and signified is arbitrary, since there is no necessary reason for one concept rather than another to be attached to a given signifier, there is therefore no defining property which the concept must retain in order to count as the signified of that signifier. The signified associated with a signifier can take any form; there is no essential core of meaning that it must retain in order to count as the proper signified for that signifier. The fact that the relation between signifier and signified is arbitrary means, then, that since there are no fixed universal concepts or fixed universal signifiers, the signified itself is arbitrary, and so is the signifier. We then must ask, as Saussure does, what defines a signifier or a signified, and the answer leads us to a very important principle: both signifier and signified are purely relational or differential entities. Because they are arbitrary they are relational. This is a principle which requires explanation.

The nature of linguistic units

Saussure attaches great importance — more so than it would appear from the published *Course* — to the fact that language is not a nomenclature, for unless we grasp this we cannot understand the full ramifications of the arbitrary nature of the sign. A language does not simply assign arbitrary names to a set of independently existing concepts. It sets up an arbitrary relation between signifiers of its own choosing on the one hand, and signifieds of its own choosing on the other. Not only does each language produce a different set of signifiers, articulating and dividing the continuum of sound in a distinctive way; each language produces a different set of signifieds; it has distinctive and thus 'arbitrary' ways of organizing the world into concepts or categories.

It is obvious that the sound sequences of *fleuve* and *revière* are signifiers of French but not of English, whereas *river* and *stream* are English but not French. Less obviously but more significantly, the organization of the conceptual plane is also different in English and French. The signified 'river' is opposed to 'stream' solely in terms of size, whereas a 'fleuve' differs from a 'rivière' not because it is necessarily larger but because it flows into the sea, while a 'rivière' does not. In short, 'fleuve' and 'revière' are not signifieds or concepts of English. They represent a different articulation of the conceptual plane.

The fact that these two languages operate perfectly well with different conceptual articulations or distinctions indicates that these divisions are not natural, inevitable or necessary, but, in an important sense, arbitrary. Obviously it is important that a language has ways of talking about flowing bodies of water, but it can make its conceptual distinctions in this area in any of a wide variety of ways (size, swiftness of flow, straightness or sinuosity, direction of flow, depth, navigability, etc.). Not only can a language arbitrarily choose its signifiers; it can divide up a spectrum of conceptual possibilities in any way it likes.

Moreover, and here we come to an important point, the fact that these concepts or signifieds are arbitrary divisions of a continuum means that they are not autonomous entities, each of which is defined by some kind of essence. They are members of a system and are defined by their relations to the other members of that system. If I am to explain to someone the meaning of *stream* I must tell him about the difference between a stream and a river, a stream and a rivulet, etc. And similarly, I cannot explain the French concept of a 'rivière' without describing the distinction between 'rivière' and 'fleuve' on the one hand and 'rivière' and 'ruisseau' on the other.

[. . .] But perhaps the easiest way to grasp this notion of the purely relational nature of linguistic units is to approach it from another angle.

Consider the problem of identity in linguistics: the question of when two utterances or portions of an utterance count as examples of a single linguistic unit. Suppose someone tells me, 'I bought a bed today', and I reply, 'What sort of bed?' What do we mean when we say that the same sign has been employed twice in this brief conversation? What is the basis on which we can claim that two examples or instances of the same linguistic unit have appeared in our dialogue? Note that we have already begged the question in transcribing a portion of the noises that each of us made as *bed*. In fact, the actual noises which were produced will have been measurably different — different from a purely physical and acoustic point of view. Voices vary; after a very few words we can recognize a friend's voice on the telephone because the actual physical signals he emits are different from those of our other acquaintances.

My interlocutor and I produced different noises, yet we want to say that we have produced the same signifier, used the same sign. The signifier, then, is not the same thing as the noises that either he or I produced. It is an abstract unit of some kind, not to be confused with the actual sequence of sounds. But what sort of unit is it? Of what does the unit consist? We might approach this question by asking how far the actual noises produced could vary and still count as versions of the same signifier. This, of course, is similar to the question we implicitly asked earlier about the signified: how far can a colour vary and still count as brown? And the answer for the signifier is very similar to the answer for the signified. The noises made can vary considerably (there is no essential property which they must possess) so long as they do not become confused with those of contrasting signifiers. We have considerable latitude in the way we utter *bed*, so long as what we say is not confused with *bad, bud, bid, bode; bread, bled, dead, fed, head, led, red, said, wed; beck, bell, bet.*

In other words, it is distinctions which are important, and it is for this reason that linguistic units have a purely relational identity. The principle is not easy to grasp, but Saussure offers a concrete analogy. We are willing to grant that in an important sense the 8.25 Geneva-to-Paris Express is the same train each day, even though the coaches, locomotive and personnel change from one day to the next. What gives the train its identity is its place in the system of trains, as indicated by the timetable. And note that this relational identity is indeed the determining factor: the train remains the same train even if it leaves half an hour late. Indeed, it might always leave late without ceasing to be the 8.25 Geneva-to-Paris Express. What is important is that it be distinguished from, say, the 10.25 Geneva-to-Paris Express, the 8.40 Geneva-to-Dijon local, etc.

Another analogy which Saussure uses to illustrate the notion of relational identity is the comparison between language and chess. The basic units of chess are obviously king, queen, rook, knight, bishop, and pawn. The actual physical shape of the pieces and the material from which they are made is of no importance. The king may be of any size and shape, as long as there are ways of distinguishing it from other pieces. Moreover, the two rooks need not be of identical size and shape, so long as they can be distinguished from other pieces. Thus, as Saussure points out, if a piece is lost from a chess set we can replace it with any other sort of object, provided always that this object will not be confused with the objects representing pieces of a different value (*Course*, 110; *Cours*, 153–154). The actual physical properties of pieces are of no importance, so long as there are differences of some kind — any kind will do — between pieces which have a different value.

Thus one can say that the units of the game of chess have no material identity: there are no physical properties necessary to a king, etc. Identity is wholly a function of differences within a system. [. . .] The actual sounds we produce in speaking are not in themselves units of the linguistic system [. . .], the linguistic unit is form rather than substance, defined by the relations which set it off from other units.

'Langue' and 'parole'

Here, in the distinction between the linguistic system and its actual manifestations, we have reached the crucial opposition between *langue* and *parole. La langue* is the system of a language, the language as a system of forms, whereas *parole* is actual speech, the speech acts which are made possible by the language. *La langue* is what the individual assimilates when he learns a language, a set of forms or 'hoard deposited by the practice of speech in speakers who belong to the same community, a grammatical system which, to all intents and purposes, exists in the mind of each speaker' (*Course*, 13–14; *Cours*, 30). 'It is the social product whose existence permits the individual to exercise his linguistic faculty' (Engler, 31). *Parole*, on the other hand, is the 'executive side of language' and for Saussure involves both 'the combinations by which the speaker uses the code of the linguistic system in order to express his own thoughts' and 'the psycho-physical mechanisms which permit him to externalize these combinations' (*Course*, 14; *Cours*, 31). In the act of *parole* the speaker selects and combines elements of the linguistic system and gives these forms a concrete phonic and psychological manifestation, as sounds and meanings.

[. . .] *La langue*, Saussure argued, must be the linguist's primary concern. What he is trying to do in analysing a language is not to describe speech acts but to determine the units, the rules of combination which make up the linguistic system. *La langue*, or the linguistic system, is a coherent, analysable object; 'it is a system of signs in which the only essential thing is the union of meanings and acoustic images' (*Course*, 15; *Cours*, 32). In studying language as a system of signs one is trying to identify its essential features: those elements which are crucial to the signifying function of language or, in other words, the elements which are functional within the system in that they create signs by distinguishing them one from another.

The distinction between *langue* and *parole* thus provides a principle of relevance for linguistics. 'In separating *langue* from *parole*', Saussure writes, 'we are separating what is social from what is individual and what is essential from what is ancillary or accidental' (*Course*, 14, *Cours*, 30). If we tried to study everything related to the phenomenon of speech we would enter a realm of confusion where relevance and irrelevance were extremely difficult to determine, but if we concentrate on *la langue*, then various aspects of language and speech fall into place within or around it. Once we put forward this notion of the linguistic system, we can then ask of every phenomenon whether it belongs to the system itself or is simply a feature of the performance or realization of linguistic units, and we thus succeed in classifying speech facts into groups where they can profitably be studied.

For example, the distinction between *langue* and *parole* leads to the creation of two distinct disciplines which study sound and its linguistic functions: phonetics, which studies sound in speech acts from a physical point of view, and phonology, which is not interested in physical events themselves but in the distinctions between the abstract units of the signifier which are functional within the linguistic system. [. . .]

The distinction between phonetics and phonology takes us back to points made earlier about the linguistic identity of the form *bed*. Phonetics would describe the actual sounds produced when one utters the form, but, as we argued above, the identity of *bed* as a unit of English does not depend on the nature of these actual sounds but on the distinctions which separate *bed* from *bet, bad, head*, etc. Phonology is the study of these functional distinctions, and 'functional' is what should be stressed here. For example, in English utterances there is a perceptible and measurable difference between the 'l-sound' which occurs before vowels (as in *lend* or *alive*) and that which occurs before consonants or at the end of words (as in *melt* or *peel*). This is a real *phonetic* difference, but it is not a difference ever used to distinguish between two signs. It is not a functional difference and therefore is not a part of the phonological system of English. On the other hand, the difference between the vowels of *feel* and *fill* is used in English to distinguish signs (compare *keel* and *kill, keen* and *kin, seat* and *sit, heat* and *hit*, etc.). This opposition plays a very important role in the phonological system of English in that it creates a large number of distinct signs.

The same distinction between what belongs to particular linguistic acts and what belongs to the linguistic system itself is important at other levels too, not just that of sound. We can distinguish, for example, between utterance, as a unit of *parole*, and sentence, a unit of *la langue*. Two different utterances may be manifestations of the same sentence; so once again we encounter this central notion of identity in linguistics. The actual sounds and the contextual meanings of the two utterances will be different; what makes the two utterances instances of a single linguistic unit will be the distinctions which give that unit a relational identity.

For example, if at some time Cuthbert says 'I am tired', *I* refers to Cuthbert, and understanding this reference is an important part of understanding the utterance. However, that reference is not part of the meaning of the sentence, for George also may utter the same sentence, and in his utterance *I* will refer to George. Within the linguistic system *I* does not refer to anyone. Its meaning in the system is the result of the distinctions between *I* and *you, he, she, it, we,* and *they*: a meaning which we can sum up by saying that *I* means 'the speaker' as opposed to anyone else.

[. . .] By separating *langue* from *parole* Saussure gave linguistics a suitable object of study and gave the linguist a much clearer sense of what he was doing: if he focused on language as a system then he knew what he was trying to reconstruct and could, within this perspective, determine what evidence was relevant and how it should be organized.

Synchronic and diachronic perspectives

There is another important consequence of the arbitrary nature of sign which has also been treated by Saussure's critics as a questionable and unnecessary imposition. This is the distinction between the *synchronic* study of language (study of the linguistic system in a particular state, without reference to time) and the *diachronic* study of language (study of its evolutionary in time). It has been suggested that in distinguishing rigorously between these two perspectives and in granting priority to the synchronic study of language, Saussure was ignoring, or at least setting aside, the fact that a language is fundamentally historical and contingent, an entity in constant evolution. But on the contrary, it was precisely because he recognized, more profoundly than his critics, the radical historicity of language that he asserted the importance of distinguishing between facts about the linguistic system and facts about linguistic evolution, even in cases where the two kinds of facts seem extraordinarily intertwined. There is an apparent paradox here, which requires elucidation.

What is the connection between the arbitrary nature of the sign and the profoundly historical nature of language? We can put it in this way: if there were some essential or natural connection between signifier and signified, then the sign would have an essential core, which would be unaffected by time or which at least would resist change. This unchanging essence could be opposed to those 'accidental' features which did alter from one period to another. But in fact, as we have seen, there is no aspect of the sign which is a necessary property and which therefore lies outside time. Any aspect of sound or meaning can alter; the history of languages is full of radical evolutionary alterations of both sound and meaning. The Old English *þing* meaning 'discussion' has gradually become the modern English *thing* with a totally different meaning. The Greek θηριακὸς (theriakos) meaning 'pertaining to a wild animal' became the modern English *treacle*. The Latin *calidum* ('hot') became the modern French *chaud* (pronounced ʃo, as in English *show*), in which meaning persists but none of the original phonological elements is preserved. In short, neither signifier nor signified contains any essential core which time cannot touch. Because it is arbitrary, the sign is totally subject to history, and the combination at a particular moment of a given signifier and signified is a contingent result of the historical process.

The fact that the sign is arbitrary or wholly contingent makes it subject to history but also means that signs require an ahistorical analysis. This is not as paradoxical as it might seem. Since the sign has no necessary core which must persist, it must be defined as a relational entity, in its relations to other signs. And the relevant relations are those which obtain at a particular time. A language, Saussure says, 'is a system of pure values which are determined by nothing except the momentary arrangement of its terms' (*Course*, 80; *Cours*, 116). Because the language is a wholly historical entity, always open to change, one must focus on the relations which exist in a particular synchronic state if one is to define its elements.

In asserting the priority of synchronic description, Saussure is pointing out the irrelevance of historical or diachronic facts to the analysis of *la langue*. Some examples will show why diachronic information is irrelevant. In modern English the second person pronoun *you* is used to refer both to one person and to many and can be either the subject or object in a sentence. In an earlier state of the language, however, *you* was defined by its opposition to *ye* on the one hand (*ye* a subject pronoun and *you* an object pronoun) and to *thee* and *thou* on the other (*thee* and *thou* singular forms and *you* a plural form). At a later stage *you* came to serve also as a respectful way of addressing one person, like the modern French *vous*. Now in modern English *you* is no longer defined by its opposition to *ye*, *thee* and *thou*. One can know and speak modern English perfectly without knowing that *you* was once a plural and objective form, and indeed if one knows this there is no way in which this knowledge can serve as part of one's knowledge of modern English. The description of modern English *you* would remain exactly the same if its historical evolution had been wholly different, for *you* in modern English is defined by its role in the synchronic state of the language.

[. . .]

Saussure argues that despite their different status, diachronic statements are derived from synchronic statements. What allows us, he asks, to state the fact that Latin *mare* became French *mer* ('sea')? The historical linguist might argue that we know *mare* became *mer* because here, as elsewhere, the final *e* was dropped and *a* became *e*. But, Saussure argues, to suggest that these regular sound changes are what create the link between the two forms is to get things backwards, because what enables us to identify this sound change is our initial notion that one form became the other. 'We are using the correspondence between *mare* and *mer* to decide that *a* became *e* and that final *e* fell' (*Course*, 182; *Cours*, 249).

In fact, what we are supposing in connecting *mare* and *mer* is this: that *mare, mer* and the intermediate forms constitute an unbroken chain of synchronic identities. At each period where, retrospectively, we can say that a change occurred, there was an old form and a new form which were phonetically different but phonologically or functionally identical. They may of course have had different associations (e.g. one form might have seemed a bit old-fashioned) but they could be used interchangeably by speakers. No doubt some would stick to the old form and others prefer the new, but since the move from one to the other would not produce a difference in actual meaning, from the point of view of the linguistic system there would be a synchronic identity between the two forms. It is in this sense that diachronic identity depends on a series of synchronic identities.

[. . .]

Thus, one cannot argue that diachronic linguistics is in some way closer to the reality of language, while synchronic analysis is a fiction. Historical filiations are derived from synchronic identities. Not only that, they are facts of a different order. Synchronically speaking, diachronic identities are a distortion, for the earlier and later signs which they relate have no common properties. Each sign has no properties other than the specific relational properties which define it within its own synchronic system. From the point of view of systems of signs, which after all is the point of view which matters when dealing with signs, the earlier and later sign are wholly disparate.

Whence the importance of separating the synchronic and diachronic perspectives, even when the facts they are treating seem inextricably intertwined. This is a point which one must stress, because linguists who oppose Saussure's radical distinction between synchronic and diachronic approaches and wish to envisage a synthetic, panchronic perspective often point to the entanglement of synchronic and diachronic facts as if it supported their case. Saussure is all too aware of the intertwining of synchronic and diachronic facts; indeed, for him the whole difficulty is one separating these elements when they are mixed, because only in this way can linguistic analysis attain coherence. Linguistic forms have synchronic and diachronic aspects which must be separated because they are facts of a different order, with different conditions of existence.

[. . .]

Language as social fact

In explaining these technical aspects of Saussure's theory of language we have not emphasized sufficiently one principle to which he gave great weight: that in analysing a language we are analysing social facts, dealing with the social use of material objects. As we have said, a language could be realized in various substances without alteration to its basic nature as a system of relations. What is important, indeed all that is relevant, are the distinctions and relations that have been endowed with meaning by a society. The question the analyst constantly asks is what are the differences which have meaning for members of the speech community. It may often be difficult to assign a precise form to those things that function as signs, but if a difference bears meaning for members of a culture, then there is a sign, however abstract, which must be analysed. For speakers of English *John loves Mary* is different in meaning from *Mary loves John*; therefore the word-order constitutes a sign, a social fact, whereas some physical differences between the way two speakers utter the sentence, *John loves Mary*, may bear no meaning and therefore be purely material facts, not social facts.

We can see, then, that the linguist studies not large collections of sound sequences but a system of social conventions. He is trying to determine the units and rules of combination which make up that system and which make possible linguistic communication between members of a society. It is one of the virtues of Saussure's theory of language to have placed social conventions and social facts at the centre of linguistic investigation by stressing the problem of the sign. What are the signs of this linguistic system? On what does their identity as signs depend? Asking these simple questions, demonstrating that nothing can be taken for granted as a unit of language, Saussure continually stressed the importance of adopting the right methodological perspective and seeing language as a system of socially determined values, not as a collection of substantially defined elements.

Note

1. Note that here, as throughout, I use italics to cite linguistic forms (e.g. *dog, tod*) and quotation marks to designate meanings (e.g. 'dog')

References

[Editor's note: the first edition of Saussure's *Cours de Linguistique Générale* was published in 1916. Text citations '*Cours*', '*Course*' and 'Engler' throughout this article refer to specific subsequent editions of Saussure's work, as listed below.]

'*Course*': de Saussure, F. (1960) *Course in General Linguistics*, translated by Wade Baskin. London, Peter Owen and London, Fontana (1974).

'*Cours*': de Saussure, F. (1973) *Cours de Linguistique Générale*, edited by Tullio de Mauro. Paris, Payot.

'Engler': de Saussure, F. (1967) *Course in General Linguistics: critical edition*, edited by Rudolph Engler. Wiesbaden: Otto Harrassowitz.

1.4 Discourse Analysis as a New Cross-Discipline

T.A. van Dijk

Source: Extracts from van Dijk, T. A. (1985) 'Introduction: Discourse analysis as a new cross-discipline'. In *Handbook of Discourse Analysis, Vol. 1 Disciplines of Discourse*. London: Academic Press, pp. 1–10.

Historical background

Discourse analysis is both an old and a new discipline. Its origins can be traced back to the study of language, public speech and literature more than 2000 years ago. One major historical source is undoubtedly classical rhetoric, the art of good speaking. Whereas the *grammatica*, the historical antecedent of linguistics, was concerned with the normative rules of correct language use, its sister discipline of *rhetorica* dealt with the precepts for the planning, organization, specific operations and performance of public speech in political and legal settings. Its crucial concern, therefore, was persuasive effectiveness. In this sense, classical rhetoric both anticipates contemporary stylistics and structural analyses of discourse and contains intuitive cognitive and social psychological notions about memory organization and attitude change in communicative contexts.

After some important revivals in the Middle Ages and the seventeenth and eighteenth centuries, however, rhetoric lost much of its importance in the curricula of schools and in academic research. The emergence of historical and comparative linguistics at the beginning of the nineteenth century and the birth of structural analysis of language at the beginning of the twentieth century replaced rhetoric as the primary discipline of the humanities. Fragments of rhetoric survived only in school textbooks of speech and communication, on one hand, and in stylistics or the study of literary language, on the other.

Yet, parallel to this decline of rhetoric as an independent academic discipline, new developments in several fields of the humanities and the social sciences took place that would eventually lead to the emergence of discourse analysis. First, the young revolution in Russia witnessed concomitant new ideas in anthropology, poetics and linguistics, an interdisciplinary development known under the label of 'Russian formalism'. Apart from research by literary scholars and linguists (and related new experiments in the theory and practice of art and film), one of the (later) most influential books of that time appeared to be *Morphology of the Folktale* by Vladimir Propp (1928; first English translation, 1958). Major structural principles of early linguistics (phonology, morphology) were here paralleled with a first structural analysis of discourse, namely the Russian folktale, in terms of a set of fixed thematic functions in which variable contents of different tales could be inserted. [. . .] Lévi-Strauss' structural analysis of culture, and especially his analysis of myths, in part inspired by Propp and by the further development of structural linguistics in Europe, was at the same time one of the sources for renewal in anthropology, poetics and other branches of the humanities and the social sciences. These early interdisciplinary developments of the middle 1960s were often captured under the new (or rather, renewed) label of 'semiotics', to which is associated the names of Barthes, Greimas, Todorov and many others engaged in the structural analysis of narrative and other discourse forms or cultural practices.

Structuralism and the analysis of texts (1964–1972)

Although of course historical developments are more continuous than is suggested here, it seems warranted to locate the origins of modern discourse analysis in the middle 1960s. The first publication of structural analyses of discourse in France, by some of the authors mentioned above, appeared in 1964 (*Communications* 4): a new critical analysis of Propp by Bremond, an application of modern linguistics and semantics to literature by Todorov, the well-known extension to the analysis of film by Metz, the famous rhetorical analysis of publicity pictures by Barthes and finally, the first introduction to the new discipline of semiotics *sémiologie*, also by Barthes. This issue of *Communications* was followed two years later by another special issue (*Communications* 8), which was completely dedicated to the structural analysis of narrative (with contributions by the same authors, but also by Greimas, Eco and Genette, among others). Although the background, orientations, objects of research and methods of all these authors were still far from homogeneous, the common interest in discourse analysis within the wider framework of a linguistically inspired semiotics influenced and provided coherence in these first attempts.

At the same time, on the other side of the ocean, 1964 also saw the publication of another influential book of readings: Hymes' *Language in Culture and Society*. Although notions such as 'discourse' or 'text' do not yet dominate the contributions to that voluminous book, there is attention to forms of 'speech', 'communication' and to specific topics such as 'forms of address', which would later develop into the discourse analytical orientation of the so-called ethnography of speaking in anthropology. Of course, there are obvious differences between this and the French brands of structuralism in the 1960s. Yet on both sides the interaction between structural linguistics and anthropology appeared to be very fruitful for the initial interest in the study of language use, discourse and communication forms. At the same time,

Hymes' collection not only contained the great names of linguistic anthropology (or anthropological linguistics), such as Boas, Greenberg, Goodenough, Lévi-Strauss, Malinowski, Firth, Sapir and many others, but also, the first collection of work from what soon would be called 'sociolinguistics' (Brown, Bernstein, Gumperz, Bright and others). That is, not only discourse, style, forms of address and verbal art, but also the social, cultural and historical contexts, and the variations of language use came to be studied systematically.

From a methodological point of view, it is interesting to note that the new linguistic paradigm that also came to be established in the mid-1960s, Chomsky's generative-transformational grammar, hardly appears in this book of classics. His name is mentioned only once in the index, merely referring to a 1955 article by him, although his *Syntactic Structures* figures in the general bibliography.

One other name that appears in Hymes' collection is that of Pike, whose tagmemic approach to language and human behaviour would soon also provide background for new developments in discourse analysis (Pike, 1967). The study of narratives in indigenous languages by him and his followers had always been closely related to the analysis of discourse (Grimes, 1975; Longacre, 1977).

Back in Europe again, 1964 also was the year in which the first linguistic appeals were made in favour of a so-called text linguistics or text grammar, first by Hartmann in a small paper, and soon by his students, such as Schmidt and others in the Germanies and the surrounding countries. In Europe, more than in the United States, the original plea by Harris (1952) for a linguistic discourse analysis was taken seriously and eventually led to a new, generative-transformational approach to the grammar of discourse. [. . .]

Another functional approach, finally, is characterized by the 'systemic grammar' developed by Halliday (1961), in which not only the thematic organization of sentences, but also the relations between sentences and discourse, were analysed. This work gave rise to several studies at the boundaries of linguistics, stylistics and poetics, both by Halliday himself and by Leech and Crystal. Besides poetry, conversation, advertising and news received systematic attention in these English studies.

From this brief historical review of the origins of modern discourse analysis, we may draw several conclusions. First, the early interest in systematic discourse analysis was essentially a descriptive and structuralist enterprise, mainly at the boundaries of linguistics and anthropology. Second, this interest primarily involved indigenous or popular discourse genres, such as folktales, myths and stories, as well as some ritual interaction forms. Third, the functional analysis of sentence and discourse structure as well as the first attempts towards text linguistics often took place independently of or against the increasingly prevailing paradigm of generative-transformational grammars. Both the formal sophistication and the inherent limitations of this approach to language would decisively influence the development of discourse analysis and other studies of language during the 1970s.

The emergence of discourse analysis as a new discipline (1972–1974)

Whereas the 1960s had brought various scattered attempts to apply semiotic or linguistic methods to the study of texts and communicative events, the early 1970s saw the publication of the first monographs and collections wholly and explicitly dealing with systematic discourse analysis as an independent orientation or research within and across several disciplines.

This development, however, did not come alone. Part of its theoretical and methodological inspiration was shared by other paradigm shifts in the study of language, for example a critical extension or refutation of formal, context-free transformational grammars. Thus, sociolinguistics, which had also begun to take shape in the late 1960s (Fishman, 1968), emphasized that the theoretical distinction between competence and performance, as it had been reintroduced by Chomsky (after Saussure's distinction between *langue* and *parole*), was not without problems. Against notions such as 'ideal speakers' and 'homogeneous speech community', sociolinguistic work stressed the importance of language variation in the sociocultural context. Apart from variations in phonology, morphology and syntax, and the dependence of stylistic variation on social factors, this reorientation also soon began to pay specific attention to discourse, for example the work of Labov (1972a, b). His studies of black English also involved analyses of forms of verbal duelling among adolescents, and his other sociolinguistic work featured analyses of natural storytelling about personal experience. This latter research was in marked contrast to the structuralist analysis of written stories mentioned above because of its interest in spoken language and the functions of discourse in the social context.

A second important development in the early 1970s was the discovery in linguistics of the philosophical work by Austin, Grice and Searle about speech acts. Whereas sociolinguistics stressed the role of language variation and the social context, this approach considered verbal utterances not only as sentences, but also as specific forms of social action. That is, sentences when used in some specific context also should be assigned some additional meaning or function, an illocutionary one, to be defined in terms of speaker intentions, beliefs or evaluations, or relations between speaker and hearer. In this way, not only could systematic properties of the context be accounted for, but also the relation between utterances as abstract linguistic objects and utterances taken as a form of social interaction could be explained. This new dimension added a pragmatic orientation to the usual theoretical components of language. [. . .]

Third, within the framework of grammatical theory itself, it was repeatedly maintained that grammars should not merely provide structural characterizations of isolated sentences. This and other arguments led to the development of text grammars, mainly in the Germanies and other European countries. The study of pronouns and other cohesion markers, of semantic coherence, presupposition, topic and comment, overall semantic macrostructures and other typical features of texts, understood as sequences of sentences, began to be studied in linguistics within a new, integrated perspective. Though demonstrating a more formal point of view, this new orientation shared with sociolinguistics and pragmatics its interest for an account of the structures of actual language use. The first books in the field, after a few articles in the 1960s, also began to appear in the early 1970s (Petöfi, 1971; Dressler, 1972; van Dijk, 1972; Schmidt, 1973), soon leading to a more widespread, interdisciplinary and broader study of textlinguistics and discourse, often independently in various countries (e.g. Halliday and Hasan, 1976).

At the same time psychology and the new field of artificial intelligence rediscovered discourse, after the early, and later influential, work on memory for stories by Bartlett (1932). More than other neighbouring disciplines, psychology and psycholinguistics developed in the shadow of transformational grammar, so that much work was concerned with the experimental testing of the psychological reality of, for example, syntactic rules. The early 1970s brought not only a decisive breakthrough — conditioned by Chomsky, Miller and others — of the cognitive and information processing paradigm against the prevailing behaviourism of the previous decades, but also a greater interest in semantic memory and the representation of knowledge (Carrol and Freedle, 1972; Lindsay and Norman, 1972). The extension of this cognitive research to models of memory for texts and of processes for text understanding and production was a natural step, and the collection edited by Carroll and Freedle, just mentioned, represents the first attempts in that direction. Work done by Kintsch, Bower, Rumelhart and others marked the beginnings of the psychological study of discourse (e.g. Kintsch, 1974) and at the same time demonstrated renewed interest for the earlier work by Bartlett (1932).

Artificial intelligence, the computer simulation of language understanding, at the same time started its important work about knowledge representations in memory. Thus, Charniak (1972) in his dissertation on children's stories showed the relevance of the vast amounts of world knowledge and the great numbers of knowledge-activation strategies needed for the understanding of even very simple children's stories. Bartlett's early notion of 'schema' now had the more sophisticated company of similar notions in artificial intelligence, such as 'script', 'scenario', 'frame', in the work by Schank, Abelson, Rumelhart and others in this new sister discipline of cognitive psychology (e.g. Schank and Abelson, 1977).

Apparently, paradigmatic shifts seldom come alone in a single discipline. The early 1970s also witnessed important developments in sociology, such as the increasing attention to the analysis of everyday conversations and other forms of natural dialogue in social interaction. Here too, the late 1960s saw a critical refutation of the prevailing macrosociological approaches to social structure: attention was turned to everyday social interaction and to commonsense interpretation categories at the microlevel of social reality.

This interpretative, phenomenological sociology was advocated by Goffman, Garfinkel and others. Work by the late Harvey Sacks (through his unpublished lecture notes and an occasional paper) primarily initiated and stimulated the soon quickly spreading analysis of everyday conversation. The early 1970s also saw the first published and widely read versions of this work (Sudnow, 1972; Cicourel, 1973; Sacks, Schegloff and Jefferson, 1974). With this approach, the predominant interest in monological discourse genres (texts, stories, myths, etc.) had found its necessary complement. Natural, mundane and spontaneous language use was primarily identified with conversation and other forms of dialogue in the social situation. People not only have implicit knowledge of the rules of grammar, but also of the rules of, for example, turn taking in conversation. In this respect, this conversational analysis recalls the early structural and formal approaches to the structures of sentences and provides the first elements of a grammar of verbal interaction. Thus, not only was a new dialogical dimension added to the earlier monological studies of discourse structures, but also a plea was made for the study of language and language use as a form of social interaction, as pragmatics or speech act theory had done in more formal and philosophical terms. Soon this work in sociology found its way into linguistics and other neighbouring disciplines. Not only conversations but also dialogues in the classroom or in other institutional settings received extensive interest, such as in the discourse analysis approach to classroom talk by Sinclair and Coulthard (1975) in England.

And finally, the circle of these independent beginnings of contemporary discourse analysis can be closed by returning again to the discipline where much of it had started in the first place: anthropology. The work by Hymes, Gumperz and others had yielded an increasingly autonomous orientation of ethnographic research on communicative events, labelled the 'ethnography of speaking' (or the 'ethnography of communication'). Under the inspiration of the influential and programmatic work of Hymes in the 1960s, new theories and fieldwork were collected in two readers (Gumperz and Hymes, 1972; Bauman and Scherzer, 1974). The boundaries between the sociolinguistics of discourse and this new branch of anthropology were fuzzy: the study of 'real' language use in the sociocultural context no longer stopped at form of address, rituals or myth, but also began to pay attention to the mundane forms of talk in different cultures, such as greetings, spontaneous storytelling, formal meeting, verbal duelling, and other forms of communication and verbal interaction. [. . .]

References Bibliography

This list of references is merely a selective bibliography of the major works and names of the people mentioned in this historical survey of the emergence of discourse analysis.

Bartlett, F. C. (1932) *Remembering*. London: Cambridge University Press.

Bauman, R., and Sherzer, J. (eds) (1974) *Explorations in the Ethnography of Speaking*. London: Cambridge University Press.

Carroll, J. S. and Freedle, R. O. (eds) (1972) *Language Comprehension and the Acquisition of Knowledge*. Washington, DC: Winston.

Charniak, E. (1972) *Towards a Model of Children's Story Comprehension*. Unpublished doctoral dissertation, Massachusetts Institute of Technology, Cambridge.

Cicourel, A. V. (1973) *Cognitive Sociology*. Harmondsworth: Penguin Books.

Communications 4 (1964) *Recherches Sémiologiques*. Paris: Seuil.

Communications 8 (1966) *Recherches Sémiologiques. L'Analyse Structurale du Rećit*. Paris: Seuil

Dressler, W. U. (1972) *Einführung in die Textlinguistik*. Tübingen: Niemeyer. (New version, with R. de Beaugrande, published as *Introduction to Text Linguistics*. London: Longman, 1981).

Fishman, J. (ed.) (1968) *Readings in the Sociology of Language*. The Hague: Mouton.

Grimes, J. E. (1975) *The Thread of Discourse*. The Hague: Mouton.

Gumperz, J. D. and Hymes D. (eds) (1972) *Directions in Sociolinguistics. The Ethnography of Communication*. New York: Holt, Rinehart & Winston.

Halliday, M. A. K. (1961) Categories of the theory of grammar, *Word*, **17**, 241–292.

Halliday, M. A. K. and Hasan, R. (1976) *Cohesion in English*. London: Longman.

Harris, Z. S. (1952) Discourse analysis. *Language*, **28**, 1–30.

Hartmann, P. (1964) Text, Texte, Klassen Von Texten. *Bogawus*, **2**, 15–25.

Hymes, D. (ed.) (1964) *Language in Culture and Society*. New York: Harper & Row.

Kintsch, W. (1974) *The Representation of Meaning in Memory*. Hillsdale, NJ: Erlbaum.

Labov, W. (1972a) *Language in the Inner City*. Philadelphia: University of Pennsylvania Press.

Labov, W. (1972b) *Sociolinguistic Patterns*. Philadelphia: University of Pennsylvania Press.

Lindsay, P. H. and Norman, D. A. (1972) *Human Information Processing*. New York: Academic Press.

Longacre, R. E. (ed.) (1977) *Discourse Grammar* (Vols. 1–3). Dallas: Summer Institute of Linguistics.

Petöfi, J. S. (1971) *Transformationsgrammatiken und eine Ko-textuelle Texttheorie*. Frankfurt: Athenaeum.

Pike, K. L. (1967) *Language in Relation to a Unified Theory of Human Behavior*. The Hague: Mouton.

Propp, V. (1958) *Morphology of the Folktale*. Bloomington, IN: Indiana University Press. (Original work published 1928.)

Sacks, H., Schegloff, E. and Jefferson, G. (1974) A simplest systematic of turntaking for conversation. *Language*, **50**, 696–735.

Schank, R. C. and Abelson, R. P. (1977) *Scripts, Plans, Goals and Understanding*. Hillsdale, NJ: Erlbaum.

Schmidt, S. J. (1973) *Texttheorie*. Munich: Fink (UTB).

Sinclair, J. McH. and Coulthard, R. M. (1975) *Towards an Analysis of Discourse. The English Used by Teachers and Pupils*. London: Oxford University Press.

Sudnow, D. (ed.) (1972) *Studies in Social Interaction*. New York: Free Press.

van Dijk, T. A. (1972) *Some Aspects of Text Grammars*. The Hague: Mouton.

1.5 Discourse in the Novel

M. M. Bakhtin

Source: Extracts from Bakhtin, M. M. (1981) 'Discourse in the novel'. In *The Dialogic Imagination*. University of Texas Press, pp. 287–422.

The principal idea of this essay is that the study of verbal art can and must overcome the divorce between an abstract 'formal' approach and an equally abstract 'ideological' approach. Form and content in discourse are one, once we understand that verbal discourse is a social phenomenon — social throughout its entire range and in each and every of its factors, from the sound image to the furthest reaches of abstract meaning.

[. . .]

Language — like the living concrete environment in which the consious-ness of the verbal artist lives — is never unitary. It is unitary only as an abstract grammatical system of normative forms, taken in isolation from the concrete, ideological conceptualizations that fill it, and in isolation from the uninterrupted process of historical becoming that is a characteristic of all living language. Actual social life and historical becoming create within an abstractly unitary national language a multitude of concrete worlds, a multitude of bounded verbal-ideological and social belief systems; within these various systems (identical in the abstract) are elements of language filled with various semantic and axiological content and each with its own different sound.

Literary language — both spoken and written — although it is unitary not only in its shared, abstract, linguistic markers but also in its forms for conceptualizing these abstract markers, is in itself stratified and heteroglot in its aspect as an expressive system, that is, in the forms that carry its meanings.

This stratification is accomplished first of all by the specific organisms called *genres*. Certain features of language (lexicological, semantic, syntactic) will knit together with the intentional aim, and with the overall accentual system inherent in one or another genre: oratorical, publicistic, newspaper and journalistic genres, the genres of low literature (penny dreadfuls, for instance) or, finally, the various genres of high literature. Certain features of language take on the specific flavour of a given genre: they knit together with specific points of view, specific approaches, forms of thinking, nuances and accents characteristic of the given genre.

In addition, there is interwoven with this generic stratification of language a *professional* stratification of language, in the broad sense of the term 'professional': the language of the lawyer, the doctor, the businessman, the politician, the public education teacher and so forth, and these sometimes coincide with, and sometimes depart from, the stratification into genres. It goes without saying that these languages differ from each other not only in their vocabularies; they involve specific forms for manifesting intentions, forms for making conceptualization and evaluation concrete. And even the very language of the writer (the poet or novelist) can be taken as a professional jargon on a par with other professional jargons.

What is important to us here is the intentional dimensions, that is, the denotative and expressive dimension of the 'shared' language's stratification. It is in fact not the neutral linguistic components of language being stratified and differentiated, but rather a situation in which the intentional possibilities of language are being expropriated: these possibilities are realized in specific directions, filled with specific content, they are made concrete, particular, and are permeated with concrete value judgements; they knit together with specific objects and with the belief systems of certain genres of expression and points of view peculiar to particular professions. Within these points of view, that is, for the speakers of the language themselves, these generic languages and professional jargons are directly intentional — they denote and express directly and fully, and are capable of expressing themselves without mediation; but outside, that is, for those not participating in the given purview, these languages may be treated as objects, as typifactions, as local colour. For such outsiders, the intentions permeating these languages become *things*, limited in their meaning and expression; they attract to, or excise from, such language a particular word — making it difficult for the word to be utilized in a directly intentional way, without any qualifications.

But the situation is far from exhausted by the generic and professional stratification of the common literary language. Although at its very core literary language is frequently socially homogeneous, as the oral and written language of a dominant social group, there is nevertheless always present, even here, a certain degree of social differentiation, a social stratification, that in other eras can become extremely acute. Social stratification may here and there coincide with generic and professional stratification, but in essence it is, of course, a thing completely autonomous and peculiar to itself.

Social stratification is also and primarily determined by differences between the forms used to convey meaning and between the expressive planes of various belief systems — that is, stratification expresses itself in typical differences in ways used to conceptualize and accentuate elements of language, and stratification may not violate the abstractly linguistic dialectological unity of the shared literary language.

What is more, all socially significant world views have the capacity to exploit the intentional possibilities of language through the medium of their specific concrete instancing. Various tendencies (artistic and otherwise), circles, journals, particular newspapers, even particular significant artistic works and individual persons are all capable of stratifying language, in proportion to their social significance; they are capable of attracting its words and forms into their orbit by means of their own characteristic intentions and accents, and in so doing to a certain extent alienating these words and forms from other tendencies, parties, artistic works and persons.

Every socially significant verbal performance has the ability — sometimes for a long period time, and for a wide circle of persons — to infect with its own intention certain aspects of language that had been affected by its semantic and expressive impulse, imposing on them specific semantic nuances and specific axiological overtones; thus, it can create slogan words, curse words, praise words and so forth.

In any given historical moment of verbal-ideological life, each generation at each social level has its own language; moreover, every age group has as a matter of fact its own language, its own vocabulary, its own particular accentual system that, in their turn, vary depending on social level, academic institution (the language of the cadet, the high school student, the trade school student are all different languages) and other stratifying factors. All this is brought about by socially typifying languages, no matter how narrow the social circle in which they are spoken. It is even possible to have a family jargon define the societal limits of a language, as, for instance, the jargon of the Irtenevs in Tolstoy, with its special vocabulary and unique accentual system.

And finally, at any given moment, languages of various epochs and periods of socio-ideological life cohabit with one another. Even languages of the day exist: one could say that today's and yesterday's socio-ideological and political 'day' do not, in a certain sense, share the same language; every day represents another socio-ideological semantic 'state of affairs', another vocabulary, another accentual system, with its own slogans, its own ways of assigning blame and praise. Poetry depersonalizes 'days' in language, while prose, as we shall see, often deliberately intensifies differences between them, gives them embodied representation and dialogically opposes them to one another in unresolvable dialogues.

Thus at any given moment of its historical existence, language is heteroglot from top to bottom: it represents the coexistence of socio-ideological contradictions between the present and the past, between differing epochs of the past, between different socio-ideological groups in the present, between tendencies, schools, circles and so forth, all given a bodily form. These 'languages' of heteroglossia intersect each other in a variety of ways, forming new socially typifying 'languages.'

[. . .] As such they all may be juxtaposed to one another, mutually supplement one another, contradict one another and be interrelated dialogically. As such they encounter one another and coexist in the consciousness of real people — first and foremost, in the creative consciousness of people who write novels. As such, these languages live a real life, they struggle and evolve in an environment of social heteroglossia. Therefore they are all able to enter into the unitary plane of the novel, which can unite in itself parodic stylizations of generic languages, various forms of stylizations and illustrations of professional and period-bound languages, the languages of particular generations, of social dialects and others (as occurs, for example, in the English comic novel). They may all be drawn in by the novelist for the orchestration of his themes and for the refracted (indirect) expression of his intentions and values.

[. . .] *To study the word as such, ignoring the impulse that reaches out beyond it, is just as senseless as to study psychological experience outside the context of that real life towards which it was directed and by which it is determined.*

By stressing the intentional dimension of stratification in literary language, we are able, as has been said, to locate in a single series such methodologically heterogeneous phenomena as professional and social dialects, world views and individual artistic works, for in their intentional dimension one finds that common plane on which they can all be juxtaposed, and juxtaposed dialogically. The whole matter consists in the fact that there may be, between 'languages', highly specific dialogic relations, no matter how these languages are conceived, they may all be taken as particular points of view on the world. However varied the social forces doing the work of stratification — a profession, a genre, a particular tendency, an individual personality — the work itself everywhere comes down to the (relatively) protracted and socially meaningful (collective) saturation of language with specific (and consequently limiting) intentions and accents. The longer this stratifying saturation goes on, the broader the social circle encompassed by it and consequently the more substantial the social force bringing about such a stratification of language, the more sharply focused and stable will be those traces, the linguistic changes in the language markers (linguistic symbols), that are left behind in language as a result of this social force's activity — from stable (and consequently social) semantic nuances to authentic dialectological markers (phonetic, morphological and others), which permit us to speak of particular social dialects.

As a result of the work done by all these stratifying forces in language, there are no 'neutral' words and forms — words and forms that can belong to 'no one'; language has been completely taken over, shot through with intentions and accents. For any individual consciousness living in it, language is not an abstract system of normative forms but rather a concrete heteroglot conception of the world. All words have the 'taste' of a profession, a genre, a tendency, a party, a particular work, a particular person, a generation, an age group, the day and hour. Each word tastes of the context and contexts in which it has lived its socially charged life; all words and forms are populated by intentions. Contextual overtones (generic, tendentious, individualistic) are inevitable in the word.

As a living, socio-ideological concrete thing, as heteroglot opinion, language, for the individual consciousness, lies on the borderline between oneself and the other. The word in language is half someone else's. It becomes 'one's own' only when the speaker populates it with his own intention, his own accent, when he appropriates the word, adapting it to his own semantic and expressive intention. Prior to this moment of appropriation, the word does not exist in a neutral and impersonal language (it is not, after all, out of the dictionary that the speaker gets his words!), but rather it exists in other people's mouths, in other people's contexts, serving other people's intentions: it is from there that one must take the word, and make it one's own. And not all words for just anyone submit equally easily to this appropriation, to this seizure and transformation into private property: many words stubbornly resist, others remain alien, sound foreign in the mouth of the one who appropriated them and who now speaks them; they cannot be assimilated into his context and fall out of it, it is as if they put themselves in quotation marks against the will of the speaker. Language is not a neutral medium that passes freely and easily into the private property of the speaker's intentions, it is populated — overpopulated — with the intentions of others. Expropriating it, forcing it to submit to one's own intentions and accents, is a difficult and complicated process.

We have so far proceeded on the assumption of the abstract-linguistic (dialectological) unity of literary language. But even a literary language is anything but a closed dialect. Within the scope of literary language itself there is already a more or less sharply defined boundary between everyday conversational language and written language. Distinctions between genres frequently coincide with dialectological distinctions (for example, the high — Church Slavonic — and the low — conversational — genres of the eighteenth century); finally, certain dialects may be legitimized in literature and thus to a certain extent be appropriated by literary language.

As they enter literature and are appropriated to literary language, dialects in this new context lose, of course, the quality of closed sociolinguistic systems; they are deformed and in fact cease to be that which they had been simply as dialects. On the other hand, these dialects, on entering the literary language and preserving within it their own dialectological elasticity, their other-languagedness, have the effect of deforming the literary language; it, too, ceases to be that which it had been, a closed sociolinguistic system. Literary language is a highly distinctive phenomenon, as is the linguistic consciousness of the educated person who is its agent; within it, intentional diversity of speech [*raznorečivost'*] (which is present in every living dialect as a closed system) is transformed into diversity of language [*raznojazyčie*]; what results is not a single language but a dialogue of languages.

The national literary language of a people with a highly developed art of prose, especially if it is novelistic prose with a rich and tension-filled verbal-ideological history, is in fact an organized microcosm that reflects the macrocosm not only of national heteroglossia, but of European heteroglossia as well. The unity of a literary language is not a unity of a single, closed language system, but is rather a highly specific unity of several 'languages' that have established contact and mutual recognition with each other (merely one of which is poetic language in the narrow sense). Precisely this constitutes the peculiar nature of the methodological problem in literary language.

Concrete socio-ideological language consciousness, as it becomes creative — that is, as it becomes active as literature — discovers itself already surrounded by heteroglossia and not at all a single, unitary language, inviolable and indisputable. The actively literary linguistic consciousness at all times and every where (that is, in all epochs of literature historically available to us) comes upon 'languages', and not language. Consciousness finds itself inevitably facing the necessity of *having to choose a language*. With each literary-verbal performance, consciousness must actively orient itself amidst heteroglossia, it must move in and occupy a position for itself within it, it chooses, in other words, a 'language.' Only by remaining in a closed environment, one without writing or thought, completely off the maps of socio-ideological becoming, could a man fail to sense this activity of selecting a language and rest assured in the inviolability of his own language, the conviction that his language is predetermined.

Even such a man, however, deals not in fact with a single language, but with languages — except that the place occupied by each of these languages is fixed and indisputable, the movement from one to the other is predetermined and not a thought process; it is as if these languages were in different chambers. They do not collide with each other in his consciousness, there is no attempt to coordinate them, to look at one of these languages through the eyes of another language.

Thus an illiterate peasant, miles away from any urban centre, naively immersed in an unmoving and for him unshakable everyday world, nevertheless lived in several language systems: he prayed to God in one language (Church Slavonic), sang songs in another, spoke to his family in a third and, when he began to dictate petitions to the local authorities through a scribe, he tried speaking yet a fourth language (the official-literate language, 'paper' language). All these are *different languages*, even from the point of view of abstract sociodialectological markers. But these languages were not dialogically coordinated in the linguistic consciousness of the peasant; he passed from one to the other without thinking, automatically: each was indisputably in its own place, and the place of each was indisputable. He was not yet able to regard one language (and the verbal world corresponding to it) through the eyes of another language (that is, the language of everyday life and the everyday world with the language of prayer or song, or vice versa).[1]

As soon as a critical interanimation of languages began to occur in the consciousness of our peasant, as soon as it became clear that these were not only various different languages but even internally variegated languages, that the ideological systems and approaches to the world that were indissolubly connected with these languages contradicted each other and in no way could live in peace and quiet with one another — then the inviolability and predetermined quality of these languages came to an end, and the necessity of actively choosing one's orientation among them began.

[. . .]

The following must be kept in mind: that the speech of another, once enclosed in a context, is — no matter how accurately transmitted — always subject to certain semantic changes. The context embracing another's word is responsible for its dialogizing background, whose influence can be very great. Given the appropriate methods for framing, one may bring about fundamental changes even in another's utterance accurately quoted. Any sly and ill-disposed polemicist knows very well which dialogizing backdrop he should bring to bear on the accurately quoted words of his opponent, in order to distort their sense. By manipulating the effects of context, it is very easy to emphasize the brute materiality of another's words, and to stimulate dialogic reactions associated with such 'brute materiality'; thus it is, for instance, very easy to make even the most serious utterance comical. Another's discourse, when introduced into a speech context, enters the speech that frames it not in a mechanical bond but in a chemical union (on the semantic and emotionally expressive level); the degree of dialogized influence, one on the other, can be enormous. For this reason we cannot, when studying the various forms for transmitting another's speech, treat any of these forms in isolation from the means for its contextualized (dialogizing) framing — the one is indissolubly linked with the other. The formulation of another's speech as well as its framing (and the context can begin preparing for the introduction of another's speech far back in the text) both express the unitary act of dialogic interaction with that speech, a relation determining the entire nature of its transmission and all the changes in meaning and accent that take place in it during transmission.

The speaking person and his discourse in everyday speech, we have said, serves as a *subject* for the engaged, practical transmission of information, and not as a *means* of representation. As a matter of fact, all everyday forms for transmitting another's discourse, as well as the changes in discourse connected with these forms — from subtle nuances in meaning and emphasis to gross externalized distortions of the verbal composition — are defined by this practical engagement. But this emphasis on engaged discourse does not exclude certain aspects of representability. In order to assess and divine the real meaning of others' words in everyday life, the following are surely of decisive significance: *who* precisely is speaking, and under *what* concrete circumstances? When we attempt to understand and make assessments in everyday life, we do not separate discourse from the personality speaking it (as we can in the ideological realm), because the personality is so materially present to us. And the entire speaking situation is very important: who is present during it, with what expression or mimicry is it uttered, with what shades of intonation? During everyday verbal transmission of another's words, the entire complex of discourse as well as the personality of the speaker may be expressed and even played with (in the form of anything from an exact replication to a parodic ridiculing and exaggeration of gestures and intonations). This representation is always subordinated to the tasks of practical, engaged transmission and is wholly determined by these tasks. This of course does not involve the artistic image of a speaking person and the artistic image of his discourse, and even less the image of a language. Nevertheless, everyday episodes involving the same person, when they become linked, already entail prose devices for the double-voice and even double-languaged representation of another's words.

These conversations about speaking persons and others' words in everyday life do not go beyond the boundaries of the superficial aspects of discourse, the weight it carries in a specific situation; the deeper semantic and emotionally expressive levels of discourse do not enter the game. The topic of a speaking person takes on quite another significance in the ordinary ideological workings of our consciousness, in the process of assimilating our consciousness to the ideological world. The ideological becoming of a human being, in this view, is the process of selectively assimilating the words of others.

When verbal disciplines are taught in school, two basic modes are recognized for the appropriation and transmission — simultaneously — of another's words (a text, a rule, a model): 'reciting by heart' and 'retelling in one's own words'. The latter mode poses on a small scale the task implicit in all prose stylistics: retelling a text in one's own words is to a certain extent a double-voiced narration of another's words, for indeed 'one's own words' must not completely dilute the quality that makes another's words unique; a retelling in one's own words should have a mixed character, able when necessary to reproduce the style and expressions of the transmitted text. It is this second mode used in schools for transmitting another's discourse, 'retelling in one's own words', that includes within it an entire series of forms for the appropriation while transmitting of another's words, depending upon the character of the text being appropriated and the pedagogical environment in which it is understood and evaluated.

The tendency to assimilate others' discourse takes on an even deeper and more basic significance in an individual's ideological becoming, in the most fundamental sense. Another's discourse performs here no longer as information, directions, rules, models and so forth — but strives rather to determine the very bases of our ideological interrelations with the world, the very basis of our behaviour; it performs here as *authoritative discourse*, and an *internally persuasive discourse*.

[. . .]

The authoritative word demands that we acknowledge it, that we make it our own; it binds us, quite independent of any power it might have to persuade us internally; we encounter it with its authority already fused to it. The authoritative word is located in a distanced zone, organically connected with a past that is felt to be hierarchically higher. It is, so to speak, the word of the fathers. Its authority was already *acknowledged* in the past. It is a *prior* discourse. It is therefore not a question of choosing it from among other possible discourses that are its equal. It is given (it sounds) in lofty spheres, not those of familiar contact. Its language is a special (as it were, hieratic) language. It can be profaned. It is akin to taboo, i.e. a name that must not be taken in vain.

We cannot embark here on a survey of the many and varied types of authoritative discourse (for example, the authority of religious dogma, or of acknowledged scientific truth or of a currently fashionable book), nor can we survey different degrees of authoritativeness. For our purposes only formal features for the transmission and representation of authoritative discourse are important, those common to all types and degrees of such discourse.

The degree to which a word may be conjoined with authority — whether the authority is recognized by us or not — is what determines its specific demarcation and individuation in discourse; it requires a *distance* vis-à-vis itself (this distance may be valorized as positive or as negative, just as our attitude towards it may be sympathetic or hostile). Authoritative discourse may organize around itself great masses of other types of discourses (which interpret it, praise it, apply it in various ways), but the authoritative discourse itself does not merge with these (by means of, say, gradual transitions); it remains sharply demarcated, compact and inert: it demands, so to speak, not only quotation marks but a demarcation even more magisterial, a special script, for instance.[2] It is considerably more difficult to incorporate semantic changes into such a discourse, even with the help of a framing context: its semantic structure is static and dead, for it is fully complete, it has but a single meaning, the letter is fully sufficient to the sense and calcifies it.

It is not a free appropriation and assimilation of the word itself that authoritative discourse seeks to elicit from us, rather, it demands our unconditional allegiance. Therefore authoritative discourse permits no play with the context framing it, no play with its borders, no gradual and flexible transitions, no spontaneously creative stylizing variants on it. It enters our verbal consciousness as a compact and indivisible mass; one must either totally affirm it or totally reject it. It is indissolubly fused with its authority — with political power, an institution, a person — and it stands and falls together with that authority. One cannot divide it up — agree with one part, accept but not completely another part, reject utterly a third part. Therefore the distance we ourselves observe vis-à-vis this authoritative discourse remains unchanged in all its projections: a playing with distances, with fusion and dissolution, with approach and retreat, is not here possible.

All these functions determine the uniqueness of authoritative discourse, both as a concrete means for formulating itself during transmission and as its distinctive means for being framed by contexts. The zone of the framing context must likewise be distanced — no familiar contact is possible here either. The one perceiving and understanding this discourse is a distant descendant; there can be no arguing with him.

These factors also determine the potential role of authoritative discourse in prose. Authoritative discourse can not be represented — it is only transmitted. Its inertia, its semantic finiteness and calcification, the degree to which it is hard-edged, a thing in its own right, the impermissibility of any free stylistic development in relation to it — all this renders the artistic representation of authoritative discourse impossible. Its role in the novel is insignificant. It is by its very nature incapable of being double voiced; it cannot enter into hybrid constructions. If completely deprived of its authority it becomes simply an object, a *relic*, a *thing*. It enters the artistic context as an alien body, there is no space around it to play in, no contradictory emotions — it is not surrounded by an agitated and cacophonous dialogic life, and the context around it dies, words dry up. For this reason images of official-authoritative truth, images of virtue (of any sort: monastic, spiritual, bureaucratic, moral, etc.) have never been successful in the novel. It suffices to mention the hopeless attempts of Gogol and Dostoevsky in this regard. For this reason the authoritative text always remains, in the novel, a dead quotation, something that falls out of the artistic context (for example, the evangelical texts in Tolstoy at the end of *Resurrection*).[3]

Authoritative discourses may embody various contents: authority as such, or the authoritativeness of tradition, of generally acknowledged truths, of the official line and other similar authorities. These discourses may have a variety of zones (determined by the degree to which they are distanced from the zone of contact) with a variety of relations to the presumed listener or interpreter (the apperceptive background presumed by the discourse, the degree of reciprocation between the two and so forth).

[. . .]

When someone else's ideological discourse is internally persuasive for us and acknowledged by us, entirely different possibilities open up. Such discourse is of decisive significance in the evolution of an individual consciousness: consciousness awakens to independent ideological life precisely in a world of alien discourses surrounding it, and from which it cannot initially separate itself; the process of distinguishing between one's own and another's discourse, between one's own and another's thought, is activated rather late in development. When thought begins to work in an independent, experimenting and discriminating way, what first occurs is a separation between internally persuasive discourse and authoritarian enforced discourse, along with a rejection of those congeries of discourses that do not matter to us, that do not touch us.

Internally persuasive discourse — as opposed to one that is externally authoritative — is, as it is affirmed through assimilation, tightly interwoven with 'one's own word'.[4] In the everyday rounds of our consciousness, the internally persuasive word is half ours and half someone else's. Its creativity and productiveness consist precisely in the fact that such a word awakens new and independent words, that it organizes masses of our words from within, and does not remain in an isolated and static condition. It is not so much interpreted by us as it is further, that is, freely, developed, applied to new material, new conditions; it enters into interanimating relationships with new contexts. More than that, it enters into an intense interaction, a *struggle* with other internally persuasive discourses. Our ideological development is just such an intense struggle within us for hegemony among various available verbal and ideological points of view, approaches, directions and values. The semantic structure of an internally persuasive discourse is *not finite*, it is *open*;

in each of the new contexts that dialogize it, this discourse is able to reveal ever newer *ways to mean.*

The internally persuasive word is either a contemporary word, born in a zone of contact with unresolved contemporaneity, or else it is a word that has been reclaimed for contemporaneity; such a word relates to its descendants as well as to its contemporaries as if *both* were contemporaries; what is constitutive for it is a special conception of listeners, readers, perceivers. Every discourse presupposes a special conception of the listener, of his apperceptive background and the degree of his responsiveness; it presupposes a specific distance. All this is very important for coming to grips with the historical life of discourse. Ignoring such aspects and nuances leads to a reification of the word (and to a muffling of the dialogism native to it).

All of the above determine the methods for formulating internally persuasive discourse during its transmission, as well as methods for framing it in contexts. Such methods provide maximal interaction between another's word and its context, for the dialogizing influence they have on each other, for the free and creative development of another's word, for a gradation of transitions. They serve to govern the play of boundaries, the distance between that point where the context begins to prepare for the introduction of another's word and the point where the word is actually introduced (its 'theme' may sound in the text long before the appearance of the actual word). These methods account for other peculiarities as well, which also express the essence of the internally persuasive word, such as that word's semantic openness to us, its capacity for further creative life in the context of our ideological consciousness, its unfinishedness and the inexhaustibility of our further dialogic interaction with it. We have not yet learned from it all it might tell us; we can take it into new contexts, attach it to new material, put it in a new situation in order to wrest new answers from it, new insights into its meaning, and even wrest from it new words of its *own* (since another's discourse, if productive, gives birth to a new word from us in response).

The means for formulating and framing internally persuasive discourse may be supple and dynamic to such an extent that this discourse may literally be *omnipresent* in the context, imparting to everything its own specific tones and from time to time breaking through to become a completely materialized thing, as another's word fully set off and demarcated (as happens in character zones). Such variants on the theme of another's discourse are widespread in all areas of creative ideological activity, and even in the narrowly scientific disciplines. Of such a sort is any gifted, creative exposition defining alien world views: such an exposition is always a free stylistic variation on another's discourse; it expounds another's thought in the style of that thought even while applying it to new material, to another way of posing the problem; it conducts experiments and gets solutions in the language of another's discourse.

Notes

1. We are of course deliberately simplifying: the real-life peasant could and did do this to a certain extent.
2. Often the authoritative word is in fact a word spoken by another in a foreign language (cf. for example the phenomenon of foreign-language religious texts in most cultures).
3. When analysing a concrete example of authoritative discourse in a novel, it is necessary to keep in mind the fact that purely authoritative discourse may, in another epoch, be internally persuasive; this is especially true where ethics are concerned.
4. One's own discourse is gradually and slowly wrought out of others' words that have been acknowledged and assimilated, and the boundaries between the two are at first scarcely perceptible.

1.6 A Framework for the Study of Verbal Art

R. Hasan

Source: extracts from Hasan, R. (1985) 'A Framework for the study of verbal art', in *Linguistics, Language and Verbal Art* (Course ECS805 *Specialized curriculum: language and learning*). Victoria, Deakin University.

[. . .]

Language and verbal art

Although there may be some exceptions to this general rule (Halliday and Hasan, 1985), our way into most of the meanings of most texts is obviously through their language: texts after all are linguistic objects, and a literature text is no exception to this rule. But in the study of verbal art the need to pay attention to language goes beyond this. It is not that there is art, and the job of language is simply to express it; rather, it is that *if* there is art, it is because how language functions in the text. In everyday life, we all know people who can tell a story well and others who just 'kill it'. What causes the difference? It is the way that the story is 'discoursed', the manner in which the patterns of language function to create the fable. This analogy is simple, and verbal art is a complex phenomenon; none the less, it does point to the important fact that in verbal art the role of language is central. Here language is not as clothing is to the body; it *is* the body (Hasan, 1964, 1971).

The importance of language in verbal art has been recognized for centuries, but the ways of talking about its role have not always been helpful. To say that the language of literature is sublime, creative, emotionally charged, mimetic, etc. is not exactly revealing. First, it is not clear what the terms signify. Is the language of a quarrel emotionally charged? If not, why do we get upset by it? If yes, then is a quarrel an instance of verbal art? Was *Das Kapital* a piece of creative writing? It certainly created a thought structure not available before to the community as a whole; and it has made an important difference to the world. You can see that the parading of epithets is in no way explanatory. But what is worse, it creates the spurious belief that the ways of talking about, and analysing, language in literature are quite distinct from those of its use elsewhere.

[. . .]

In the early 1960s, the heyday of transformational linguistics, much was made of deviation and ungrammaticality as a crucial characteristic of the genre of literature (Levin, 1962). This too seems wrong. The notion of deviation is not as self-evident as some linguists would like to believe. Is *He took exception to what I said* a deviant clause? Is it deviant to say, as Mundle (1971) does, *I had failed to notice something which must have stared me in the face on hundreds of occasions* (p. 7). If things can 'stare one in the face', why can flowers not dance? If we can talk about the bitterness of our memories, the depth of our affection, and the barrenness of a philosophy, why should a line such as *Love is a barren sea, bitter and deep* (Swinburne, 'A leave taking') be dubbed deviant? Today's deviation is tomorrow's norm — it is, seen positively, an extension of the resources of a language to mean. So the concept of deviation tends to tell us more about the limitations of a linguistic model — of its underlying approach to human language — than it does about the work that is being studied. Moreover, it leaves us with two important questions: first, how can deviant utterances have any meaning? and second, why do they attract attention in literature?

A wording that plays with the current norms of language, in the way that the Swinburne line does, is still meaningful; we are never at a loss to interpret it. So it is more important to examine its relation to the system of language to establish what aspects of the system are being exploited in it to create a novel meaning, than it is to show how it fails to conform. [. . .]

The example I quoted from Mundle is not from the genre of literature. Outside this genre, the so-called deviation thrives too. You only need to open any book on science, on economics, philosophy, or any field of expertise to see that we often explain one thing by another. When we talk about some *approach shedding a great deal of light on some problem,* we are combining distinct domains of experience to create a unity: an approach is not light, but it reveals as light does; a problem is not a concrete object, but it is tangible like one. The attributes of one domain enhance those of the other. The need for this way of talking is obviously great, for in natural creation of texts we are always led to such expressions, as you will see if you examine this paragraph. It is, however, only in literature that these new modes of expression draw particular attention to themselves even though the frequency of their occurrence varies both with genre and with individual authors. In this respect, the new modes of expression are not very different from such patterns as repetition, parallelism and contrast. Each of these patterns occurs a good deal in everyday non-literature use of language. Below is a note that my son brought from the school a couple of years ago.

> EXCURSION XX: NOTE TO PARENTS
> Travel will be train and ferry.
> Dawes Point will be the venue for lunch.
> Children must be at School for departure at 8:30;
> They will be back for dismissal at normal time.

Compare this with the opening lines of D. J. Enright's 'A polished performance':

Citizens of the polished capital
Sigh for the towns up country,
And their innocent simplicity.
People in the towns up country
Applaud the unpolished innocence
Of the distant villages.

Although the parallelism in the Enright quote is greater, that in the school notice is also striking. But people socialized into the study of canonical literature are much more likely to notice the parallelism of the second, than of the first. A cursory glance at any daily newspaper yields scores of examples of alliteration and metaphor, and other such patterns. I found the following in the *Sydney Morning Herald* (21 June 1984) without actively searching for them:

Melbourne man fathered Rios embryos
Contempt case coverage permitted
Chopsticks begin to lose their grip

Two things follow from the above discussion: we cannot characterize literature by reference to isolated patterns of language; and, we must explain why we pull out the patterning of patterns as significant in literature, while ignoring its occurrences elsewhere. I suggest we need a shift of focus: the search for the language *of* literature is misguided; we should look instead at language *in* literature.

This is not simply a play on words. The phrase 'language in literature', when expanded, would read 'functions of language in literature'. As Mukarovsky (1977, p. 3) said: 'Poetic language is permanently characterised only by its function; however, function is not a property but a mode of utilising the properties of a given phenomenon'. [. . .]

Language and art in verbal art

The assertions above may appear a little cryptic, particularly since, in talking about language, the 'function' is used in so many senses. How does language contribute to the creation of verbal art?

The notion of *Foregrounding*, first evolved by the Prague School linguists and developed greatly by Mukarovsky, is essential to a discussion of this question. The concept basic to foregrounding is that of contrast; and as applied to a text, the contrast is a contrast to the norms of that text. [. . .]

'Contrast' is a very general notion: given any two sentences, you can always find some parameters along which they could be said to contrast. We therefore need to know when contrast is significant, because it is only significant contrast that is called foregrounding. Secondly, if *a* contrasts with *b*, then *b* contrasts with *a*: if future contrasts with past then the reverse too is a correct statement. Which of these is foregrounded, and why? Third, the contrast between future and past is one, valid everywhere in the use of language, just as repetition of /k/ in initial position is alliteration even if it occurs in *contempt case coverage*. At what point does a formal pattern become so significant as to be given the name of foregrounding?

We think of something as foregrounded when it stands out against an established tendency. In the two sentences *I might go there tomorrow. At least I'll try*, the question of foregrounding does not arise because no expectation has yet been established. [. . .] Foregrounding would be impossible without the existence of a consistent background: Mukarovsky referred to this background as 'automatization', i.e. the automatic quality of some pattern(s). This quality is not inherent in the pattern as such; it is the textual deployment of that pattern in that text that gives it the status of the automatized phenomenon.

I believe that the effect of foregrounding extends to the automatized aspect of the text as well. By being itself highlighted, foregrounding also brings to attention that against which it is highlighted. Thus it is not simply the foregrounded 'bits' that are important to the understanding of the meanings of the text, but rather the opposition that is being set up by the contrast. Seen thus, foregrounding is a device by which the attention of the reader is directed to the organization of the various strands of meaning in the text. [. . .]

While the notion of foregrounding is made explicit by describing its formal characteristics, its significance resides elsewhere: foregrounding becomes noticeable because of its consistency. [. . .] There are two aspects to this consistency: the stability of its semantic direction, and the stability of its textual location. By stability of semantic direction, I mean that the various foregrounded patterns point towards the same general kind of meaning. [. . .] The meanings highlighted by the foregrounded patterns converge towards the same direction. Butt (1983) has coined the happy expression 'semantic drift' to refer to much the same kind of phenomenon.

By stability of textual location, I mean that the significant patterns of foregrounding have a tendency to occur at a textually important point. I would emphasise that 'textual location' does not refer to material location in the text, for example, every other paragraph, at the end of every fifth line, and so on; it refers rather to some significant point in the organisation of the text as a unity.

We pay attention to the patterning of patterns when it is significant; and in order to be significant the foregrounding must have a semantic consequence. The reason parallelism attracts no attention in the school notice is because we cannot attach any significance to it — it does not contribute to the meanings of that particular text. Even within a literature text, there must be some patternings of patterns [. . .] which do not attract attention to themselves. These turn out to be precisely the kind of patterns that do not display the type of consistency that I have described above. Such consistency permits the foregrounding to do a job in verbal art — it enables it to play a part in the semantic organization and articulation of the meanings of the literature text. So it is not the patterns per se that are artistic; it is the mode of their utilization that creates an important parameter of artfulness in verbal art. This provides one reason for the centrality of language in the study of verbal art.

We can, in fact, think of verbal art as a semiotic system, which can be described generally as having an internal design similar to that of the semiotic system of language. Human language is a multiple coding system (Halliday, 1985b; Halliday and Hasan 1985), consisting of three strata:

Folk label	**Technical label**
Meaning	Semantics
Wording	Lexico-grammar
Sound	Phonology

Meaning is coded as wording, while wording itself is coded as sound. So the relationship between the strata is that of realization, or manifestation, of one through the other. You could think of this from the point of view of accessibility: meanings become accessible through wording; and wording becomes accessible through sound. However, sound itself has no significance unless it is paired with meaning; and in this pairing, the stratum of wording plays a decisive role: it is through the systematicity of the relationship between the units at this stratum that meanings are created and sound-patterns associated with them. As we cannot go into greater details here, you will need to consult Halliday (1985b) for a fuller explanation.

I have suggested elsewhere (Hasan, 1964, 1967, 1971, 1975) that we need to recognize three strata in verbal art, amongst which the relationship is analogous to that amongst the strata of language. The strata in verbal art would be as follows

Theme
Symbolic articulation
Verbalization

What are these strata, and what is the relationship amongst them? Let us begin from the lowest stratum — that of *verbalization*. This is the point of primary contact with the work. We can begin to know a piece of verbal art only if we know the language. (Note the important difference here between verbal art and painting or sculpture.) Knowing a language implies knowing the relations between the meanings, wordings and the sounds. At this level the literature text is like any other text: you need to know the language to know the meanings encoded in the text; and relevant to this stratum is the entire linguistic resource of the community. An individual will understand a text only to the extent that she or he possesses a sensitivity to the lexico-grammatical patterns as the creator of the meaning potential of the language in question.

It is at the stratum of verbalization that statements such as the meaning of English future, present and past tenses, and their relation to each other, are located. These meanings are available in varying degrees to the speakers of English. However, the fact that these meanings are available does not imply that the speakers can provide explicit descriptions of these patterns, just as the child's enjoyment of sound patterns does not imply the ability to produce a coherent and correct description of such categories as alliteration, rhyme and assonance. What it does permit is the reformulation of some strands of the meanings of a text.

If the analysis of literature were limited to just this stratum, the most that one could do would be to say what kind of linguistic patterns occurred, at the three strata of semantics, lexico-grammar and phonology: the reader would have an idea what the individual clauses of the text mean and what logical relations unite them. This would permit a paraphrase of the text. [. . .] Up to a certain stage in the school system, the 'teaching' of literature consists simply of getting the pupils to do precisely this kind of paraphrase.

The ability to paraphrase is most probably an important stage in socialization into the study of verbal art; but it is far from everything. In the analyses produced above, we went beyond the assertion of meanings that are the aggregate of the individual messages of the texts. Whenever we ask about a story, a poem, a novel, etc.: What is it about?, there can be two, not mutually exclusive, answers. One may say, 'The widower' is about the daily routine of a man living all by himself in the Australian outback, or Frost's 'The road not taken' is about someone choosing to go down one road in the hope of coming back to the other, but never being able to do so. These would be correct descriptions of what the poems are about — but simply by reference to the stratum of verbalization. However, without denying the validity of these responses, one might say that 'The widower' [a poem by the Australian poet L.A. Murray] is about the centrality of community to individuality, and 'The road not taken' is about the limitations and immutability of human choices. And these too would be correct descriptions — but these are at the highest level of abstraction; they pertain to the stratum of *theme*. The stratum of theme is the deepest level of meaning in verbal art; it is what a text is about when dissociated from the particularities of that text. In its nature, the theme of verbal art is very close to a generalization, which can be viewed as a hypothesis about some aspect of the life of social man. I believe Aristotle had this aspect of verbal art in mind when he declared that art is truer than history. And although the framework I am presenting here is my own, there is no doubt that the need for this stratum is recognized in most schools of literary criticism.

I have now described two of the three strata from the semiotic system of verbal art — the lowest, and the highest. The two are brought into contact with each other through the stratum of *symbolic articulation*. This level is analogous to that of lexico-grammar in the semiotic system of human language. It consists of the system of signs that create the meanings of the highest stratum — theme. How is this achieved?

It has to be recognized that the doings/happenings/states etc. in a literature text have a dual status: they are themselves, i.e. they are assertions of such and such a state of affairs; for example, the widower will split off wood, go inside, boil water and make tea. These are themselves meanings. But a meaning can be attached to these meanings. If this is possible, then the first-order meanings are like signs or symbols, which in their turn possess a meaning — a second order, perhaps more general meaning. In 'The widower' I have interpreted them as activities that dwindle into a catalogue of ineffectual movements against the cosmic movement of time. I also suggested that the utter predictability of the widower's day is relevant to our perception of him as an automaton-like being. But predictability does not have to be seen this way: it could have been interpreted as the security of certainty. In giving the interpretation I have done, I am influenced by the aching paddocks, the bright webbed visions smeared on the dark of his thoughts to dance and fade away, the remorseless progression of time, the utter aloneness of the widower, sitting all by himself at the head of an unoccupied table, confronted with the memory of a nebulous nightmare. But each of these elements of meaning was highlighted for me by the patterns of foregrounding. If I am prevented from interpreting the predictability of 'events' in the widower's life as a symbol signifying security, this is largely because of the consistency of foregrounding in the poem.

So the stratum of symbolic articulation is where the meanings of language are turned into signs having a deeper meaning. Foregrounding and patterning of patterns play an important role in ascribing the second-order meanings to the patterns of the first-order meanings; and in doing this, they provide a principle for discriminating between the crucial and the incidental. The exact identity of the acts the widower plans to undertake matters little, their predictability is crucial. And predictability itself does not have just one meaning; it achieves a definite status by its systematic relation to the ineffectuality of his actions, to the movements of time and to the camouflaged emotions. Together they function as a set of artistic metaphors, enunciating the meaning of complete isolation from humanity. And it is in this sense that we can describe pieces of verbal art as extended metaphors. In all verbal art there exist two levels of semiosis: one that is the product of the use of natural language, itself a semiotic system; and the other which is the product of the artistic system through foregrounding and repatternings of the first-order meanings. This is why paraphrase is never sufficient to describe the meanings of a literature text. The art of verbal art consists of the use of language in such a way that this second-order semiosis becomes possible.

The two semiotic systems — of verbal art and of human language — can be brought together as in Figure 1. Figure 1 summarizes the preceding discussion, which shows that language is central to verbal art in two

Figure 1 Verbal art and language.

important ways: it is the writer's point of departure, and the reader's point of entry; and, secondly, the element of art in verbal art resides in the second-order semiosis, achieved through the consistency of foregrounding. So this framework can be used to explain how a literature text comes to mean what it does (Hasan, 1971, 1975, 1979). And through its implications the framework also addresses the question of the community's evaluation of verbal art (Hasan, 1971, 1975, 1980; Halliday, 1982). We examine some of the implications below.

The status of verbal art

In the discussion of verbal art many oppositions are presented as irreconcilables, with the implication that if literature is one it cannot be the other. I believe it is somewhat simplistic to argue that if literature is aesthetic then it cannot be pragmatic, that truth and falsehood are decided once for all, that fiction is as different from fact as day from night. When examined in the light of the above framework, the insistence on mutual exclusion appears misguided.

I said above that theme is like a general hypothesis about some aspect of social man. If interpretation can probe this deepest level of meaning, the work is productive of reflection about humanity. Seen from this point of view, Jakobson's claim (1960) that the function of verbal art is aesthetic, not pragmatic, is open to question. As Mukarovsky remarked, the 'observer of poetry' should not 'lose sight of the various shadings of the communicative function and its significance for the poetic structure' (Mukarovsky, 1964, p. 33). I believe that the source of the problem might lie in the rather loose use of the term 'function', which in the writings of the Prague School linguists can sometimes be interpreted as 'the essential attribute' and sometimes simply as 'use'. In the latter interpretation, it would be absurd for us to claim, for example, that Bennett's *The Old Wives' Tale* or Malouf's *Fly Away Peter* are aesthetic objects without any communicative or referential value or purpose. One of the reasons that verbal art can never be dissociated from the community in which it was created is precisely because the stratum of theme is closest to a community's ideology.

The nature of theme in literature raises serious doubts about the classification of verbal art as 'fiction' — something to which the concept of truth cannot be applied. The paradox to which Aristotle drew attention is precisely that while at one level, a literature text may be simply fictional — so not true in the literal sense — at another level, it embodies precisely the kind of 'truths' that most communities are deeply concerned with. It is not only in literature that hypotheses about the life of social man are constructed; they obviously form the basis of social sciences. In these specialist domains, the hypotheses are presented and explored explicitly, whereas in verbal art they are inferred, and generally not debated explicitly. Just as the set of hypotheses in social sciences is not static, but grows through a complex relation of 'fact' and imagination, so also the 'truths' in verbal art are not just the known, communally given ones: they can be, and often are, an exploration of the possible. One parameter for the originality of a piece of verbal art is precisely in the novel conception of its theme.

However, it is well to remember that there exist genres devoted to the development of the same kind of thought structures that characterize theme in verbal art. If a piece of verbal art is valued in a particular way by (some) members of a community, this cannot be simply because of its theme. No matter how novel it is, it is very likely to be better elaborated and more explicitly debated in some specialist domain. The value of Shakespeare is not simply in the picture of the Elizabethan view of the universe that his writings build for us; otherwise, with better documented material on the same topic, his plays would lose value. So there must be more to the continued value of a piece of verbal art than just the quality of its deepest meanings. It is in this rather special sense that we can say that the value of literature does not lie entirely in its pragmatic function.

What is characteristic of verbal art — but not of the specialist domains bearing the closest resemblance to theme — is that in the former, the patterning of patterns becomes a vehicle for a second-order semiosis, so that one order of meaning acts as metaphor for a second order of meaning: the art of verbal art resides in its symbolic articulation. Now if the events/happenings/characters etc. of a literature text are metaphors, it makes very little sense to ask if these are true or fictional. To ask this question is to miss the point. Nothing much depends upon their truthfulness, so from the point of view of their status as art, their fictionality is as much beside the point as their historical truthfulness. The more important question is whether in the specific events etc. — whether imagined or real — one is able to perceive some general meaning; and having perceived this, whether one is able to share this perception communally, by utilizing and extending the modes of meaning provided by human languages.

The principle of second-order semiosis is relevant to another distinction that has been difficult to pin down. Once a novel patterning of patterns is introduced, it can become a currency — something that is available to the community for use in other textual environments. So one might use parallel structure, simile, metaphor, alliteration and so on, not as significant foregrounding for second-order semiosis, but simply as embellishment. The degree to which patterning of patterns is encouraged in the writing styles of genres other than literature, varies from time to time, and is probably very closely related to the community's notions about knowledge and knowledgeable persons. Burke's speeches, Gibbon's *Rise and Fall of the Roman Empire*, Johnson's letters and Browne's *Religio Medici* are examples often cited to prove the impossibility of defining literature conclusively (Eagleton, 1983). But it is highly doubtful that in actual practice — i.e. in how people talked about texts — these have been ever regarded as identical with, say, Shakespeare, Defoe or Chaucer.

I would suggest that it is useful to make a systematic distinction. If the patterning of patterns is consistently utilized for a second-order semiosis, resulting in metaphorization, then the text in question is a *literature text*. If, however, such a role is not played by the patternings, then we have a *literary text*. The recognition of this distinction is important, not least because the techniques for the study and evaluation of the two are not identical.

Literature, language and community

The *autonomy* of literature text became an axiom with the advent of modern critical theories. Simplified, the principle of autonomy means that the text itself provides cues for deciding what extra-textual phenomena are relevant to it, if they are. So Elsa Morante's *History* is not to be judged by reference to the actual events of the Second World War. And we do not need to discover her intentions and her life history before we turn to the study of her novel to decide what it means and how, and whether it is successful in achieving its 'artistic intention' (Mukarovsky, 1977). This is a welcome change; and the framework presented above provides explicit motivation for insisting on the autonomy of the literature text. However, it would be an error to convert autonomy into anomie: literature is not a self-motivated activity, divorced from the concerns of the community in which it is created. A correct understanding of the nature of language, which is central to verbal art, would guard against this attitude.

Languages need communities to live in; they develop and change through their use in the living of life, and this characteristically takes place in social contexts of culture. The relationship between language and culture is symbiotic: the one lives through the other. Because language is instrumental in the creation, maintenance and change in societies (Whorf, 1956; Bernstein, 1971; Douglas, 1975; Halliday, 1977; Hasan, 1984), and society of language, language cannot help carrying the social meanings of its speech community. Whenever we use language, we invoke far more of our social reality than people give the utterance credit for in describing its meanings. These facts have consequences both for the maker and the receiver of the message. Literature is no exception to this; in fact, the situation here is further compounded since literature texts 'span' distinct social stages.

Let us take the maker of the literature text first. An understanding of the context of a text's creation is important. There are at least three major perspectives from which the context of creation can be viewed. First, the language itself: no matter how many novel modes of expression a poet creates, the point of her departure is given by the language of her community. One consideration in the valuation of a literature text is precisely this: how have the meaning resources of the language been extended? But no author lives alone with the language; she is surrounded by the taken-for-granted realities of her community. The assumptions that insidiously flow into the writing speak of the culture. Why is the destruction of Rodney's ego ascribed to his mother, more than to his father? Is Wilson an anti-feminist? Or is he simply voicing the same social pressures that even today make a mother feel that the well-being of her child is largely her responsibility? What is the value of filial piety today compared with the Elizabethan ideal? Considerations of this type are far more important to the understanding of a literature text than determining whether Hamlet really existed, or if Shakespeare was really Shakespeare. Finally, even though the artist is a creator, he cannot create in a vacuum. Despite the great value attached to originality, art creates its own conventions. This too is an important part of the context of creation. No one is going to be greatly impressed by the use of the 'flash back' technique in narratives any more; it has become a part of the trappings. The changing forms of the English lyric are a source of enlightenment to anyone who would want to study changes in artistic conventions. It is not an accident that the theme, the symbolic articulation, and the patterns of language display a great deal of similarity within any one period of verbal art.

You will notice that I have said nothing about the individual who has the role of the author. Here, there are no clear-cut boundries between the social and the private; the emotional and the intellectual; and the creator and the person of the creator. We know very little about how these forces combine in the creative process. For the reader, the author lives through the text, much as in everyday life our image of a person emerges from that person's texts. In this sense, there can be no 'death of the author' (Barthes, 1977), it is only the writing hand that dies. So long as some members of the community find the artistic structures worth while, the author has defied the oblivion imposed by death. Barthes' striking title is a good reminder that our concern is not with the person of the author; it is only with the creator of the artistic structure, whose milieu, whose communal affinities speak through his text, almost despite him rather than because of him: they constantly take us back to his original community.

The context of a literature text's reception acts upon the meanings of that text for the reader. This is one reason why there can never be one single reading of a literature text. Hamlet in the bush (Bohannan, 1974) is not exactly the same thing as Hamlet in today's lecture room; and that is again different from Hamlet on the Elizabethan stage. This is a vast topic and I shall only sketch the most important parameters here. Generally speaking, the greater the distance between the context of creation and reception, the more inaccessible the meanings of the text become. In the first place, language itself is subject to change, and this change may be such as to prevent even a rudimentary understanding of the text. For me, Old English literature texts are as inaccessible as the Arabic ones; less dramatically, many of the conventions of Chaucer's language are no longer currency. Even in the case of Elizabethan English, we are likely to perceive linguistic signs as carrying meanings that would not be in keeping with the Elizabethan understanding. The presence of artistic conventions impinges on the reader as well. We cannot read Defoe today as if Austen, Brontë and Elliot never existed. With increasing distance between the context of creation and reception, cultural differences assume an important role. In an age where broken homes, single parents and reshuffling of sexual partners become a norm to at least some section of the community, the meaning of Hamlet's trauma at Gertrude's hasty marriage to Claudius is somewhat different from that for the Elizabethan. In a sense, there is no such being as *the* reader. Each reader is a unique person; and a reader's own life-situation plays an important part in her understanding of a text. However, we still cannot announce blithely: texts are dead; long live readers. The reasons for this are, again, closely related to the nature of language and its relation to the life of its speech community. The following section elaborates on this remark.

Linguistics, literature and readers

The context of creation and reception merge in the reading of a text. From a limited point of view, a text already produced is an inert object, incapable of achieving anything by itself. Readers are the medium for a text's achievement; and in this sense, the role of the reader (Eco, 1979) is paramount. But it is important to recognize that a reader is not an entirely free agent. No matter how unique a person I am, I could not justifiably ascribe the same thematic import to *Pride and Prejudice* as to *Necessity's Child*. The language of the text, if I understand it as the English speech community does, is an insurance against this.

The present emphasis on the private nature of writing and reading tends to obscure the fact that both are a form of dialogue, in which the turns are separated by the social import of time and place. In a dialogue, you are never free to say just what you like; the nature of the other's turn acts upon the nature of your turn. Just as in some sense, in the writing turn, the (projected) reader is the other, so in the reading turn of this dialogue, the text plays the role of the other. Through its language it positions us into taking account of the many aspects discussed so far — both those internal to the text — its theme, symbolic articulation and verbalization — and those external to the text, implicated through the relation of a language to its speech community.

In the dialogue of reading, the knowledge of language is an essential ingredient, as it is in any linguistic participation. And it is generally agreed that reading is understanding. But understanding is not an all-or-none phenomenon: there can be different degrees of understanding. We need to make a distinction between reading for private purposes and reading as a stage in the study of literature. Private reading can afford to stop at a level of understanding, far removed from that required for engaging in a public debate. For the former, the operational knowledge of language is enough, to bring us to the point of paraphrase. The child listening to the nursery rhyme has just this kind of knowledge. True that such reading will create sensitivity, but sensitivity unaccompanied by an explicit analysis does not turn the private into public. If all we are interested in are the private deliberations and reactions of someone to a poem or a novel then the privateness of this enterprise absolves it from public scrutiny. What they understand — i.e. how they read and how they react to it — is their personal business. In the study of literature, by contrast, the understanding must necessarily become an object of scrutiny.

[. . .] When what is up for debate is the very understanding of a text, one can no longer rely on just the operational knowledge of language. First, there must be a vocabulary for talking about that which is being interpreted in the act of reading. It is not much use talking about the headlong rush of sentences, or crunchy consonants: such descriptions eloquently prove the need for a technical language, which can permit reference to categories of language, without mixing personal reaction with the objective nature of the phenomena. Secondly, and more importantly, knowledge about language is needed to describe the techniques of symbolic articulation employed in the text. And this involves the construction of hypotheses about the second-order semiosis, permitted by the consistency of foregrounding. The semantic value of foregrounding depends at least partly upon the workings of the existing system of language. Unless we know how that system works, the interpretation of those patterns becomes problematic, which are essentially attempts at extending the system's meaning resources. The specialist domain that enables us to acquire knowledge about language is linguistics; without linguistics, the study of literature must remain a series of personal preferences, no matter how much the posture of objectivity is adopted: being objective implies knowing the nature of that which one is being objective about. An understanding of the nature of language, of how the system works, is essential and it is not a natural by-product of knowing how to use language. That is a necessary condition but not a sufficient one. And the degree to which a linguistic model permits systematic statements of meaning will determine the success of its use in such studies. Further I would claim that a better understanding of the patterns of language through which the meanings of the text came into being has contributed to a different reading; and by doing this the analysis has enhanced my appreciation of the work (O'Toole, 1982). Understanding about language has consequences for understanding the meanings of the work of literature.

In recent years the notion of 'literary competence' has been introduced (Culler, 1975) by analogy with linguistic competence. It is well to remember that linguistic competence does not entail ability to describe language explicitly, as even those who favour the concept would readily admit. Literary competence is not produced by exposure to literature — what is produced by exposure to literature is a taste for the type of literature one is exposed to. This follows from the difference between competence to study literature and competence to read it as a private enterprise. To create the ability to study literature, a person has to be exposed to *studies* of literature, and the more explicit the methods of such a study, the more likely it is that the exposure would be fruitful. In the school system, where literature is 'taught', it is difficult to see what form the teaching can take — if it is concerned with the interpretation of the work — without an explicit understanding of the basis of one's appraisal.

I believe that the foundation of appraisal is laid upon an initial appreciation, but that this appreciation is enhanced through study, so that by the time we come to mature students of literature, appreciation and appraisal become intertwined. [. . .] Exposure to nursery rhymes, and other forms of verbal art, is a valuable starting point. The humble nursery rhyme is a rich resource for drawing attention to essentially the same characteristic of language that is employed so effectively in the valued pieces of literature — namely its ability to construct meanings for us, its ability to turn back upon itself as in:

> There was a little guinea-pig
> Which, being little, was not big.

The 'self-evident' nature of the assertion in this couplet is an invitation to ask: why are little things not big? It is an effective introduction to the principle of arbitrariness of the linguistic sign (Saussure, 1966; Culler, article 1.3 of this volume; Hasan, 1985). And from the arbitrariness of the sign follows its community-based nature, its dependence on social contexts, its truly creative aspect — namely our social reality. While exposure to such a corpus can sensitize us to the nature of language as a potential for meaning, this sensitivity needs to be enhanced by explicit discourse.

There are many misconceptions about linguistics. One, encouraged by many linguists themselves, is that linguistics is concerned simply with lexicogrammar — with structure and lexicon. I believe with Whorf (1956) that linguistics is 'essentially a quest for meaning'. And meanings cannot be studied in isolation from people who engage in the processes of meaning. This view clearly argues for a model of linguistics wherein one studies not only language in society — with society an optional extra — but also society in language — how our structures of knowledge, our personalities, our social and political institutions are created and maintained by language.

In his recent publication Culler (1983, p. 21) has remarked: 'The categories and methods of linguistics, whether applied directly to the language of literature or used as the model for a poetics, enable critics to focus not on the meanings of a work and its implications or value but on the structures that produce meaning'. I hope I have demonstrated through my analysis that given the right model of linguistics, a scholar can use it for focus on the 'meaning of a work and its implication'. The evaluation of the work is not independent of either the interpretation or the kinds of consideration to which I drew attention earlier in this chapter.

You will note that my point of entry into considerations relevant to the evaluation of literature texts is through appeal to the nature of language. If language were oblivious of culture, and if artistic conventions were universal and independent of the system of language, the evaluation of a work of literature would be a very different matter. [. . .]

References

Barthes, R. (1977) 'The death of the author'. In *Image, Music, Text*, tr. S. Heath, Hill & Wang.

Bernstein, B. B. (1971) *Class, Codes and Control, Vol. 1*. London: Routledge & Kegan Paul.

Bohannan, L. (1974), 'Shakespeare in the bush'. In Spradley J. P. and McCurdy D. W. (eds) *Conformity and Conflict*, 2nd ed. Boston, Mass: Little Brown & Co.

Butt, D. G. (1983) 'Semantic drift in verbal art', *Australian Review of Applied Linguistics*, **6** (1), 38–48.

Culler, J. (1975) *Structuralist Poetics: Structuralism, Linguistics and the Study of Literature*. Ithaca, NY: Cornell University Press.

Culler, J. (1983) *On Deconstruction: Theory and Criticism after Structuralism*. London: Routledge & Kegan Paul.

Douglas, M. (1975) *Implicit Meanings*, London: Routledge & Kegan Paul.

Eagleton, T. (1983), *Literary Theory: An Introduction*. Oxford: Basil Blackwell.

Eco, U. (1979) *The Role of the Reader: Explorations in the Semiotics of Texts*. Bloomington, Ind.: Indiana University Press.

Halliday, M. A. K. (1977) 'Language as social semiotic: Towards a general sociolinguistic theory', In Makkai A., Makkai V. B. and Heilmann L. (eds) *Linguistics at the Crossroads*. Lake Bluff, III.: Jupiter Press.

Halliday, M. A. K. (1982) 'The de-automatization of meaning: From Priestley's *An Inspector Calls*'. In Anderson J. (ed.) *Current Issues in Linguistic Theory, Vol. 15*. John Benjamins.

Halliday, M. A. K. (1985b) *Spoken and Written Language* (ECS805 Specialised Curriculum: Language and Learning). Deakin University, Vic.

Halliday, M. A. K. and Hasan, R. (1985) *Language, Context, and Text: Aspects of Language in a Social-semiotic Perspective* (ECS805 Specialised Curriculum: Language and Learning). Deakin University, Vic.

Hasan, R. (1964) A Linguistic Study of Contrasting Linguistic Features in the Style of Two Contemporary English Prose Writers. Unpublished PhD thesis, University of Edinburgh, Edinburgh.

Hasan, R. (1967) 'Linguistics and the study of literary texts'. *Etudes de Linguistique Applique* (5).

Hasan, R. (1971), 'Rime and reason in literature'. In Chatman S. (ed.) *Literary Style: A Symposium*, London: Oxford University Press.

Hasan, R. (1975) 'The place of stylistics in the study of verbal art'. In Ringborn H. (ed.) *Style and Text*. Skriptor.

Hasan, R. (1979) 'Language in the study of literature'. In Halliday M. A. K. (ed.) *Working Conference on Language in Education: Report to Participants*. University of Sydney Extension Program, Sydney.

Hasan, R. (1984) 'What kind of resource is language?' *Australian Review of Applied Linguistics*, **7** (1), 57–85.

Hasan, R. (1985) 'Meaning, text and context — fifty years after Malinowski'. In Greaves W. S. and Benson J. D. (eds) *Systemic Perspectives on Discourse: Selected Theoretical Papers from the Ninth International Systemic Workshop*. Norwood, NJ: Ablex.

Jakobson, R. (1960) 'Concluding statement: Linguistics and poetics'. In Sebeok T. A. (ed.), *Style in Language*. New York, John Wiley.

Levin, S. R. (1962) *Linguistic Structure in Poetry* (Janua Linguarum 23). The Hague: Mouton.

Mukarovsky, J. R. (1964) 'Standard language and poetic language'. In Garvin P. L. (ed. and tr.) *A Prague School Reader on Esthetics, Literary Structure, and Style*. Washington, DC: Georgetown University Press.

Mukarovsky, J. (1977) 'On poetic language'. In Burbank J. and Steiner P. (eds and trs) *The Word and Verbal Art*. New Haven, Conn.: Yale University Press.

Mundle, C. W. K. (1971) *Perception: Facts and Theories*. Oxford: Oxford University Press.

O'Toole, L. M. (1982) *Structure, Style and Interpretation in the Russian Short Story*. New Haven, Conn.: Yale University Press.

Saussure, F. de (1966) *Course in General Linguistics*. New York: McGraw-Hill. First published 1916.

Whorf, B. L. (1956) *Language, Mind and Reality*, ed. J. B. Carroll. Cambridge, Mass.: MIT Press.

1.7 Some Issues over which Linguists Can Agree

R. Hudson

Source: Hudson, R. (1982) 'Some issues over which linguists can agree'. In Carter, R. (ed.) *Linguistics and the Teacher*. London: Routledge and Kegan Paul, pp. 54–64.

The following is a list of 83 points which seem to be acceptable to most if not all linguists in Britain, and possibly in other countries too. The basis for claiming that they are so widely acceptable is that the list has been seen and commented on by a reasonably large number of British linguists, and I think the revisions I have made to successive versions of the list mean that it should be compatible with the views expressed by those who gave me their comments. Specifically, I had comments on at least one of the half-dozen versions which were circulated from each of the following linguists (some of whom would probably be happier to be referred to as applied linguists): J. Aitchison, R. Allwright, M. Breen, A. Brookes, G. Brown, K. Brown, C. Brumfit, C. Candlin, N. Collinge, G. Corbett, A. Cruse, A. Cruttenden, L. Davidson, M. Deuchar, N. Fairclough, D. Ferris, A. Fox, M. French, P. Gannon, G. Gazdar, M. Harris, R. Hartmann, R. Hogg, J. Hurford, G. Knowles, R. Le Page, J. Lyons, J. Mountford, W. O'Donnell, K. Perera, G. Pullum, S. Pulman, R. Quirk, M. Riddle, R. Robins, S. Romaine, G. Sampson, D. Sharp, M. Short, N. Smith, M. Stubbs, G. Thornton, L. Task, G. Wells, M. Wheeler, D. Wilson, J. Windsor Lewis. Between them, these linguists cover just over half the linguistics departments in British universities (15 out of 26), and there is no reason to think that the other departments would have presented a significantly different set of views. (All departments were in fact circulated with copies of the list, and a request for comments.) Moreover, any reader who knows the work of linguists in the list will agree that they cover a very wide range of views on such questions as the proper balance between theory and description and the pros and cons of competing linguistic theories. This diversity of views on controversial questions makes me all the more confident about the list of views on which they can all, apparently, agree. I should like to take this opportunity of thanking them all for their help.

1 The linguistic approach to the study of language

a Linguists describe language empirically — that is, they try to make statements which are testable, and they take language as it is, rather than saying how it should be. (In other words, linguistics is descriptive, but not prescriptive or normative.) (See 2.1a, 2.3a, 2.4b, 3.2e.)

b The primary object of description for linguists is the structure of language, but many linguists study this in relation to its functions (notably, that of conveying meaning) and in relation to other psychological and cultural systems. (See 2.1b, 2.7a)

c Linguists construct theories of language, in order to explain why particular languages have some of the properties that they do have. Linguists differ in the relative emphasis they put on general theory and on description of particular languages. (See 2.1d.)

d An essential tool of linguistics (both descriptive and theoretical) is a meta-language containing technical terms denoting analytical categories and constructs. None of the traditional or everyday meta-language is sacrosanct, though much of it is the result of earlier linguistic scholarship, but many traditional terms have in fact been adopted by linguists with approximately their established meanings. (See 3.2a, 3.3e, 3.4a.)

e The first aim of linguists is to understand the nature of language and of particular languages. Some linguists, however, are motivated by the belief that such understanding is likely to have practical social benefits, e.g. for those concerned professionally with the teaching of the mother tongue or of second languages, or with the treatment of language disorders.

2 Language, society and the individual

2.1 Language

a Language is amenable to objective study, with regard both to its structure and to its functions and external relations. (See 1a, 3.2c.)

b We learn our language from other individuals, so language is a property both of the individual and of the community from which he learns it. Consequently, both social and psychological approaches to its study are necessary.

c A language consists partly of a set of interacting general constraints, or rules, and partly of a vocabulary of lexical items. (Some linguists prefer to take a language as a set of sentences, and would apply the preceding description to the grammar of a language, rather than to the language itself.) (See 2.3d,f, 2.5a, 2.6e, 3.)

d There are features common to all languages (linguistic universals) which involve the organization of their grammars and also the types of patterning found in sentences. (See 1c, 2.2d, 2.4a, 2.6e,f, 3.)

e Although all speakers know at least one language, and use this knowledge ('competence') in speaking and understanding, very little of their knowledge is conscious. Knowledge of structural properties (e.g. rules of syntax) is particularly hard to report in an organized way. (See 2.5.)

2.2 Languages

a There is no clear or qualitative difference between so-called 'language-boundaries' and 'dialect-boundaries'. (See 2.3c,d, i.)

b There are between 4000 and 5000 languages (though no precise figure is possible because of the uncertainty referred to in (a) above). They differ widely in their number of speakers, ranging from a few individuals to hundreds of millions; and nations differ widely in the number of languages spoken natively in them, ranging from one to many hundreds.

c In many communities it is normal for every speaker to command two or more languages more or less fluently. Such communities exist in Britain, both in the traditional Celtic areas and in areas of high immigration. (See 2.3b.)

d There is no evidence that normal human languages differ greatly in the complexity of their rules, or that there are any languages that are 'primitive' in the size of their vocabulary (or any other part of their language), however 'primitive' their speakers may be from a cultural point of view. (The term 'normal human language' is meant to exclude on the one hand artificial languages such as Esperanto or computer languages, and on the other hand languages which are not used as the primary means of communication within any community, notably pidgin languages. Such languages may be simpler than normal human languages, though this is not necessarily so.) (See 2.1d, 3.3i.)

e Only a minority of languages are written, and an even smaller minority are standardized (i.e. include a variety which is codified and widely accepted as the variety most suitable for formal writing and speech). English belongs to this small minority. (See 2.3a,h, 2.4c, 3.2.)

f The present position of English as a world language is due to historical accidents rather than to inherent superiority of the language's structure. (Similar remarks apply to other world languages, notably French, Spanish and Russian, and to the 'Classical' languages such as Greek, Latin, Arabic and Sanskrit). (See 2.3e, 3.5e.)

2.3 Varieties of languages

a Spoken language developed before written language in the history of mankind, and it also develops first in the individual speaker; moreover, many languages are never written. These factors lead most linguists to believe that in linguistic theory priority should be given to spoken language, and many linguists give further priority to the most casual varieties of spoken language, those which are least influenced by normative grammar. (See 1a, 2.2a,e, 2.4e.)

b Every society requires its members to use different varieties of language in different situations. (See 2.2c, 2.3h, 3.1d.)

c The different 'varieties' referred to in (b) may be so-called 'languages', 'dialects' or 'registers' (i.e. roughly 'styles'). (See 2.2a, 3.4c.)

d All varieties (including the most casual speech) are 'languages', in that they have their own rules and vocabulary, and they are all subject to rules controlling their use. (See 2.1c, 2.2a.)

e The prestige of a variety derives from its social functions (i.e. from the people and situations with which it is associated) rather than from its structural properties. (See 2.2f, 2.7b, 3.4b.)

f All normal speakers are able to use more than one variety of language. (See 2.2c, 2.5f.)

g Different varieties are often associated with different social statuses, whether these are the result of birth (e.g. sex, region of origin, race) or of later experience (e.g. occupation, religion, education). (See 2.5g, 2.7b.)

h There is no reason for considering the variety called 'Standard English' the best for use in all situations. (See 2.2e.)

i Standard English subsumes a wide range of varieties, and has no clear boundaries vis-à-vis non-standard varieties. (See 2.2a.)

j In particular, there are many different ways of pronouncing Standard English (i.e.

different 'accents'), one of which is particularly prestigious in England and Wales, namely 'received pronunciation' ('RP'). (See 3.1a, 3.2f.)

2.4 *Change*

a The only parts of a language which are immune to change are those which it shares with all other human languages. (See 2.ld, 2.6b, 3.5d.)

b Change in a language is normally a matter of becoming different, rather than better or worse. (See 1a, 2.4d.)

c It is normal for language to change from generation to generation even when subject to the conservative influence of a standardized variety. (See 2.2e, 2.6c, 3.2e.)

d Change in the language may reflect the influence of non-standard varieties on the standard one as well as vice versa. (See 2.4b, 2.6a.)

e Language changes for different types of reason: sociolinguistic, as when one variety influences another, or communicative needs change, or institutions such as schools intervene; psycholinguistic, as when one group misperceives or misanalyses the speech of another; structural, as when disrupted patterns are restored. (See 2.3a, 2.5a, 2.6a, 2.7a, 3.5c.)

2.5 *Acquisition*

a When children learn to speak, they learn a language (in the sense of rules plus vocabulary) which is an increasingly good approximation to the language of their models; however, direct repetition of model utterances plays only a minor part in their speech. (See 2.1c, 2.4e, 3.1b,c, 3.2.)

b In learning their language, children's main source of information about the model is the speech of older people. No explicit instruction by the latter is needed, though parents often simplify their speech when talking to children, and correct some of the children's mistakes in a haphazard way. (See 2.4f.)

c By primary school age, children are commonly taking their peers rather than their parents as their dominant linguistic models. (See 2.5g,h.)

d There are considerable differences between children in the speed at which they acquire active use of specific parts of language. Such differences may be in part due to differences in their experience of language used by older people. (See 2.7a,c.)

e A child's poor performance in formal, threatening or unfamiliar situations cannot be taken as evidence of impoverished linguistic competence, but may be due to other factors such as low motivation for speaking in that situation, or unfamiliarity with the conventions for use of language in such situations. (See 2.7c, 3.4c.)

f By primary school age children already command a range of different varieties for use in different situations. (See 2.3f.)

g Some parts of the language of children are indicators of the status of being a child, and will be abandoned by the time the child reaches adulthood. Some such features are learned almost exclusively from peers, and may have been handed on in this way for many centuries. (See 2.3g, 2.5c.)

h Mere exposure to a model different from that of his peers or his parents will not in itself lead a child to change his own speech; the child must also want to accept the model as the standard for his own behaviour. Many people go on using varieties which they know are low in prestige, and which they believe are deficient, because these varieties are the only ones which they can accept. (See 2.5c, 2.6a, 2.7b.)

i The amount of knowledge involved in mastering a language is very great, although its extent is masked from ordinary adult speakers for various reasons, such as the unconscious nature of much of the knowledge. Children normally acquire a high proportion of this knowledge before they reach school age. (See 2.2d, 3.3d.)

2.6 Relations between languages and dialects

a Whenever speakers of two languages or dialects are in contact with one another, the languages or dialects concerned may be expected to influence each other in proportion to the extent of the contact, the social relations between the speakers, and the practical benefits of such influence for the recipients. (See 2.4c,d, 2.5h.)

b Such influence may be profound, going well beyond the borrowing of individual lexical items. (See 2.4a, 2.6g.)

c Since languages and dialects are indicators of group membership it is common for a community to resist and criticize such influence, and to pick out particular aspects of it for explicit complaint. (See 2.4c, 2.7b.)

d Some aspects of language are more susceptible to external influence than others. Possibly certain areas of vocabulary are the most susceptible, and the least susceptible may be inflectional morphology (i.e. variation in the form of a word to reflect its number, tense, case, etc.). (See 3.3c, 3.4a,b.)

e Alongside the similarities among languages, there are many gross differences. Such differences are most obvious in the arbitrary relations between the pronunciation of a word and its meaning and/or its syntactic properties, which are covered partly by the vocabulary and partly by the rules of morphology. (See 2.1c,d, 3.3a, 3.4d.)

f Apparent similarities between languages may turn out on thorough investigation to conceal significant differences, and vice versa. (See 2.1d.)

g If two languages are similar in their structures this need not be because they developed historically from the same earlier language, nor need historically related languages be similar in their structures. (See 2.4a, 2.6b.)

2.7 Speech as behaviour

a There are many possible reasons for speaking, only one of which is the desire to communicate ideas to an addressee. Other purposes include the establishing or maintaining of relations with the addressees, and the sorting out of the speaker's own thoughts. (See 1b, 2.4e, 2.5d, 3.5a.)

b The variety of language which a speaker uses on a particular occasion serves as an indicator of the speaker's group-membership and also of the speaker's perception of the type of situation in which the speech is taking place. A speaker's choice of variety is not wholly determined by social factors beyond his control, but may be manipulated by him to suit his purposes. (See 2.3e,g, 2.5c,h, 3.1a,c.)

c No speaker uses speech equally fluently or effectively for all functions (i.e. for all purposes and in all situations). Skill in speaking depends in part on having the opportunity to practise speech in quite specific functions, rather than on general linguistic ability. (See 2.5d, 3.2b.)

d When people comprehend speech, they may actually need to perceive only a proportion of the total utterance, since they can fill in the gaps with what they expect to hear.

3 The structure of language (see 2.1c, d)

3.1 Pronunciation

a Pronunciation differences are especially closely associated with social group membership differences, and consequently they are especially value-loaded. (See 2.3j, 2.7b.)

b Pronunciations which deviate from the prestige variety are generally learned from other speakers, and are not the result of 'slovenly speech habits'. (See 2.5a, 3.1d.)

c The precision with which speakers unconsciously conform to the linguistic models which they have adopted in pronunciation (as in other areas of language) goes beyond what is required for efficient communication (e.g. for the avoidance of ambiguity.) (See 2.5a, 2.7b.)

d All speakers, in all varieties, use pronunciations in fast speech which differ considerably from those used in slow, careful speech, and other aspects of the situation, such as its formality, may have similar effects. Rapid casual speech is skilled rather than 'slovenly'. (See 2.3b, 2.7d, 3.1b.)

e The analysis of pronunciation takes account of at least the following: phonetic features of vowels and consonants, the order in which these occur, and the larger patterns which they form (syllables, words, intonation patterns, etc.)

f Intonation does not only reflect the speaker's attitude, but is a particularly important indicator in spoken language of an utterance's structure, and also of its contribution to the discourse. (See 3.2b.)

g Intonation is regulated by norms which vary from variety to variety. Children start to learn the intonation patterns of their community's variety in the first year of life.

3.2 Writing

a Written language reflects a linguistic analysis in terms of categories (e.g. sentence, letter) some of which are not related simply or directly to categories needed for spoken language. (See 1d.)

b The skills needed for successful reading and writing are partly distinct from those needed for speaking and listening, and the relevant linguistic patterns are also partly different. Such skills and patterns have to be learned as part of the acquisition of literacy, so the latter involves much more than learning to spell and to recognize single words. (see 2.7c,d.)

c The English writing system is only one of many such systems, each of which is amenable to objective and systematic study. Not all writing systems are alphabetic, and not all alphabetic systems are like English in the way they relate writing to other parts of language structure. (See 2.1a.)

d Spelling is only one part of the English writing system, which also includes for example punctuation, handwriting and the numerals. (See 3.3c.)

e Spelling is probably the most immutable part of English, and the part where prescriptivism is most easily accepted by linguists. (See 1a, 2.4c.)

f English spelling does not reflect RP any more directly than it does other accents, so it is no easier for RP speakers to learn. (See 2.3j.)

3.3 Vocabulary

a The relation between the meaning of a word and the pronunciation (or spelling) of its root is usually arbitrary. (See 2.6e, 3.4d.)

b Items of vocabulary ('lexical items') include not only single words but also idioms (combinations of words whose meaning cannot be derived from the meanings of the individual words) and other longer structures such as clichés. (See 3.5b.)

c The specification of a lexical item must refer to at least the following types of information: its pronunciation (and its spelling, if the language is a written one), its meaning, the syntactic and semantic contexts in which it may occur, and how inflectional morphology affects its form (at least if it is irregular in this respect). (See 2.6d, 3.2d.)

d There is no known limit to the amount of detailed information of all such types which may be associated with a lexical item. Existing dictionaries, even large ones, only specify lexical items incompletely.

e The syntactic information about a lexical item may be partially given in terms of word-classes, some of which correspond closely to traditional parts of speech. However, a complete syntactic specification of a lexical item needs much more information than can be given in terms of a small set of mutually exclusive word-classes like the parts of speech. (See 1d.)

f The boundaries between word-classes tend to be unclear even when defined by linguists.

g Many lexical items have meanings which cannot be defined without reference to the culture of the language's speakers.

h Vocabulary varies greatly between registers, so a child may use in the classroom only a small portion of his or her total vocabulary. (See 3.4c.)

i It is very difficult to measure a person's vocabulary meaningfully, partly because of the difference between active and passive vocabulary, partly because it is possible to know different amounts of detail about any given item, and partly because it is possible to know more vocabulary relevant to one area of experience than to another, so that measures based on just one kind of vocabulary do not give a sound basis for estimating the total vocabulary. (See 2.2d, 3.3d,h.)

3.4 Syntax

a The analysis of syntactic structure takes account of at least the following factors: the order in which words occur, how they combine to form larger units (phrases, clauses, sentences, etc.), the syntactic classes to which the words belong (including those marked by inflectional morphology), and the specifically syntactic relations among the words or other units, such as the relations referred to by the labels 'subject' and 'modifier'. (See 1d, 2.6d, 3.5b.)

b Although English base has little inflectional morphology, it has a complex syntax (i.e. it is not true that 'English has no grammar'). This is true of all dialects of English. (See 2.3e, 2.6d.)

c Syntax, like vocabulary, is particulary sensitive to register differences, so a child's use of syntactic constructions in the classroom may reflect only part of the total range of constructions that the child knows, and uses under other circumstances. (See 2.3c, 2.5e, 3.3h.)

d The relations between meanings and syntactic structures are less arbitrary than those between the meaning and pronunciation of a single word. However, even this limited arbitrariness allows very different syntactic structures to be associated (either by different languages, or within the same language) with similar meanings, and vice versa. (See 2.6e, 3.3a.)

e Syntactic complexity is only one source of difficulty in understanding spoken or written language. (See 2.7e, 3.2b.)

3.5 Meaning

a The information conveyed by an utterance of a sentence on a particular occasion may cover many different types of 'meaning', relating to the conditions for the sentence's being true, the assumptions made by the speakers, the utterance's social function as a statement, a suggestion, a request, etc., and other factors. (See 2.7a.)

b Part of this information is the literal meaning of the sentence uttered, which reflects the meanings of the lexical items in it and the syntactic relations between them. Part of it, however, derives from the context in which the sentence is used. (See 3.3b, 3.4a.)

c To a greater extent than other parts of language, meaning may be negotiated by speakers and addresser, e.g. by defining terms or by modifying established meanings to suit special circumstances. (See 2.4e.)

d The meanings of lexical items change with time, and there is no reason to take the etymological meaning of a word as its true one, or indeed as part of its meaning at all. (See 2.4a,f.)

e There is no evidence that any language is any more 'logical' than any other. (See 2.2f.)

SECTION II

The Development of Language and Thought

Introduction

Much psychological research on the acquisition of language and cognitive development has focused on the very earliest childhood years. One explanation for this focus on infancy has been offered by Durkin (1978), who suggests that 'widespread interest in the origins of language seems to have led the research community to pursue ever younger subjects' (p. 1). Certainly, the development of language and thought during the later years of childhood is a relatively neglected field of study.

One striking exception to this tradition in cognitive psychology is the work of Jerome Bruner. This breadth of interest has linked early development to that of later years, and he has attempted more than most cognitive psychologists to bring out the educational relevance of his field of study. In the first of two articles, Bruner defines two distinct ways of thinking, and shows how they are tied to different kinds of discourse.

Bruner's work owes much to that of his predecessors Jean Piaget and L. S. Vygotsky. Indeed, Bruner has played a significant role in releasing Vygotsky's ideas from near obscurity in the early 1950s, and disseminating them to a wider, and increasingly receptive, academic audience. Bruner's second article combines a personal account of his involvement in this dissemination with an introduction to some of Vygotsky's most influential ideas about the development of language and thought.

Much academic discussion of the development of language and thought seems to be based on the tacit assumption that children are monolingual, although for much of the world's population bilingualism is a normal part of everyday social life. In the last article in this section, Barbara Mayor discusses the nature of bilingualism and its possible cognitive significance.

Reference

Durkin, K. (ed.) (1978) *Language Development in the School Years*. London: Croom Helm.

2.1 Vygotsky: A Historical and Conceptual Perspective

J. Bruner

Source: Bruner, J. (1985) 'Vygotsky: a historical and conceptual perspective'. In Wertsch, J. V. (ed.) *Culture, Communication and Cognition: Vygotskyan Perspectives*. Cambridge: Cambridge University Press, pp. 21–34.

It might be appropriate for me to begin with some historical, indeed autobiographical, notes. For quite by chance, I lived through some of the events that may have led to Vygotsky having an impact on psychology in America. He is, I believe, going through a second cycle now. But we can come to that later.

Let me tell you of a distinction I used to make, half jokingly, between paleo- and neo-Pavlovian psychology. Like most Westerners before 1956, I knew only the former. It was about conditioned reflexes in the classic mold. As an undergraduate I had assisted Karl Zener in his conditioning experiments. They were, at least technically and on the surface, in the paleo-Pavlovian: the salivary response of dogs was conditioned to the usual array of bells and buzzers. But Karl Zener was no paleo-Pavlovian in spirit. He had gone as a postdoctoral fellow to study at the Kaiser Wilhelm Institute in Berlin with Wolfgang Köhler and Kurt Lewin, and Pavlov's connectionism was anathema to this young Harvard-trained Gestaltist. His particular bogeyman was the stimulus-substitution theory of conditioning, that an old response remains intact and is simply captured by a new stimulus that takes over the triggering functioning of the old. For Zener, the central idea was 'action in a field': when a response becomes conditioned, it is not simply 'transferred' to the control of a new stimulus. Rather, the context changes and with it the nature of the task and of the signalling properties of the stimuli and the response as well. Isolated responses and isolated stimuli were rejected in the view, their place taken by means–end structures that changed in the course of conditioning. And he proved his point, as I shall presently relate.

It was 1936. I was not yet old enough to vote. But I was old enough to take sides. I thought Karl Zener admirable for using the classic Pavlovian conditioning situation as the battlefield on which to defeat the old 'switchboard theory'. I even did my part by learning the surgery needed to turn the parotid salivary duct of the dog outward to the cheek so that its salivary flow could be measured through a capillary system attached to the dog's cheek by a drilled silver dollar glued there by a mix of bee's wax and sealing wax applied hot and soft and allowed to cool hard and adhesive. We needed that tough adhesive joint, for Zener's dogs did not just stand there at the tray awaiting food delivery (as they had in Moscow). When the buzzer sounded, they had to cross from another table, around the barrier of a whirring fan, and then position themselves at the tray. A dog conditioned in the classical Pavlovian task just standing there and waiting in the old harness would have no difficulty transferring to the new obstacle course. He didn't have to be taught when to start salivating: not when the buzzer sounded, but after you got round the obstacle. The whole response pattern was reorganized. Surely this was no simple matter of a response being transferred from one stimulus to another. With hardly a qualm, I became a thorough and mocking revisionist. Little did I know that the fates were preparing me to become an ally to the psychologists in Russia who were reacting in much the same way towards simplistic Pavlovianism.

I began to learn about all of this in a more first-hand way when I attended the International Congress of Psychology in Montreal in 1954. There was a Russian delegation. Their presented papers characteristically started with a genuflection to Pavlov, followed quickly by some rather interesting studies of attention or problem solving or whatever that had little to do with the Pavlov I had read. They seemed to represent some other interest whose nature I could not quite discern. And then there was a classically Russian reception towards the end of the week, replete with vodka and a barrel of caviar. It was at that reception (and at an informal party afterward at Wilder Penfield's) that I first encountered talk of Vygotsky, of the role of language in development, of the 'zone of proximal development', and (of all things) a Second Signal System attributed to Pavlov. The Second Signal System was the world encoded in language: nature transformed by history and culture. Vygotsky's work, I learned that evening, was widely circulated though it was officially banned. The Second Signal System, I thought, was a splendid way of getting beyond Pavlov while still maintaining a posture of high respect.

Vygotsky's *Thought and Language* appeared in 1934, shortly after his death of tuberculosis at the age of 37. It so deeply disturbed the guardians of proper Marxist interpretation that it was suppressed two years later, in 1936, the year of my engagement with the Pavlovian dogs in the obstacle course. As Luria and Leont'ev said of the book years later (1956), 'The primary and fundamental task of that time [the late 1920s and 1930s when the "battle for consciousness" raged] consisted of freeing oneself on the one hand from vulgar behaviourism and, on the other, from the subjective understanding of mental phenomena as exclusively internal subjective states that can only be investigated through introspection' (p. 6). It was not for another 20 years that the book could appear openly in Russian. It was published in 1956. It was the same year that another volume on thought appeared, *A Study of Thinking*, by Bruner, Goodnow and Austin (1956). It is a year, 1956, that has recently become a popular candidate as the year of birth of the cognitive sciences. Something was going on in the intellectual atmosphere.

Vygotsky's book finally appeared in English in 1962. I was asked to write an introduction to it. By then I had learned enough about Vygotsky from accounts of his work by Alexander Romanovich Luria, with whom I had become close friends, so that I welcomed this added goad to close study. And I read the book not only with meticulous care, but with growing astonishment. For Vygotsky was plainly a genius. Yet it was an elusive form of genius, his. Unlike, say, Pavlov or Piaget, there was nothing massive or glacial about the corpus of his thought and its development. Rather, it was like the later Wittgenstein: at times aphoristic, often sketchy, vivid in its illuminations.

To begin with, I liked his instrumentalism. That is to say, I admired his way of interpreting thought and speech as instruments for the planning and carrying out of action. Or as he puts it in an early essay, 'Children solve practical tasks with the help of their speech, as well as with their eyes and hands. This unity of perception, speech and action, which ultimately produces internalization of the visual field, constitutes the central subject matter for any analysis of the origin of uniquely human forms of behavior' (1978, p. 26). Language is (in Vygotsky's sense as in Dewey's) a way of sorting out one's thoughts about things. Thought is a mode of organizing perception and action. But all of them, each in their way, also reflect the tools and aids available for use in carrying out action. Or to take his epigraph from Francis Bacon, 'Nec manus, nisi intellectus, sibi permissus, multam valent; instrumentis et auxilibus res perficitur'. But what a curious epigraph: 'Neither the hand nor the mind alone left to themselves, would amount to much'. And what are these prosthetic devices that perfect them (if you will allow me a modern gloss on 'instrumentis et auxilibus')?

Well, for one thing, it would seem that there are concepts and ideas and theories that permit one to get to higher ground. Take the following quotation: 'The new higher concepts in turn transform the meaning of the lower. The adolescent who has mastered algebraic concepts has gained a vantage point from which he sees arithmetic concepts in a broader perspective' (Vygotsky, 1934, p. 115). There seems, then, to be some interesting way in which it becomes possible to turn around upon one's thoughts, to see them in a new light. This is, of course, mind reflecting on itself. It is not very surprising that, given the plodding, *lumpen* nature of Marxist criticism and interpretation in those days, Vygotsky should have been banned for 20 years . Yet again there is something sibylline about this pronouncement too, it seems to be about consciousness and, indeed, about what today we call 'metacognition'. So let us pursue the matter a step further.

About consciousness he says: 'Consciousness and control appear only at a late stage in the development of a function, after it has been used and practised unconsciously and spontaneously. In order to subject a function to intellectual control, we must first possess it' (1934, p. 90). This suggests that prior to the development of self-directed, conscious control, action is, so to speak, governed by a more direct mode of responding to environmental events. This again is a rather dark way of talking about the issue. It suggests that consciousness or (in the classical sense) reflection is a way of buffering immediate responses so that the situation can be better appraised from higher ground. And how it that achieved?

This brings us, then, to the heart of the matter: to Vygotsky's ideas about the famous zone of proximal development. It has to do with the manner in which we arrange the environment such that the child can reach higher or more abstract ground from which to reflect, ground on which he is enabled to be more conscious. Or to use his words, the zone of proximal development is '*the distance between the actual developmental level as determined by independent problem solving and the level of potential development as determined through problem solving under adult guidance or in collaboration with more capable peers*' (1978 p. 86). Or to put it even more concretely, he says: 'Human learning presupposes a specific social nature and a process by which children grow into the intellectual life of those around them' (1978, p. 88). And óne final leap: 'Thus the notion of a zone of proximal development' he says, 'enables us to propound a new formula, namely that the only "good learning" is that which is in advance of development' (1978, p. 89).

Now, if one takes this quite literally, there is a contradiction in Vygotsky's proposal. On the one hand the zone of proximal development has to do with achieving 'consciousness and control'. But consciousness and control come only after one has already got a function well and spontaneously mastered. So how could 'good learning' be that which is in advance of development and, as it were, bound initially to be unconscious since unmastered? I have puzzled about this matter for many years, and I think I understand what Vygotsky might have meant. Or at least, I understand the matter somewhat as follows, and it is this point that I will want to develop. If the child is enabled to advance by being under the tutelage of an adult or a more competent peer, then the tutor or the aiding peer serves the learner as a vicarious form of consciousness until such a time as the learner is able to master his own action through his own consciousness and control. When the child achieves that conscious control over a new function or conceptual system, it is then that he is able to use it as a tool. Up to that point, the tutor in effect performs the critical function of 'scaffolding' the learning task to make it possible for the child, in Vygotsky's words, to internalize external knowledge and convert it into a tool for conscious control.

Vygotsky then comments that the acquisition of language provides the paradigm case for what he is talking about. It is mastered at first in collaboration with an adult or a more competent peer solely with the objective of communicating. Once mastered sufficiently in this way, it can then become internalized and serve under conscious control as a means of carrying out inner speech dialogues. I quite agree with Vygotsky that language acquisition may provide an interesting paradigm case and, like him, I will presently consider some parallels and disanalogies between language acquisition and the way in which we enable children, by our calculated aid, to get ahead of their present levels of development into a new zone.

Before I do that, however, I would like to comment in passing on one point that has usually been overlooked or given second billing in our own achievement-orientated Western culture. It is inherent in his conviction that passing on knowledge is like passing on language — his basic belief that social transaction is the fundamental vehicle of education and not, so to speak, solo performance. But alas, he did not live long enough to develop his ideas about the subject. I believe that it was his eventual hope to delineate the transactional nature of learning, particularly since learning for him involved entry into a culture via induction by more skilled members. But though he did not live long enough to carry out this programme, it seems to me that it remains an important one to pursue. Too often, human learning has been depicted in the paradigm of a long organism pitted against nature — whether in the model of the behaviourist's organism shaping up responses to fit the geometries and probabilities of the world of stimuli, or in the Piagetian model where a lone child struggles single-handed to strike some equilibrium between assimilating the world to himself or himself to the world. Vygotsky was struck, rather, with how much learning is quintessentially assisted and vicarious and about social conventions and intellectual prostheses in the manner of Popper's World Three.

There are, I think, three kinds of concepts that would be needed in order to carry out a Vygotskian project on 'learning by transaction', and there is enough extant in his writings to suggest how he would pose them. One has to do with 'props' and 'instruments' that make it possible for the child to go beyond his present 'level of development' to achieve higher ground and, eventually, new consciousness. The second is some specification of the kinds of processes that make the child sensitive or receptive to vicarious or transactional learning. The third has to do with procedures that the more proficient partner in a transaction uses in order to ease the way for the intending (or even the initially unintending) learner. It takes no particular imagination to see that the three — props, processes and procedures — are at the heart of what we ordinarily think of as education — curriculum, learning and teaching. For Vygotsky, they were matters that grew out of his theory of development. I shall touch on these in passing and come back to them at the end.

Let me now return to the perspective of language, where Vygotsky felt we should begin. For all that there is a great deal of disagreement on how language acquisition occurs — and we need not review the contending views here — there are certain points on which there is consensus. I think we would all agree now that the input of speech to the language-acquiring child is highly tailored by adults to match the child's level of speech development and that it is altered systematically to stay matched with the child's progress. There are certain conventional and/or natural ways in which this fine-tuning is accomplished, and the result is the baby talk (BT) register or 'motherese' — exaggerated stress, simpler segmentation, reduced syntactic complexity, and so forth. It is difficult to imagine that it is all merely conventional, since four-year-olds use BT in speaking to two-year-olds, and that seems a rather early age for acquiring so subtle a convention. Let me quickly add that there is no agreement (and little evidence) as to whether the existence of fine-tuning matters much or little in helping the child master the language. What we certainly do know is that language must be acquired across a wide range of variation in the degree of tunedness of adult tutors. This has led some to believe that language is not taught, only learned. A more correct inference would be that *learning to know* a language must be possible with a minimum instantiation of its constructive rules. That is, linguistic competence in the old sense of the word is not any obvious product of any obvious teaching.

What is altogether less clear is whether *learning to use* a language can be mastered with exposure to only scanty or degenerate input of instances. It would, I suppose, be impossible to master such things as the conditions on speech acts, how to handle the given-new contract in discourse, how to fulfill adjacency requirements, even how to appreciate deictic shifters like *me–you* and *here–there* without having entered into a considerable amount of contingent communication with a more expert speaker of the language who had in mind some pedagogical aims. I think that with the exception of some old-fashioned purists, most students of language acquisition would agree that the amount of explicit guidance or teaching in language transmission is probably inversely proportional to the formal structure of what has to be mastered. The loose rules and maxims of pragmatics — Grice's (1975) cooperative principles, Searle's (1969, 1975) speech acts, and so on — are worked over and negotiated in contingent discourse and at some length. Syntax, however, is hardly ever the object of explicit pedagogy or negotiation; phonology rarely. Semantics is the middling case. It would seem, then, that it is as a byproduct of learning to *use* language in discourse that the child masters its *structure*. As Roger Brown suggests in his discussion of BT (1977), there is indeed a point of the mother talking with her child in language that he has already mastered. It is not redundant. It keeps communication going in a way that assures the child will know how to *use* the new instrument in a variety of contexts with some effectiveness.

Indeed, there is even a continuity in pragmatic mastery that is quite uncharacteristic of the mastery of formal syntax. That is to say, the bulk of research — Halliday (1975), Bates and the Rome group (1976, 1979), Dore (1974, 1975, 1977), Bruner (1981, 1983) — suggests that there is a slow accretion of skill in carrying out such elementary functions as referring, requesting and offering. It begins before the onset of lexicogrammatical speech by the use of gesture, intonation and so on, and as the child learns the structures of language, these are used to further the child's efforts 'to do things with words'. But before he has words, he does his things with gestures and babbles and stylized intonation contours. Communicative intent seems to be present from the start or very near the start. And intent of this kind uses whatever props are available. It is almost always in the interest of fulfilling his communicative intentions that the child recognizes and picks up new structural tricks relating to language. Only late in the day do the new tricks suggest new functions — like Michael Halliday's (1975) more elaborated mathematic functions or John Searle's (1979) commissives like promising.

One last point about language acquisition that will be crucial to the argument I want finally to make. A great deal of it occurs in highly framed or formated situations: familiar and routinized settings in which the two members of the pair are operating in a highly known microcosm, with fairly easily recognized intentions, and where the adult can most easily caliberate his or her hypotheses about what the child means. Michael Silverstein has suggested that these microcosms are often so tiny that they deserve to be called 'nanocosms'. A good example of such a developing format is provided by Ninio and Bruner (1978) for the mastery of labelling and simple topic-comment structures. Its main procedural characteristics is that the adult maintains a very constant routine over time to which the child responds with increasing skill and decreasing variability. In the Ninio–Bruner case, the adult has a standard way of requesting of the child the names of objects in picture books and the like and manages it in such a way that the child learns the names of things and how to comment on things named without ever making an error. The only errors recognized or responded to by the mother are regressions or backslidings that she knows the child knows he can correct if challenged. I would liken the procedure in such formats to the constructing of scaffolds. In effect, the child is permitted to do as much as he can spontaneously do; whatever he cannot do is filled in or 'held up' by the mother's scaffolding activities. When he cannot respond to her request for a label save by uttering an extended babble, she accepts what he has on offer and then provides the word — until such a time as he can produce a lexeme-length babble, at which point she will no longer accept extended babbles in response to her stylized *What's that, Jonathan*? Formats of this kind are very characteristic of the settings in which errorless learning occurs in many indigenous societies. Such 'errorless learning' has been notably well described by Fortes (1938) in a remarkable monograph on education among the Tale of West Africa.

The last thing to say about language acquisition of this formated, pragmatically paced kind is that it is governed by a rule of 'voluntary handover and willing receipt'. Anything the child masters is his to use and there is no question about whether, how or why it should be used in speech. All such decisions are left to the learner. There are astonishingly few cases on record suggesting normal resistance to learning. When resistance occurs, it seems to accompany profound pathology. I have never heard anybody say, even in the most deeply anti-intellectual times, 'What a waste of time learning to speak'. The only exceptions to this general case are to be found in matters of truth, sincerity and felicity, all of which are negotiable in terms of criteria that are inherently extralinguistic.

All that I have said thus far about language acquisition has led me to conclude that there is a Language Acquisition Support System (LASS) that is at least partly innate. I see it as a counterpart to some sort of Language Acquisition Device (LAD). LAD is what makes it possible for the child to master the constitutive rules of his native language without a sufficient sample of instances to support his inductive leaps. Without it we would be sunk, for there is no unique grammar that can be logically induced from any finite sample of utterances in any language. The function of LASS is to assure that input will be a form acceptable to the recognition routines of LAD, however, those recognition routines may eventually be described. Although I think there are enormous differences between the way a language is acquired and the way other forms of knowledge and skill are acquired, I agree with Vygotsky that there is a deep parallel in all forms of knowledge acquisition — precisely the existence of a crucial match between a *support system* in the social environment and an *acquisition process* in the learner. I think it is this match that makes possible the transmission of the culture, first as a set of connected ways of acting, perceiving and talking, and then finally as a generative system of taking conscious thought, using the instruments of reflection that the culture 'stores' as theories, scenarios, plots, prototypes, maxims and so on. The fact that we learn the culture as readily and effectively as we do must give us pause — considering how poorly we do at certain artificial, 'made-up' subjects that we teach in schools and whose use is *not* imbedded in any established cultural practice.

I can only sketch roughly some examples of the match I have in mind. Let me take first a study of three- and five-year-old children being 'tutored' in the task of putting together sets of interlocking wooden blocks, a study by Wood, Bruner and Ross (1976) that I am only beginning to understand. We were exactly in the position of most schools that set out to teach a subject without the advice or consent of the pupils involved and without the task having any contextualization in the children's lives. The task was to build a pyramid out of interlocking wooden blocks that could, of course, have been used for any number of other, perhaps more engaging activities — like building castles or radar installations. The subjects were three- and five-year-olds, and they were in the hands of a tutor who was to help them build a pyramid. The tutor, I must report, was genuinely fascinated by what children did in such tasks, was highly sophisticated about both problem solving and children, and in general radiated interest and responsive goodwill. The details are not important, but there are some generalities worth noting about the ways in which the tutor had to behave in order to do her job. Let me spell out some of these inevitabilities of acting as a support system for the child's foray into the zone of proximal development.

After the child is induced into taking on the task — even three-year-olds follow the universal rule of doing what people ask of them, particularly if the people are the likes of Gail Ross — the main tasks of the tutor are these. First is to model the task, to establish that something is possible and interesting. In this case, it consisted of constructing the pyramid slowly, with conspicuous marking of the subassemblies that the child will need later. At that moment, the tutor has a monopoly on foresight. She is consciousness for two. The child, somehow, is induced to try. That is surely a crucial part of what the more experienced do for the less experienced, and let us not confuse ourselves with words like *identification* or whatever: it is very obscure how an adult gets a child to venture into the zone. I think it is easiest when the venture is seen as play, but that is too large a topic (see Bruner et al., 1976). It relates to minimizing the cost, indeed the possibility, of error. Once the child is willing to try, the tutor's general task is that of scaffolding — reducing the number of degrees of freedom that the child must manage in the task. She does it by segmenting the task and ritualizing it: creating a format, a nanocosm. Like the adults in the Fortes study in Taleland, she sees to it that the child does only what he can do and then she fills in the rest — as in slipping the pegs of certain blocks into the holes of others to which they are mated, the child having brought them next to each other. She limits the complexity of the task to the level that the child can just manage, even to the point of shielding his limited attention from distractors.

Recall what Vygotsky said about leading the child on ahead of his development. This is done with some prudence by the tutor. Once the child has mastered some routine that was modular to the task, putting together a subassembly of blocks for example, the tutor then tempted the child to use his skill to build a higher-order assembly. That, of course, was structurally built into the nature of the blocks as we had constructed them. Yet it is often enough observed, this 'raising the ante', whatever the nature of the materials of a task (including language), that it merits being considered as a candidate for a principle. Curiously, it is what keeps the child 'in the zone' and, at the same time, what keeps him from getting bored.

Now, after all this has been accomplished, then and only then do the child and the tutor interact in a way that fits the title 'instruction'. Instruction — telling the child what to do or what he might try next or what he is doing that is getting in his way, and the like — instruction in words comes only after the child knows how to do the problem. Vygotsky somewhere notes that at first language and action are fused and it is for this reason that the child talks to himself while carrying out a task. Eventually, language and action become separated, and the latter (the task) can be represented in the medium of the former (words). It is when that stage is reached that one can incorporate what one knows into words, and thereby into the process of dialogue.

There are only a few studies on the role of dialogue in problem solving although there are many claims to the effect that thought is internalized dialogue — claims by writers as various as Vygotsky, George Herbert Mead, and many contemporary hermeneuticists who believe in the negotiated nature of meaning and are therefore bound to abide by a social definition of the thought processes. We do not know what dialogue about a problem does during problem solving, before problem solving or after — although there are some tempting clues in the literature such as it is [see Zivin (1979) for a review and evaluation of this literature]. I want to present a hypothesis about the internalization that is based on a reinterpretation of Vygotsky presented by Wertsch (1979).

Once dialogue is made possible by the child now being able to represent linguistically the aspects and elements of the operations he has mastered that he can share with an assisting adult, a powerful discourse device becomes available. It is a device that permits the taking for granted what is known and shared between speaker and listener and going beyond it to what is a comment on what is shared and known. This is sometimes called the topic–comment structure of language and it has most recently been revitalized by the linguist Chafe (1974, 1976) and the psycholinguists Clark and Haviland (1977) under the interesting rubric the 'given–new contract'. It is a rather old idea that was originally formulated by the Prague School of linguists to embody a discourse-sensitive version of the subject–predicate distinction. In their functional view, a subject (or topic) is that which is shared in the consciousness (or intersubjectivity, to use the more fashionable term) of speaker and listener. A predicate is that which introduces something new, a comment upon the topic or subject that is in joint consciousness. The given in discourse is the unstressed, the unmarked, the easily pronominalized, the background. The new is the stressed, the marked, the fully nominalized, the foregrounded. It is the means whereby language permits (even encourages) the adult to lure the child into the zone of proximal development, and of course, it likewise permits the child to put questions of his own to the adult about what is beyond the information given. It is obviously a reciprocal process for adult and child, as we know from a recent study by Tizard and her colleagues (Tizard et al., 1980) that shows that the children (three to five) who ask the most searching questions are the ones whose parents are most likely to answer them fully and, of course, the parents who are most likely to answer are the ones with children most likely to ask!

So what does this tell us about the internalization of dialogue? How can the child internalize a procedure for distinguishing what is shared consciousness and what is asymmetric with respect to an addressee? Let me go back for a moment to a comment I made in passing earlier: that at the earliest stage of inducting a child into a new activity, the adult serves almost as the vicarious consciousness of the child in the sense of being the only one who knows the goal of the activity in which the two of them are engaged. When the child masters a new task, he masters its means–end structure: he too now knows the goal, although at any moment he may be unclear about how to get there. It seems to me to be the case (and I cannot yet put it more strongly than that) that the given–new discourse pattern becomes converted when internalized into a system for distinguishing the givens and the knowns of a situation from that which is problematic, new and uncertain. It becomes the medium for the sort of task analysis that all who are concerned with metacognition brood about–from Feuerstein and Jensen (in press) and Edward deBono (in press) at one side, such artificial intelligence people as Hays (in press) at the other, with Ann Brown (in press) and Courtney Cazden (1981) in the middle.

You will know, of course, that Vygotsky had some very evocative, rather puzzling things to say about the structure of inner speech. It was he who commented upon the fact that inner speech was principally predicative, the the subject dropped out. Along with Wertsch (and with Roman Jakobson who first introduced me to the idea) I think Vygotsky was using subject–predicate in the Prague sense of given and new rather than in the strictly syntactic or the derived case grammatical sense. Inner speech, on this view, so exaggerates the unmarked–unstressed–backgrounded versus marked–stressed–foregrounded distinction of the given–new as to ban the former altogether. It becomes, if you will forgive me a weakness for nautical metaphors, an ideal navigational instrument for operating in the zone of proximal development, beyond the information given. Who needs a navigational instrument that tells you that you are where you already know you are? Wertsch (1979) puts it well:

> In the case of private speech, given information is that knowledge that is in the speaker's consciousness at the time of the utterance. So-called new information is what is being introduced into the speaker's consciousness as a result of the action he is carrying out. (p. 95)

And he means by action, of course, intended action where there is some representation of a goal and a set of alternative means for getting to it.

Let me conclude with a few final remarks about where things stand. As you can see, I have been attempting to follow the spirit of the Vygotskian project to find the manner in which aspirant members of a culture learn from their tutors, the vicars of their culture, how to understand the world. That world is a symbolic world in the sense that it consists of conceptually organized, rule-bound belief systems about what exists, about how to get to goals, about what is to be valued. There is no way, none, in which a human being could possibly master that world without the aid and assistance of others for, in fact, that world *is* others. The culture stores an extraordinarily rich file of concepts, techniques and other prosthetic devices that are available (often in a highly biased way, for the file constitutes one of the sources of wealth in any society and most societies do not share their wealth equally among all). The prosthetic devices require for their use certain fundamental skills, notable among them the ability to use the language as an instrument of thought — natural language, and eventually such artificial languages as mathematics, Polish logic, Fortran, sprung rhythms and especially written language. As Vygotsky said, it is a matter of using whatever one has learned before to get to higher ground next. What is obvious and, perhaps, 'given' in this account is that there must be, needs be at any given stage of voyaging into the zone of proximal development a support system that helps learners get there. If tutors are seen not as partners in advancement, but, as reported in some recent research (Hood et al., 1980), as sources of punishment, then it may have disastrous consequences for the candidate learner. That problem has not been at the centre of my attention, although I know how desperately important it is. Rather, I have tried to address myself to the issue of how we learn from others and I have chosen Vygotsky as my model because he was the first to look. I hope I have convinced the reader that his project is still worth pursuing.

References

Bates, E. (1976) *Language and Context: The Acquisition of Pragmatics.* New York: Academic Press.

Bates, E. (1979) *The Emergence of Symbols: Cognition and Communication in Infancy.* New York: Academic Press.

Brown, A. L. (in press). 'The importance of diagnosis in cognitive skills instruction'. In Chipman S., Segal J. W., and Glaser R. (ed) *Thinking and Learning Skills: Current Research and Open Questions, Vol. 2* Hillsdale, NJ: Erlbaum.

Brown, R. (1977) Introduction. In Snow C. E. and Ferguson C. A. (eds) *Talking to Children: Language Input and Acquisition.* Cambridge: Cambridge University Press.

Bruner, J. (1981) 'Interaction and language acquisition'. In Deutsch W. (ed.) *The Child's Construction of Language.* New York: Academic Press.

Bruner, J. (1983) *Child's Talk.* New York: Norton.

Bruner J., Goodnow, J. and Austin, G. (1956) *A Study of Thinking.* New York: Wiley.

Bruner, J. S., Jolly, A. and Sylva, K. (eds) (1976) *Play: Its Role in Evolution and Development.* London: Penguin.

Cazden, C. (1981) 'Performance before competence: Assistance to child discourse in the zone of proximal development', *Quarterly Newsletter of the Laboratory of Comparative Human Cognition,* **3**,(1), 5–8.

Chafe, W. L. (1974) 'Language and consciousness'. *Language,* **50**, 111–113.

Chafe, W. L. (1976) 'Givenness, contrastiveness, definiteness, subjects, topics, and point of view'. In Li C. N. (ed.) *Subject and Topic.* New York: Academic Press.

Clark, H. H. and Haviland, S. E. (1977) 'Comprehension and the given-new contract'. In Freedle R. (ed.) *Discourse Production and Comprehension.* Norwood, NJ: Ablex.

DeBono, E. (in press) 'The Cort thinking program'. In Segal J. W., Chipman S. and Glaser, R. (eds) *Thinking and Learning Skills: Current Research and Open Questions, Vol. 1.* Hillsdale, HJ: Erlbaum.

Dore, J. (1974) 'A pragmatic description of early language development'. *Journal of Psycholinguistic Research,* **3**, 343–350.

Dore, J. (1975) 'Holophrases, speech acts, and language universals'. *Journal of Child Language,* **2**, 21–40.

Dore, J. (1977) ' "Oh them sheriff": A pragmatic analysis of children's responses to questions'. In Ervin-Tripp S. and Mitchell-Kernen C. (eds.) *Child Discourse.* New York: Academic Press.

Feuerstein, R. and Jensen, M. (in press) 'Instrumental enrichment: An intervention program for low-functioning adolescents'. In Segal J. W., Chipman, S. and Glaser, R. (eds.) *Thinking and Learning Skills: Relating Instruction to Basic Research, Vol. 1.* Hillsdale, NJ: Erlbaum.

Fortes, M. (1938) 'Social and psychological aspects of education in Taleland' *Africa* **11**(4), Supplement. International Institute of African Languages and Cultures, Memorandum 7.

Grice, H. P. (1975) 'Logic and conversation'. In Cole, P. and Morgan J. (eds) *Syntax and Semantics, Vol. 3.* New York: Academic Press.

Halliday, M. A. K. (1975) *Learning How to Mean: Explorations in the Development of Language.* London: Edward Arnold.

Hays, J. R. (in press) 'Three problems in teaching general skills'. In Chipman S., Segal J. W. and Glaser R. (eds) *Thinking and Learning Skills: Current Research and Open Questions, Vol. 2.* Hillsdale, NJ: Erlbaum.

Hood, L., McDermott, R. and Cole, M. (1980) ' "Let's try to make it a good day" — Some not so simple ways'. *Discourse Processes,* **3**,155–168.

Luria, A. R. and Leont'ev, A. N. (1956) 'Introduction to L. S. Vygotsky, *Izbrannie*

Psikhologicheskie Issledovaniya [Selected Psychological Research]. Moscow: Izdatel'stvo Akademii Pedagogicheskikh Nauk.

Ninio, A. and Bruner, J. S. (1978) 'The achievement and antecedents of labelling'. *Journal of Child Language,* **5**, 1–16.

Searle, J. R. (1969) *Speech Acts: An Essay in the Philosophy of Language.* Cambridge: Cambridge University Press.

Searle J. R. (1975) 'Indirect speech acts'. In Cole P. and Morgan, J. L. (eds) *Syntax and Semantics,* Vol. **3**. New York: Academic Press.

Searle, J. R. (1979) *Expression and Meaning: Studies in the History of Speech Acts.* Cambridge: Cambridge University Press.

Tizard, B., Griffiths, B. and Atkinson, M. (1980) 'Children's questions and parents' answers'. Paper presented at the annual meeting of the Psychology Section, British Association, Salcombe, England.

Vygotsky, L. S. (1934) *Myshlenie i Rech'* [Thinking and speech]. Moscow: Sotsekriz (English translation: *Thought and Language.* Cambridge: MIT Press, 1962.)

Vygotsky, L. S. (1956) *Izbrannie Psikhologicheskie Issledovaniya* [Selected psychological research]. Moscow: Izdatel'stvo Akademii Pedagogicheskikh Nauk.

Vygotsky, L. S. (1978) *Mind in Society: The Development of Higher Psychological Processes.* Cambridge: Harvard University Press.

Wertsch, J. V. (1979) 'The regulation of human action and the given-new organization of private speech'. In Zivin G. (ed.) *The Development of Self-Regulation Through Private Speech.* New York: Wiley.

Wood, D., Bruner, J. S. and Ross, G. (1976) 'The role of tutoring in problem solving'. *Journal of Child Psychology and Psychiatry,* **17**, 89–100.

Zivin, G. (ed.) (1979) *The Development of Self-regulation Through Private Speech.* New York: Wiley.

2.2 Two Modes of Thought

J. Bruner

Source: Edited version of Bruner, J. (1968) 'Two modes of thought'. *In Actual Minds, Possible Worlds*. Cambridge, Mass.: Harvard University Press, pp. 11–29.

Let me begin by setting out my argument as baldly as possible, better to examine its basis and its consequences. It is this. There are two modes of cognitive functioning, two modes of thoughts, each providing distinctive ways of ordering experience, of constructing reality. The two (though complementary) are irreducible to one another. Efforts to reduce one mode to the other or to ignore one at the expense of the other inevitably fail to capture the rich diversity of thought.

Each of the ways of knowing, moreover, has operating principles of its own and its own criteria of well-formedness. They differ radically in their procedures for verification. A good story and a well-formed argument are different natural kinds. Both can be used as means for convincing another, yet what they convince *of* is fundamentally different: arguments convince one of their truth, stories of their lifelikeness. The one verifies by eventual appeal to procedures for establishing formal and empirical proof. The other establishes not truth but verisimilitude. It has been claimed that the one is a refinement of or an abstraction from the other. But this must be either false or true only in the most unenlightening way.

They function differently, as already noted, and the structure of a well-formed logical argument differs radically from that of a well-wrought story. Each, perhaps, is a specialization or transformation of simple exposition, by which statements of fact are converted into statements implying causality. But the types of causality implied in the two modes are palpably different. The term *then* functions differently in the logical proposition 'if x, then y' and in the narrative *recit* 'The king died, and then the queen died'. One leads to a search for universal truth conditions, the other for likely particular connections between two events — mortal grief, suicide, foul play. While it is true that the world of a story (to achieve verisimilitude) must conform to canons of logical consistency, it can use violations of such consistency as a basis of drama — as in the novels of Kafka, where non-logical arbitrariness in the social order provides the engine of drama, or in the plays of Pirandello or Beckett, where the identity operator, a = a, is cunningly violated to create multiple perspectives. And by the same token, the arts of rhetoric include the use of dramatic instantiation as a means of clinching an argument whose basis is principally logical.

But for all that, a story (allegedly true or allegedly fictional) is judged for its goodness as a story by criteria that are of a different kind from those used to judge a logical argument as adequate or correct. We all know by now that many scientific and mathematical hypotheses start their lives as little stories or metaphors, but they reach their scientific maturity by a process of conversion into verifiability, formal or empirical, and their power at maturity does not rest upon their dramatic origins. Hypothesis creation (in contrast to hypothesis testing) remains a tantalizing mystery — so much so that sober philosophers of science, like Karl Popper, characterize science as consisting principally of the falsification of hypotheses, no matter the source whence the hypothesis has come. Perhaps Richard Rorty is right in characterizing the mainstream of Anglo-American philosophy (which, on the whole, he rejects) as preoccupied with the epistemological question of how to know truth — which he contrasts with the broader question of how we come to endow experience with meaning, which is the question that preoccupies the poet and the storyteller.

Let me quickly and lightly characterize the two modes so that I may get on more precisely with the matter. One mode, the paradigmatic or logico-scientific one, attempts to fulfill the ideal of a formal, mathematical system of description and explanation. It employs categorization or conceptualization and the operations by which categories are established, instantiated, idealized and related one to the other to form a system. Its armamentarium of connectives includes on the formal side such ideas as conjunction and disjunction, hyperonymy and hyponymy, strict implication, and the devices by which general propositions are extracted from statements in their particular contexts. At a gross level, the logico-scientific mode (I shall call it 'paradigmatic' hereafter) deals in general causes, and in their establishment, and makes use of procedures to assure verifiable reference and to test for empirical truth. Its language is regulated by requirements of consistency and non-contradiction. Its domain is defined not only by observables to which its basic statements relate, but also by the set of possible worlds that can be logically generated and tested against observables — that is, it is driven by principled hypotheses.

We know a very great deal about the paradigmatic mode of thinking, and there have been developed over the millennia powerful prosthetic devices for helping us carry on with its work: logic, mathematics, sciences, and automata for operating in these fields as painlessly and swiftly as possible. We also know a fair amount about how children who are weak initially at the paradigmatic mode grow up to be fairly good at it when they can be induced to use it. The imaginative application of the paradigmatic mode leads to good theory, tight analysis, logical proof, sound argument and empirical discovery guided by reasoned hypothesis. But paradigmatic 'imagination' (or intuition) is not the same as the imagination of the novelist or poet. Rather, it is the ability to see possible formal connections before one is able to prove them in any formal way.

The imaginative application of the narrative mode leads instead to good stories, gripping drama, believable (though not necessarily 'true') historical accounts. It deals in human or human-like intention and action and the vicissitudes and consequences that mark their course. It strives to put its timeless miracles into particulars of experience, and to locate the experience in time and place. Joyce thought of the particularities of the story as epiphanies of the ordinary. The paradigmatic mode, by contrast, seeks to transcend the particular by higher and higher reaching for abstraction, and in the end disclaims in principle any explanatory value at all where the particular is concerned. There is a heartlessness to logic: one goes where one's premises and conclusions and observations take one, give or take some of the blindnesses that even logicians are prone to. Scientists, perhaps because they rely on familiar stories to fill in the gaps of their knowledge, have a harder time in practice. But their salvation is to wash the stories away when causes can be substituted for them. Paul Ricoeur argues that narrative is built upon concern for the human condition: stories reach sad or comic or absurd dénouements, while theoretical arguments are simply conclusive or inconclusive. In contrast to our vast knowledge of how science and logical reasoning proceed, we know precious little in any formal sense about how to make good stories.

Perhaps one of the reasons for this is that story must construct two landscapes simultaneously. One is the landscape of action, where the constituents are the arguments of action: agent, intention or goal, situation, instrument, something corresponding to a 'story grammar'. The other landscape is the landscape of consciousness: what those involved in the action know, think or feel, or do not know, think or feel. The two landscapes are essential and distinct: it is the difference between Oedipus sharing Jocasta's bed before and after he learns from the messenger that she is his mother.

In this sense, psychic reality dominates narrative and any reality that exists beyond the awareness of those involved in the story is put there by the author with the object of creating dramatic effect. Indeed, it is an invention of modern novelists and playwrights to create a world made up entirely of the psychic realities of the protagonists, leaving knowledge of the 'real' world in the realm of the implicit. So writers as different as Joyce and Melville share the characteristic of not 'disclosing' aboriginal realities but leaving them at the horizon of the story as matters of supposition — or, as we shall see, of *pre*supposition.

Science — particularly theoretical physics — also proceeds by constructing worlds in a comparable way, by 'inventing' the facts (or world) against which the theory must be tested. But the striking difference is that, from time to time, there are moments of testing when, for example, light can be shown to be bent or neutrinos must be shown to leave marks in a cloud chamber. It may indeed be the case, as Quine has urged, that physics is 99 per cent speculation and 1 per cent observation. But the world making involved in its speculations is of a different order from what story making does. Physics must eventuate in predicting something that is testably right, however much it may speculate. Stories have no such need for testability. Believability in a story is of a different order than the believability of even the speculative parts of physical theory. If we apply Popper's criterion of falsifiability to a story as a test of its goodness, we are guilty of misplaced verification.

Having said that much about how the two modes can be distinguished one from the other, let me now focus almost entirely on the less understood of the pair: on narrative. [. . .] I shall want to concentrate on narrative, so to speak, at its far reach: as an art form. William James comments in his Gifford Lectures, *The Varieties of Religious Experience*, that to study religion one should study the most religious man at his most religious moment. I shall try to follow his advice with respect to narrative but, perhaps, with a Platonic twist. The great works of fiction that transform narrative into an art form come closest to revealing 'purely' the deep structure of the narrative mode in expression. The same claim can be made for science and mathematics: they reveal most plainly (and purely) the deep structure of paradigmatic thought. And perhaps James intended his dictum in the same sense, in spite of his anti-Platonism.

There is another reason, aside from the Platonic, for pursuing this course. If one takes the view [. . .] that human mental activity depends for its full expression upon being linked to a cultural tool kit — a set of prosthetic devices, so to speak — then we are well advised when studying mental activity to take into account the tools employed in that activity. As primatologists tell us, this amplification by cultural tools is the hallmark of human skills, and we overlook it in our research with peril. And so, if one wishes to study the psychology of mathematics (as, say G. Polya did), one studies the works of trained and gifted mathematicians, with particular emphasis on the heuristics and the formalisms they use to give form to their mathematical intuitions.

By the same token, one does well to study the work of trained and gifted writers if one is to understand what it is that makes good stories powerful or compelling. Anybody (at almost any age) can tell a story — and it is altogether good that story grammarians, so called, are studying the minimal structure needed to create a story. And anybody (again, at almost any age) can 'do' some mathematics. But great fiction, like great mathematics, requires the transformation of intuitions into expressions in a symbolic system — natural language or some artificialized form of it. The forms of expression that emerge, the discourse that carries the story, or the calculus that depicts a mathematical relation — these are crucial for understanding the differences between an inchoate account of a bad marriage and *Madame Bovary*, between a clumsily argued justification and an elegant and powerful derivation of a logical proof. I think I have said all that needs saying on this point, a point addressed more to psychologists than to literary theorists. The former, perhaps, will quarrel with the point out of deference to the reductionism of science. The latter will almost certainly find the point almost bizarrely obvious.

Narrative deals with the vicissitudes of human intentions. And since there are myriad intentions and endless ways for them to run into trouble — or so it would seem — there should be endless kinds of stories. But, surprisingly, this seems not to be the case. One view has it that lifelike narratives start with a canonical or 'legitimate' steady state, which is breached, resulting in a crisis, which is terminated by a redress, with recurrence of the cycle an open possibility. Literary theorists as various as Victor Turner (an anthropologist), Tzvetan Todorov, Hayden White (an historian) and Vladimir Propp (a folklorist) suggest that there is some such constraining deep structure to narrative, and that good stories are well-formed particular realizations of it. Not all literary scholars take this view — Barbara Herrnstein-Smith being a notable dissenting voice.

If it were the case that there are limits on the kinds of stories, it could mean either that the limits are inherent in the minds of writers and/or readers (what one is able to tell or to understand), or that the limits are a matter of convention. If it were the former, if the limits on story were innate, then it would be difficult to explain the eruptions of innovation that illuminate the course of literary history. And if it were the latter, the heavy hand of convention, that limited the nature of story, then it would be just as difficult to explain why there is so much recognizable similarity in tales from all lands, and so much historical continuity within any particular language whose literatures have gone through changes as dramatic as, say, the French or English or Russian.

The arguments pro and con are, somehow, more interesting than conclusive. Their conclusiveness is flawed not only by literary innovation but, I suspect, by the impossibility of deciding whether, say, Joyce's *Ulysses* or Beckett's *Molloy* trilogy fits a particular formula or not. Aside from all that, what level of interpretation of a story shall we take to represent its 'deep structure' — litera, moralis, allegoria or anagogia? And whose interpretation: Jung's, Foucault's, Northrop Frye's? And when, as with anti-novels, a writer (like Calvino, say) exploits his reader's story expectations by flouting them artfully, does that count as violating or conforming to the canonical form?

And as if this were not enough, there is the question of the discourse into which the story is woven and the two aspects of story (to which we have already alluded): the *fabula* and the *sjuzet*, the timeless and the sequences. Which is constrained, and in what ways? That there may be a structure to time-worn folktales or to myths, a matter to which I shall revert later, nobody will deny. But do these narratives provide a universal structure for all fictions? For Alain Robbe-Grillet or, to take an instance where it is even difficult to decide whether the book is a novel or an exercise in criticism, for Julian Barnes' *Flaubert's Parrot*?

I think we would do well with as loose fitting a constraint as we can manage concerning what a story must 'be' to be a story. And the one that strikes me as most serviceable is the one with which we began: narrative deals with the vicissitudes of intention.

I propose this not only because it leaves the theorist with a certain flexibility but because it has a 'primitiveness' that is appealing. By primitive I mean simply that one can make a strong argument for the irreducible nature of the concept of intention (much as Kant did for the concept of causation.) That is to say, intention is immediately and intuitively recognizable: it seems to require for its recognition no complex or sophisticated interpretive act on the part of the beholder. The evidence for such a claim is compelling.

There is a celebrated monograph, little known outside academic psychology, written a generation ago by the Belgian student of perception, Baron Michotte. By cinematic means, he demonstrated that when objects move with respect to one another within highly limited constraints, we *see* causality. An object moves towards another, makes contact with it, and the second object is seen to move in a compatible direction: we see one object 'launching' another. Time–space relations can variously be arranged so that one object can be seen 'dragging' another, or 'deflecting' it, and so on. These are 'primitive' perceptions, and they are quite irresistible: we *see* cause.

To answer Humes's objection that such causal experiences derive from association, Alan Leslie repeated the Michotte demonstrations with six-month-old babies. His procedure measured signs of surprise in the infant, which expressed itself in a variety of registerable ways from facial expression to changes in heart rate and blood pressure. Leslie showed the infants a sequence of cinematic presentations that in their space–time arrangement were seen by adults as caused. He would then intersperse one non-causal presentation that was outside the prescribed Michotte space–time limits — and the baby would show startled surprise. The same effect could be achieved by following a non-causal sequence of presentations with a causal one. In each case, Leslie argued, there was some qualitative change in the experience of the infant that led to 'dishabituation' and surprise. Note that a change in space–time arrangement of the displays that was as large as the one used to shift category produced no effect if it was within the category of causality. Michotte's work and Leslie's follow-up provide powerful argument for the irreducibility of causality as a 'mental category' in the Kantian sense.

Can intentionality as a concept be shown to be as primitive? Fritz Heider and Marianne Simmel have also used a 'bare' animated film to demonstrate the irresistibility of 'perceived intention' in the form of a scenario involving a small moving triangle, a small moving circle, a large moving square and a box-like empty rectangle — whose movements are irresistibly seen as two lovers being pursued by a large bully who, upon being thwarted, breaks up the house in which he has tried to find them. Judith Ann Stewart, more recently, has shown that it is possible to arrange the space–time relationship of simple figures to produce apparent intention or 'animacy'. We plainly *see* 'search', 'goal seeking', 'persistence in overcoming obstacles' — see them as intention-driven. Interestingly, from the point of view of Propp's pioneering work on the structure of folktales (to which we shall come presently), the perception of animacy is induced by varying direction and speed of motion of an object with respect to an obstacle.

Unfortunately, we do not yet have the analogue experiment on apparent intention for Leslie's baby experiments on apparent causality. It will come soon enough. If it should yield positive results, then we would have to conclude that 'intention and its vicissitudes' constitute a primitive category system in terms of which experience is organized, at least as primitive as the category system of causality. I say 'at least' for the fact remains that the evidence of children's animism suggests that their more primitive category is intention — physically caused events being seen as psychically intended, as in the early experiments that earned Piaget his first worldwide acclaim.

But such experiments, while they tell us about the primitiveness of the idea of intention, tell us nothing about the discourse that converts an unworded narrative into powerful and haunting stories. What is it in the telling or writing of a tale that produces Jakobson's *literaturnost*? In the *telling* there must be 'triggers' that release responses in the reader's mind, that transform a banal fabula into a masterpiece of literary narrative. Obviously, the language of the discourse is critical, but even before that there is plot, plot and its structure. Whatever the medium — whether words, cinema, abstract animation, theatre — one can always distinguish between the fabula or basic story stuff, the events to be related in the narrative, and the 'plot' or sjuzet, the story as told by linking the events together. The plot is how and in what order the reader becomes aware of what happened. And the 'same' story can be told in different sequence. This means, of course, that there must be transformations of some kind that permit a common base structure of story to be handled in different meaning-preserving sequences.

What can we say about the deep structure of stories — the story stuff, or fabula, that lends itself to different orders of presentation? Could it be the kind of structure that I examined a moment ago and earlier attributed to Victor Turner, Hayden White, Vladimir Propp and Tzvetan Todorov? That is to say, one 'primitive' fabula involves the breach of a legitimate state of affairs, the break then creating a crisis that is nipped in the bud or that persists intil there is redress? If there were a corresponding structure in the minds of the readers, cinema viewers and playgoers, then such a fabula could be plotted in linear order, in flashbacks, or even *in medias res*, starting virtually anywhere (as Robbe-Grillet succeeds in doing for film and novel, and as, say, Michel Leiris does in his 'experimental' antinarrative autobiography)? We do not have to take a stand on how many such fabula there are (as many, for example, as Jung's archetypes?), only that they have some sort of being in the beholder's mind that permits him to recognize them in whatever expression encountered.

But there is something more to it than that. Kenneth Burke argues that 'story stuff' involves *characters* in *action* with intentions or *goals* in *settings* using particular *means*. Drama is generated, he claims, when there is an imbalance in the 'ratio' of these constituents. That is to say, a character (say Nora in *A Doll's House*) is in an inappropriate setting, or an action does not warrant the goal to which it is leading a character.

Yet, neither breach, crisis and redress, nor imbalances in a Burkeian pentad, are sufficient descriptions of 'story stuff'. For there are elements of story that rest not upon action and interaction but upon character as such. Conrad's novels provide a good example. Jim's inscrutability (even to the narrator who 'tells' his story) is central to the drama of *Lord Jim*. In *The Secret Sharer*, the young captain's fascinated obsession with Leggart drives the story. Some readers actually propose that Leggart is an imaginary *Doppelganger* who exists only in the captain's mind. Perhaps, as with Aristotle's recipe for tragedy in the *Poetics*, drama is a working out of character in action in a plot constrained by a setting.

Yet this too cannot be a full account if we heed Propp's argument that, in the folktale, character is a *function* of a highly constrained plot, the chief role of a character being to play out a plot role as hero, false hero, helper, villain, and so on. For while it may be the case that in the time-smoothed folktale story stuff determines character (and therefore character cannot be central), it is equally true that in a 'modern' novel plot is derived from the working out of character in a particular setting (one of the earliest theorists of modernism, therefore, being Aristotle on tragedy!).

Greimas's view is that a primitive or irreducible feature of story (whatever else it may include) is that it occurs jointly on the plane of action and in the subjectivity of the protagonists. And perhaps this is why deceit, guile and misunderstanding are to be found so often in myths and folktales from 'Little Red Riding Hood' to 'Perseus and the Gorgon' and, at the same time, lie at the heart of so many modern novels and plays.

Psychologically, the 'dual landscape' view is appealing in suggesting how the reader is helped to enter the life and mind of the protagonists: their consciousness are the magnets for empathy. The matching of 'inner' vision and 'outer' reality is, moveover, a classic human plight. It grips the child hearing how the Big Bad Wolf tries to deceive and then is unmasked by Red Riding Hood, or the adult reading Joyce's 'Araby', suffering the humiliation of the young boy when his dreams of a gift for the neighbour girl fade in the tawdry atmosphere of the fairground closing.

In any case, the fabula of story — its timeless underlying theme — seems to be a unity that incorporates at least three constituents. It contains a *plight* into which *characters* have fallen as a result of intentions that have gone awry either because of circumstances, of the 'character of characters' or most likely of the interaction between the two. And it requires an uneven distribution of underlying consciousness among the characters with respect to the plight. What gives the story its unity is the manner in which plight, characters and consciousness interact to yield a structure that has a start, a development and a 'sense of an ending'. Whether it is sufficient to characterize this unified structure as *steady state, breach, crisis, redress* is difficult to know. It is certainly not *necessary* to do so, for what one seeks in story structure is precisely how plight, character and consciousness are integrated. Better to leave the issue open and to approach the matter with an open mind.

Language, to whatever use it may be put, has the design feature of being organized on different levels, each level providing constituents for the level above which dominates it. As Jakobson noted in his classic analysis of the sound system of speech, the distinctive features of speech sound are determined by the phonemes that they constitute at the next level up; phonemes are combined according to rules at the next level up, the morpheme, and so on.

So too at the levels above sound, for morphemes, lexemes, sentences, speech acts and discourse. Each level has its form of order, but that order is controlled and modified by the level above it. Since each level is dominated by the level above it, efforts to understand any level on its own have inevitably led to failure. The structure of language is such that it permits us to go from speech sounds through the intermediate levels to the intentions of speech acts and discourse. The path by which we travel that route varies with our objective, and storytelling is a special objective.

In putting any particular expression together, one *selects* words and one *combines* them. *How* one selects and combines will depend on the uses to which one wishes to put an utterance. Jakobson calls these two primitive language-forming acts, selecting and combining, the *vertical* and the *horizontal* axes of language. The vertical axis of selection is dominated by the requirement of preserving or modifying meaning by substituting appropriate words or expressions for one another: *boy, immature male, lad,* and so on. But the rule of substitution goes beyond synonymy to metaphor. What of *colt, lamb, fawn*? Do they fit *boy*? We say it depends on context and objective. And what of larger-order substitutions? Which does better for New York: 'the biggest city in North America' or 'the harbour at the mouth of the Hudson'? Again, it depends. And what of substituting for *depression: 'black mood'* or 'ragged claws scuttling across the floors of silent seas'? There is forever a matter of choice about the vertical axis: whether to preserve reference as literally as possible, whether to create an atmospheric change by metaphor, whether (as Jakobson and the Prague School urged upon poets) to 'make it strange' so as to overcome automatic reading.

It is probably the case that scientific or logical writing — or, rather, writing governed by requirements of a scientific argument — tends to choose words with the object of assuring clear and definite reference and literal sense. It is required by the felicity conditions of speech acts of this kind. Litera dominates over moralis and the others. In the telling of a story, one has the selection restriction of representing a referent in the eye of a protagonist-beholder, with a perspective that fits the subjective landscape on which the story is being unfolded, and yet with due regard for the action that is going on. So from the start, the selection of expressions must meet the special requirement of that special form of speech act that is a story — of which more presently, when I consider a crucial idea proposed by Wolfgang Iser.

The second axis, the horizontal axis of combination, is inherent in the generative power of syntax to combine words and phrases. Its most elementary expression is predication or, even more primitively, the juxtaposition of a comment on a topic, when the topic is 'given' or taken for granted and the comment is something new added to it. I see a new species of bird and say to my partner: 'Some bird. Fantastic'. The first element is the topic; the second the comment. Predication is a more evolved form of making comments on topics that permits us to assign a 'truth function' to the expression, as in such ordinary sentences as:

The boy has a ball.
The boy has a secret.
The boy has a burning ambition.
The boy has a bee in his bonnet.

The boy is the given; the predicate is new. The sentence can now be translated into a formal or logical proposition and tested for its truth value in the context in which the utterance was made.

To the degree that a subject and predicate are 'transparent' they can easily be converted into verifiable propositional form: indeed, one common theory of meaning, the verificationist theory, equates meaning with the set of verifiable propositions a predicational statement generates. But there are statements or utterances that combine given and new in a manner that is 'strange' or that, in Henry James' sense, contains gaps, or where there is difficult distance between the two. A good case in point is Eliot's lines:

I should have been a pair of ragged claws
Scuttling across the floors of silent seas.

To render these lines literally as 'I am depressed with aging' (taking into account the context of the whole of 'Prufrock', from which they are extracted) fails to capture the horizontal given-new combination of the poem. Yet, on one interpretation, that may be what they mean — noting that in the vertical axis we have translated 'ragged claws . . .' into 'depression over aging'. To be sure, as Jakobson also insisted, meaning always involves translation. But there is some sense in which neither the literal translation of the new term nor the resulting combination of it with the given term succeeds as a poetic translation. And if we take predicate-like utterances in which both the subject and the predicate are non-literal, the failure is even more evident, as in these lines from MacNeice:

The sunlight on the garden
Hardens and grows cold.
We cannot cage the minute
Within its nets of gold;
When all is told
We cannot beg for pardon.

It is not only 'unclear' how to manage the vertical axis — to what does 'sunlight on the garden' refer, and 'harden' in this context? 'Cage'? And then, 'cage the minute', etcetera.

The language of poetry, or perhaps I should say the language of evocation, substitutes metaphors for both given and new, leaving it somewhat ambiguous what they are substitutes for. When the terms are combined, the resulting given–new combination is no longer amenable to being converted into ordinary truth functional propositions. Indeed, at crucial moments it even departs from the 'contract' that specifies a clear distinction between given and new in predicative combinations.

So neither vertically nor horizontally does the evocative language of poetry and story conform to the requirements of plain reference or of verifiable predication. Stories of literary merit, to be sure, are about events in a 'real' world, but they render that world newly strange, rescue it from obviousness, fill it with gaps that call upon the reader, in Barthes' sense, to become a writer, a composer of a virtual text in response to the actual. In the end, it is the reader who must write for himself what *he* intends to do with the actual text. How, for example, to read these lines from Yeats:

> The brawling of a sparrow in the eaves,
> The brilliant moon and all the milky sky,
> And all that famous harmony of leaves,
> Had blotted out man's image and his cry.

Which brings us directly to Wolfgang Iser's reflections in *The Act of Reading* on what manner of speech act is narrative. I want to touch on only one part of his argument, one that is central to my own. With respect to narrative, he says, 'the reader receives it by composing it'. The text itself has structures that are 'two-sided': a *verbal* aspect that guides reaction and prevents it from being arbitrary, and an affective aspect that is triggered or 'prestructured by the language of the text'. But the prestructure is underdetermined: fictional texts are 'inherently indeterminate'.

> Fictional texts constitute their own objects and do not copy something already in existence. For this reason they cannot have the full determinacy of real objects, and indeed, it is the element of indeterminacy that evokes the text to 'communicate' with the reader, in the sense that they induce him to participate both in the production and the comprehension of this work's intention.

It is this 'relative indeterminacy of a text' that 'allows a spectrum of actualizations'. And so, 'literary texts initiate "performances" of meaning rather than actually formulating meaning themselves'.

And that is what is at the core of literary narrative as a speech act: an utterance or a text whose intention is to initiate and guide a search for meanings among a spectrum of possible meanings. Storytelling, besides, is a speech act whose felicity conditions are unique. The speech act is initiated by giving some indication to a listener or reader, first, that a story is to be recounted; second, that it is true or fictional; and third (optionally), that it fits some genre — a sad story, a moral fable, a comeuppance tale, a particular scandal, a happening in one's life. Beyond that, there is a condition of style: that the form of the discourse in which the story is actualized leaves open the 'performance of meaning' in Iser's sense. It is this last condition that brings us directly to the discourse of stories, to which I turn now.

Discourse, if Iser is right about narrative speech acts, must depend upon forms of discourse that recruit the reader's imagination — that enlist him in the 'performance of meaning under the guidance of the text'. Discourse must make it possible for the reader to 'write' his own virtual text. And there are three features of discourse that seem to me to be crucial in this enlistment process.

The first is the triggering of *presupposition*, the creation of implicit rather than explicit meanings. For with explicitness, the reader's degrees of interpretive freedom are annulled. Examples abound, but Primo Levi's recent *The Periodic Table* provides a particularly striking case. His subtle setting forth of the properties of a particular element in each 'story' — argon, hydrogen, zinc, and so on — provides a presuppositional background in terms of which the stories may be 'interpreted'. How the presuppositional background triggers interpretation is a matter I shall come to shortly.

The second is what I shall call *subjectification:* the depiction of reality not through an omniscient eye that views a timeless reality, but through the filter of the consciousness of protagonists in the story. Joyce, in the stories of *Dubliners,* rarely even hints at how the world really *is.* We see only the realities of the characters themselves — leaving us like the prisoners in Plato's cave, viewing only the shadows of events we can never know directly.

The third is *multiple perspective:* beholding the world not univocally but simultaneously through a set of prisms each of which catches some part of it. Auden's poem on the death of Yeats is a brilliant example: the poet's death is seen in the instruments of winter airports, on the floor of the Bourse, in the sickroom, in the 'guts of the living'. Roland Barthes argues in *S/Z* that without multiple codes of meaning a story is merely 'readerly,' not 'writerly'.

There are doubtless other means by which discourse keeps meaning open or 'performable' by the reader — metaphor among them. But the three mentioned suffice for illustration. Together they succeed in *subjunctivizing reality,* which is my way of rendering what Iser means by a narrative speech act. I take my meaning of 'subjunctive' from the second one offered by the *OED*: 'Designating a mood (L. *modus subjunctivus*) the forms of which are employed to denote an action or state as conceived (and not as a fact) and therefore used to express a wish, command, exhortation, or a contingent, hypothetical, or prospective event'. To be in the subjunctive mode is, then, to be trafficking in human possibilities rather than in settled certainties. An 'achieved' or 'uptaken' narrative speech act, then, produces a subjunctive world. When I use the term *subjunctivize,* I shall mean it in this sense. What then can we say in any technical way about the means whereby discourse portrays a 'subjunctive reality'? For surely that is the key to the issue of discourse in great fiction. Let me turn to some of the more systematic ways in which this is accomplished.

Begin with the familiar case of speech acts and Paul Grice's extension of the idea to what he calls the 'Cooperative Principle' governing ordinary conversation. He proposes maxims of quantity (saying only as much as is necessary), of quality (saying only the truth, and saying it with perspicuousness), and of relevance (saying only what is to the point). However needed such maxims may be for regulating conversational cooperation, in fact they are guides to banality: to be brief, perspicuous, truthful and relevant is to be drab and literal. But the existence of such maxims (however implicit our awareness of them), Grice argues, provides us with the means of violating them for purposes of *meaning more than we say* or for meaning something other than what we say (as in irony, for example) or for meaning less than we say. To mean in this way, by the use of such intended violations or 'conversational implicatures', is to create gaps and to recruit presuppositions to fill them . As in:

> Where's Jack?
> Well, I saw a yellow VW outside Susan's

The reader-hearer, if he is to stay on the narrative scene, must fill in, and under the circumstances he is made complicitous with the characters in the exchange. Why doesn't the respondent say outright (perspicuously) that Jack is visiting Susan? Is it an illicit visit? Is Jack 'going the rounds'? Cookbooks on story writing urge the use of implicatures to increase 'narrative tension', and they can easily lose their effect when overused. Yet they provide the means for the kind of indirect talk that forces 'meaning performance' upon the reader.

Presupposition is an ancient and complex topic in logic and linguistics, and one that deserves closer study by the student of narrative. A presupposition, formally defined, is an implied proposition whose force remains invariant whether the explicit proposition in which it is embedded is true or false. Their nature and operations have been set forth brilliantly by Stephen Levinson, by L. Karttunen and Richard Peters, and by Gerald Gazdar, and their discussions of presuppositional triggers, filters, plugs and holes are richly suggestive for literary text analysis. They deal with what are called 'heritage expressions' and with how a presupposition is built up over discourse in order to project itself into later statements. Triggers effect such projection. Four simple examples will serve to illustrate their manner of operating.

Trigger	Presupposition
Definite descriptions:	
John saw/didn't see the chimera.	There exists a chimera.
Factive verbs:	
John realized/didn't realise he was broke.	John was broke.
Implicative verbs:	
John managed/didn't manage to open the door.	John tried to open the door.
Iteratives:	
You can't get buggy whips anymore.	You used to be able to get buggy whips.

There are many other triggers. I think it is plain (though the details are not easy) that triggering presuppositions, like intentionally violating conversational maxims, provides a powerful way of 'meaning more than you are saying', or going beyond surface text, or packing the text with meaning for narrative purposes.

The use of presupposition is greatly facilitated by an informal 'contract' that governs language exchanges. As Dan Sperber and Deirdre Wilson have noted, we characteristically assume that what somebody says *must* make sense, and we will, when in doubt about *what* sense it makes, search for or invent an interpretation of the utterance to give it sense. Example on a London street (after Sperber and Wilson):

> Will you buy a raffle ticket for the Royal Naval Lifeboat Institution?
> No thanks, I spend summers near Manchester.
> Ah yes, of course.

Obviously, you cannot press a reader (or listener) to make endless interpretations of your obscure remarks. But you can go a surprisingly long way — provided only that you start with something approximating what Joseph Campbell called a 'mythologically instructed community'. And, in fact, most of the devices and tropes that we use in the telling and writing of stories are not substantively as demanding as the one in Sperber and Wilson's example.

To revert to the beginning discussion of paradigmatic and narrative modes of thought, both of them surely trade on presupposition, if only for the sake of brevity. If the scientist or analytic philosopher or logician should be found to be triggering presuppositions in a covert way, he will become the butt of jokes about making a hard sell rather than letting things speak for themselves. His presuppositions should be unpackable, easily so. The writer of fiction who does *not* use such triggering will simply fail. His story will be 'flat'. [. . .]

2.3 What Does It Mean To Be Bilingual?

B. Mayor

Introduction

Throughout the world people grow up, receive an education and live their daily lives through the medium of more than one distinct language or language variety. Even those who are exposed to a single language in the home may acquire a second on entering school. In other cases a second language is formally learned at later stages of schooling. Still others acquire or learn an additional language in later life because of occupational needs or personal interest. The resulting bilingualism of all these individuals will differ in crucial respects but they will all be developing two important skills:

1 They will be learning to recognize their various languages as separate systems and to keep them apart when necessary.
2 They will be learning how to choose the appropriate language for the circumstances (who is there, what they're talking about, etc.).

Such skills are not unique to bilinguals. So-called 'monolinguals' (who may in fact command several varieties of their single language) are also learning to make such distinctions and choices among the language varieties available to them. In the case of bilingualism, however, we are talking about language varieties which may be mutually incomprehensible to monolingual speakers of each, and where a *gradual* transition from one variety to the other is less likely. We need to remember, moreover, that bilinguals normally have access to more than one register and possibly more than one dialect within each of their languages, so that their overall repertoire is even greater than the term '*bi*lingual' might suggest.

How many languages

It is not always easy to determine how many languages a person knows, let alone which he or she knows 'best'. One reason is that the term 'language' itself has social rather than scientific reality. (When does a 'dialect' count as a separate language, and why?) Second, what is meant by 'knowing' a language is a matter of personal judgement. For example, a *passive* command of a language (understanding most of what is said, without necessarily feeling confident enough to speak the language) tends to get overlooked altogether. And yet, if we accept the definition of bilinguals used by the Linguistic Minorities Project (1983), namely 'regular *users* of two languages' (p. 13), we cannot ignore this level of skill altogether.

Even having established that speaker X uses languages Y and Z, we lack an accurate terminology to describe the role played by these two languages in the speaker's life. Most of the terms that are in common use prove difficult to apply with any precision because they tend to emphasize certain features to the exclusion of others. The term '*mother tongue*', for example, can be quite misleading, since it may literally not be the same thing as 'father tongue' or 'grandmother tongue' and so on. Similar reservations apply to the terms '*home language*'. In a multilingual household, a child may have a range of productive and receptive competencies in a variety of languages and/or dialects of languages even before starting school. '*Native language*' is even more problematic, because it seems to imply a value judgement about a speaker's credentials. What level of linguistic competence does one need to reach to qualify as a native speaker? Can one be a native speaker of more than one language? '*First language*' seems to be a less ambiguous term but, like home language, it needs to be used with caution when referring to children from multilingual families, many of whom will be brought up to be bi- or trilingual in some degree. What is more useful to know is who speaks what language to whom and under what circumstances: for example, playing with siblings (sex and chronological position in the family will be crucial factors here) versus formal family gatherings versus religious ceremonies and so on. Such information is, however, hard to come by. Survey data can be unreliable, in that speakers are often unaware of what they do in practice.

'*Community language*' and '*heritage language*' are rather different terms, referring to languages which serve a function in the local (or even national) minority community, without necessarily being spoken as a language of the home. Thus, depending on their religious affiliation, British speakers of a language best described as a dialect of Punjabi may regard either standard Urdu (the national language of Pakistan) or standard Punjabi (an official language of the Indian Punjab) as their community language, since both have wide currency nationally and internationally. 'Heritage language' is used similarly, but with an even broader scope, to encompass languages which are no longer actively used in the home, for example Italian for many Italian-Americans. We are dealing here with issues of ethnic identity, which are essentially concerned with the speaker's attitudes and therefore particularly hard to measure in any objective way.

Balance between languages

Perhaps the most important point to emphasize is that the balance between a bilingual person's two (or more) languages is constantly shifting throughout life — a phenomenon very vividly described by the bilingual subjects interviewed for Miller's book *Many Voices* (1983), and by the contributors to Grosjean's (1982) *Life with Two Languages*. Any description of a bilingual person's language use is therefore in the nature of a snapshot in time. The so-called 'first language' may not remain the dominant language throughout life and may not be the preferred language in a wide range of contexts. Truly 'balanced' bilingualism is probably the exception rather than the norm. However, this is not to say that a first language must inevitably wither away as a second is acquired (a situation sometimes called 'subtractive' bilingualism): given the right combination of circumstances, a second language can be acquired while the first continues to develop ('additive' bilingualism).

Switching between languages

In multilingual societies there is often quite an elaborate pattern of appropriateness, which either indicates or strongly influences the choice of a particular language in a particular context. Thus languages, or particular registers of them, may become polarized to cover different ranges of experience: one, for example, will become the language of literacy and formal education, another the language of family intimacy or fun. A bilingual speaker once likened this to putting on a different set of clothes according to the situation. (This does not, of course, rule out the possibility, as for the monolingual speaker, of choosing *against* the norm for special effect.)

As a result of this, the languages of a bilingual speaker often come to symbolize different areas of human experience, different cultural values, even different stages in the child's development. This can lead, especially in adolescence, to a situation where the language of the home becomes associated solely with the culture of the home and local community and not with the possibility of success or acceptance in the wider society. This is not an inevitable state of affairs in a bilingual community, but rather the result of a particular kind of society in which one language group dominates all the formal institutions. Schools have a critical role to play here.

In the company of other bilinguals, the bilingual speaker also has the option of incorporating features of one language within the other (*code mixing*) or even of changing language completely within a single utterance (*code switching*). Bilingual code switching and mixing should in no way be seen as defective versions of monolingual language use. On the basis of extensive observation and analysis, Gumperz (1982) has concluded that 'only in relatively few [cases] is code alteration motivated by speakers' inability to find words to express what they want to say in one or the other code' (pp. 64–65) but rather that 'motivation for code switching appears to be stylistic and metaphorical . . . code switching signals contextual information equivalent to what in monolingual settings is conveyed through prosody or other syntactic or lexical processes' (pp. 72, 98). Gumperz found that most code switches fell into the following broad categories:

(1) Direct quotation from another speaker
(2) Addressing a point to a particular person
(3) Interjection of a point
(4) Repetition or rephrasing of a point
(5) A sign of the speaker's involvement

This is by no means an exhaustive list of the possibilities. Nor does it imply that bilingual speakers are always conscious of the fact, or the significance, of their language switches, any more than monolingual speakers are aware of, say, shifts in pronunciation or rate of delivery. Nevertheless such features have communicative value. In other words there is normally a message implicit in the *choice* of language — although listeners may not always agree precisely as to its interpretation. (This, as always, depends on how far they share cultural assumptions.)

However, there is one important qualification to this argument. In some communities code switching has become so much a part of the linguistic norm that it can probably be regarded as a code in its own right. Poplack, in her extensive study (1980) of an established Puerto Rican community in New York City, maintains that this type of code switching is more 'intimate', i.e. more likely to take place *within* a sentence. It is also less likely to form part of a conscious or unconscious discourse strategy, as claimed by Gumperz. Poplack argues that 'there is no need to require any social motivation for this type of code switching, given that, as a discourse mode, it may itself form part of the repertoire of a speech community. It is then the choice (or not) of this mode which is of significance to participants rather than the choice of switch points' (p. 164).

Language development in the bilingual child

There have been several studies of the *simultaneous acquisition* of two languages by young children (see Saunders, 1983, for an overview). A more familiar situation, however, and that of most bilingual children in Britain, is *consecutive acquisition*, whereby one language is established to a greater or lesser degree before a second is acquired.

There are several crucial distinctions between the process of acquiring a first language as a baby and that of acquiring a second language in later life, however young. The various aspects of language develop at a differential rate throughout life — in very broad terms there is a rapid development of the sound system at an early age, overlapping with and followed by a rather slower development of grammatical sensitivity, and a development of meaning and the strategies of discourse that continues throughout life. As a result, each of these aspects will be more or less established in the first language at the time when the child encounters the second. To illustrate the point, consider the case of the monolingual baby, who is learning how to talk, in the sense of physically articulating sounds, at the same time as learning to distinguish the sounds of one particular language; learning to make sense of language *per se* at the same time as learning the rules of one particular system. In the case of the child acquiring a second language, these two processes — the general and the specific — are separated.

Where the learning of *meaning* is concerned, the situation is a little more complicated because the process of learning to mean is ongoing throughout life. A baby is forming concepts at the same time as acquiring linguistic means of expressing those concepts. Adult second-language learners, on the other hand, have an existing set of quite sophisticated meanings against which to measure the new linguistic data, and initially their ability to express themselves in the second language is likely to be inadequate for their communicative needs. Young bilingual children fall somewhere between these two extremes in that they may, depending on their age and circumstances, be acquiring some concepts via one language, some via another, and some simultaneously via *both* in those areas of their life where the two languages interact. (There is a good discussion of this process in Grosjean, 1982; see also Saunders, 1983.) This is not to say that it is ever simply a case of grafting new labels onto old concepts, as anyone who has any experience of learning a second language will know. There are some words and phrases which simply do not have their translation equivalents in other languages. (The whole question of whether concepts are language dependent or whether they exist independently in the brain with language labels attached has been debated; see, for example, Carroll, 1956; Albert and Obler, 1978).

Finally, the baby is likely to be surrounded by linguistic input almost every waking hour, whereas input for the second-language learner may be more limited. Indeed, many bilingual children will need to get most of their practice in speaking English during school hours.

On the other hand, there are several ways in which acquiring the second language will be similar to acquiring the first. Inevitably input will need to precede output, in other words the developing bilingual child will need a language model, or models, and plenty of chance to listen before one could reasonably expect any speech in the second language. Even then, the child will need to experiment a good deal in the process of working out the rules of the language. And it is unlikely that the child will speak at all unless he or she has real need to communicate something.

Making sense of it all

What, then, is going on when a developing bilingual is confronted by a mass of input in a second language? Edwards (1983) has argued that 'Children are essentially pattern learners whether in the acquisition of their mother tongue or a second language. But they operate their own rule systems aiming only gradually at the adult model of the target language' (p. 83). The young monolingual's use of 'mans' for 'men' or 'goed' for 'went' is clearly a valuable stage in working out a rule. The difference between the first- and the second-language learner is that the latter already has a linguistic system against which to judge the new input and will be developing a sensitivity to what the two languages have in common and where they differ. On the basis of past linguistic experience, the child may begin by expecting certain linguistic cues which are absent in the second language. But this is all part of an active strategy. As Corder (1978) says 'It is one of the strategies of learning to find out just how far down the scale it is going to be necessary to go before starting to build up again' (p. 90). Naturally, a speaker of a language such as Cantonese is going to have to go a great deal further 'down the scale' to find common linguistic rules with English — whether of pronunciation, grammar or vocabulary — than is a speaker of a more closely related language such as, say, Spanish.

As the developing bilingual speaker attempts to make sense of the new language input, a phenomenon known as 'interlanguage' often occurs, reflecting the learner's attempt to integrate the old with the new. It would be unfortunate to see this in purely negative terms. Trial and error, by definition, involve experimenting and making mistakes. As the child has access to more and more input, the provisional hypotheses will gradually be refined until the language approximates more closely to the idiomatic usage of a native speaker. However, the notion of 'interference' or 'transference' is not always helpful, since many 'errors' made by second-language learners resemble the developmental stages of first-language learning, such as simplification of syntax, overgeneralization of rules, and so on. For example, an analysis of the acquisition of English by two small groups of Norwegian and Spanish speakers (see Cancino et al., 1974; Ravem, 1974) revealed expressions like the following, which were neither based on the speakers' first language nor yet authentic English:

Expression in first language	*Expression used*	*English 'target' expression*
Where go Daddy?	Where Daddy is going?	Where is Daddy going?
I no can understand.	I don't understand.	I can't understand.

The important thing is that a child should be given space to experiment and take risks with the language, on the principle that fluency is more likely to lead to accuracy than vice versa.

Biliteracy

Many of the issues affecting the acquisition of two (or more) languages apply equally to the learning of two (or more) writing systems. As with spoken language, we need to distinguish between the acquisition of literacy *per se* and learning to read a particular language. Lado (1975) describes the distinction in the following terms: 'Learning to write his first language he has to master the great abstraction involved in representing the sounds of a language by marks on paper. Learning to write a second language, he already knows that marks on paper can represent sounds' (p. 106; also quoted in Downing, 1973, p. 72). Again, as with spoken language, there is some evidence (e.g. Kaufmann, 1968; Modiano, 1968) of positive transfer of skills, especially where the scripts are the same, and only a little evidence of interference, mainly at the spelling level (see Grosjean, 1982, pp. 306–307).

Some children have the opportunity of acquiring their biliteracy, like their bilingualism, naturally through exposure to written language in the home. In most cases, however, biliteracy is the result of formal teaching. The question facing educators is which language and/or script is most appropriate for the acquisition of initial literacy. Often (as with the related issue of dialect difference within a single language) the question is simply not addressed, and literacy, like oracy, is taught through the medium of the nationally prestigious language variety. However, this ignores some important psychological factors. Edelsky (1981, p. 90) has described literacy as 'an orchestration of multiple cueing systems', involving grapho-phonic, syntactic and semantic/pragmatic levels. The child whose language (or dialect) is different from the language of formal literacy may have to cope with a mismatch of input at all these levels, and will have to try and reconcile an unfamiliar symbol with an unfamiliar sound in an unfamiliar structure referring to an unfamiliar concept.

Let us look in a little more detail at each of these levels, beginning with the different writing systems. There is evidence that, especially in the early stages of reading, different strategies may be needed for different types of representation (e.g. logographic or alphabetic), but this does not appear to affect ease of reading once the system has been mastered. What may be more significant is the number of different symbols which a learner has to cope with and the number of distinguishing features between the symbols. In this respect some scripts have a distinct advantage over others for the teaching of initial literacy. (See Downing's *Comparative Reading* (1973), which draws on research from thirteen countries involving seven different scripts.) Still more significant, and of direct pedagogic relevance, is the sound–symbol correspondence between the script and a particular spoken language. In some languages, such as Spanish, Welsh and syllabically written Japanese, there is a close and fairly regular correspondence between the spoken and written word. In others, such as English and French, there is a far greater gulf to bridge (although there may be more *morphemic* regularity in these systems). It can be argued, in the case of children who are already bilingual, that initial literacy is best acquired via the language with the closest sound–symbol correspondence, since reading skills can subsequently be transferred to the language with less regular spelling. Thus teachers in Wales often claim an advantage of Welsh over English for the teaching of initial literacy in bilingual schools.

Turning to Edelsky's syntactic level, languages also differ in the extent to which grammatical information is coded in the spoken versus the written language. In an inflected language such as Spanish or German, grammatical information is present in the spoken language to which the child is exposed prior to formal schooling. In these cases writing (at least in the early stages) is simply a matter of recoding familiar information in written form. In other inflected languages, notably French, a great deal of grammatical information (such as verb endings and plurals) is not expressed at all in the spoken language and is encountered first in the written form. This poses an additional hurdle for the learner.

The issue is further complicated by the fact that many bilingual children of linguistic minority groups are taught literacy via their weaker language. There is a strong case for saying that initial literacy is best acquired via the child's first language or dialect, thus moving from the familiar to the unfamiliar. In some instances the competing demands of the more regular script versus the more familiar language will be irreconcilable, and in those instances the case for familiarity will be the stronger. Moreover, this usually has the advantage of drawing on the support of the home and community. Cowan and Sarmad (1976), in a very thorough study of the acquisition of biliteracy in Persian–English bilingual schools, found that reading progress was enhanced in the language that was reinforced in the home. It is impossible to say how far this is simply a result of the child encountering the written form of familiar *words*, or how far we have moved across into Edelsky's semantic/pragmatic level. Perhaps it is rather, as Goodman (1969) has argued, that readers (or more specifically, beginning readers) 'can't comprehend materials which are based on *experience* and *concepts* outside their background' (quoted in Downing, 1973 p. 68; my italics).

Even verbal code switching has its written equivalent, which seems to operate according to similar principles. Edelsky (1981) gives us an interesting insight into how a class of bilingual Hispanic American children learn these principles:

> Almost all of the code-switching we have found so far occurs in Spanish texts. With rare exceptions, when the children write in English, they do not code switch. Even when they mentioned a song learned in Spanish ('La Vibora del Mar'), they labelled it *the snake in the ocean*. When we look at the in-classroom print available to them in each language, this discrepancy seems more understandable. Although children have access to trade books in Spanish, much of the Spanish print is 'home made' (teacher-made posters, dittoed reading materials, etc.). Print in English is overwhelmingly commercially produced. Therefore, perhaps Spanish texts are seen as more informal, and thus hospitable to code-switching. (p. 77)

Bilingualism: an advantage or a disadvantage?

Many claims have traditionally been made for the benefits of 'foreign' language learning. Here are a few of them:

1 Another language gives access to another people and their culture, and thus helps to broaden one's view of the world.
2 Knowing a second language can give insights into the workings of language as a system.
3 It is good mental discipline in itself.
4 It is a marketable skill.

However, these arguments are rarely applied (by Europeans) to non-European languages. The bilingualism of most of Britain's linguistic minority communities is therefore devalued:

> Whereas learning a foreign language and even one or two dead ones as well has always been the *sine qua non* of a 'good' education, and whereas a child who picks up fluent French and Italian, say, because her father has been posted abroad, is likely to be thought fortunate, at an advantage, even 'finished', a child with two or three non-European languages, in some of which he may be literate, could be regarded as quite literally languageless when he arrives in an English school, where 'not a word of English' can often imply 'not a word'. (Miller, 1983, p. 5)

In this case, the bilingualism of the child, if it is recognized at all, tends to be seen as a disadvantage, on the arguable grounds that it puts too much strain on the child's brain and hence has a detrimental effect on other learning ('cognitive overload'), or that it results in a relative lack of fluency or limited competence in both languages. But how valid are these claims in reality?

Problems of assessment

What is the actual *evidence* of any benefits or disadvantages attaching to bilingualism? During the past 50 years or so there has been a great deal of research on this topic, and some conflicting results. (Good overviews of the research can be found in Hornby, 1977; Albert and Obler, 1978; Swain and Cummins, 1979; Grosjean, 1982; Cummins and Swain, 1986). The problem with much of the early research was that it failed to control for any socioeconomic factors and thus drew faulty conclusions about the relative performance of the (generally disadvantaged) bilingual group as compared to that of the (generally advantaged) monolingual group. Moreover, the tests on which these judgements were based were often culturally biased and conducted in only one — usually the bilingual subject's weaker — language. Awareness of the bias in such testing was till lacking in the 1970s:

> Under the headline 'Startling Admission on IQ Tests' the *San Francisco Chronicle* of January 4th 1970 reported that 45% of the elementary children with Spanish surnames who had been in classes for the mentally retarded in one school system had been found to be of average or above average intelligence when tested in Spanish. One child's IQ rose from 67 when tested in English to 128 when tested in Spanish. The average score gained by the 35 pupils who had been labelled mentally retarded as a result of tests given in their weaker language was 17 points.
>
> The retesting in Spanish took place only as a result of a federal judge ordering it to be done (after teachers, psychologists, parents and students had filed affidavits). (Quoted in Wright, 1982, pp. 25–26)

United States Public Law 142 now requires that 'evaluation must be provided and administered in the child's native language or other mode of communication'. Of course the full linguistic potential of the bilingual child can only ever be revealed when testing takes account of *both* the child's languages. (For a fuller discussion of assessment issues, see Cummins, 1984b; Williams, 1984.)

The potential benefits of bilingualism

There has always been a more positive school of thought in the literature on bilingualism. This is best exemplified by Vygotsky (1962), who argued that being able to express the same thought in different languages would enable a child to 'see his language as one particular system among many, to view its phenomena under more general categories', leading to 'awareness of his linguistic operations' (p. 110), a skill we might call *metalinguistic awareness*. Recently more evidence has been forthcoming to support this conjecture, notably in the work of Peal and Lambert (1962) with French–English children in Canada; Ben Zeev (1977) with Hebrew–English and Spanish–English bilingual children in the United States; and Ianco-Worrall (1972) with Afrikaans–English bilingual children in South Africa.

Other researchers have demonstrated more general cognitive benefits in being bilingual. Saunders (1983, pp. 17–20), reviewing all the available research evidence, has summarized the advantages of bilingual children over monolinguals, *when matched on other criteria*, as follows:

1 Earlier and greater awareness of the arbitrariness of language (i.e. the realization that there is no intrinsic connection between, say, the word 'dog' and the animal it symbolizes).
2 Earlier separation of meaning from sound (e.g. a tendency to group words according to their semantics rather than their phonology; thus cap–hat, rather than cap–can).
3 Greater adeptness at evaluating non-empirical contradictory statements (i.e. elementary logic).
4 Greater facility in concept formation.
5 Greater adeptness at divergent thinking (e.g. 'Tell me all the things I could do with a paper clip').
6 Greater social sensitivity (especially sensitivity to the effectiveness of communication, such as the needs of a listener who cannot see what the speaker can see).

All of these skills, especially 1–4, which might be said to constitute 'disembedded' thinking (Donaldson, 1978), are highly valued by the formal education system and might lead us to believe that bilinguals would automatically achieve greater educational success. However, this would be to ignore the pre-existing inequalities of race, ethnicity and social class, which have traditionally led to a correspondingly low status for certain types of bilingualism.

The role of bilingual education

It is often said that priority should be given to developing bilingual children's competence in English if they are to have a fair chance of contributing to British society on equal terms. This is a persuasive argument, especially as it is often advanced by parents who wish to see their children succeed in this society. But none of the research evidence would lead us to believe that supporting a child's first language will have any detrimental effect on the acquisition of a second; indeed it is far more likely to enhance it by building on firm foundations and leading to a greater awareness of how language works.

If bilingual children are to fulfil their intellectual potential, it is important that both their languages, and in particular the potentially more vulnerable language, should be recognized and supported within school. In recent years several formal projects have been set up to investigate the effects of educating children of primary age bilingually, with English (sometimes the children's first language, sometimes their second) as one of the two languages of education. These are:

- Schools Council Bilingual Education in Wales Project 1968–77 (Price and Dodson, 1978)
- Bedford, EC Mother Tongue Project 1976–79 (Bedfordshire Education Services, 1980)
- DES Mother Tongue and English Teaching Project in Bradford 1978–80 (MOTET, 1981)
- Various studies in the USA and Canada (Swain and Lapkin, 1982; Cummins, 1984a).

The following broad conclusions can be drawn from these studies:

1 The children's general intellectual development did not suffer and in some respects benefited.
2 Second-language proficiency was promoted at no long-term cost to the development of proficiency in the first language.
3 In addition, the children had acquired functional competence in their second language.

It is thus misleading to think of language skills as a matter of either/or. The aim of education should surely be to extend and not to restrict a child's range of options, and 'we should be fostering an environment which enables bilingual children to continue, if they wish, to make links and contacts across communities, rather than the one-way journey away from their parents.' (*Issues*, 1982, p. 5).

References

Albert, M. L. and Obler, L. K. (1978) *The Bilingual Brain*, New York & London: Academic Press.

Bedfordshire Education Service (1980) *EC Mother Tongue and Culture Pilot Project 1976–1980*. A report prepared for the colloquium at Cranfield Institute of Technology, 24–27 March 1980.

Ben Zeev, S. (1977) 'Mechanisms by which childhood bilingualism affects understanding of language and cognitive structures'. In Hornby, P. A. (ed.) *Bilingualism: Psychological, Social and Educational Implications*. New York: Academic Press, pp. 29–55.

Cancino, H., Rosansky, E. J. and Schumann, J. H. (1974) 'Second language acquisition: the negative'. Paper presented at the 1974 Summer meeting of the Linguistic Society of America in Amherst, Mass.

Carroll, J. B. (ed.) (1956) *Language, Thought and Reality: Selected Writings of Benjamin Lee Whorf*, Cambridge, Mass.; MIT Press.

Corder, S. P. (1978) 'Language-learner language'. In Richards, J. C. (ed.) *Understanding Second and Foreign Language Learning : Issues and Approaches*. Rowley, Mass.: Newbury House, pp. 71–93.

Cowan, J. R. and Sarmad, Z. (1976) 'Reading performance of bilingual children according to type of school and home language'. *Language Learning*, **26**(2), 353–376.

Cummins, J. (1984a) 'Mother tongue maintenance for minority language children: some common misconceptions'. *Forum 2*, London, ILEA, Languages Inspectorate, Spring.

Cummins, J. (1984b) *Bilingualism and special Education: Issues in Assessment and Pedagogy*. Clevedon, Avon; Multilingual Matters.

Cummins, J. and Swain, M. (1986) *Bilingualism in Education*. London: Longman.

Donaldson, M. (1978) *Children's Minds*. London: Fontana.

Downing, J.(1973) *Comparative Reading: Cross National Studies of Behaviour and Processes in Reading and Writing*. New York: Macmillan.

Edelsky, C. (1981) 'From "Jimosalcsco" to "7 Narangas se calleron y el arbol-est-triste en lagrymas": writing development in a bilingual program'. In Cronnell, B. (ed.) *The Writing Needs of Linguistically Different Students*. Proceedings of a research/practice conference held at SWRL Educational Research and Development, Los Alamitos, Cailfornia, June.

Edwards, V. (1983) *Languages in Multicultural Classrooms*. London: Batsford Academic and Education.

Goodman, K. S. (1969) 'Dialect barriers to reading comprehension'. In Baratz, J. C. and Shuy, R. W. (eds) *Teaching Black Children to Read*. Washington DC: Centre for Applied Linguistics.

Grosjean, F. (1982) *Life with Two Languages: an Introduction to Bilingualism*. Cambridge, Mass.: Harvard University Press.

Gumperz, J. (1982) *Discourse Strategies*, London: Cambridge University Press.

Hornby, P. A. (ed.) (1977) *Bilingualism: Psychological, Social and Educational Implications*. New York: Academic Press.

Ianco-Worrall, A. D. (1972) 'Bilingualism and cognitive development'. *Child Development*, **43**, 1390–1400.

Issues (1982) 'Mother tongue: politics and practice'. *Issues in Race and Education*, **35**, Spring.

Kaufmann, M. (1968) 'Will instruction in reading Spanish affect ability in reading English?' *Journal of Reading*, **11**, April, 521–527.

Lado, R. (1957) *Linguistics Across Cultures*. Ann Arbor, Mich.: University of Michigan Press.

Linguistic Minorities Project (1983) *Linguistic Minorities in England*, A Report for the Department of Education and Science, Linguistic Minorities Project. University of London Institute of Education.

Miller, J. (1983) *Many Voices: Bilingualism, Culture and Education*. London: Routledge and Kegan Paul.

Modiano, N. (1968) 'National or mother language in beginning reading: a comparative study'. *Research in the Teaching of English*, **2**, Spring, 32–43.

MOTET (1981) *Mother Tongue and English Teaching for Young Asian Children in Bradford*, Report to the Department of Education and Science, *Digest*, *Vols. I & II*, Bradford University.

Peal, E. and Lambert, W. (1962) 'The relation of bilingualism to intelligence'. *Psychological Monographs*, **76**(27), whole number 547.

Poplack, S. (1980) 'Sometimes, I'll start a sentence in Spanish y termino en espanol (sic)'. *Linguistics*, **18**, 581–618.

Price, E. and Dodson, C. J. (1978) *Bilingual Education in Wales 5-11*. London: Evans Methuen and Schools Council.

Ravem, R. (1974) 'The development of wh-questions in first and second language learners'. In Richards, J. (ed) *Error Analysis: Perspectives on Second Language Acquisition*. London: Longman.

Saunders, G. (1983) *Bilingual Children: Guidance for the Family*. Clevedon, Avon: Multilingual Matters.

Swain, M. and Cummins, J. (1979) 'Bilingualism, cognitive functioning and education'.

Language Teaching and Linguistics Abstracts, **12**(1), 4–8. London: Cambridge University Press.

Swain, M. and Lapkin, S.(1982) *Evaluating Bilingual Education: a Canadian Case Study*. Clevedon, Avon: Multilingual Mattcrs.

Vygotsky, S. (1962) *Thought and Language*. Cambridge, Mass.: MIT Press.

Williams, P. (ed.) (1984) *Special Education in Minority Communities*. Milton Keynes: Open University Press.

Wright, J. (1982) *Bilingualism in Education*. London: Issues in Race and Education, 11 Carleton Gardens, Brecknock Road, London N19 5AQ. (A shorter version of this paper was published as 'Mother tongues in British schools' in *The English Magazine*, **3**, Spring 1980).

SECTION III

Language and Social Processes

Introduction

This section begins with a general, introductory discussion by John Gumperz and Jenny Cook-Gumperz of how people use language, albeit unselfconsciously, to define and maintain social identities. They also identify some ways in which the cultural and linguistic conventions followed by members of different social groups can, in contact, lead to communication failures and misunderstandings.

The next three articles (all considerably shortened versions of their originals) were selected to represent the continuing debate about one of the most contentious issues in the study of language in education — the possible influence of children's acquisition and use of mother tongues that are 'non-standard' varieties of language on their achievement within a school system which only recognizes the legitimacy of a 'standard' language variety. First, we have one of the most influential articles in the history of this debate — William Labov's 'The logic of non-standard English' — in which he argues against the view, popular among educationalists in the 1970s, that children from certain social backgrounds fail in school because they are 'linguistically deprived'. He attacks the research on which this view is based, and asserts the linguistic equality and cognitive equivalence of the language varieties of different social groups.

This is followed by an extract from one of the most vehement rebuttals of Labov's position, John Honey's *The Language Trap*. He argues that the 'linguistic equality case remains unproven, and that if taken seriously will act against the best educational interests of those very children its exponents claim to champion'. This debate is then taken one stage further through the article by J. R. Edwards, whose review of *The Language Trap* provides a careful, rational re-examination of the major themes introduced by both Labov and Honey.

The final article in this section should serve to remind us that there are other important social factors influencing language use besides social class and ethnicity. French and French review the recently developed field of sociolinguistic research into language and gender.

3.1 Language and the Communication of Social Identity

J.J. Gumperz and J. Cook-Gumperz

Source: Extracts from Gumperz, J. J. and Cook-Gumperz, J. (1982) 'Introduction: language and the communication of social identity'. In Gumperz, J. J. (ed.) *Language and Social Identity*. Cambridge: Cambridge University Press, pp. 1–21.

[. . .] Our basic premise is that social processes are symbolic processes but that symbols have meaning only in relation to the forces which control the utilization and allocation of environmental resources. We customarily take gender, ethnicity and class as given parameters and boundaries within which we create our own social identities. The study of language as interactional discourse demonstrates that these parameters are not constants that can be taken for granted but are communicatively produced. Therefore to understand issues of identity and how they affect and are affected by social, political and ethnic divisions we need to gain insights into the communicative processes by which they arise.

However, communication cannot be studied in isolation; it must be analysed in terms of its effect on people's lives. We must focus on what communication does: how it constrains evaluation and decision making, not merely how it is structured. We therefore begin with materials or texts collected in strategic research sites which exemplify the problems we seek to deal with. Rather than concentrating on ethnography, grammar, semantics or linguistic variation alone, we want to find ways of analysing situated talk that brings together social, sociocognitive and linguistic constructs, and to develop relevant analytic methods that build on the perspective of sociolinguistic theory outlined in the previous work on discourse strategies (Gumperz, 1982). We are attempting to provide for the integration of individual consciousness, face-to-face processes of social activity, and situated group communication processes within contexts selected for their importance in the life space of the people studied.

These goals raise a further basic question. What is it about modern bureaucratic industrial society that increases the importance of communication processes? Perhaps the most important characteristic of the social environments in which we live is their unprecedented cultural and ethnic diversity. Social conflict during the past decades has increasingly come to be characterized as ethnic, class or religious conflict. But cultural pluralism is not new. Why is it that social distinctions which in other times were taken for granted and accepted as intrinsic to social order have suddenly become points of contention? What distinguishes today's urban situation is that the modes of interaction among subgroups and the ways in which individuals of different backgrounds must relate to each other and to the system by which they are governed have changed. The old forms of plural society in which families lived in island-like communities, surrounded and supported by others of similar ethnic or class background, are no longer typical.

In our daily lives we have become increasingly dependent on public services and on cooperation with others who may not share our culture. Yet unforeseen difficulties tend to arise when individuals of different cultural backgrounds communicate in public speech events such as committee meetings, interviews, employment situations and similar types of goal-directed verbal interaction. This can be true, even in cases where we find no overt conflict of values and goals. We all know that it is much easier to get things done when participants share the same background. When backgrounds differ, meetings can be plagued by misunderstandings, mutual misrepresentations of events and misevaluations. It seems that, in intergroup encounters, judgements of performance and of ability that on the whole are quite reliable when people share the same background may tend to break down. Interactions that are normally seen as routine often meet with unforeseen problems. Accepted strategies of persuasion and argumentation may no longer be successful. Furthermore, the difficulties occurring in such situations do not disappear with the increasing intensity of intergroup contact. On the contrary, they seem to increase and often become most acute after the groups involved have been in contact for several years and initial grammatical difficulties have disappeared. When this situation persists over time, what starts as isolated situation-bound communication differences at the individual level may harden into ideological distinctions that then become value laden, so that every time problems of understanding arise they serve to create further differences in the symbolization of identity.

One might argue that some urban residents acquire styles of speaking that serve them well in home and peer-group situations but are likely to be misunderstood in intergroup settings, while others of different backgrounds do not have these problems. This would suggest that once linguistic sources of misunderstanding are isolated and situated norms of language usage specified, appropriate behaviour can be taught. Yet the issue cannot be as simple as this because talk itself is constitutive of social reality. Where communicative conventions and symbols of social identity differ, the social reality itself becomes subject to question. On the other hand, however, both talk and social reality are part of and serve to maintain an ideology which takes on a historical life of its own. However, this is not a completely deterministic argument. We do not intend to claim that ideology shapes language and that since language shapes social reality there is no way out. Our main goal [. . .] is to show how ideology enters into face-to-face speaking practices to create an interactional space in which the subconscious and automatic sociolinguistic processes of interpretation and inference can generate a variety of outcomes and make interpretations subject to question. Thus we are not separating meaning and actions in their abstract analytical form, but we are looking at how they are realized in practices and how this process of realization can influence seemingly value-free assessments. To that end we begin with a more detailed discussion of institutional and socioecological forces that affect communication.

The social relevance of communicative processes

Post-industrial society in the urbanized regions of both Western and non-Western countries is characterized by the bureaucratization of public institutions and by the increasingly pervasive penetration of these institutions into the day-to-day lives of individuals. These phenomena produce certain characteristics that serve to differentiate present-day communicative environments from those of the past. What we are referring to here is a major historical change in the relationship of the individual to public institutions. This change has created a context where the public life of society members is materially affected by public agencies like educational and industrial institutions, union organizations, social welfare or health services.

Technological specialization of function complicates life in many ways, but what is of special interest here is the communicative maze society erects as part of the process of producing demonstrably public rationality of decision making. In job selection, for example, replacing a practical demonstration of the applicant's ability to do a particular job are elaborate procedures involving complex verbal tasks. From the filling out of application forms, the career counselling session, the job interview and the salary negotiation, assumptions about how information is to be conveyed are critical and these are assumptions which may vary widely even within the same socioeconomic group in the same community. Objective tests replace personal discretion. Hence candidates who do well may or may not be as competent to do the job as the non-successful test-taker. Finally, personnel judgements, and many other societal evaluations, are grounded on the individual's ability to talk well and to make a good presentation of him/herself, as well as the ability to pass tests. Many situations may only be entered by way of a written demonstration of verbal and mathematical skills, but, once demonstrated, these written skills must be reinforced orally, in interviews. In other words, what counts is the ability to conform to the principles of rhetoric by which performance is judged in bureaucratic systems.

The role communicative skills play has thus been radically altered in our society. The ability to manage or adapt to diverse communicative situations has become essential and the ability to interact with people with whom one has no personal acquaintance is crucial to acquiring even a small measure of personal and social control. We have to talk in order to establish our rights and entitlements. When we are at work we often rely on interactive and persuasive skills to get things done. Communicative resources thus form an integral part of an individual's symbolic and social capital, and in our society this form of capital can be every bit as essential as real property resources were once considered to be (Bourdieu, 1973).

The conditions we have described have brought about major changes in the nature and significance of ethnic and social boundaries. The term 'ethnicity' has traditionally been used to refer to relationships based on the linkage of similar people, whose social identity was formed by influences from outside the society in which they now live; but increasingly it has come to indicate relationships based on differences distinguishing one, new, indigenous group from another (Glazer and Moynihan, 1975). We shall refer to these two concepts as the *old* and the *new* ethnicity, respectively. The old ethnicity was supported both regionally and interpersonally through reinforced social networks which joined people through clusters of occupational, neighbourhood, familial and political ties. People of the same ethnicity often lived near each other and supported each other within their work and their political groups. Marriage and families continued these network linkages. In the large urban centres of the industrial world, the consciousness of immigrant groups' separate historical past was reinforced in the present by physical-geographical, friendship and occupational ties.

The new ethnicity depends less upon geographical proximity and shared occupations and more upon the highlighting of key differences separating one group from another. Michael Hechter (1978), in developing a general theory of ethnicity that accounts for changes in the modern urban world, has referred to the dual basis of modern urban concepts of ethnicity as (1) *interactive* group formation, whereby one group is distinguished from another by its similarities and overlapping networks; and (2) *reactive* group formation whereby an ethnic group reasserts its historically established distinctions from other groups within a common national polity. The new ethnicity is more a product of the second process, because this ethnic identity is defined more as a need for political and social support in the pursuit of common interest than as regional similarity or sharedness of occupational ties.

Individuals build upon residual elements of shared culture to revive a common sentiment upon which to found ethnically based interest groups. Ethnic identity thus becomes a means of eliciting political and social support in the pursuit of goals which are defined within the terms of reference established by the society at large. Because of the complex communicative environment in which individuals must exist, the cohesiveness of the new ethnic groups cannot rest on co-residence in geographically bounded or internally homogeneous communities. Even established immigrant communities are no longer able to survive in communicatively isolated separate islands, inner-city ethnic neighbourhoods may limit resident's access to public resources, but they no longer insulate.

The old ethnic ties found their linguistic expression in loyalty to a language other than that of the major society. The new ethnic identities rely on linguistic symbols to establish speech conventions that are significantly different. These symbols are much more than mere markers of identity. Increasing participation in public affairs leads to the introduction of terminologies and discourse patterns modelled on those of the community at large, which come to exist and be used alongside more established forms. New communicative strategies are created based on the juxtaposition of the two sets of forms which symbolize not only group membership but adherence to a set of values. These communicative conventions are largely independent of the actual language, i.e. they may be used whether the minority or the majority language is spoken. Even where the original native language is lost the new discourse conventions tend to persist and to be taken over into the groups's use of majority language. In fact these conventions come to reflect the identity of the group itself and can act as powerful instruments of persuasion in everyday communicative situations for participants who share its values (Gumperz, 1982, chapter 2).

For example, in the United States, American English is the primary language of the indigenous population but this common language hides an underlying diversity in values and discourse conventions. These differences were for a long time dismissed as non-standard language practices that detracted from the potential effectiveness of the group as communicators, even though the first language of the group was English. But the fact that these linguistic and discourse differences seem to persist in the face of pressure for standardization has forced a re-evaluation of their social and communicative significance.

It is in these ways that we can see how the social and political conditions of modern life favour the creation of new linguistic symbols which can serve as the rallying point for interest group sharing. This reliance on in-group symbols, however, conflicts with the equally strong need for control of the rhetorical strategies of the bureaucratically accepted modes of communication. The bureaucratic system can thus be seen as a major structural source of the communicative complexity we have been discussing. Bureaucracy relies on the existence of what are seen as uniform meritocratic criteria of evaluation to control access to scarce resources. Meritocratic standards must be independent of the evaluator's individual preference. In theory at least, they must stand above ethnic and cultural variation. Such standards must ultimately be defensible in a public arena where courts and public hearings are the final arbiters of legitimacy.

Without an increasingly ethnically diverse population, bureaucracy might be far less of an issue than it is. A common ethnicity that includes a common communicative history would ensure the transmission of strategies of negotiation which would be shared by most. But pluralism complicates the problem immeasurably.

The key point of our argument is that social identity and ethnicity are in large part established and maintained through language, yet it is because of the historical character of the process through which groups are formed and the symbols of identity created that we have the particular characteristics of the way of speaking that we will be analysing. This argument therefore serves to attenuate the explanatory relationship between language, ideology and speaking practices. Only by understanding the specific historical roots of language divergence can we adequately account for the specific character of the communicative practices and monitor ongoing processes of social change.

[...]

The empirical basis: creating situations and texts

The first step in attacking these problems, which by their very nature are difficult to document and to analyse in detail, is to gain qualitative insights. Our analysis therefore seeks to emphasize interpretive methods of in-depth study, rather than relying on survey techniques to enumerate behaviours or compiling self-reports. What we need to do is find typical instances of key situations or speech events which are critical given our analysis of the social and ethnographic background.

In terms familiar from recent work in ethnography of communication, we would argue that the developments of our recent past, perhaps as recent a past as the last few decades, have created, or at least brought to central importance, new *kinds* of speech events. Some of these new events are (1) interviews (job, counselling, psychiatric, governmental), (2) committee negotiations, (3) courtroom interrogations and formal hearings, (4) public debates and discussions.

While different in detail, such events share certain important features. Although on the surface an air of equality, mutuality, and cordiality prevails, participant roles, i.e., the right to speak and the obligation to answer, are predetermined, or at least strictly constrained. In interviews the interviewer chooses questions, initiates topics of discussions, and evaluates responses. The interviewees respond, i.e., they answer. Often they are expected to volunteer information but what it is they can say is strictly constrained by expectations which are rarely made explicit. When they venture into the interviewers' territory, interviewers may comment: "*I'm* interviewing *you*, not vice versa." In committee meetings and to some extent in debates and discussions, tacitly understood rules of preference, unspoken conventions as to what counts as valid and what information may or may not be introduced prevail. The participant structure of such events thus reflects a real power asymmetry underneath the surface equality, a serious problem when the lesser communicator does not know the rules. The issue is compounded by the fact that what is evaluated appears to be neutral. Evaluators tend to concentrate on presentation of facts and information, or problem solving and reasoning abilities, so that underlying sources of ambiguity are not ordinarily discovered.

Although evaluation may ultimately be subjective, whatever judgments are made must be made relative to explicit meritocratic and demonstrably objective standards of ability and achievement where decisions are appealable. Hence standards must, in theory at least, be publicly available.

Judgments must be defensible in the public arena. But since appeals require rhetorical sophistication, including acquaintance with often unstated assumptions specific to the dominant culture or to the organization doing the judging, the weaker participant, who lacks the requisite verbal knowledge, is always at a disadvantage.

The initial task in the analysis is basically an ethnographic one of collecting actual instances of interactive situations containing all the internal evidence to document outcomes. Recordings of public meetings or on-the-spot public broadcasts provide a good first source of materials. Since it is often impossible to collect the background information necessary for further stages of analysis, field work is also required.

Yet ethnographic work in modern urban settings involves a great deal of time. Individuals involved in interethnic relations are often quite ready to be interviewed and to talk about communication problems. However, the structural conditions of the situations we need to explore make it impossible for them to be too closely involved in the research without changing the very nature of the social context. And besides, interviews alone, apart from the information they yield about attitudes, cannot provide the data we need.

In order to understand and evaluate a situation from a member's perspective, the researchers need to be fully involved in the everyday affairs of the organization. They need to know what participants' aims and expectations are in addition to observing what happens. Ethnographers of communication have the difficult task of experiencing in order to uncover the practical strategies of others while at the same time becoming so involved that they themselves become one of the main focuses of their own inquiries. What involvement does is create the practical knowledge which enables us to know which situations are best exemplars of the practices we need to analyse. But the ethnographers' presence in the situation is not necessarily a sufficient trigger to lead to the critical situations that reveal the relevant social and environmental forces coming together at the same time.

[. . .] Where, for ethical reasons, direct recording is not possible, actual situations can be recreated through play to gain an insight into the subconscious communicative phenomena. Experience with a wide range of natural situations can serve as the basis for recreating socially realistic experimental conditions where individuals are asked to re-enact events such as job interviews with which they have become familiar in everyday life. If these naturalistic situations are skilfully constructed and not too carefully predetermined, rhetorical strategies will emerge automatically without conscious planning, as such strategies are so deeply embedded in the participants' practices. Since it is these rhetorical devices that we want to analyse, eliciting such constructed texts does not necessarily entail a loss of validity.

[. . .]

The analysis of cultural expectations

The speech situations that we deal with [. . .] share common characteristics. They are goal oriented in the sense that each aims to *get* something done, i.e. to reach an agreement, to evaluate abilities or to get advice. These goals are a defining characteristic of the situation in question. The fact that these overall goals exist and are shared by the participants provides us with a participants' viewpoint for judging when something goes wrong. Thus as a first step in the analysis, by simply looking at the content of what transpires, it is possible to judge to what extent communication has succeeded or failed.

No two events of course are perfectly comparable. One way of dealing with this is to abstract from time bound sequences to certain recurring activities and communicative tasks, such as (1) narrating, (2) explaining, (3) arguing, (4) emphasizing, (5) instructing, (6) directing.

'Communicative task' is an abstract semantic concept defined in terms of semantic ties among component utterances. Inferences about what these ties are underlie interpretations of what is going on, what is intended and what is being accomplished (Gumperz, 1982, chapter 7). The list of tasks we have given is in large part universal in that all natural activities can be seen as consisting of these tasks or various combinations thereof. By identifying these tasks, we reach a level of abstraction which, like the linguists' abstraction to grammar, is independent of content and of particular situations.

Although the pragmatic conditions of communicative tasks are theoretically taken to be universal, the realizations of these tasks as social practices are culturally variable. This variation can be analysed from several different perspectives, all of which of course co-occur in the actual practices.

(1) Different cultural assumptions about the situation and about appropriate behaviour and intentions within it.
(2) Different ways of structuring information or an argument in a conversation.
(3) Different ways of speaking: the use of a different set of unconscious linguistic conventions (such as tone of voice) to emphasize, to signal logical connections and to indicate the significance of what is being said in terms of overall meaning and attitudes.

By 'different cultural assumptions' we refer to the fact that, even though people in situations such as we study agree on the overall purpose of the interaction, there are often radical differences as to what expectations and rights are involved at any one time. [. . .]

The second perspective, 'ways of structuring', relates to issues traditionally covered in rhetorical analysis and deals with such phenomena as sequencing of arguments and with decisions about what needs to be stated and what must be conveyed indirectly. [. . .]

By 'ways of speaking' we refer to the actual linguistic cues used through which information relevant to the other two perspectives is signalled. This level includes grammar and lexicon as well as prosody, pausing, idioms and other formulaic utterances. Our basic assumption is that in conversation we simultaneously interpret and communicate at several levels of generality, i.e.

we simultaneously signal both content and about content. [. . .]

[. . .] The linguistic conventions signalling communicative tasks, particularly the interplay of contextualizing and content signs, are much more sensitive to the ethnic and class backgrounds of the participants than one might expect. Speakers may have similar life styles, speak closely related dialects of the same language, and yet regularly fail to communicate.

More importantly, the nature of the interactive situations that our society mandates, and the evaluative criteria employed, stand in direct conflict with the subtleties of conversational interpretation and the inability of people to be aware of the fact that [. . .] speakers who produce grammatical sentences in English can nevertheless show systematic differences in rhetorical strategies.

Sociolinguistic methods in the study of face-to-face interaction

It has often been assumed that ethnically different speakers are not able to handle the formal criteria for giving information or producing contextually relevant talk in situations with which they have little direct experience, such as job interviews, public debates or discussions. Much of the discussion has proceeded as if speaking appropriately required the learning of a different script, and a different set of semantic and lexical options. The real problem is that whatever the situation, whether a formal interview or an informal meeting, the need in all communication for all people who are relative strangers to each other is to achieve a *communicative flexibility*, an ability to adapt strategies to the audience and to the signs, both direct and indirect, so that the participants are able to monitor and understand at least some of each other's meaning. Meaning in any face-to-face encounter is always negotiable; it is discovering *the grounds* for negotiation that requires the participants' skill. Many of the meanings and understandings, at the level of ongoing processes of interpretation of speakers' intent, depend upon culturally specific conventions, so that much of the meaning in any encounter is indirect and implicit. The ability to expose enough of the implicit meaning to make for a satisfactory encounter between strangers or culturally different speakers requires communicative flexibility.

Some initial insights into how we can study the achievement of communicative flexibility come from work on non-verbal communication. Through frame-by-frame microanalysis of film it can be shown that communication depends upon usually unnoticed behavioural cues and postures which have interactional, i.e. social, significance, Birdwhistell (1970) and Hall (1959) have demonstrated that (1) taken-for-granted and subconsciously given non-verbal signs play an integral part in signalling of attitudes and intent in non-verbal communication, and (2) misunderstandings can arise in cross-cultural communication when the relevant signalling conventions differ. Considerable systematic analysis in this area has concentrated on isolating the actual physical behaviours that could potentially play a communicative role. A distinction was made between three basic kinds of signals: (1) microsignals, such as eye blinks or the contraction of facial muscles, which often go unnoticed, (2) proxemic signals such as gaze direction, posture and body orientation, and (3) complexes of signs that carry meanings in isolation, emblems such as winking, handshakes and nods (Ekman and Friesen, 1969). A second research approach has explored the role that these often subconscious signals play in conversational coordination (Kendon, 1970). It has been demonstrated that all natural conversations are characterized by interspeaker coordination of signals. There is further evidence that non-verbal signs are rhythmically coordinated with verbal signs, both at the micro level of syllables and at the macro level of utterances (Condon and Ogsten, 1969).

The usefulness of this non-verbal work is that it suggests behavioural ways of studying what Goffman (1961) calls 'conversational involvement' and what we refer to as 'communicative flexibility'. It enables us to tell, by looking only at actual performance features and without knowing the content, whether two speakers are actively communicating.

Erickson in his studies of counselling sessions (Erickson and Schultz, 1982) has demonstrated that (a) the ability to establish rhythmic coordination of non-verbal signals was partially a function of participants' ethnic background, and (b) interviews characterized by rhythmic coordination were most successful in terms of the information interviewees received from the session. Even where sentence level meaning and grammar are shared, therefore, failure to communicate is not just a matter of individual ability or willingness to make the effort. Apart from grammar proper there seems to be a second, equally automatic, level of interactive signs and conventions which must be shared if communication is to take place.

Little in linguistic research on syntax, grammar or discourse deals explicitly with the question of what these discourse signals are and how they are acquired. Although psycholinguists and applied linguists concerned with problems of bilingualism have done considerable work on second-language acquisition (Ervin-Tripp, 1970), and on problems of the phenomena of interference — i.e. the tendency of second-language learners to transfer patterns from their first language to the second language — research in this area concentrates on the phonology and grammar of isolated sentences. Phoneticians have done a great deal of work on the phonology of intonation, rhythm and stress. But they tend to look at these suprasegmental features of language as channels for expression of emotion which add to, but are separate from the main information-carrying functions of language (Crystal, 1975). Work by dialectologists on Afro-American and other minority dialects of English has similarly concentrated on describing differences. To the extent that communication problems are discussed in this literature, they are seen in purely referential terms as failure to understand words or sentences (Shuy, 1974) at the level of phonology, grammar and lexicon.

In yet another area, considerable work has been done during the last ten years on phenomena of discourse. Story structures, the nature of narratives

(Propp, 1958; Labov, 1973), and the linguistic signs that mark the relationships between sentences in longer passages (Halliday and Hasan, 1976) have been investigated in some detail. The main concern here has been to demonstrate that there are systematic features of language that go beyond the sentence, i.e. that stories can be analysed as having rule-governed grammars (Van Dijk, 1977). The effort has been to describe and analyse structure, rather than to deal with the question of what makes communication effective.

These studies have moved linguistic inquiry in directions that are of great value for the study of face-to-face communication. But a sociolinguistic approach to communication must show how these features of discourse contribute to participants' interpretations of each other's motives and intents and show how these features are employed in maintaining conversational involvement.

The theoretical tradition in modern linguistics that has most explicitly dealt with processes of interpretation of intent and attitude in language use is that work in linguistic pragmatics which, building on philosophy of language, has concentrated on investigation speech and on Grice's definition of meaning as intention (Cole and Morgan, 1975). Although linguistic pragmatics is explicitly concerned with presuppositions in the interpretations of intent, the data analyses are based on situations where presuppositions are shared. Analysis moreover is largely sentenced-based. While it is concerned with the logical structure of communicative events, it does not attempt to deal with the role of language in interactive processes.

The notion of intent is crucial and has carried us far beyond the older, purely abstract, structural approaches to language, to enable us to show how people build upon social knowledge in interaction. The concept of intent itself, however, if it is to be adapted to our goals, needs some modification. In dealing with conversational exchanges we do not and need not treat the psychological issue of what an individual has in mind, but rather we focus on how intent is interpreted by ordinary listeners in a particular context. We assume such interpretation is a function of (a) listener's linguistic knowledge, (b) contextual presuppositions informed by certain cues, and (c) background information brought to bear on the interpretation. Our main concern is with systematic or patterned differences in interpretation that can be traced to socially determined differences in contextual presuppositions as they relate to particular conversational conventions. When we talk about intent, therefore, we mean the socially recognized communicative intent that is implied in particular kinds of social activities signalled in discourse. Our guiding problematic is to discover what is necessary for the maintenance of conversational cooperation.

Conversational cooperation is commonly understood to refer to the assumptions that conversationalists must make about each other's contributions and to the conversational principles on which they rely. Cooperation, however, involves not only communication through the use of words in their literal meanings, but construction across time of negotiated and situationally specific conventions for the interpretation of discourse tasks as well as the speaker's and listener's knowledge of how to conduct and interpret live performances. The features previously referred to as paralinguistic, intonation, stress, rhythm and contrastive shifts of phonetic values are all ways of conveying meaning that add to or alter the significance of semantic choices. To the extent that we can talk about conversations being governed and controlled by shared expectations, we must assume that these expectations are signalled, and sharedness is negotiated as part of the interaction itself. We refer to those signalling cues that are seen to operate systematically within specific communicative traditions and to the communicative strategies to which they give rise as *contextualization conventions*.

One way in which contextualization conventions function is to serve as guide posts for monitoring the progress of conversational interaction. We use our knowledge of grammar and lexicon, along with contextualization conventions and whatever background information we have about settings and participants, to decide what discourse task is being performed and what activity is being signalled, and this provides information about likely communicative goals and outcome. We then build on these predictions to identify the communicative intent that underlies particular utterances. Contextualization conventions *channel* interpretations in one direction or another. The basic assumption is that something is being communicated. What is at issue is *how it is to be interpreted*. The judgements made at any one time are contingent judgements; they are either confirmed or disproved by what happens subsequently. If they are confirmed, our expectations are reinforced; if they are disconfirmed, we try to recode what we have heard and change our expectations of goals, outcomes or speakers' intent.

Contextualization conventions are acquired as a result of a speaker's actual interactive experience, i.e. as a result of an individual's participation in particular networks of relationship (Gumperz, 1982, chap. 2). Like grammatical knowledge, they operate below the level of conscious choice. Where these networks differ, as they do in ethnically mixed settings, conventions differ and communication can break down. The relevant differences in conventions may not present serious problems when individuals are at ease or in routine situations, but when the situation is stressful, i.e. when much depends on the outcome as in a job interview or in a formal negotiation, they are quite likely to affect communication. This is a largely unrecognized type of communicative problem and most people, therefore, interpret the other person's way of speaking according to their own conventions. This means that a person may draw totally incorrect inferences about someone else. For example s/he may conclude that someone is being rude, irrelevant, boring or not talking sense at all. Or often hearers become lost in a maze of words or ideas that do not seem to cohere. They also lack the means to sort out the difficulties which will inevitably occur. So the strategies necessary for solving the misunderstanding which we ordinarily rely on to remedy and re-evaluate communicative situations do not convey the necessary information. Our discussion of contextualization implies that to the extent that communicative breakdowns and miscommunications are the result of linguistic factors they can be attributed to the operation of processes which work below the level of awareness, and are no more available to the casual observer than are the eye blinks and facial cues discovered through microanalysis of non-verbal signs.

[. . .]

References

Birdwhistell, R. (1970) *Kinesics and Context: Essays on Body Motion Communication.* Philadelphia: University of Pennsylvania Press.

Bourdieu, P. (1973) 'Cultural reproduction and social reproduction'. In Brown, R. (ed.) *Knowledge, Education and Cultural Change.* London: Tavistock.

Cole, P. and Morgan, J L. (eds) (1975) *Syntax and Semantics, Vol. 3: speech acts*, New York: Academic Press.

Condon, J. C. and Ogsten, D. (1969) 'Speech and body motion. In Kjeldergaard, P. (ed.) *Perception of Language.* Columbus, Ohio: Charles Merrill.

Crystal, D. (1975) *The English Tone of Voice.* London: Edward Arnold.

Ekman, P. and Friesen, W. (1969) 'The repertoire of non-verbal behaviour: origins, usage, coding and categories'. *Semiotica*, 1, 49–98.

Erickson, F. and Schultz, J. J. (1982) *The Counselor as Gatekeeper.* New York: Academic Press.

Ervin-Tripp, S. (1970) 'Structure and process in language acquisition'. In Alatis, J. E. (ed.) *21st Annual Roundtable Monograph Series on Language and Linguistics.* Washington DC: Georgetown University Press.

Glazer, N. and Moynihan, D. P. (1975) *Beyond the Melting Pot.* Chicago: University of Chicago Press.

Goffman, E. (1961) *Encounters.* Indianapolis: Bobbs Merrill.

Gumperz, J J. (1982) *Discourse Strategies.* Cambridge: Cambridge University Press.

Hall E. T. (1959) *The Silent Language.* New York: Doubleday.

Halliday, M. A. K. and Hasan, R. (1976) *Cohesion in English.* London: Longmans.

Hechter, M. (1978) 'Considerations on Western European ethnoregionalism. Paper presented at conference on Ethnicity and Economic Development, University of Michigan, Ann Arbor, October 1978.

Kendon, A. (1970) 'Movement coordination in social action'. *Psychologica,* **32,** 100–124.

Labov, W. (1973) *Language in the Inner City.* Philadelphia: University of Pennsylvania Press.

Propp, V. (1958) *Morphology of the Folktale.* Ed. with an introduction by S. Pirkova-Jacobson. Trans. L. Scott. Bloomington: Indiana University Research Center in Anthropology, Folklore and Linguistics. No. 10.

Shuy, R. (1974) 'Problems of communication in the cross-cultural medical interview'. *Working Papers in Sociolinguistics* 19. Austin, Texas: Southwest Educational Development Laboratory.

Van Dijk, T. A. (1977) *Text and Context.* London: Longmans.

3.2 The Logic of Non-standard English

W. Labov

Source: excerpts from Labov, W. (1969) 'The logic of nonstandard English' *Georgetown Monographs on Language and Linguistics*, **22**. Washington, D.C.: Georgetown University Press.

In the past decade, a great deal of federally sponsored research has been devoted to the educational problems of children in ghetto schools. In order to account for the poor performance of children in these schools, educational psychologists have attempted to discover what kind of disadvantage or defect they are suffering from. The viewpoint which has been widely accepted, and used as the basis for large-scale intervention programmes, is that the children show a cultural deficit as a result of an impoverished environment in their early years. Considerable attention has been given to language. In this area, the deficit theory appears as the concept of 'verbal deprivation': Negro children from the ghetto area receive little verbal stimulation, are said to hear very little well-formed language, and as a result are impoverished in their means of verbal expression: they cannot speak complete sentences, do not know the names of common objects, cannot form concepts or convey logical thoughts.

Unfortunately, these notions are based upon the work of educational psychologists who know very little about language and even less about Negro children. The concept of verbal deprivation has no basis in social reality: in fact, Negro children in the urban ghettos receive a great deal of verbal stimulation, hear more well-formed sentences than middle-class children, and participate fully in a highly verbal culture; they have the same basic vocabulary, possess the same capacity for conceptual learning, and use the same logic as anyone else who learns to speak and understand English.

The notion of 'verbal deprivation' is a part of the modern mythology of educational psychology, typical of the unfounded notions which tend to expand rapidly in our educational system. In past decades linguists have been as guilty as others in promoting such intellectual fashions at the expense of both teachers and children. But the myth of verbal deprivation is particularly dangerous, because it diverts attention from real defects of our educational system to imaginary defects of the child; and as we shall see, it leads its sponsors inevitably to the hypothesis of the genetic inferiority of Negro children which it was originally designed to avoid.

The most useful service which linguists can perform today is to clear away the illusion of 'verbal deprivation' and provide a more adequate notion of the relations between standard and non-standard dialects. [. . .]

Verbality

The general setting in which the deficit theory has arisen consists of a number of facts which are known to all of us: that Negro children in the central urban ghettos do badly on all school subjects, including arithmetic and reading. In reading, they average more than two years behind the national norm. Furthermore, this lag is cumulative, so that they do worse comparatively in the fifth grade than in the first grade. Reports in the literature show that this bad performance is correlated most closely with socioeconomic status. Segregated ethnic groups, however, seem to do worse than others: in particular, Indians, Mexican-Americans and Negro children. Our own work in New York City confirms the fact that most Negro children read very poorly; however, our studies in the speech community show that the situation is even worse than has been reported. If one separates the isolated and peripheral individuals from the members of the central peer groups, the peer-group members show even worse reading records, and to all intents and purposes are not learning to read at all during the time they spend in school (Labov and Robins, 1969).

In speaking of children in the urban ghetto areas, the term 'lower class' is frequently used as opposed to 'middleclass'. In the several sociolinguistic studies we have carried out, and in many parallel studies, it is useful to distinguish a 'lower-class' group from 'working-class'. Lower-class families are typically female-based or 'matri-focal', with no father present to provide steady economic support, whereas for the working-class there is typically an intact nuclear family with the father holding a semi-skilled or unskilled job. The educational problems of ghetto areas run across this important class distinction; there is no evidence, for example, that the father's presence or absence is closely correlated with educational achievement.[1] The peer groups we have studied in South Central Harlem, representing the basic vernacular culture, include members from both family types. The attack against 'cultural deprivation' in the ghetto is overtly directed at family structures typical of lower-class families, but the educational failure we have been discussing is characteristic of both working-class and lower-class children.

In the balance of this paper, I will therefore refer to children from urban ghetto areas, rather than 'lower-class' children: the population we are concerned with are those who participate fully in the vernacular culture of the street and who have been alienated from the school system.[2] We are obviously dealing with the effects of the caste system of American society — essentially a 'colour marking' system. Everyone recognizes this. The question is, by what mechanism does the colour bar prevent children from learning to read? One answer is the notion of 'cultural deprivation' put forward by Martin Deutsch and others: the Negro children are said to lack the favourable factors in their home environment which enable middle-class children to do well in school (Deutsch et al., 1967, 1968.) These factors involve the development of various cognitive skills through verbal interaction with adults, including the ability to reason abstractly, speak fluently and focus upon long-range goals. In their publications, these psychologists also recognize broader social factors. However, the deficit theory does not focus upon the interaction of the Negro child with white society so much as on his failure to interact with his mother at home. In the literature we find very little direct observation of verbal interaction in the Negro home; most typically, the investigators ask the child if he has dinner with his parents, and if he engages in dinner-table conversation with them. He is also asked whether his family takes him on trips to museums and other cultural activities. This slender thread of evidence is used to explain and interpret the large body of tests carried out in the laboratory and in the school.

The most extreme view which proceeds from this orientation — and one that is now being widely accepted — is that lower-class Negro children have no language at all. The notion is first drawn from Basil Bernstein's writings that 'much of lower-class language consists of a kind of incidental "emotional" accompaniment to action here and now' (Jensen, 1968, p. 118). Bernstein's views are filtered through a strong bias against all forms of working-class behaviour, so that middle-class language is seen as superior in every respect — as 'more abstract, and necessarily somewhat more flexible, detailed and subtle'. One can proceed through a range of such views until one comes to the practical programme of Carl Bereiter, Siegfried Engelmann and their associates (Bereiter and Engelmann, 1966; Bereiter et al., 1966). Bereiter's programme for an academically oriented preschool is based upon their premise that Negro children must have a language with which they can learn, and their empirical finding that these children come to school without such a language. In his work with four-year-old Negro children from Urbana, Bereiter reports that their communication was by gestures, 'single words' and 'a series of badly-connected words or phrases', such as *They mine* and *Me got juice*. He reports that Negro children could not ask questions, that 'without exaggerating . . . these four-year-olds could make no statements of any kind'. Furthermore, when these children were asked 'Where is the book?', they did not know enough to look at the table where the book was lying in order to answer. Thus Bereiter concludes that the children's speech forms are nothing more than a series of emotional cries, and he decides to treat them 'as if the children had no language at all'. He identifies their speech with his interpretation of Bernstein's restricted code: 'the language of culturally deprived children . . . is not merely an underdeveloped version of standard English, but is a basically non-logical mode of expressive behavior' (Bereiter et al., 1966, p. 113). The basic programme of his preschool is to teach them a new language devised by Engelmann, which consists of a limited series of questions and answers such as *Where is the squirrel? The squirrel is in the tree*. The children will not be punished if they use their vernacular speech on the playground, but they will not be allowed to use it in the schoolroom. If they should answer the question *Where is the squirrel?* with the illogical vernacular form *In the tree* they will be reprehended by various means and made to say, *The squirrel is in the tree*.

Linguists and psycholinguists who have worked with Negro children are apt to dismiss this view of their language as utter nonsense. Yet there is no reason to reject Bereiter's observations as spurious: they were certainly not made up: on the contrary, they give us a very clear view of the behaviour of student and teacher which can be duplicated in any classroom. In our own work outside of the adult-dominated environments of school and home,[3] we do not observe Negro children behaving like this, but on many occasions we have been asked to help analyse the results of research into verbal deprivation in such test situations.

Here, for example, is a complete interview with a Negro boy, one of hundreds carried out in a New York City school. The boy enters a room where there is a large, friendly white interviewer, who puts on the table in front of him a block or a fire engine, and says 'Tell me everything you can about this'. (The interviewer's further remarks are in parentheses.)

[*12 seconds of silence*]
(What would you say it looks like?)
[*8 seconds of silence*]
A space ship.
(Hmmmm.)
[*13 seconds of silence*]
Like a je-et.
[*12 seconds of silence*]
Like a plane.
[*20 seconds of silence*]
(What colour is it?)
Orange. [*2 seconds*] An' whi-ite. [*2 seconds*] An' green.
[*6 seconds of silence*]
(An' what could you use it for?)
[*8 seconds of silence*]
A je-et.
[*6 seconds of silence*]
(If you had two of them, what would you do with them?)
[6 seconds of silence]
Give one to somebody.
(Hmmmm. Who do you think would like to have it?)
[*10 seconds of silence*]
Cla-rence.
(Mm. Where do you think we could get another one of these?)
At the store.
(Oh ka-ay!)

We have here the same kind of defensive, monosyllabic behaviour which is reported in Bereiter's work. What is the situation that produces it? The child is in an asymmetrical situation where anything he says can literally be held against him. He has learned a number of devices to *avoid* saying anything in this situation, and he works very hard to achieve this end. One may observe the intonation patterns which Negro children often use when they are asked a question to which the answer is obvious. The answer may be read as 'Will this satisfy you?' [. . .]

If one takes this interview as a measure of the verbal capacity of the child, it must be as his capacity to defend himself in a hostile and threatening situation. But unfortunately, thousands of such interviews are used as evidence of the child's total verbal capacity, or more simply his 'verbality'; it is argued that this lack of verbality *explains* his poor performance in school. Operation Headstart and other intervention programmes have largely been based upon the 'deficit theory' — the notions that such interviews give us a measure of the child's verbal capacity and that the verbal stimulation which he has been missing can be supplied in a preschool environment.

The verbal behaviour which is shown by the child in the test situation quoted above is not the result of the ineptness of the interviewer. It is rather the result of regular sociolinguistic factors operating upon adult and child in this asymmetrical situation. In our work in urban ghetto areas, we have often encountered such behaviour. Ordinarily we worked with boys 10–17 years old; and whenever we extended our approach downward to 8- or 9-year olds, we began to see the need for different techniques to explore the verbal capacity of the child. At one point we began a series of interviews with younger brothers of the 'Thunderbirds' in 1390 5th Avenue. Clarence Robins returned after an interview with 8-year-old Leon L., who showed the following minimal response to topics which arouse intense interest in other interviews with older boys.

CR: What if you saw somebody kickin' somebody else on the ground, or was using a stick, what would you do if you saw that?
LEON: Mmmm.
CR: If it was supposed to be a fair fight —
LEON: I don' know.
CR: You don' know? Would you do anything . . . huh? I can't hear you.
LEON: No.
CR: Did you ever see somebody got beat up real bad?
LEON: . . . Nope ? ? ?
CR: Well — uh — did you ever get into a fight with a guy?
LEON: Nope.
CR: That was bigger than you?
LEON: Nope.
CR: You never been in a fight?
LEON: Nope.
CR: Nobody ever pick on you?
LEON: Nope.
CR: Nobody ever hit you?
LEON: Nope.
CR: How come?
LEON: Ah 'on' know.
CR: Didn't you ever hit somebody?
LEON: Nope.
CR: [*incredulous*] You never hit nobody?

LEON: Mhm.
CR: Aww, ba-a-a-be, you ain't gonna tell me that.

[. . .] This non-verbal behaviour occurs in a relatively *favourable* context for adult–child interaction; since the adult is a Negro man raised in Harlem, who knows this particular neighbourhood and these boys very well. He is a skilled interviewer who has obtained a very high level of verbal response with techniques developed for a different age level, and he has an extraordinary advantage over most teachers or experimenters in these respects. But even his skills and personality are ineffective in breaking down the social constraints that prevail here.

When we reviewed the record of this interview with Leon, we decided to use it as a test of our own knowledge of the sociolinguistic factors which control speech. We made the following changes in the social situation: in the next interview with Leon, Clarence

1 brought along a supply of potato chips, changing the 'interview' into something more in the nature of a party;
2 brought along Leon's best friend, 8-year-old Gregory;
3 reduced the height imbalance (when Clarence got down on the floor of Leon's room, he dropped from 6ft 2in. to 3ft 6in.);
4 introduced taboo words and taboo topics, and proved to Leon's surprise that one can say anything into our microphone without any fear of retaliation.

The result of these changes is a striking difference in the volume and style of speech.

CR: Is there anybody who says *your momma drink pee*?
{ LEON: [*rapidly and breathlessly*] Yee-ah!
{ GREG: Yup!
LEON: And your father eat doo-doo for breadfas'!
CR: Ohhh!! [*laughs*]
LEON: And they say *your father — your father eat doo-doo for dinner*
GREG: When they sound on me, I say *CBM*.
CR: What that mean?
{ LEON: Congo-booger-snatch! [*laughs*]
{ GREG: Congo booger-snatcher! [*laughs*]
GREG: And sometimes I'll curse with *BB*.
CR: What that?
GREG: Black boy! [*Leon — crunching on potato chips*] Oh that's a *MBB*.
CR: MBB. What's that?
GREG: 'Merican Black Boy!.
CR: Ohh . . .
GREG: Anyway, 'Mericans is same like white people, right?
LEON: And they talk about Allah.
CR: Oh yeah?
GREG: Yeah.
CR: What they say about Allah?

LEON: Allah — Allah is God.
GREG: Allah —
CR: And what else?
LEON: I don't know the res'.
GREG: Allah i — Allah is God, Allah is the only God, Allah —
LEON: Allah is the *son* of God.
GREG: But can he make magic?
LEON: Nope.
GREG: I know who can make magic.
CR: Who can?
LEON: The God, the *real* one.
CR: Who can make magic?
GREG: The son of po' — [CR: Hm?] I'm sayin' the po'k chop God! He only a po'k chop God! [*Leon chuckles*][4]

The 'non-verbal' Leon is now competing actively for the floor; Gregory and Leon talk to each other as much as they do to the interviewer.

One can make a more direct comparison of the two interviews by examining the section on fighting. Leon persists in denying that he fights, but he can no longer use monosyllabic answers, and Gregory cuts through his façade in a way that Clarence Robins alone was unable to do.

CR: Now, you said you had this fight, but I wanted you to tell me about the fight that you had.
LEON: I ain't had no fight.
GREG: Yes, you did! He said Barry,
CR: You said you had one! you had a fight with Butchie,
GREG: An he say Garland . . . an' Michael.
CR: an' Barry . . .
LEON: I di'n'; you said that, Gregory!
GREG: You did.
LEON: You know you said that!
GREG: You said Garland, remember that?
GREG: You said Garland! Yes you did!
CR: You said Garland, that's right.
GREG: He said Mich — an' I say Michael.
CR: Did you have a fight with Garland?
LEON: Uh-uh.
CR: You had one, and he beat you up, too!
GREG: Yes he did!
LEON: No, I di — I never had a fight with Butch! . . .

The same pattern can be seen on other local topics, where the interviewer brings neighbourhood gossip to bear on Leon and Gregory acts as a witness.

CR: . . . Hey Gregory! heard that around here . . . and I'm 'on' tell you who said it, too . . .
LEON: Who?

CR: about you . . .
LEON: Who?
GREG: out you . . . Who? I'd say it!

CR: They said that — they say that the only person you play with is David Gilbert.

LEON: Yee-ah! yee-ah! yee-ah! . . .
GREG: That's who you play with!

LEON: I 'on' play with him no more!
GREG: Yes you do!

LEON: I 'on' play with him no more!

GREG: But remember, about me and Robbie?

LEON: So that's not —

GREG: and you went to Petey and Gilbert's house, 'member? *Ah haaah*!!

LEON: So that's — so — but I would — I had came back out, an' I ain't go to his house no more . . .

The observer must now draw a very different conclusion about the verbal capacity of Leon. The monosyllabic speaker who had nothing to say about anything and cannot remember what he did yesterday has disappeared. Instead, we have two boys who have so much to say they keep interrupting each other, who seem to have no difficulty in using the English language to express themselves. An we in turn obtain the volume of speech and the rich array of grammatical devices which we need for analysing the structure of non-standard Negro English (N N E): negative concord [*I 'on' play with him no more*] the pluperfect [*had came back out*], negative perfect [*I ain't had*], the negative preterite [*I ain't go*], and so on.

One can now transfer this demonstration of the sociolinguistic control of speech to other test situations — including IQ and reading tests in school. It should be immediately apparent that none of the standard tests will come anywhere near measuring Leon's verbal capacity. On these tests he will show up as very much the monosyllabic, inept, ignorant, bumbling child of our first interview. The teacher has far less ability than Clarence Robins to elicit speech from this child; Clarence knows the community, the things that Leon has been doing, and the things that Leon would like to talk about. But the power relationships in a one-to-one confrontation between adult and child are too asymmetrical. This does not mean that some Negro children will not talk a great deal when alone with an adult, or that an adult cannot get close to any child. It means that the social situation is the most powerful determinant of verbal behaviour and that an adult must enter into the right social relation with a child if he wants to find out what a child can do: this is just what many teachers cannot do.

The view of the Negro speech community which we obtain from our work in the ghetto areas is precisely the opposite from that reported by Deutsch, Engelmann and Bereiter. We see a child bathed in verbal stimulation from morning to night. We see many speech events which depend upon the competitive exhibition of verbal skills: sounding, singing, toasts, rifting, louding — a whole range of activities in which the individual gains status through his use of language.[5] We see the younger child trying to acquire these skills from older children — hanging around on the outskirts of the older peer groups, and imitating this behaviour to the best of his ability. We see no connecting between verbal skill at the speech events characteristic of the street culture and success in the schoolroom.

Verbosity

There are undoubtedly many verbal skills which children from ghetto areas must learn in order to do well in the school situation, and some of these are indeed characteristic of middle-class verbal behaviour. Precision in spelling, practice in handling abstract symbols, the ability to state explicitly the meaning of words, and a richer knowledge of the Latinate vocabulary, may all be useful acquisitions. But is it true that *all* of the middle-class verbal habits are functional and desirable in the school situation? Before we impose middle-class verbal style upon children from other cultural groups, we should find out how much of this is useful for the main work of analysing and generalizing, and how much is merely stylistic — or even dysfunctional. In high school and college middle-class children spontaneously complicate their syntax to the point that instructors despair of getting them to make their language simpler and clearer. In every learned journal one can find examples of jargon and empty elaboration — and complaints about it. Is the 'elaborated code' of Bernstein really so 'flexible, detailed and subtle' as some psychologists believe (Jensen, 1968, p. 119)? Isn't it also turgid, redundant and empty? Is it not simply an elaborated *style*, rather than a superior code or system?

Our work in the speech community makes it painfully obvious that in many ways working-class speakers are more effective narrators, reasoners and debaters than many middle-class speakers who temporize, qualify and lose their argument in a mass of irrelevant detail. Many academic writers try to rid themselves of that part of middle-class style that is empty pretension, and keep that part that is needed for precision. But the average middle-class speaker that we encounter makes no such effort; he is enmeshed in verbiage, the victim of sociolinguistic factors beyond his control.

I will not attempt to support this argument here with systematic quantitative evidence, although it is possible to develop measures which show how far middle-class speakers can wander from the point. I would like to contrast two speakers dealing with roughly the same topic — matters of belief. The first is Larry H., 15-year-old core member of the Jets, being interviewed by John Lewis. Larry is one of the loudest and roughest members of the Jets, one who gives the least recognition to the conventional rules of politeness. For most readers of this paper, first contact with Larry would produce some fairly negative reactions on both sides: it is probable that you would not *like* him any more than his teachers do. Larry causes trouble in and out of school; he was put back from the eleventh grade to the ninth, and has been threatened with further action by the school authorities.

JL: What happens to you after you die? Do you know?
LARRY: Yeah, I know.
JL: What?
LARRY: After they put you in the ground, your body turns into — ah — bones, an' shit.
JL: What happens to your spirit?
LARRY: Your spirit — soon as you die, your spirit leaves you.
JL: And where does the spirit go?
LARRY: Well, it all depends . . .
JL: On what?
LARRY: You know, like some people say if you're good an' shit, you spirit goin' t' heaven . . . 'n if you bad, your spirit goin' to hell. Well, bullshit! Your spirit goin' to hell anyway, good or bad.
JL: Why?
LARRY: Why? I'll tell you why. 'Cause you see, doesn' nobody really know that it's a God, y'know, 'cause I mean I have seen black gods, pink gods, white gods, all colour gods, and don't nobody know it's really a God. An' when they be sayin' if you good, you goin' t' heaven, tha's bullshit, 'cause you ain't goin' to no heaven, 'cause it ain't no heaven for you to go to.

Larry is a paradigmatic speaker of non-standard Negro English as opposed to standard English (S E). His grammar shows a high concentration of such characteristic N N E forms as negative inversion [*don't nobody know . . .*], negative concord [*you ain't goin' to no heaven . . .*], invariant *be* [*when they be sayin' . . .*], dummy *it* for S E *there* [*it ain't no heaven . . .*], optional copula deletion [*if you're good . . . if you bad . . .*], and full forms of auxiliaries [*I have seen . . .*]. The only S E influence in this passage is the one case of *doesn't* instead of the invariant *don't* of N N E. Larry also provides a paradigmatic example of the rhetorical style of N N E: he can sum up a complex argument in a few words, and the full force of his opinions comes through without qualification or reservation. He is eminently quotable, and his interviews give us many concise statements of the N N E point of view. One can almost say that Larry *speaks* the N N E culture (see Labov et al., 1968, vol. 2, pp. 38, 71–73, 291–292).

It is the logical form of this passage which is of particular interest here. Larry presents a complex set of interdependent propositions which can be explicated by setting out the S E equivalents in linear order. The basic argument is to deny the twin propositions.

(A) If you are good, (B) then your spirit will go to heaven.
(– A) If you are bad. (C) then your spirit will go to hell.

Larry denies (B), and asserts that *if* (A) or (– A), *then* (C). His argument may be outlined as follows:

1 Everyone has a different idea of what God is like.
2 Therefore nobody really knows that God exists.
3 If there is a heaven, it was made by God.
4 If God doesn't exist, he couldn't have made heaven.
5 Therefore heaven does not exist.
6 You can't go somewhere that doesn't exist.
B Therefore you can't go to heaven.
C Therefore you are going to hell.

The argument is presented in the order: (C), because (2) because (1), therefore (– B) because (5) and (6). Part of the argument is implicit: the connection (2) therefore (2), therefore (– B) leaves unstated the connecting links (3) and (4), and in this interval Larry strengthens the propositions from the form (2) *Nobody knows if there is* . . . to (5) *There is no* . . . Otherwise, the case is presented explicitly as well as economically. The complex argument is summed up in Larry's last sentence, which shows formally the dependence of (– B) on (5) and (6):

An' when they be sayin' if you good, you goin' t' heaven, [*The proposition, if* A, *then* B]
Tha's bullshit,
[*is absurd*]
'cause you ain't goin' to no heaven
[*because* – B]
'cause it ain't no heaven for you to go to.
[*because* (5) *and* (6)].

This hypothetical argument is not carried on at a high level of seriousness. It is a game played with ideas as counters, in which opponents use a wide variety of verbal devices to win. There is no personal commitment to any of these propositions, and no reluctance to strengthen one's argument by bending the rules of logic as in the (2–5) sequence. But if the opponent invokes the rule of logic, they hold. In John Lewis' interviews, he often makes this move, and the force of his argument is always acknowledged and countered within the rules of logic. In this case, he pointed out the fallacy that the argument (2–3–4–5–6) leads to (– C) as well as (– B), so it cannot be used to support Larry's assertion (C):

JL: Well, if there's no heaven, how could there be a hell?
LARRY: I mean — ye — eah. Well, let me tell you, it ain't no hell, 'cause this is hell right here, y'know!
JL: This is hell?
LARRY: Yeah, this is hell right here!

Larry's answer is quick, ingenious and decisive. The application of the (3–4–5) argument to hell is denied, since hell is here, and therefore conclusion (C) stands. These are not ready-made or preconceived opinions, but new propositions devised to win the logical argument in the game being played.

The reader will note the speed and precision of Larry's mental operations. He does not wander, or insert meaningless verbiage. The only repetition is (2), placed before and after (1) in his original statement. It is often said that the non-standard vernacular is not suited for dealing with abstract or hypothetical questions, but in fact speakers from the NNE community take great delight in exercising their wit and logic on the most improbable and problematical matters. Despite the fact that Larry H. does not believe in God, and has just denied all knowledge of him, John Lewis advances the following hypothetical question:

JL:. . . But, just say that there is a God, what colour is he? White or black?
LARRY: Well, if it is a God . . . I wouldn' know what colour, I couldn' say, — couldn' nobody say what colour he is or really *would* be.
JL: But now, jus' suppose there was a God —
LARRY: Unless'n they say . . .
JL: No, I was jus' sayin' jus' suppose there is a God, would he be white or black?
LARRY: He'd be white, man.
JL: Why?
LARRY: Why? I'll tell you why. 'Cause the average whitey out here got everything, you dig? And the nigger ain't got shit, y'know? Y'understan'? So — um — for — in order for *that* to happen, you know it ain't no black God that's doin' that bullshit.

No one can hear Larry's answer to this question without being convinced that they are in the presence of a skilled speaker with great 'verbal presence of mind', who can use the English language expertly for many purposes. Larry's answer to John Lewis is again a complex argument. The formulation is not SE, but it is clear and effective even for those not familiar with the vernacular. The nearest SE equivalent might be: 'So you know that God isn't black, because if he was, he wouldn't have arranged things like that.'

The reader will have noted that this analysis is being carried out in standard English, and the inevitable challenge is: why not write in NNE, then, or in your own non-standard dialect? The fundamental reason is, of course, one of firmly fixed social conventions. All communities agree that SE is the 'proper' medium for formal writing and public communication. Furthermore, it seems likely that SE has an advantage over NNE in explicit analysis of surface forms, which is what we are doing here. We will return to this opposition between explicitness and logical statement in the section on grammaticality. First, however, it will be helpful to examine SE in its primary natural setting as the medium for informal spoken communication of middle-class speakers.

Let us now turn to the second speaker, an upper-middle-class, college educated Negro man being interviewed by Clarence Robins in our survey of adults in Central Harlem.

CR: Do you know of anything that someone can do, to have someone who has passed on visit him in a dream?

CHARLES M.: Well, I even heard my parents say that there is such a thing as something in dreams some things like that, and sometimes dreams do come true. I have personally never had a dream come true. I've never dreamt that somebody was dying and they actually died, (Mhm) or that I was going to have ten dollars the next day and somehow I got ten dollars in my pocket. (Mhm). I don't particularly believe in that, I don't think it's true. I do feel, though, that there is such a thing as — ah — witchcraft. I do feel that in certain cultures there is such a thing as witchcraft, or some sort of *science* of witchcraft; I don't think that it's just a matter of believing hard enough that there is such a thing as witchcraft. I do believe that there is such a thing that a person can put himself in a state of *mind* (Mhm), or that — er — something could be given them to intoxicate them in a certain — to a certain frame of mind — that — that could actually be considered witchcraft.

Charles M. is obviously a 'good speaker' who strikes the listener as well educated, intelligent and sincere. He is a likeable and attractive person — the kind of person that middle-class listeners rate very high on a scale of 'job suitability' and equally high as a potential friend. His language is more moderate and tempered than Larry's; he makes every effort to qualify his opinions, and seems anxious to avoid any misstatements or over-statements. From these qualities emerges the primary characteristic of this passage — its *verbosity*. Words multiply, some modifying and qualifying, others repeating or padding the main argument. The first half of this extract is a response to the initial question on dreams, basically:

1 Some people say that dreams sometimes come true.
2 I have never had a dream come true.
3 Therefore I don't believe (1).

Some characteristic filler phrases appear here: *such a thing as, some things like that, particularly*. Two examples of dreams given after (2) are afterthoughts that might have been given after (1). Proposition (3) is stated twice for no obvious reason. Nevertheless, this much of Charles M.'s response is well directed to the point of the question. He then volunteers a statement of his beliefs about witchcraft which shows the difficulty of middle-class speakers who (a) want to express a belief in something but (b) want to show themselves judicious, rational and free from superstitions. The basic proposition can be stated simply in five words:

But I believe in witchcraft.

However, the idea is enlarged to exactly 100 words, and it is difficult to see what else is being said. In the following quotations, padding which can be removed without change in meaning is shown in brackets.

1 'I [do] feel, though, that there is [such a thing as] witchcraft.' *feel* seems to be a euphemism for 'believe'.

2 '[I do feel that] in certain cultures [there is such a thing as witchcraft].' This repetition seems designed only to introduce the word *culture*, which lets us know that the speaker knows about anthropology. Does *certain cultures* mean 'not in ours' or 'not in all'?

3 '[or some sort of *science* of witchcraft.]' This addition seems to have no clear meaning at all. What is a 'science' of witchcraft as opposed to just plain witchcraft? The main function is to introduce the word *science*, though it seems to have no connection to what follows.

4 'I don't think that it's just [a matter of] believing hard enough that [there is such a thing as] witchcraft.' The speaker argues that witchcraft is not merely a belief; there is more to it.

5 I [do] believe that [*there is such a thing that*] a person can put himself in a state of *mind* . . . that [*could actually be considered*] witchcraft.' Is witchcraft as a state of mind different from the state of belief denied in (4)?

6 'or that something could be given them to intoxicate them [to a certain frame of mind] . . . ' The third learned word, *intoxicate*, is introduced by this addition. The vacuity of this passage becomes more evident if we remove repetitions, fashionable words and stylistic decorations:

But I believe in witchcraft.
I don't think witchcraft is just a belief.
A person can put himself or be put in a state of
mind that is witchcraft.

Without the extra verbiage and the OK words like *science*, *culture* and *intoxicate*, Charles M. appears as something less than a first-rate thinker. The initial impression of him as a good speaker is simply our long-conditioned reaction to middle-class verbosity: we know that people who use these stylistic devices are educated people, and we are inclined to credit them with saying something intelligent. Our reactions are accurate in one sense: Charles M. is more educated than Larry. But is he more rational, more logical or more intelligent? Is he any better at thinking out a problem to its solution? Does he deal more easily with abstractions? There is no reason to think so. Charles M. succeeds in letting us know that he is educated, but in the end we do not know what he is trying to say, and neither does he.

In the previous section I have attempted to explain the origin of the myth that lower-class Negro children are non-verbal. The examples just given may help to account for the corresponding myth that middle-class language is in itself better suited for dealing with abstract, logically complex and hypothetical questions. These examples are intended to have a certain negative force. They are not controlled experiments: on the contrary, this and the preceding section are designed to convince the reader that the controlled experiments that have been offered in evidence are misleading. [. . .] Since the crucial intervening variables of interpretation and motivation are uncontrolled, most of the literature on verbal deprivation tells us nothing about the capacities of children. They are only the trappings of science: an approach which substitutes the formal procedures of the scientific method for the activity itself. With our present limited grasp of these problems, the best we can do to understand the verbal capacities of children is to study them within the cultural context in which they were developed.

It is not only the N N E vernacular which should be studied in this way, but also the language of middle-class children. The explicitness and precision which we hope to gain from copying middle-class forms are often the product of the test situation, and limited to it. [. . .]

It is true that technical and scientific books are written in a style which is markedly 'middle class'. But unfortunately, we often fail to achieve the explicitness and precision which we look for in such writing; and the speech of many middle-class people departs maximally from this target. All too often, 'standard English' is represented by a style that is simultaneously overparticular and vague. The accumulating flow of words buries rather than strikes the target. It is this verbosity which is most easily taught and most easily learned, so that words take the place of thought, and nothing can be found behind them.

When Bernstein described his 'elaborated code' in general terms, it emerges as a subtle and sophisticated mode of planning utterances, achieving structural variety, taking the other person's knowledge into account, and so on. But when it comes to describing the actual difference between middle-class and working-class speakers, we are presented with a proliferation of 'I think', of the passive, of modals and auxiliaries, of the first person pronoun, of uncommon words; these are the bench marks of hemming and hawing, backing and filling, that are used by Charles M., devices which often obscure whatever positive contribution education can make to our use of language. When we have discovered how much middle-class style is a matter of fashion and how much actually helps us express our ideas clearly, we will have done ourselves a great service; we will then be in a position to say what standard grammatical rules must be taught to non-standard speakers in the early grades.

Grammaticality

Let us now examine Bereiter's own data on the verbal behaviour of the children he dealt with. The expressions *They mine* and *Me got juice* are cited as examples of a language which lacks the means for expressing logical relations – in this case characterized as 'a series of badly connected words' (Bereiter et al., 1966, pp. 133 ff.). In the case of *They mine,* it is apparent that Bereiter confuses the notions of logic and explicitness. We know that there are many languages of the world which do not have a present copula, and which conjoin subject and predicate complement without a verb. Russian, Hungarian and Arabic may be foreign; but they are not by that same token illogical. In the case of non-standard Negro English we are not dealing with even this superficial grammatical difference, but rather with a low-level rule which carries contraction one step farther to delete single consonants representing the verbs *is, have* or *will* (Labov et al., 1968, sect. 3.4). We have yet to find any children who do not sometimes use the full forms of *is* and *will*, even though they may frequently delete it. Our recent studies with Negro children four to seven years old indicate that they use the full form of the copula *is* more often than pre-adolescents 10 to 12 years old, or the adolescents 14 to 17 years old.

Furthermore, the deletion of the *is* or *are* in non-standard Negro English is not the result of erratic or illogical behaviour: it follows the same regular rules as standard English contraction. Wherever standard English can contract, Negro children use either the contracted from or (more commonly) the deleted zero form. Thus *They mine* corresponds to standard *They're mine*, not to the full form *They are mine*. On the other hand, no such deletion is possible in positions where standard English cannot contract: just as one cannot say *That's what they're* in standard English, *That's what they* is equally impossible in the vernacular we are considering. The internal constraints upon both of these rules show that we are dealing with a phonological process like contraction, sensitive to such phonetic conditions as whether or not the next word begins with a vowel or a consonant. The appropriate use of the deletion rule, like the contraction rule, requires a deep and intimate knowledge of English grammar and phonology. Such knowledge is not available for conscious inspection by native speakers: the rules we have recently worked out for standard contraction (Labov et al., 1968, sect. 3.4) have never appeared in any grammar, and are certainly not a part of the conscious knowledge of any standard English speakers. Nevertheless, the adult or child who uses these rules must have formed at some level of psychological organization clear concepts of 'tense marker', 'verb phrase', 'rule ordering', 'sentence embedding', 'pronoun' and many other grammatical categories which are essential parts of any logical system.

[. . .]

What's wrong with being wrong?

If there is a failure of logic involved here, it is surely in the approach of the verbal deprivation theorists, rather than in the mental abilities of the children concerned. We can isolate six distinct steps in the reasoning which has led to programmes such as those of Deutsch, Bereiter and Engelmann:

1 The lower-class child's verbal response to a formal and threatening situation is used to demonstrate his lack of verbal capacity, or verbal deficit.
2 This verbal deficit is declared to be a major cause of the lower-class child's poor performance in school.
3 Since middle-class children do better in school, middle-class speech habits are seen to be necessary for learning.
4 Class and ethnic differences in grammatical form are equated with differences in the capacity for logical analysis.
5 Teaching the child to mimic certain formal speech patterns used by middle-class teachers is seen as teaching him to think logically.
6 Children who learn these formal speech patterns are then said to be thinking logically

and it is predicted that they will do much better in reading and arithmetic in the years to follow.

In the previous sections of this paper, I have tried to show that these propositions are wrong, concentrating on (1), (4) and (5). Proposition (3) is the primary logical fallacy which illicitly identifies a form of speech as the *cause* of middle-class achievement in school. Proposition (6) is the one which is most easily shown to be wrong in fact, as we will note below.

However, it is not too naïve to ask, 'What is wrong with being wrong?' There is no competing educational theory which is being dismantled by this programme; and there does not seem to be any great harm in having children repeat *This is not a box* for 20 minutes a day. We have already conceded that N N E children need help in analysing language into its surface components, and in being more explicit. But there are serious and damaging consequences of the verbal deprivation theory which may be considered under two headings: (1) the theoretical bias, and (2) the consequences failure.

1 It is widely recognized that the teacher's attitude towards the child is an important factor in his success or failure. The work of Rosenthal on 'self-fulfilling prophecies' shows that the progress of children in the early grades can be dramatically affected by a single random labelling of certain children as 'intellectual bloomers' (Rosenthal and Jacobson, 1968). When the everyday language of Negro children is stigmatized as 'not language at all' and 'not possessing the means for logical thought', the effect of such a labelling is repeated many times during each day of the school year. Every time that a child uses a form of N N E without the copula or with negative concord, he will be labelling himself for the teacher's benefit as 'illogical', as a 'nonconceptual thinker'. Bereiter and Engelmann, Deutsch and Jensen are giving teachers a ready-made, theoretical basis for the prejudice they already feel against the lower-class Negro child and his language. When they hear him say *I don't want none* or *They mine*, they will be hearing through the bias provided by the verbal deprivation theory: not an English dialect different from theirs, but the primitive mentality of the savage mind.

But what if the teacher succeeds in training the child to use the new language consistently? The verbal deprivation theory holds that this will lead to a whole chain of successes in school, and that the child will be drawn away from the vernacular culture into the middle-class world. Undoubtedly this will happen with a few isolated individuals, just as it happens in every school system today, for a few children. But we are concerned not with the few but the many, and for the majority of Negro children the distance between them and the school is bound to widen under this approach.

Proponents of the deficit theory have a strange view of social organization outside of the classroom: they see the attraction of the peer group as a 'substitute' for success and gratification normally provided by the school. For example, Whiteman and Deutsch (1968) introduce their account of the deprivation hypothesis with an eye-witness account of a child who accidentally dropped his school notebook into a puddle of water and walked away without picking it up.

A policeman who had been standing nearby walked over to the puddle and stared at the notebook with some degree of disbelief. (pp. 86–87)

The child's alienation from school is explained as the result of his coming to school without the 'verbal, conceptual, attentional and learning skills requisite to school success'. The authors see the child as 'suffering from feelings of inferiority because he is failing; . . . he withdraws or becomes hostile, finding gratification elsewhere, such as in his peer group'.

To view the peer group as a mere substitute for school shows an extraordinary lack of knowledge of adolescent culture. In our studies in South Central Harlem we have seen the reverse situation: the children who are rejected by the peer group are quite likely to succeed in school. In middle-class suburban areas, many children do fail in school because of their personal deficiencies; in ghetto areas, it is the healthy, vigorous popular child with normal intelligence who cannot read and fails all along the line. It is not necessary to document here the influence of the peer group upon the behaviour of youth in our society; but we may note that somewhere between the time that children first learn to talk and puberty, their language is restructured to fit the rules used by their peer group. From a linguistic viewpoint, the peer group is certainly a more powerful influence than the family (Gans, 1962). Less directly, the pressures of peer group activity are also felt within the school. Many children, particularly those who are not doing well in school, show a sudden sharp down turn in the fourth and fifth grades, and children in the ghetto schools are no exception. It is at the same age, at nine or ten years old, that the influence of the vernacular peer group becomes predominant. Instead of dealing with isolated individuals, the school is then dealing with children who are integrated into groups of their own, with rewards and value systems which oppose those of the school. Those who know the sociolinguistic situation cannot doubt that reaction against the Bereiter–Engelmann approach in later years will be even more violent on the part of the students involved, and that the rejection of the school system will be even more categorial.

The essential fallacy of the verbal deprivation theory lies in tracing the educational failure of the child to his personal deficiencies. At present, these deficiencies are said to be caused by his home environment. It is traditional to explain a child's failure in school by his inadequacy: but when failure reaches such massive proportions, it seems to us necessary to look at the social and cultural obstacles to learning, and the inability of the school to adjust to the social situation. Operation Headstart is designed to repair the child, rather than the school; to the extent that it is based upon this inverted logic, it is bound to fail.

2 The second area in which the verbal deprivation theory is doing serious harm to our educational system is in the consequences of this failure, and the reaction to it. If Operation Headstart fails, the interpretations which we receive will be from the same educational psychologists who designed this programme. The fault will be found not in the data, the theory, nor in the methods used, but rather in the children who have failed to respond to the

opportunities offered to them. When Negro children fail to show the significant advance which the deprivation theory predicts, it will be further proof of the profound gulf which separates their mental processes from those of civilized, middle-class mankind.

[. . .] It may seem that the fallacies of the verbal deprivation theory are so obvious that they are hardly worth exposing; I have tried to show that it is an important job for us to undertake. If linguists can contribute some of their available knowledge and energy towards this end, we will have done a great deal to justify the support that society has given to basic research in our field.[6]

Notes

1 There are a number of studies reported recently which show no relation between school achievement and presence of a father in the nuclear family. Preliminary findings to this effect are cited from a study by Bernard Mackler of C U E in Thos. S. Langer and Stanley T. Michaels, *Life Stress and Mental Health* (New York: Free Press), Chapter 8. Jensen (1969) cites James Coleman's study *Equality of Educational Opportunity*, p. 506, and others to illustrate the same point.

2 The concept of 'non-standard Negro English' (N N E), and the vernacular culture in which it is embedded, is presented in detail in Labov et al. (1968), sections 1, 2, 3 and 4.1. See Volume 2, section 4.3, for the linguistic traits which distinguish speakers who participate fully in the N N E culture from marginal and isolated individuals.

3 The research cited here was carried out in South Central Harlem and other ghetto areas in 1965–1968 to describe structural and functional differences between non-standard Negro English and standard English of the classroom. It was supported by the Office of Education as Co-operative Research Projects 3091 and 3288. Detailed reports are given in Labov et al. (1965), Labov (1967) and Labov et al. (1968).

4 The reference to the *pork chop God* condenses several concepts of black nationalism current in the Harlem community. A *pork chop* is a Negro who has not lost the traditional subservient ideology of the South, who has no knowledge of himself in Muslim terms, and the *pork chop God* would be the traditional God of Southern Baptists. He and his followers may be pork chops, but he still holds the power in Leon and Gregory's world.

5 For detailed accounts of these speech events, see Labov et al. (1968, section 4.2).

6 The negative report of the Westinghouse Learning Corporation and Ohio University on Operation Headstart was published in the *New York Times* (on 13 April 1969). This evidence for the failure of the programme was widely publicized and it seems likely that the report's discouraging conclusions 'will be used by conservative Congressmen as a weapon against any kind of expenditure for disadvantaged' children, especially Negroes.

References

Bereiter, C. and Engelmann, S. (1966) *Teaching Disadvantaged Children in the Pre-School*. Englewood Cliffs, NJ: Prentice-Hall.

Bereiter, C. et al. (1966) 'An academically oriented pre-school for culturally deprived children'. In Hechinger, F. M. (ed.) *Pre-School Education Today*. New York: Doubleday, pp. 105–137

Deutsch, M. et al. (1967) The Disadvantaged Child. New York: Basic Books.

Deutsch, M., Katz, I. and Jensen, A. R. (eds) (1968) *Social Class, Race and Psychological Development*. New York: Holt.

Gans, H. (1962) 'The peer group society'. In *The Urban Villagers*, New York: Free Press.

Jensen, a. (1968) Social class and verbal learning. In Deutsch et al., op. cit.

Jensen, A. (1969) 'How much can we boost I Q and scholastic achievement?' *Harvard Educational Review*, **39**, 1.

Labov, W. (1967) Some sources of reading problems for Negro speakers of non-standard English'. In Frazier, A. (ed.) *New Directions in Elementary English*. National Council of Teachers of English, pp 140–167. Reprinted in Barat, Joan C. and Shuy, R. W (eds) *Teaching Black Children to Read*. Washington D C, Center for Applied Linguistics, pp. 29–67.

Labov, W. and Robins, C. (1969) 'A note on the relation of reading failure to peer-group status in urban ghettos, *The Teachers' College Record*, **70**, 5.

Labov, W., Cohen, P. and Robins, C. (1965) *A Preliminary Study of the Structure of English Used by Negro and Puerto Rican Speakers in New York City*. Final Report, Co-operative Research Project no. 3091. Office of Education. Washington D C.

Labov, W., Cohen, P., Robins, C. and Lewis, J. (1968) *A Study of the Non-Standard English of Negro and Puerto Rican Speakers in New York City*. Final Report, Co-operative research Project no. 3288, Office of Education, Washington, D C, vols. 1 and 2.

Rosenthal, R. and Jacobson, L. (1968) 'Self-fulfilling prophecies in the classroom: teachers' expectations as unintended determinants of pupils' intellectual competence'. In Deutsch et al. (1968), op. cit.

Whiteman, M. and Deutsch, M. (1968) 'Social disadvantage as related to intellective and language development'. In Deutsch et al. (1968), op. cit.

3.3 The Language Trap: Race, Class and 'Standard English' in British Schools

J. Honey

Source: Extracts from Honey, J. (1983) *The Language Trap: Race, Class and 'Standard English' in British Schools.* Kenton, Middx: National Council for Educational Standards.

Threatened standards in English

In the past two decades there has been increasing concern, on both sides of the Atlantic, over the standards of written and spoken English achieved by the products of our school systems. Complaints from employers have been backed up with many examples of the unfavourable impression created by candidates for jobs in their letters of application or at interview, or afterwards in the course of their jobs; and anyone involved in processing forms of any kind, including insurance claims where clarity of exposition may be crucial, will tell the same story. A glance at the errors and unintended ambiguities on the handwritten cards displayed in newsagents' windows will confirm this point. All this is a sad commentary on more than a century of publicly provided education for all.

[. . .]

Producing semi-literates

It is a serious matter that our educational system (and others) continue to turn out, as they do, an annual crop of total illiterates,[1] and no less serious that from otherwise able pupils we produce students who are in some sense semi-literate. Yet the inability of our schools to turn out pupils with satisfactory standards of English is not simply due to the legacy of an inappropriate English curriculum or to a shortage of appropriately qualified teachers. Another powerful factor has been at work, especially over the past decade, and its effect has been to undermine attempts by teachers to meet the demands of parents and employers that pupils should be able to speak and write 'good English'. This is the notion, propounded originally by a group of specialists in linguistics, and widely influential among educationists and especially among teachers of English and those who train them, that for schools to foster one variety of English is contrary to the findings of the science of linguistics. For has that newly established discipline not demonstrated that all languages, and all varieties of any one language, are *equally good?* Therefore, to emphasize any one variety, i.e. standard English, in preference to the dialect spoken in the pupil's home, is not only unjustifiable in scientific terms, but it does irreparable harm to the self-esteem of the child whose dialect is discriminated against.

[. . .]

The following collection of quotations shows how the hypothesis about the nature of language variety has been stated by prominent linguists and by others, both in relation to the different languages spoken in entirely different societies, and in relation to different varieties or dialects of the same language. It is also an interesting illustration of how a pseudo-scientific theory is handed down by incautious academics first to school teachers and their like, ultimately to become the stock-in-trade of lightly educated politicians:

The oracles: Crystal to Ken Livingstone

1 'We cannot measure one language against the yardstick provided by another. . . . It is ridiculous to think that a language could exist where there were insufficient words for the people to talk about any aspect of the environment they wished. *Language always keeps pace with the social development of its users'* (Professor David Crystal, *What is Linguistics?*, 1968, p. 15 (and in all subsequent editions since then), (my italics).

2 'Every language has sufficiently rich vocabulary for the expression of all the distinctions that are important in the society using it' (Professor John Lyons, *Chomsky*, 1970/77, p. 21).

3 'All varieties of a language are structured, complex, rule-governed systems which are *entirely adequate* for the needs of their speakers' (Dr. Peter Trudgill, *Sociolinguistics*, 1974, p. 20), (my italics).

4 'All languages and dialects are adequate as communicative systems. The social acceptability of a particular language or dialect, considered nonstandard because of its association with a subordinate social group, is *totally unrelated* to its *adequacy for communication*' (Walt Wolfram, chapter on Dialect Divergence in John F. Savage (ed.) *Linguistics for Teachers* (U S A), 1973, p. 69), (my italics).

5 'It is accepted by linguists that no language or dialect is inherently superior or inferior to any other, and that all languages and dialects are *suited to the communities they serve*' (Michael Stubbs, *Language, Schools and Classrooms*, 1976, p. 24), (my italics).

6 'It is an established fact that no language or dialect is superior to another' (Dr V. K. Edwards, *The West Indian Language Issue in British Schools*, 1979, p. 105).

7 'As research shows, dialects are inherently equal' (Donna Christian, *Language Arts and Dialect Differences*, pamphlet for teachers sponsored by U S Department of Health, Education and Welfare, 1979, p. 5).

8 'There is virtually unanimous recognition among linguists that one language or dialect is as *good* as another' (David Sutcliffe, *British Black English*, 1982, p. 76), (my italics).

9 'All linguists agree that all dialects of English are equally *efficient*, complex and rule-

governed systems' (John Richmond (teacher-adviser, Inner London Education Authority), chapter in David Sutcliffe (1982), op. cit. (my italics).[2]

10 'No one system of language is better than any other' (Ken Livingstone, leader of Greater London Council, in discussion on English language use on *Any Questions*, BBC Radio 4, 8/1/82).[3]

'All languages are equally good'

What sort of authority have these statements got? The layman would readily tend to assume that speakers of different language have different potentialities open to them: that if you belong to a 'primitive' tribe whose language has a total vocabulary of a few thousand words or less, there are things you simply cannot say, compared with speakers from modernized societies whose dictionaries list hundreds of thousands of words, many of which are each capable of being used in a number of subtly different senses. Some might go further and suggest that there are thoughts you cannot think (or are unlikely to), concepts which your mind cannot get a hold on, simply because of the limitations of the language of your tribe. Didn't the early missionaries have difficulties in communicating their simplest (to them) theological ideas in some such communities; how can speakers of such languages cope, *in their own language*, with the concepts of higher mathematics, or Wittgensteinian philosophy, not to speak of biochemistry or nuclear physics.

Yet one powerful school of linguistic thought has, as we have seen from that list, dismissed such misgivings. Their rulings on the functional irrelevance of differences between language, and between dialects or other varieties of a given language, are set out on that list. Every language or dialect, they claim, has a sufficiently rich vocabulary; always keeps pace with its speakers' social development; is entirely adequate for all their needs, and as a communicative system; and is as good and as efficient as any other. What is especially noteworthy about these theorists is that they offer no proofs for their rulings, nor even any empirical evidence. The absence of evidence or attempted proof is no deterrent to the repetition of their proclamation: it is as if they believe that by simply repeating someting often enough, it will somehow become true. But if, in place of ritual incantation, we stop to examine the implications of what these theorists and their acolytes are saying, we can begin to judge the validity of those quotations and of the conclusions they are used to support.

We saw that Professor Lyons, Professor Crystal and Dr Trudgill dismiss as naïve our catalogue of doubts. Some of the key words in their quotations are *important, user* and *needs*. The third of these is the most revealing: all varieties of a language are asserted to be entirely adequate for all their speakers' *needs*. Thus, if a speech community is found whose language does not already possess the extensive vocabulary which would enable its members to handle any given aspect of modern technology (say), or modern medicine, or modern communications, then we are presumably to infer that the members of that community do not *need* any of those commodities. Now, I can think of all kinds of philosophical arguments why the members of a given society should be thought 'better off' or 'happier' without electricity, or penicillin, or telephones, but I doubt whether the presence or absence of these items in their existing linguistic system would be widely supported as a valid or relevant argument. Nor does the fact of whether those members themselves already consider the linguistic distinctions involved to be sufficiently *important* to them (Professor Lyons' point) convince me either: in judging what is 'important' to a given society, as also in judging what a given society 'needs', I will not fall in the trap of simply referring to what that society has considered important or needful in the past. [. . .]

There is, in fact, absolutely no evidence that languages keep pace with the social development of their users. Certainly they may stay abreast of the *general* needs of their speakers to discuss current aspects of their environment, but there are two exceptions even to this. First, there is normally a time-lag before new concepts, new activities or new institutions are given names which are incorporated into the vocabulary of the language; and secondly there are always individual users of that language who are ahead of the rest of the community in inventing or perceiving some new phenomenon for themselves, or copying it from another society, and are for an initial period bereft of the vocabulary for naming it, and in some cases even describing it, in their own language.

The need to prove that linguistic diversity has such implications would seem absurd to anyone who has actually tried to translate a scholarly paper in physics, psychology or semantics from a major world language into the speech of a preliterate jungle tribe or into the local dialect of a remote province, which may even lack the linguistic means of measuring or classifying distance or time in anything like the precision required in those disciplines — where (for example) the only two terms in the language for indicating distance might be those corresponding to *quite a long way* and *very nearby*.[4]

Why is it, then, that certain linguists on both sides of the Atlantic propagate these theories about all languages and dialects being equally good? Here we must begin by trying to understand the particular intellectual and social climate which has been so urgently receptive of these ideas that few have stopped to ask the necessary awkward questions, for fear of treading upon the 'forbidden ground'[5] of linguistic differences.

First, we note the attitude which was fashionable among social scientists in a number of disciplines in the 1960s and 1970s, which held that one cannot really understand, and certainly cannot pass judgement on, societies (or specific aspects of societies) other than one's own. Since it was considered improper or 'unscientific' to judge aspects of other societies as good or bad, just or unjust, so it was equally improper to consider that the languages or dialects of different societies or subgroups might be subjected to qualitative judgements. A good example of the 'relativist' position is the classic statement by a professor at the Open University, D. F. Swift, in a book about race, in 1972: 'We cannot accept quality distinctions between cultures'.[6] Nowadays this type of 'relativists' approach tends to be rejected by many social scientists, who hold that we have indeed not only a right but a *duty* to pass comparative value-judgements in relation to aspects of different societies, or even whole societies — so that the crimes of Nazi Germany or Stalinist Russia cannot be excused because those who perpetrated them might be represented as acting acceptably within the terms of their own cultural values. [. . .]

Chomsky and language theory

A second reason for the prevalence of these unsubstantiated theories relates to the influence in modern linguistics of the work of the American linguist Noam Chomsky. A professor at the Massachusetts Institute of Technology since 1955, Chomsky has been the most important name in linguistic theory for nearly two decades, and it was only towards the end of the 1970s that his theories began to be seriously called into question, to the extent that the American philosopher J. R. Searle has recently declared that 'the Chomskyan paradigm has broken down'.[7] [. . .]

Not all of Chomsky's contribution to linguistics is now in danger of being overthrown, and in particular the essentials of his work on syntax may prove to have lasting value. But one aspect of Chomskyan linguistics which concerns us here is his distinctive view of how children acquire language, which is called 'nativism'. Whatever different language or dialect the child happens to come to speak, his ability to learn it is held to be essentially due to his having inherited genetically a piece of 'complex fixed mental machinery', a 'set of mental tramlines programmed into our brain since birth'.[8] Chomsky offers no firm empirical evidence for his theory of the innate basis of all human linguistic behaviour, and the whole idea is much disputed among those linguists who dare to challenge the Chomskyan position. This particular hypothesis is closely allied with a further Chomskyan theory which he shared with another notable twentieth-century linguist working in America, Roman Jakobson, which holds that certain aspects of grammar and sound systems are *universal* in all languages, and for Chomskyans 'it is only by assuming that a child is born with the highly restrictive principles of universal grammar, and the predisposition to make use of them in analysing the utterances he hears about him, that we can make sense of the process of language learning'.[9]

It is especially paradoxical that supporters of extreme egalitarian and 'progressive' notions in the social sciences should be willing to swallow, without any substantial evidence, a set of hypotheses based on human heredity — since the assertion that innate characteristics may be more crucial than acquired ones (for example, in the development of intelligence) has long been condemned by exactly such people as giving scope to 'racist' conclusions (as in the Jensen controversy). An important corollary of Chomsky's theory of 'nativism' is that other assumption that all human languages are cut to a common pattern, since they are all, of course, determined by the psychological structuring which is innate to our species.[10]

The reader will readily see how these two interdependent and effectively circular hypotheses, widely proclaimed by a powerful group of academics, should lend support to that notion that all human languages and dialects are 'equally good'. [. . .]

Pidgin, creole and dialect

One positive development in modern linguistics in which Chomskyans (as well as linguists from other schools) have taken a prominent part, should be mentioned here. This is the attention which has been given to the study of less prestigious languages and varieties — e.g. pidgins, creoles and dialects — which scholars had hitherto been too ready to dismiss as merely debased forms of the standard languages to which they were closely related. Though the claims of such linguistic studies need to be closely scrutinized, they have in certain instances lent support to that part of the quotation from Dr Trudgill [on p. 164] that dialects such as Cockney or West Country possess their own grammatical rules which may be every bit as rigorous as those of standard English, and are 'structured, complex, rule-governed systems',[11] though the implications of their *complexity* need further elaboration. What we have already disputed is that particular linguist's presuppositions about the *needs* of such dialect speakers, and what we will further be disputing is his claim, and that of others, about their *functional adequacy*.

There is, as other quotations on that list clumsily imply, a widespread recognition among linguists that when a Cockney child says 'I don't know nuffink [nothing]', or a West Country speaker 'Ee be some taissey, ee be', or a speaker of Jamaican creole says 'dem gal a sharp',[12] that utterance may be obeying strict and perhaps very complex grammatical rules which are just as regular and systematic as the requirement of a standard English speaker to say 'I don't know anything', or 'He's in a very bad mood indeed' or 'Those girls are getting sharp'. What *is* in dispute among linguists are the intellectual, social and educational implications of using these different language varieties rather than the standard language.

The suggestion that there may be any intellectual implications of saying the equivalent of 'I don't know nothing' will come as a surprise to all except the old guard of grammatical purists who used to stamp on this kind of utterance in elementary school classrooms with the scornful claim that two negatives always make a positive, which is clearly not always the case in the Cockney dialect, in Jamaican creole or indeed in French (*je ne sais rien*, etc.) and many other languages. So we now know better than to say that Cockney (or creole or French) speakers must tend to be intellectually defective because their variety of language offends the rules of logic, since closer linguistic analysis shows their grammar on that point to be internally consistent and regular. What we have *not* disposed of is the much wider question of whether some languages (or, to some extent, some varieties of one language) might be less well equipped as vehicles of certain kinds of intellectual activity than others, with consequent intellectual disadvantage to those people who can only handle effectively that one language or dialect, and not any other, less limiting, form.

Does language define experience?

The problem we are dealing with here is the famous 'Sapir–Whorf' hypothesis, much discussed among linguists and social scientists generally. Though there are traces of this idea in many previous thinkers, its first explicit formulation was by the American academic linguist Edward Sapir (d. 1939) and it was further elaborated by Benjamin Lee Whorf (d. 1941), a brilliant amateur linguist who collaborated with him. Sapir's conclusion was that 'human beings . . . are very much at the mercy of the particular language which has become the medium of expression for their society', and that 'Language . . . actually *defines* experience for us . . .'[13] Whorf claimed that American Indian languages which (like other languages we have already noted) do not recognize time as being measurable, and have no grammatical tenses comparable with European languages, nor for that reason any concept of speed, impose upon their speakers intellectual limitations which would have prevented their speakers from independently evolving sophisticated scientific theories (in, for example, physics) and must, by implication, impose handicaps upon the progress of their speakers in learning the science subjects of modern educational systems, or in adjusting to an industrial economy where the measurement of time and speed — or simply obedience to a timetable — are important.

[. . .]

An open question

We may now grant that Sapir and Whorf may have overstated the extent and nature of the 'tyrannical hold that linguistic form has upon our orientation in the world'.[14] It is easier to accept Whorf's case that language *influences* how one perceives the universe, than his stronger case that the language one speaks *determines* one's conception of the universe.[15] Linguists have rightly pointed to the ability individuals possess, and have actually demonstrated, in breaking the 'conceptual fetters other men have forged',[16] as pioneers in every culture take one intellectual step outside the system evolved within that culture and embodied in its language. Yet for the *mass* of speakers round the world, development in their native culture and their attempt to adjust to other cultures will be heavily conditioned by the strengths and limitations of their native language or dialect. What earlier we were told was nonsense — a slur on other cultures — does now seem to be true. There may be whole areas of experience which are not covered by a given language or variety. It does not necessarily follow that speakers of that language cannot comprehend those new ideas or share that experience, but it is reasonable to assume that there are difficulties in the way of their doing so. A language which has a rich vocabulary *can* express subtleties of meaning which a language with a few words cannot; it is at least reasonable to suggest that some of these delicate nuances are unlikely to exist in the minds of those speakers unless the words exist by which to express them.[17] (The fact that some preliterate societies may already have a richer vocabulary for some natural or mystical phenomena will only help its members if those phenomena are important to the present stage of their cultural evolution.[8]) Similarly, the differences between languages in preliterate societies and in societies which have developed writing systems will reflect intellectual differences between those cultures, and in particular the access of their speakers to more advanced stages of intellectual development such as those described by some analysts as 'objective knowledge' and 'critical thinking'.[19] The studies known as 'science', as pursued in high schools and universities around the world, simply do not exist in the majority of the world's languages.[20]

Nor is it only the comparison between the languages of 'primitive' and 'advanced' societies which suggests implications for the intellectual processes of their respective speakers. As an Oxford classicist has recently written, 'In studying Japanese one is forced to recognise that what one had lazily assumed to be fundamental categories of human thought are merely local habits'[21] and another British scholar has even claimed that differences between the varieties of English spoken in Britain and in America carry differences of thought.[22] Actual examples of the intellectual consequences of the structures of specific languages are now being offered by the American scholar Alfred H. Bloom, who has produced evidence suggesting that educated Chinese speakers tend not to entertain certain kinds of theoretical speculation because their language does not contain the grammatical construction which would enable them to do so.[23]

So it is simply not true that all languages and dialects are equally 'good'. At best it is an open question, at worst it is fallacious and certainly all the formulations of the proposition which I have listed are dangerously misleading. [. . .]

A single shred

One consequence of the rejection of the 'all languages and dialects are equally good' theory would be to call in question the relationship between standard English and other varieties within our educational system, since we can now see that the use of different types of language can entail differential intellectual consequences and this could surely affect educational progress. It would be wrong to give the impression that those who reject this reasoning do so without a single shred of empirical evidence, for they do in fact point to a powerful study by an American sociolinguist, William Labov, which has exercised a seminal influence on both sides of the Atlantic. This [article 3.2 of this volume] first appeared as an article 'The logic of nonstandard English' in 1969, was reprinted as a chapter in his important book *Language in the Inner City* (1972) and has been republished again and again in numerous collections and sets of 'Readings' since then, in Britain and the U S A, including the Open University's source book *Language and Education* (1972). Indeed, it is referred to on many of the Open University's courses, its general argument has been made the basis of language policies in several countries besides the USA, and it may fairly be said to have passed into the sacred canon of modern linguistics.[24]

[. . .]

The crucial interview

Since the characteristics of non-standard Negro speech have been taken by some educational psychologists, as part of the theory of linguistic deprivation, to indicate deficiencies in the ability to handle logical argument, Labov is at great pains to prove that the black English vernacular is in no way inferior to standard English as a vehicle of logical discourse. This yields the most contentious, and the most significant, part of his whole article. He proceeds to offer a comparison between one interview with a 15-year-old black gang member, Larry, on the topic of life after death, with a single interview with a middle-class, college-educated black adult, Charles, on the subject of belief in witchcraft. Larry is said to be a typical speaker of the black English vernacular (B E V) as opposed to standard English, and to represent the typical rhetorical style of the B E V speaker. Larry's contribution to the interview requires a full grammatical explication by Labov, and also an extensive re-ordering by Labov of Larry's arguments into logical form and into standard English. [. . .]

By contrast the middle-class young black adult speaker of standard English, Charles, is quoted as having delivered one paragraph on witchcraft which (Labov claims) shows him to be intelligent, sincere, but tending to use more moderate and tempered language than Larry, and making every effort to qualify his opinions. This endows the quoted passage with what for Labov is its 'primary characteristic' — its verbosity.

There we have it, then. The comparison of these two interviews is used to support the key contention of Labov's article on 'the logic of non-standard English'. So far from being deficient in logic, speakers like Larry present their argument in ways which show them to be 'quick, ingenious and decisive',[25] where standard English speakers like Charles are 'enmeshed in verbiage',[26] 'simultaneously overparticular and vague',[27] cluttering up their assertions with qualifications like 'I think', with modal verbs (like 'may' and 'might'), humming and hawing, and using 'uncommon words', so that in the end 'words take the place of thoughts'.[28] The contrast is between the *precision* of the black English vernacular and the *empty pretension* of standard English.[29]

'More effective' English

Labov thus claims to have exploded two myths: that lower-class black children suffer any linguistic deficit; and that the standard English of the middle classes and of the school system 'is in itself better suited for dealing with abstract, logically complex, or hypothetical questions'[30] Indeed, Labov's claim goes further than that. This non-standard variety of English is not merely proved to be every bit as usable for the expression of logical argument as standard English, it is indeed superior: its speakers are '*more effective* narrators, reasoners and debaters' than many speakers of standard English.[31]

This sweeping judgement has been enormously influential, as I have indicated, among specialists in linguistics, among educationists, and on educational policies in the U S A, and has in turn had considerable influence on this side of the Atlantic. So let us remind ourselves of the research methods which underpin these conclusions. What Labov gives us is a comparison of the edited extracts of *two* taped interviews, followed by his own interpretation and comments. No *evidence* is presented on whether the interviews, or their subjects, can be regarded as representative. Labov's interpretation of what he claims is the essence of the argument of each speaker is Labov's own, and purely subjective. Given Labov's earlier insistence on the atmosphere of an interview as being crucial to its success in eliciting verbal behaviour which is genuinely typical of the speaker, it is odd that we are given no evidence on how far these conditions were satisfied in the case of the interview with Charles, the speaker of standard English. It is very noticeable that the development of the supposed 'logic' of Larry's brilliant argument (as interpreted for us by Labov) depends heavily on answers elicited from Larry in the course of a sustained two-way exchange in which it is the interviewer who opens up a number of key stages of the argument. But in the interview with the standard English speaker, the whole of the passage of argument attributed to Charles (and analysed adversely by Labov) is a sustained and extended answer to a single question from the interviewer, and the development of its argument does not depend on constant prompts from the interviewer. Yet it is Larry, whose 'argument' does require such prompts, who is credited with 'great verbal presence of mind'.

We are simply not comparing like with like. With a disingenuousness so colossal that it almost disarms, Labov at one point concedes that he is not offering systematic quantitative evidence,[32] yet the whole of the rest of his article presupposes that his analysis of these two interviews proves his case; and the whole of his attempt to assert the 'logic of non-standard English' depends on the comparison of these two interviews. At a later point in the article he uses his admission that these interviews are not controlled experiments as though it were some kind of merit, because they will help convince the reader that controlled experiments which have been offered in support of his *opponents*' case are misleading.[33]

An alternative explanation

What we have seen here is a travesty of scientific method. But even if Labov had provided proof of properly conducted experiments using representative sampling techniques under controlled interview conditions, he might still have come up with evidence suggesting that in comparison with less educated speakers of whatever variety of English, those who have experienced more education tend to indulge in longer sentences, with longer stretches of extended and unprompted explanation; and that part of this length and apparent 'verbosity' is contributed by forms such as 'I think', the use of modal verbs like 'may' and 'might', and many other signs of hesitation and, above all, of the need to qualify stated opinions. Everyone knows that it is easy to be 'spontaneous', 'direct' and 'precise' in your arguments if your education has not given you a knowledge of the complexity which surrounds any of the great issues — such as the existence of the supernatural — on which there is no consensus either among the uneducated or among the world's greatest thinkers. It is those who, like Charles, are at an intermediate but advancing stage of their intellectual development who are most susceptible to qualification, hesitation, repetition and thus verbosity. They have enough knowledge to perceive that a bold and precise answer is open to dissection and possible ridicule, yet their intellectual maturity has not yet reached the stage where they can expound a case which acknowledges both their own conclusions and their awareness of possible intellectual objections to their case, and other subtleties. A 15-year-old gang member who has turned his back on education and the things of the mind is only too ready to rush in with dogmatic statements which may merely reflect his own ignorance and prejudice.

[. . .]

The implications of academic credulity

What have we established so far about the list of quotations about the characteristics of different languages which represent the new orthodoxy in sociolinguistics and which underlie the attack on the teaching of standard English in schools?

We have seen how some of their most crucial assumptions are unproven. We can accept the important case that all languages and all varieties of any one language are likely to have a regular and consistent grammatical structure, and that specific ones should not be simply written off as debased, though we have not been given any evidence that all languages or dialects have grammatical structure of *equal* complexity. (This may be important, since there is mounting evidence that certain types of complexity of language may reflect corresponding complexity of thought.[34]

[. . .]

The standardization of English

Let us examine some of the implications of linguistic variation in Britain. Here we consider only the varieties of one language, English (since Welsh, Gaelic and the languages of twentieth-century immigrant groups are a separate problem). A specific form of English used for governmental purposes, and among the most educated, had emerged by the sixteenth century and the standardization of its written form was assisted by the development of the printing press. Regional dialects (with their own distinctive grammar, vocabulary and accent) continued to be spoken by all classes of society, though their decline, in competition with standard English, was rapid in the nineteenth century in the face of geographical mobility, the spread of mass education, and the mass-readership press. In the twentieth century, with the intensification of all these factors, and the standardizing influence first of sound broadcasting and the cinema and then of television, this decline became a rout.

Outside the odd Hovis TV commercial, there are almost no 'pure' dialect speakers left in Britain, though many people are still influenced by traces of the grammar, vocabulary and idiom of the original dialect of their region, and even more by its pronounciation. For a variety of reasons, this is likely to be truest of those with least education and those in the lowest social classes. Thus what used to be classified as a *regional* 'dialect' might nowadays more appropriately be described as a *social-class* dialect, or 'sociolect', though such sociolects will, of course, be distinguishable from each other by carrying traces of the dialects which were once spoken by all social classes in that region. Meanwhile there had emerged a standard form of accent, technically known as R P ('received pronunciation') and by around 1900 this form, or one very close to it and containing only a few vestigial features of one's original local accent, had come to be widely regarded as the only form compatible with 'educatedness'.[35]

In addition, large-scale immigration in the past three decades has brought into the country two main groups of speakers of other varieties of English: West Indians, who speak various forms of patois or creole, among whom speakers of the Jamaican English creole are the most numerous; and immigrants originating in the subcontinent of India (either direct, or via East Africa) whose varieties of English, developed during more than two centuries of contact between English and at least 16 major languages and more than 1700 dialects in that subcontinent, show marked differences of grammar, idiom and pronunciation (especially intonation) compared with all forms of British English.[36]

What are the consequences of speaking one of these dialects or sociolects rather than standard English? According to that school of linguistics which dismisses the concepts of linguistic or intellectual 'deficit', there can be no consequences for those speakers' intellectual progress. But we have seen how fallible the views of that school are — as I have stressed, this is still at the very least an open question. Ten years ago a whole generation of teachers in Britain were being trained up on the theories (or garbled versions of them) of the London University sociolinguist Basil Bernstein, who attempted to describe the different linguistic 'codes' — *elaborated* and *restricted* — which he claimed are characteristic of middle-class and working-class children respectively. Because of apparent shifts in Bernstein's own position on these, and the paucity of extended documentation of the syntactic and other ingredients of the two linguistic codes,[37] it is difficult to regard Bernstein's case as conclusive, and it is the fashion among the 'all languages are equal' theorists whom we have listed and examined, to dismiss Bernstein's case with scorn. But many teachers claim that his proposed analysis helps both to describe features of the sociolect of many of their disadvantaged pupils and to understand the conceptual difficulties which such pupils appear to face in some of their school subjects. They may, of course, be simply reading his analysis into experiences which deserve quite other explanations, but certainly Bernstein's case, despite all these reservations, can be said to have been more plausibly — and in some respects more 'scientifically' — argued than the contrary case put by Labov and his disciples.

So we do not know *for sure* what consequences there might be for the intellectual progress of a pupil in Britain who spoke a non-standard variety of English, though it has been pointed out that difficulties can arise for such speakers in the early stages of learning to read, from the greater mismatch between their pronunciation system and the orthography of standard English.[38] As there is a clearly established correspondence between a child's ability to learn to read and write, and his linguistic ability,[39] we just do not know how far that correspondence may be adversely affected by the child's speaking a non-standard variety of English.

What we *can* say is that the whole of our educational system, as at present constituted, presupposes the ability to handle standard English. This is the variety of English used by teachers themselves and it is the one in relation to which they tend, rightly or wrongly, to make judgements about their pupils. Among innumerable powerful pressures in this direction are the public examination system, the fact that all textbooks are written in standard English, and the general point, from which it seems impossible to escape, that there is a long-standing and now overwhelming association, right across British society, between the use of the grammar, vocabulary and idiom of standard English and the concept of 'educatedness'.

Dialect in school

Some of the experts whose statements we have examined would wish to challenge this — to dispute, not the fact that this *is* so, but that it *should* be so. They advocate the use of dialects and creoles in public examinations such as 'O' and 'A' levels and for university degrees. Dr Peter Trudgill, for example, has claimed that a high-level discussion of the poetry of Keats, written in such a non-standard dialect, is *just as good* as one written in standard English.[40] This point is also made by David Sutcliffe, whose study of varieties of Jamaican patois spoke in Britain likewise presupposes the unanimous recognition among linguists about all languages or dialects being equally good (see list, p. 164). In order to demonstrate that Jamaican creole is, like any other non-standard variety of English, capable of conveying the same nuances, and of entering into exactly the same degree of abstraction, as standard English, Sutcliffe shows how a portion of an academic thesis presented for a Master's degree of a British university could be written in Jamaican creole. [. . .] Readers might find it instructive to work out similar examples of academic argumentation transacted in (say) full-blown Cockney, or in a West Country dialect. It is not disputed here that this could be done, though we would need some hard evidence that the same nuances could be conveyed, the same degree of abstraction entered into. What is more clearly demonstrable, however, is the fact that it *is* not done: that these non-standard varieties are not, in actual practice, used as the vehicle of academic discourse. It may be pure social convention that tends to inhibit London-based Fellows of the Royal Society from beginning paragraphs in academic papers 'This 'ere bloke Einstein, wot done them experiments . . .', but that social convention is, in itself, a sociolinguistic *fact*.

This leads on to a second sociolinguistic fact: to foster the use of non-standard varieties such as these, at the expense of standard English, is to confront that convention in ways which cannot be to the benefit of the already disadvantaged speakers of non-standard forms. Because our society (like all known societies) does not respect all subcultures equally, and further, because of the inescapable connexions which have grown up between the concept of 'educatedness' and the ability to handle standard English, the non-standard speaker is put at an unfair disadvantage in any crucial encounter outside his own immediate speech-community — and, increasingly often, within his own speech-community as well. Since our citizens no longer live out their lives in the village, or even region, in which they grew up, they are constantly involved in exchanges — spoken or written — when their ability to be articulate in standard English is of vital importance to them. This may be at the trivial level of ordering a meal in a restaurant or, more seriously, having to ask for credit in a restaurant or shop, being stopped by a policeman or arguing with an official, voicing a grievance or making an effective complaint, giving evidence in a court of law or just generally asserting one's rights[41] — indeed, in any situation where authority, respectability or credibility are at issue. It is only too well known that that most superficial of all distinguishing aspects of language variety, accent, can be crucial at interviews for jobs, because of the prevalence of evaluations about the acceptability of various accents and their relative compatibility with 'educatedness' — evaluations which have long persisted across British society, show no real signs of abating, and moreover tend to be shared by the speakers of the most disparaged varieties of accent themselves.[42]

Accent is not the real issue here, since the majority of speakers with non-standard accents use standard English grammar and vocabulary. Thus the triumph of a London taxi-driver, who speaks with marked traces of a Cockney accent, in a *Mastermind* TV quiz series does not herald a sudden reversal of the long-established national prejudice which regards Cockney speech as incompatible with 'educatedness', since Mr Fred Housego's knowledgeable answers (and his other subsequent radio contributions) reflect an exemplary command of the grammar, vocabulary and indeed all the idioms and allusions that are characteristic of standard English.

[. . .]

A cruel trick

For schools to foster non-standard varieties of English is to place their pupils in a trap. To persuade such speakers that their particular non-standard variety of English is in no way inferior, nor less efficient for purposes of communication, but simply *different*, is to play a cruel trick. All the evidence we have suggests that listeners filter the messages they receive from utterances of other speakers in accordance with perceptions of those speakers which are heavily influenced by the standard or non-standard nature of the language of the utterance in question. Quite apart from this filter mechanism, we know that the use of non-standard English has the power to *distract* from the speaker's intended message. The 'adequacy for communication' of any language or dialect is therefore, at least in part, a function of those socio-linguistic factors which we have seen dictating the acceptability of such a language or dialect in specific situations, for specific functions, and specific audiences. Those quotations on our list (p. 164 above) which refer to *adequacy for communication* (especially, for example, Walt Wolfram's) must therefore be judged in the light of their neglect of this decisive consideration.

But social conventions about grammar or style (and it was partly style or 'register' which influenced our reactions to the 'academic' uses of creole or Cockney on previous pages) — and, even more, prejudices about accents — can and do change. For this reason it is argued, by those whose views have been criticized above, that it is simply a matter of education: all we need to do is to teach pupils in schools, and students in colleges, that the adverse reactions of society at large to particular aspects of specific language varieties are essentially the result of social or aesthetic prejudice. Thus it has become the fashion for a new generation of school textbooks on the English language to teach children to doubt whether standard English is in any way 'more correct', more elegant or a finer variety than any other, whereas 'it is just as correct as any other dialect'.[43]

Our first objection to this must be that, insofar as adverse judgements on specific language varieties *are* merely a matter of social convention or aesthetic prejudice, the task of altering long-held and widespread opinions in any society may be a formidable one, and this will be especially true in matters of aesthetic judgement. [. . .] It is true that gradual change, on a small scale, is always possible — indeed it is apparent now in regard to the notion of the 'standard' or 'correct' for both spoken and written English, which is changing in small ways all the time, and especially widening the range of variation it regards as acceptable compared with the past: it is becoming more tolerant, less 'posh', and in some matters less prescriptive. But that is entirely different from the quantum leap which is presumed by these theorists to be possible. What is more, while the concept of standard English becomes in some respects more accommodating, the prejudices against non-standard become, if anything, even stronger.

Dialect and communication

Our second objection must be that we have not conceded that the disabilities attaching to non-standard varieties of English are entirely a matter of convention or taste. Leaving aside the possibly 'open question' of any intellectual implications of such differences, we may ask whether it is just snobbery that causes teachers to encourage their pupils to move away from traditional non-standard speech forms, or might there be some inherent limitations in communication involved in their use? Consider the following utterance overheard in a London playground. Since some of my readers may be unfamiliar with the International Phonetic Alphabet I offer a rough-and-ready transcription into a kind of standard English spelling of one child's narration of an incident to another:

> *Ee ih er en she ih im sroy inih*

In Labov's terms, we could pronounce this an admirable utterance which exemplifies the child's completely regular and rule-governed phonological and grammatical system. On the model of Labov's explication of a passage of B E V, we could say in technical linguistic terms that, compared with standard English, this speaker has a different consonant system in word-initial position, here involving *h* (*he, her, him, hit*) and regular glottal stop for the alveolar plosive in certain intervocalic and word-final positions (*it, hit, right*) and a rule permitting deletion of the lenis dental fricative in certain environments, including word-initial position (*th* in *then*), a completely regular 'oy' for 'igh' (*right*); grammatically, the contraction of standard English's 'that's right' (*sroy*) and the application of a similar editing rule for standard English's tag-question 'isn't it?'

Though only one element in that utterance ('she') is completely recognizable as standard English, there is clearly no doubt of the communicative adequacy of the 'dialect' version of standard English's 'He hit her, then she hit him — that's right, isn't it?' among speakers of that self-same 'dialect', which is reasonably representative of one of the commonest varieties of non-standard English in an area where a recent survey found more than 50 different major languages and 24 overseas dialects of English in a sample of pupils studied.[44] But the adequacy for communication *outside* the limited community of speakers of this non-standard variety of English, like that of any one West Indian creole or any other of the distinctive dialects and sociolects currently spoken in Britain, is strictly limited; and the consequence of promoting the use of such language varieties in our school system, at the expense of standard English, might be to increase their facility to communicate with members of their own subgroup but must also disadvantage them outside it. If we accept the conclusion of the American scholar David Laitin that 'speaking that language of the state is often the critical condition enabling the citizen to participate in the political arena of the state',[45] and the further fact that, whether we like it or not the 'language of the state' in Britain is standard English, then any action which impairs the ability of any future citizen to communicate adequately in that medium is an act of political emasculation, quite apart from any specific threat it poses to that individual's likely success in the educational system.

[. . .]

The *real* logic of non-standard English

It is the parents among the underprivileged who understand all this better than anyone else — better even than their sons and daughters. When, 90-years ago, an inspector of schools in Rochdale urged the use of dialect in local elementary schools, the response of one dialect-speaking parent summed up their misgivings — (I translate): 'Keep the old Lancashire dialect out of the schools, Mr Wylie, for I want my children to talk smart when they grow up'.[46] In the U S A, black parents feel cheated and resentful over attempts to promote the use of 'black' English in the schools,[47] and even Labov has been forced to concede that 'both black and white sections of the community strongly endorse the proposition that schools should teach standard English to all children'.[48] On an 'open entry' programme for the underprivileged at a New York university, recent attempts to have the 'rich black American dialects' accepted for use in course work and exams in place of standard English, were rejected following representations from both students and black staff that standard English 'is the language of the Constitution and reaches more people globally'.[49]

In Britain, those groups who are at most risk of adverse discrimination purely by virtue of the colour of their skin, contain individuals who have already learned the same lesson. Almost without exception those members of ethnic minorities who aspire to more than local political prominence — as councillors on large authorities, or as parliamentary candidates — disdain the use of Caribbean patois, West African English or the English of the subcontinent of India, and contrive to speak standard English, some of them in fact with notably 'posh' accents. Exactly the same is true of those members of the same ethnic minorities who have achieved success on television, as actors or actresses, programme presenters, reporters or newsreaders.

Why, despite this kind of reaction from so many of the 'consumers' — the intended beneficiaries — do some educationists continue to propagate these dubious linguistic theories? One clue is provided by something the anthropologist (Sir) Edmund Leach wrote nearly 30 years ago:

> For a man to speak one language rather than another is a ritual act, it is a statement about one's personal status: to speak the same language as one's neighbour expresses solidarity with one's neighbours, to speak a different language from one's neighbours expresses social distance or even hostility.[50]

Let us take two specific varieties of non-standard English whose use in schools is now being actively promoted by some educationists with the support of the specialists in linguistics whose views we have analysed — Jamaican creole in Britain and the black English vernacular in America: two varieties which have in common the fact that their speakers are black. In both countries, the use of these forms of 'black English' is cultivated for the most part among the disaffected young and, at least in present-day Britain, this variety is actually learned as a second language by adolescent blacks (who already speak standard English or one of its regional variants) in order to assert their subgroup's differences from mainstream culture and their scorn for those who identify or collaborate with that culture. Its use is often accompanied by other anti-authority behaviour, including gang membership which is sometimes crime-oriented and involved in drug use; and the creole may be used on occasions specifically in order to irritate and confuse police or other representatives of authority such as teachers or youth club workers who happen to be white. Labov extensively documents the behaviour and attitudes which are associated with speakers of B E V: they tend to be anti-school — 'causing trouble in and out of school'; perhaps, like Larry, effective manipulators of their fellows; and they reject the formal educational offering of the school. They also reject as 'lames' those of their peer group who do collaborate with the educational system and attempt to succeed in it, and who resist pressures to steal, smoke, 'shoot up dope', etc.[51] In these, as in many other groups, the conscious choice of non-standard forms in preference to standard English also serves 'sexist' purposes, emphasizing the more dubious forms of *machismo* and male exclusiveness.[52]

A commentator in Britain has shown how this variety of 'black English' is used here by members of certain subcultures 'as a particularly effective way of resisting assimilation and preventing infiltration by members of the dominant [sic] groups. . . . As a living index of the extent of the black's alienation from the cultural norms and goals of those who occupy high positions in the social structure, the Creole language is unique'.[53] Another researcher in Britain suggests that those of West Indian origin who identify with British culture will show few Creole features in their speech; those who reject British society will show marked Creole features.[54]

It is understandable that some should argue for the promoting of specific language forms as a means of asserting one's ethnic identity and preserving one's cultural heritage. But it is illogical that those who do so should then complain if the assertion of that ethnic identity and cultural heritage is simultaneously used in order to reject the offerings of the educational system, *and* to complain of lack of success in that educational system or in the world of work to which such success provides the entrée. And the implications for race relations of promoting social divisiveness, aggression and even criminality have simply not been argued through.

[. . .]

It is this identification of standard language with 'authority', and the tendency to see the activity of teaching its grammar systematically to non-standard speakers as the imposition of adult authority, which have helped cause the welcome with which the anti-standard English campaign has been received among those who dispute the right of adults to set firm standards for the young. There are those who argue that to teach standard English is to impose the 'language of oppression', and it has been suggested that the support by liberal groups in the U S A for the use of 'black English' in schools is a form of expiation of guilt feelings over the nation's past record of slavery.[55] Yet, as we have seen, a far greater oppression lies in *not* giving proper opportunities of access to standard English. Ironically, there is evidence that in the days of the slave trade between West Africa and North America, measures were taken to ensure that boatloads of slaves did not all speak the same language, since linguistic diversity put them more readily at the mercy of the slavers.[56] [. . .] To sociolinguists like me, for whom all the speech forms of the dialects and other varieties of English in contemporary Britain are a source of fascination and joy, it is hard to have to face the sad but true fact that in a plural society the handicaps of disadvantaged groups can be increased by promoting linguistic diversity, as they can be reduced by fostering greater linguistic uniformity.

What can be done?

We have seen how a great industry has grown up, dedicated to disparaging standard English,[57] and we have seen how far that industry, manned by mutually supportive theorists, has been based on fantasies, fabrications and unproven hypotheses. Once that industry is shown up for what it is, we can make a start on reasserting the importance to all pupils in all British schools of achieving a ready facility in standard English.

For two decades and more, British teachers of English, aided and abetted by the public examination boards, have abandoned the formal teaching of grammar, to the extent that it has become common for pupils (even those proceeding to university to read English) not to know the names for parts of speech, or how to describe such basic linguistic phenomena as the functions of cases for the pronoun or tenses for the verb. If they come to know of these at all, it may well be because their teacher of French or German (or, for a tiny proportion of pupils, Latin) has been forced to take time out of his course to introduce these basic notions, whose use is obviously important to the handling of the properties of standard English and to describing the ways in which it differs from other varieties. The reassertion of the place of standard English in schools thus implies renewed attention to the teaching of grammar, though we have to recognize that this poses problems, not the least of which is the scarcity of teachers (whether notionally qualified in 'English' or not) who are able to teach it. During the years of neglect of this subject, the methodology of teaching the formal grammar of English to native English speakers has not made the progress evident[58] in the methods of teaching many other subjects, and it is only too well recognized that the old drills had serious limitations. As long ago as 1845 one of Her Majesty's earliest inspectors of elementary schools, Mr F. C. Cook, reported that 'it appears very questionable whether grammar should be taught as a separate subject', and 30 years later an even more famous HMI, Matthew Arnold, remarked that 'all that relates to language, that familiar but wonderful phenomenon, is naturally interesting if it is not spoiled by being treated pedantically'.[59]

It may well be that an inductive approach, which allows pupils to perceive how the grammar of the standard language works in actual use, is more effective than the once traditional grammar exercise, though the process of induction is unlikely to make much progress unless the child is introduced to some framework of basic grammatical classification, and the rest of the 'highway code' of spelling, punctuation, sequence of tenses and so on, which for the vast majority of children certainly do not develop 'spontaneously'.[60] Because the children of the privileged classes start out with more opportunities for absorbing painlessly the grammar and idiom of standard English in the home, it is the underprivileged who have suffered most from the fact that Britain is virtually the only advanced country in the world which does not teach the grammar of its language explicitly in its schools.[61] As a Cambridge don has recently put it, the only thing worse than teaching children the grammar of standard English is *not* to teach it.[62]

[. . .]

One consequence of the Bullock Report is that the 'study of language' now forms a more substantial ingredient in the training of many teachers, and the benefits of this will doubtless filter down eventually into primary and secondary schools. Yet we have this paradox: how can we seek to promote awareness among our pupils of how language works when the 'experts' in linguistics to whom they turn for guidance show themselves to be, on specific issues, so unscientific, so uncritical and so dangerously misleading? For the experts whose views we have examined are not the lunatic fringe of this important academic discipline: William Labov is one of the most distinguished sociolinguists working in the U S A and his contribution in some areas of this discipline — not least in methodology — is of major importance. This only makes the sleight-of-hand which we have examined in his most seminal article the more difficult to understand. Prof. David Crystal is likewise a leader in his own field, and has made particularly valuable contributions to the analysis of aspects of spoken English. Among those who have mediated these questionable theories to the teaching profession, the work of Michael Stubbs is notably well written and well (if perversely) argued.

[. . .] The aberrations we have exposed must serve, not to discredit the study of linguistics in education, but rather to emphasize the need for a more open and questioning approach, and certainly a more critical one than seems to be characteristic of the texts and courses of the Open University.[63]

Suppression or versatility?

What, then, would be a proper attitude on the part of teachers and schools towards the non-standard dialects and sociolects of their pupils? Must the child leave behind him at the school gates all traces of the subculture in which he grew up? The traditional approach of many British teachers, especially in the old grammar schools, was straightforward suppression: the non-standard forms were virtually outlawed in school and attempts were made, often with great insensitivity, to make pupils conform to a one-and-only 'correct' variety of written and spoken English.

Both in Britain and in the U S A, many of those educationists who have been influenced by the 'all varieties are equally good' theory have proposed a programme that has come to be called 'bidialectalism', which is designed to foster the child's use of his own non-standard language while giving him competence in a second dialect — standard English — whose use he will need for certain specific functions. Attention needs to be given, therefore, to exploring the functions or situations in which standard English is — not 'better' or 'more correct' — but more appropriate, more *acceptable*. This approach, it is claimed, has the merit that it avoids damage to the child's self-esteem which can in turn lead to confusion, lack of confidence and ultimately hostility to school.[64]

Even this compromise, however, does not satisfy those theorists who consider that to concede that the use of standard English in any situation in preference to one's original non-standard variety is more *appropriate* or more *acceptable* is to help prop up a hierarchy of social evaluation of language varieties, when all it needs is a campaign of boycott for the whole edifice to come tumbling down. (To quote the epic words of Dr Trudgill: 'Who is to say what is "acceptable" — and "acceptable" to who?').[65]

Since society has already answered that question in ways which Dr Trudgill and others are apparently unable to recognize, we must return to the problem of what approach we can realistically adopt. If I call my suggestion *bilectalism*, it is not merely because they are varieties of 'lects' at issue — social class varieties (socio*lects*) as well as regional dia*lects* — but because the difference between my proposal and the 'bi-dialectalism' that has been advocated so far, is that my starting-point is not any assumption about the 'equality' or 'equal goodness' or 'equal communicative adequacy' of the non-standard compared with the standard forms. It is, rather, a firm recognition that — as has been argued in this paper — the ends of social justice, the promotion of the underprivileged to success in our educational system, and the fostering of their ability to be articulate communicators *outside* their immediate social group, require that they achieve a ready facility in standard English, even at the expense of their development in their original non-standard variety. Even at the expense, I am tempted to add, of their self-esteem, though I am not excessively impressed by the argument that the teaching of standard English need cause all the consequences of shame, confusion, linguistic insecurity, alienation, etc. that have been made much of by the writers quoted. Any form of education which offers a child the possibility of moving away from his underprivileged origins involves numerous potential opportunities for initial embarrassment, and of learning to cope with new social situations; and most children take these in their stride. It would ultimately be crueller and more damaging to them if one succeeded in fooling them in believing that society will accord their non-standard language patterns that equality of treatment which certain theorists say they 'deserve'.

Nothing I have said on this need prejudice the quite separate issue of 'mother-tongue instruction' — the provision for immigrant children, at an early stage of their schooling, of teaching in their home language in ways which, some evidence suggests, may act as a useful bridge to their learning of English and the other subjects of the curriculum. The evidence is not yet conclusive, and may reveal that not all such foreign languages are equally effective when used in this way in British schools. Parents will need a great deal of convincing, certainly if Canadian experience is any guide. As a Toronto newspaper put it: 'Immigrants want their children forced to speak English at school, not given special programs in their own language . . . If native languages are used at school, it only makes it harder for children to learn English'.[66]

'Bilectalism' assumes that most children are capable of coping with a number of different linguistic styles, especially spoken styles,[67] and it is the aim of such teaching to extend their repertoire so that they can handle at least two — standard English, and the variety used at home and among friends (though home and friends may in turn involve two different kinds). If successful exploration of varieties of English leads some children to be able to handle yet other varieties, then our bilectalism becomes in effect multilectalism, and part of the exercise is to become sensitive to the situations in which the use of this variety, or that, is appropriate. But as yet we simply do not know enough about the distribution of these abilities among our pupils, and what considerations are likely to favour or limit their versatility — what I call the 'Y' factor: the ability, like the entertainer Mike Yarwood, to put on different 'voices' or linguistic styles. Though there is an enormous literature on bilingualism,[68] we know almost nothing about the implications of learning, or trying to keep up, two different varieties of the same language. Why is it that some people who have mastered standard English cannot continue to talk their native non-standard variety — or, if they do, are thought to sound partronizing? Do varieties of English which are more similar to each other present more problems than varieties which are very different,[69] on the principle enunciated by psycholinguists, that interference is most likely to occur where the languages are closely related? How can 'oracy' — the term popularized by the debate on the Bullock Report — be developed without a concerted effort to break down what two Glasgow researchers correctly described as the schools' 'taboo' surrounding social judgements about accent — 'a taboo subject even less mentionable than sex or money'?[70] Since we have put so much effort in the past two decades into changing the concept of the teacher as the central 'performer' into one of an 'enabler of learning', often presiding silently over mixed-ability classes working at different stages on work-sheets or interminable 'projects', how do we recapture the concept of the 'teacher as model' — perhaps the only exemplar of the rich resources of the educated and articulate speaker of standard English with whom some children will come into sustained two way contact throughout their early lives?

But it is difficult to see how my proposed 'bilectalism' can be used to encourage the use of dialects in spoken and written work to the extent demanded by the writers whose theories we have examined. The sheer multiplicity of language and dialect varieties, spread in uneven concentrations in certain specific parts of Britain and hardly present in many schools, makes it difficult to train enough teachers whose knowledge of the particular dialect concerned enables them to 'make a distinction between forms [used by pupils] arising from dialect, and forms which would be wrong in any dialect';[71] or teachers who could handle the fact that the speech of many young people in (say) Greater London may consist of a mixture of standard English, Jamaican patois and Cockney forms. The contention by John Richmond's collaborator, the London teacher-trainer Alex McLeod, that 'most young people enjoy writing in dialect'[72] may be true; his claim that this can make it easier for them to write 'good English' might also be true, though it is not yet proven.[73] But even he has to concede the volume of opposition he has met from parents and from teachers 'in London, Melbourne and Auckland', in 'Islington, St Vincent and Port of Spain', who think that bringing dialect into the English classroom is dangerous and subversive in that it undermines the rules of 'good English' and causes confusion. 'Another view is that it is a kind of trespass on private property, infringing on [sic] territory that dialect minorities want to keep to themselves'.[74] Unless teaching which incorporates the use of dialect can also convey sympathetically the realities of the relationship between standard and non-standard English in our society, the misgiving of those parents and teachers will surely be confirmed, and the handicaps of those pupils compounded.

'Educatedness' re-examined

For many reasons besides the issue of linguistic diversity, it is now proper — and some would say urgent — that we should reconsider the ingredients of our traditional British concept of 'educatedness' and question how far each strand is appropriate to the realities of a changed world. Ultimately we will have to face up to the fact that important elements of the common culture which shaped our model of the educated person's language are fast being lost — the influence of the Authorised Version of the Bible, of the Book of Common Prayer, and of *Hymns Ancient and Modern*. New elements with great pervasive potential are represented by the idiom of *Crossroads*, of *Coronation Street*, even of the jingles and catch-phrases of well-known television commercials; and the royal James who sponsored that influential translation of the Bible now counts for less than several other Jameses — like Jimmy Young, Jimmy Hill, Jimmy Saville. But at least it is true that what these new 'models' have in common is that, despite diverse regional origins, they exploit the resources of standard English — otherwise they could never be understood outside a very limited area of the United Kingdom.[. . .]

Notes

1 It is usually reckoned that there are over two million adult illiterates in Britain, most of whom are products of the school system.
2 This chapter, which originally appeared in *The English Magazine*, vol. 2, Autumn 1979 (published by the I L E A English Centre) was also reproduced as Chapter 2.2 in Alan James and Robert Jeffcoate (eds) (1981) London: *The School in the Multiracial Society*. London: Harper & Row/Open University Press.
3 Further examples continue to come to hand, e.g. the article in the *Educational Review* (Birmingham, **34**(1), 1982) which begins: 'It is now generally accepted amongst educationists that standard English has no inherent linguistic superiority over other regional and social varieties of English' (Jenny Cheshire, 'Dialect Features and linguistic conflict in schools'). See also J. C. B. Gordon (1981) *Verbal Deficit: A Critique*, p. 62; and Leo Loveday (1982) *The Sociolinguistics of Learning and Using a Non-native language*.
4 *Times Educational Supplement*, 21 May 1982, p. 18.
5 Levic Jessel (1978) *The Ethnic Process: An Evolutionary Concept of Languages and Peoples*. Hague, p. 125.
6 D. F. Swift, in Ken Richardson and David Spears (eds) (1972) *Race, Culture and Intelligence*. Harmondsworth: Penguin, p. 156.
7 J. R. Searle, TV interview with Bryan Magee, BBC 2, 26 March 1978.
8 Geoffrey Sampson. (1980) *Schools of Linguistics*, pp. 239, 77.
9 Ibid., p. 131; also John Lyons (1970/77) *Chomsky* , pp. 128, 135
10 Sampson (1980) op. cit., p. 96
11 Peter Trudgill, loc cit. The functional significance of different kinds of grammatical complexity is a poorly explored area among the linguistic theorists discussed here, though these questions were being asked 40 years ago by, for example, L. Bodmer in *The Loom of Language* (1944), esp. Chap. V I.
12 David Sutcliffe (1982) *British Black English*, pp. 99. For 'some', 'Taissey' ('teasy'), see

K. C. Phillipps (1976) *West Country Words and Ways*, pp. 40, 98.

13 E. Sapir (1931) 'Conceptual categories in primitive languages', in *Science*, **74**, p. 578, quoted in G. Sampson (1980), op. cit., p. 83.

14 Sampson (1980), op. cit., p. 83.

15 David D. Laitin, (1977), *Politics, Language and Thought*. Chicago op. cit., p. 143.

16 Sampson (1980) op. cit., p. 102.

17 It is revealing that some of the theorists cited imagine that they have disposed of possible limitations of specific languages by the argument that since evidence of what such speakers think can only be obtained via that language, this evidence is not testable by speakers of other languages.

18 Many linguists have referred in standard works to the more refined vocabularies of certain preliterate societies in respect of, for example, colour terms, snow, etc.

19 Michael Stubbs (1980) *Language and Literacy*, pp. 104–106; Jack Goody (ed) (1968) *Literacy in Traditional Societies*; Jack Goody (1977) *The Domestication of the Savage Mind*.

20 Pauline Robinson (1980) *ESP: English for Specific Purposes*, p. 25.

21 See H. B. Nisbet's review of two books by Prof. Hugh Lloyd Jones, *Times Higher Education Supplement*, 3 September 1982, p. 14.

22 J. G. Weightman, *Times Educational Supplement*, 25 January 1980.

23 Alfred H. Bloom (1981), Chapter I.

24 The original article appeared in *Georgetown Monographs in Languages and Linguistics* No. 22 (USA 1969). In addition to its inclusion as Chapter 5 in *Language in the Inner City* (1972) and the Open University source book *Language and Education* (1972, p. 198–212), as cited, its other reprintings, in whole or in part, include F. Williams (ed.) (1970) *Language and Poverty* (U S A); Nell Keddie (ed.) (1973) *Tinker, Tailor . . . The Myth of Cultural Deprivation* (Penguin); P. P. Giglioli (ed.) (1972) *Language and Social Context* (Penguin).

25 Ibid., p. 216.

26 Ibid., p. 214.

27 Ibid., p. 222.

28 Loc. cit.

29 Ibid., p. 214.

30 Ibid., p. 220.

31 Ibid., p. 213.

32 Ibid., p. 214.

33 Ibid., p. 220.

34 Lee Kok Cheong, *Syntax of Scientific English* (1978) (Singapore Unversity Press). pp. 7, 162 *et passim*. This important book has not been given the attention it deserves.

35 J. R. de S. Honey, 'Talking proper: aspects of the changing English concept of "educatedness" '. In G. Nixon and J. Honey (eds) *Studies in English Linguistics in memory of Barbara Strang* (forthcoming).

36 David Sutcliffe (1982) *British Black English*; R. K. Bansal (1969) *The Intelligibility of Indian English*; J. C. Wells (1982), *Accents of English*, Vol. III, pp. 624–631; Paroo Nihalani, R. K. Tongue & Priya Hosali, (1979) *Indian and British English (OUP)*; Joy Parkinson, (1979) 'English Language problems of overseas doctors working in the U K', in ELTJ, **XXXIV**, 2, January.

37 For critiques of Bernstein see, for example, J. R. Edwards (1979) *Language and Disadvantage* (Edward Arnold) pp. 33–49; M. Stubbs (1976) *Language, Schools and Classrooms* (Methuen), p. 46; N. Dittmar (1976) *Sociolinguistics* (Edward Arnold), Chapter I.

38 We refer to greater differences than those presented to all learners from the non-correspondence of British spelling to standard pronunciation. See M. Stubbs, (1980) *Language and Literacy*, esp, Chap. II

39 *Times Higher Education Supplement*, 10 September 1982, review by Prof. Peter Bryant of Oxford, p. 17.

40 P. Trudgill, (1975) *Accent, Dialect and the School*, p. 80.

41 See, for example, E. A. Lind and W. M. O'Barr in H. Giles and R. St. Clair (eds) (1979) *Language and Social Psychology*.

42 See for example, H. Giles, 'Our reactions to accents', *New Society*, 14 October 1971; H. Giles and P. F. Powesland (1975) *Speech Style and Social Evaluation*; R. A. Hudson (1980) *Sociolinguistics*, esp. pp. 195–206; K. R. Scherer and H. Giles (1979) *Social Markers in Speech*; J. R. Edwards (1979), pp. 93–95.

43 Maura Healy, *Your Language (I)* (1981), Macmillan Education (1981), p. 59.

44 H. Rosen and T. Burgess (1980) *Languages and Dialects of London School Children*, pp. 61–66.

45 David Laitin (1977: see note 15 above), p. 3.

46 B. Hollingworth (1977) 'Dialect in school, an historical note'. *Durham Research Review*, **VIII**, (39) pp. 17.

47 J. L. Jaffney and R. Shuy (1973) *Language Differences — Do They Interfere?* (U S A), p. 150.

48 W. Labov (1972), p. 241.

49 L. Kitchen, 'Billy Budd in a Brooklyn School', *Times Higher Education Supplement*, 2 April 1982.

50 E. R. Leach (1954) *Political Systems of Highland Burma*, p. 39.

51 W. Labov (1972), p. 258; Stephen Eyers and John Richmond (1982) *Becoming our own experts* (Vauxhall Manor School/Talk Workshop Group/Schools Council), p. 61.

52 For a discussion of the work of Labov and Trudgill on sex differences among non-standard English speakers, see J. R. Edwards (1979), pp. 90–93.

53 D. Hebdige (1976), quoted in V. K. Edwards (1979),*The West Indian Language Issue in British Schools* (London: Routledge and Kegan Paul). p. 88.

54 V. K. Edwards (1979: note 53 above), p. 89.

55 This view is also hinted at in, for example, N. Postman (1970) 'The politics of reading'. *Harvard Educational Review*, **40** (2), May 1970.

56 Quoted in D. Bolinger, *Language, the Loaded Weapon* (1980) p. 46.

57 John Richmond, teacher-adviser in the Inner London Education Authority, writes of 'the prestige dialect misleadingly known as Standard English' (1979: see note 2 above).

58 Yet the analysis of English grammar itself has made great strides in recent years: cf. especially the work of Randolph Quirk, J. McH. Sinclair, M. A. K. Halliday and the late Barbara Strang (to whose teaching I acknowledge a personal debt).

59 Matthew Arnold, General Report for 1876.

60 Bullock Report (1975), pp. 170–172.

61 See also John Haycraft (1982) 'English at work in the World (II), *Journal of the Royal Society of Arts*, No. 5311, Vol. CXXX, June 1982, p. 410.

62 Jonathan Steinberg, (1982) 'No more grammar'. *New Society*, 25 March 1982.

63 The largest single occupational category represented among the student body of the Open University are school teachers.

64 Trudgill (1975: note 40 above); V. K. Edwards (1979: note 53 above). p. 101.

65 Trudgill (1975), p. 77.

66 *Toronto Star*, 3 October 1975.

67 J. R. Edwards (1979), pp. 66–67; see also Mercer and Maybin 'Community language and education', in N. Mercer (ed.) *Language in School and Community* (Edward Arnold) (p. 86), cited note 69 *infra*.

68 For an overview and select bibliography see E. Glyn Lewis (1981) *Bilingualism and Bilingual Education*; T. S. Donahue (1982) 'Toward a broadened context for modern bilingual education'. *Journal of Multilingual and Multicultural Development, Vol.* **III**, 2, 1982 (esp. bibliography, pp. 86–87).

69 This possibility is dismissed by two Open University course writers who describe such difficulties as a 'strange notion' comparable to the suggestion that 'learning French entailed forgetting English, or learning Rugby entailed forgetting soccer' (Mercer and Maybin: note 67 above). But cf. Einar Haugen's comment that such bilectalism 'may actually be harder to acquire than bilingualism', because 'it is harder to keep two similar languages apart than two very different ones' ('Bilingualism and bidialectalism', in R. Shuy (ed.) *Social Dialects and Language Learning*, N. C. T. E., Illinois, 1965).
70 Quoted in M. Stubbs (1976), p. 30.
71 Stephen Eyers and John Richmond (eds) (1982: see note 51 above), p. 434.
72 Ibid., p. 435
73 Loc. cit.
74 Loc. cit.

3.4 A Review of *The Language Trap*

J. R. Edwards

Source: Edited version of Edwards, J. R. (1983) 'A review of The Language Trap'. *Journal of Language and Social Psychology*, Vol. 2, No. 1, pp. 67–76.

In the 11 June 1982 issue of the *Times Higher Education Supplement*, Professor John Honey reviewed Sutcliffe's recent book on black English (1982). He was especially critical about the 'now statutory incantation' that all languages and dialects are equally good, and of the desire to *foster* Black English at school. Honey implied that, in some senses, equivalent goodness may not be a feature of linguistic varieties; and, on the second point, he presented practical and philosophical reasons why schools should not *foster* this nonstandard English. I place the word *foster* in italics because Honey uses it twice in his short review (and several more times in the monograph under review here) and because it reflects an important distinction to which I shall be turning later. Given that the tone of Honey's review was so unlike the usual linguistic/sociolinguistic line, I found it surprising that it evoked only two responses, neither of them particularly incisive.

Now, Honey has expanded his line of argument into a short monograph, provocatively titled. His main points are easily grasped and, in fact, are exactly those noted above. He claims that recent linguistic theory, supporting the view that all varieties of language are equally good, is without any basis whatever. And this, especially in the current climate of unease over allegedly poor standards of written and spoken English at school, is most pernicious for it undercuts any attempt to reintroduce 'standards'. Consequently, disadvantaged speakers of non-standard English (N S E) are the victims of a 'cruel trick' and fall into the 'language trap'; they need help in standard English (S E) so as to make real socioeconomic advance, yet the modern linguistic paradigm insists that, out of respect for their indigenous linguistic forms (which are of equal status to S E) and group identity, schools should encourage the use of N S E.

I must say that, in my own recent excursions into linguistic difference-deficit controversy (Edwards, 1979), I have often felt that the linguistic difference position, although philosophically on sound ground, carried with it an overly sanguine, perhaps naive, view. Just get disadvantaged speakers to realize the linguistic and aesthetic worth of their N S E, just change the prevailing attitudes towards their varieties (first at school, and then at large), and the sociolinguistic problems of the N S E speaker will vanish. Such a view absurdly underestimates the continuing power of what we may term *social* deficits. That is, we may fully espouse the difference position, yet may also realize that, for all intents and purposes, differences *are* deficits if that is how they are generally seen. Linguists and others have been too optimistic in thinking that public opinion will be significantly and quickly altered, merely on the basis of objective data. Precedents for this are thin on the ground, and all we know about preferences, prejudices and stereotypes leads to the observation that, once adopted, they are clung to tenaciously for reasons which social psychologists have been describing for a long time.

I therefore welcomed the chance to read and think about Honey's monograph, since a scholarly critique of prevalent trends in educational linguistics is somewhat overdue. We have, of course, had any amount of popular reaction in the press to these trends. When, for example, Trudgill — a linguist particularly singled out for attack by Honey — was interviewed in the *Sunday Times* (29 February 1976), he reported receiving a great many letters opposing his ideas. Indeed, there are almost regular philippics nowadays about poor levels of English ability, about the need to return to some sort of standards, and about the insidious influences of modern linguists. However, all of this might be sidestepped as uneducated opinion or a reflection of ignorance of subtle linguistic arguments. But now we have a professor of education enter the arena, and we expect a more equal contest.

I find Honey's argument a very curious one, not because it is at all unclear but because, after attacking many theorists who I have supported in my own summary of the area (Edwards, 1979), Honey arrives at a conclusion apparently quite similar to my own. This suggests that the shaping of Honey's argument is, in the present sociolinguistic climate, worth a close look. For he reads Labov, Trudgill, Crystal, Lyons and others, rejects their positions, and proposes 'bilectalism' as the solution to the educational problems of N S E speakers. I read these same writers, generally accept their views, and argue for 'bidialectalism'. Since there is little substantive difference between the two terms in quotation marks, it is of interest to me — and to others, I presume, especially those who have ranged themselves on the side of Labov et al. — to discover just how Honey proceeds. To anticipate my conclusions here, I can say that he tends to exaggerate somewhat the claims of contemporary linguistics, refutes these exaggerations, and arrives finally at a position which not only seems quite reasonable but is also one which many sociolinguists would not reject. Honey's task is eased here by the fact that some of the individuals whose work he criticizes are indeed guilty of inflated and naive statements, statements which unfortunately detract from what is, in my view, the generally positive influence of modern forces in educational linguistics. I propose, therefore, to proceed straightforwardly through Honey's argument, attempting to show the weaknesses of *both* the criticizer and the criticized.

Honey's basic argument

[...]

Honey begins by attacking the notion that all languages (and, by extension, dialects) are equally good. He provides quotations from ten writers (including Crystal, Lyons, Trudgill, Stubbs, V. Edwards and Sutcliffe) who claim, among other things, that language is always sufficient for the needs of its speakers, and that no variety is superior to another. But how, says Honey, can speakers in primitive tribes cope with higher mathematics, or Wittgenstein, or biochemistry? Secondly, if all varieties are adequate for group needs, then Honey argues that groups lacking the necessary vocabulary do not *need*, for example, modern technology or medicine.

In both cases, Honey confuses concepts with words. If a group, for example, begins to take an interest in simple arithmetic and, five hundred years later, develops a theory of quantum mechanics it is surely reasonable to see that words will grow with increasing sophistication. This is, in fact, what happens. There is, as well, no need to look at primitive societies (in whatever sense 'primitive' is construed) here: consider our own intellectual and linguistic development. Secondly, and relatedly, it is the lack of the prerequisite conceptual understanding which prevents a group from possessing modern medical procedures. Words themselves are only indicators. Thus, the real meaning of a statement like 'language is adequate for its speakers' needs' refers to the fact that language keeps pace with conceptual advancement, which in turn determines the needs which speakers can even be aware of. While it is true that some of the statements by linguists cited by Honey do state the language–needs relationship too naively, it is unworthy to respond in kind.

Honey next contends, *contra* the linguists, that there is no evidence that languages keep pace with the social development of their users (a view cited from Crystal). But surely (and see above) the evidence of life is compelling here. Honey says, specifically, that there is a time lag between conceptual and linguistic advance, and that some advanced individuals within a group find themselves without vocabulary for naming or describing a new phenomenon. On these points, I would say simply that there must obviously be a finite lag between new ideas and new terms, but this lag varies inversely with the general importance of the idea. How long did it take for 'astronaut' to catch on? And, even while it was still to make its entrance, there were all sorts of other descriptive terms to fill the temporary void (we no longer hear 'spaceman' very much). Description, albeit rough, is always possible. Thus, while the scientist searches for the word 'laser' he is perfectly able to convey the *idea* of what the word represents to others; in fact, if he could not, the new word itself would be empty. All of this rests upon accumulated conceptual advancement, and we have not, so far at least, had an instance of such a gigantic leap forwards that description has proved impossible.

[...]

Honey's opening arguments fail, therefore, because he confuses words with concepts, although he is abetted here by less than careful statements from the 'experts'. If we understand the state of a group's conceptual development — and this applies to groups more *or* less advanced (in any given sense) than us — then language *does* keep pace with social development and in that way is as 'good' as any other. Perhaps if Honey had looked further in linguistic literature, beyond the almost motto-like statements he cites, he would have come across more careful assessments. Hymes (1974), for example, has noted that languages are not all equal in complexity and Keenan (1974), more carefully still, that they are not equivalent in expressive power across the same range of contexts.

Since Honey claims there is no real evidence for the 'all-varieties-are-equally-good' position, how does he explain its retention? First, he says that it has become *unfashionable* to judge other societies and groups and, by implication, their languages. Secondly, he cites the influence of Chomsky. On the first point, Honey remarks that this view is now changing, and that we now feel more and more a *duty* to pass comparative judgements. He gives two examples, neither of which will have any relevance if my preceding points have been accepted; however, they may be illustrative of his approach. The crimes of the Nazis and the Stalinists, Honey notes, cannot be excused simply because those committing them might have acted within their own cultural values; and cannibal tribes should not escape value judgements because eating people is traditional practice for them. These examples, of course, are some way removed from linguistic matters. If we are able to condemn murder in a foreign society should we then feel more entitled to question the 'goodness' of its language? At the individual and the social level, we wrestle more often with questions of degree than with ones of principle. Criticism of language and criticism of murder both involve making judgements, but the similarity pretty well ends there.

Chomsky is discussed here because of his theory of innate predispositions for language (a theory which Honey feels lacks firm experimental backing — a bit unfair, perhaps, under the physiological circumstances). This implies that all languages are essentially similar at some deep level. Honey claims that this theory lends support to the 'equal goodness' idea since, if all human beings share an underlying linguistic patterning, qualitative judgements are unacceptable across languages. I suppose this is true but, unlike Honey, I don't think that if all of Chomsky's 'innate' theory were completely swept away the arguments that all varieties are adequate for their users would be seriously weakened. This is because to counter *this* argument — bearing in mind the association noted above between conceptual advancement and language development — one would have to claim that different groups of human beings differ appreciably in their innate conceptual powers. I feel that Honey himself would not wish to claim this (especially given his remarks on Jensen, below).

Before I leave Honey's treatment of Chomsky, however, I must reproduce one curious quotation [pp. 167–8]:

> It is especially paradoxical that supporters of extreme egalitarianism and 'progressive' notions in the social sciences should be willing to swallow, without any substantial evidence, a set of hypotheses based on human heredity — since the assertion that innate characteristics may be more crucial than acquired ones (for example, in the development of intelligence) has long been condemned by exactly such people as giving scope to 'racist' conclusions (as in the Jensen controversy).

This seems very perverse. With regard to language, it is because of the *equal* hereditary contribution proposed by Chomsky that the 'egalitarian' sociolinguists (and others) may feel on firmer ground. But, with regard to intelligence, Jensen's proposal was of an *unequal* hereditary distribution across groups. So, to support a Chomskian innate-language notion and to reject Jensen's innate-intelligence one is not paradoxical at all.

Honey continues by further examining the possibility that some languages are poorer than others for certain intellectual tasks. Given what I've said already, we can clearly state that some *are* poorer — if we consider intellectual activities which are not themselves comparable across groups. Enter the Whorfian hypothesis. If we accepted its strong form — that language *determines* thought — we could agree that certain varieties impose real limitations upon their speakers. But this form is not generally accepted. The easiest evidence against it is the fact that speakers of a 'limiting' variety can and do adjust to new conditions [. . .] It is one thing to say that there may be adjustment problems, or that progress may initially be slow for speakers of certain varieties when placed in a new context; it is another to claim that adjustment is impossible.

The weaker Whorfianism — that language influences our habitual activities — is more reasonable, and Honey accepts it (although his implication that the earlier, strong form faded because it became 'unfashionable' is hardly fair to a reasoned evolution from strong to weak Whorfianism). He thus notes again that a given variety may not cover certain aspects of experience, that speakers of that variety may have difficulties comprehending these aspects, and that certain nuances are likely to evade them. All true, but irrelevant to the 'goodness' of the variety in question. So, when Honey states that 'cultural biases of different societies shape thought, and linguistic structures contribute to this' [p. 12 of original], he is either reverting to the strong Whorfianism ('shaping' is not, after all, 'influencing') — which is itself wrong — or he is endorsing the weaker form (in which case he *should* have said 'influencing'), which is irrelevant to his argument.

Before going on from his rejection of the 'equally good' argument, Honey refers to Labov's famous article on Black English (1973). He claims that this supplies the only real shred of evidence for the modern linguistic case; however, the evidence is spurious and, Honey asserts, Labov's study is a 'travesty of scientific method' [p. 173]. Although Labov would not, I am sure, claim that his work is the only support for the case in question, it is fair to say that it has been very important and influential. How can Honey so scathingly denounce a study which approches sacred status in sociolinguistics?

There are four important aspects to Labov's article: (a) his criticism of the usual interview methods which led to labelling black children as verbally deprived; (b) his claim that the black community is a verbally rich one; (c) his comparison of lower-class and middle-class black speech patterns, and his support for the former; (d) his demonstration of the regular, rule-governed nature of black English. Honey accepts that Labov's first point is plausible — threatening atmospheres may well lead to poor oral performance — but that it is not backed up by much firm evidence. However, there is considerable evidence on this point, deriving not only from linguistic studies but also from broader investigations of lower-class and minority group life-styles and attitudes (on reactions to authority figures, for example). The evidence comes from groups other than black English speakers, too (see Shuy, 1971; Philips, 1972; Edwards, 1979; see even Bernstein, 1973). On the second point, Honey again claims that Labov's verbally rich black culture is without documentation and, again, this is inaccurate. A great deal of evidence shows Labov to be right (see, e.g. Kochman, 1972; Abrahams, 1976; Edwards, 1979). There is some indication that Honey does not care for the *form* this quality takes among black speakers, but that is another question entirely.

When we turn to the third aspect of Labov's article — a comparison of interviews, on the subjects of the existence of God and witchcraft — I do agree with Honey that Labov has overstated his case. Labov feels that the direct, unqualified response of the lower-class adolescent, compared to the qualified and uncertain reply of the middle-class adult, shows the power and, indeed, the superiority of the former. The lower-class patterns are quick and decisive; the middle-class ones, verbose and redundant. As I have noted (Edwards, 1979), however, qualification and redundancy probably reflect an educated awareness of the longstanding complexities attaching to abstract and important problems. This awareness is completely lacking in the adolescent's jejune comments. This in itself, of course, says nothing about the adequacy of Black English, although it may be revealing of the abilities of 15-year-olds, black or white. As well, as Honey points out, Labov gives us only two interviews here — hardly an exhaustive survey.

Honey errs, however, when he claims that Labov's analysis of the logic of non-standard English rests on the interview data alone. Much more important are Labov's investigations of the grammatical regularities of Black English (1973; see also Labov, 1976). Honey acknowledges that these are 'defensible' but gives them only a sentence or two [. . .], thereby missing the real force of Labov's work. This leads him (Honey) to state that Labov's efforts have been 'swallowed whole', where a fairer assessment would indicate that careful sociolinguistic scrutiny has convinced many that the arguments of Labov (and others) for dialectal validity are compelling. Honey also swipes at the value of the demonstration of rule-governed regularity by saying that 'it is unfortunate that not all linguists agree on what these rules are' [p. 16 of original]. This, however, is equally true for all varieties, including S E, and misses the essential point that linguists *do* tend to agree that the rules exist.

[. . .]

Educational implications

In the second half of his monograph, Honey turns to the educational consequences of the argument that, since linguistic varieties are *not* equally good, verbal deficit (which may entail intellectual deficit) remains a possibility. I can be briefer here in my comments on Honey's remarks since his case now rests upon the foundations which I have tried to show are without solid support. Still, there are some matters of interest.

Honey suggests that proponents of the 'difference' position feel that speaking N S E has no consequences for intellectual progress. But, of course, it has great consequences and difference theorists recognize this — the thrust of their position is simply that these rest upon social attitudes which may see linguistic difference as linguistic deficit. Honey is confused if he cannot see that linguistic difference can be *social* deficit.

The position of Bernstein — and the elaborated and restricted codes — has been a controversial one and (whatever Bernstein's present or past intentions) has fuelled the linguistic deficit argument (Edwards, 1979). Consequently it has been rejected, as Honey notes, by difference theorists. Yet he claims that, for many teachers, Bernstein's analysis helps to describe pupils' dialects and aids in the understanding of their conceptual difficulties. Of course it does — although here Honey, so critical of lack of evidence in others, gives no data for his assertion about teachers — since if a theory doesn't *seem* to make sense to at least some people, it evaporates. This has nothing to do with its correctness. Ptolemaic astronomy described things quite well, but it was quite wrong. The fact is that a deficit position, whether associated with Bernstein's restricted code or not, is simply untenable in the light of available linguistic evidence.

Honey next notes that the present educational system is built upon SE, and that some linguists wish that this were otherwise. I agree completely with Honey that this wish is misplaced. It is undoubtedly true that some difference theorists, hoping to push their arguments of linguistic equivalence to the logical extreme, claim that schools should cater for and *foster* N S E. However, things should only be pushed to logical extremes within systems of logic, and society is not such a system. Apart entirely from the impracticality of schools thus promoting N S E varieties, the power of social preference (or prejudice), which renders difference into deficit, would make such a policy a 'cruel trick' as Honey rightly states. But here I can finally explain why Honey's frequent use of the term *foster* confuses things. The gist of my argument so far is that, based upon linguistic evidence, schools must accept N S E varieties as valid systems. It follows that teachers should not try to stamp out these varieties, nor should children be stigmatized for using them. However, because of social realities, it does *not* follow that schools should *foster* N S E — they should, in fact, continue to provide S E models and to promote awareness of the subtleties and uses of this form, within an atmosphere of tolerance and respect for all other forms (this, of course, is a delicate undertaking; see Edwards, 1979).

So, I agree with Honey that for schools to actively promote N S E would be counterproductive. However, I reject his line of argument insofar as it implies that a difference position leads *only* to this business of fostering. I don't deny at all that many of the people he criticizes *do* see active school promotion of N S E as the outcome of their theoretical position — but that is their weakness. It is in this way that Honey — who, as I do, endorses a policy of linguistic addition which does not involve active educational promotion of N S E — incorrectly makes his final rejection of the difference position and the one conclusion to which he thinks it leads.

On some other related matters, I find myself agreeing with Honey again. He correctly notes the glibness with which some call for altering social views of speech; he sees the limitations which an active knowledge of *only* a non-standard variety can impose — and acknowledges that those most aware of these limitations are the parents of NSE-speaking children; he points to the idiocy of an American programme for rewriting textbooks in many varieties of NSE. Yet, in nearing his conclusion, Honey implies something organized, perverse and even sinister in the theories and statements of those of whom he is critical:

> We have seen how a great industry has grown up, dedicated to disparaging standard English, and we have seen how far that industry, manned by mutually supportive theorists, has been based on fantasies, fabrications, and unproven hypotheses. [p. 181]

This is surely an unwarranted and emotional statement which, even if Honey's arguments were correct and those of the others wrong, can do his case no good.

Concluding remarks

At the end, as I have mentioned, Honey proposes 'bilectalism' as the desired outcome for N S E speakers. There is really no difference between this and the 'bidialectalism' which I (and others) have endorsed, although Honey mistakenly thinks, as noted above, that bidialectalism implies fostering N S E at school. In some ways, though, his bilectalism is rather curious. For example, he considers facility in SE to be clearly pre-eminent over N S E development, even at the expense of children's self-esteem. Since the idea that attempted eradication of NSE can lead to psychological damage has been a powerful contemporary argument (see, e.g., Halliday, 1968), it is a bit surprising to see Honey treat the matter lightly. He states [p. 184]:

> I am not excessively impressed by the argument that the teaching of standard English need cause all the consequences of shame, confusion, linguistic insecurity, alienation . . . any form of education which offers a child the possibility of moving away from his underprivileged origins involves numerous potential opportunities for initial embarrassment.

While I agree that the teaching of S E, if done in a tolerant atmosphere, does not necessarily lead to damage (indeed, I strongly support the teaching of the standard at school), the second part of the quotation is intriguing. Can bilectalism — involving, according to Honey himself, linguistic repertoire *extension* — really include *moving away from* origins?

I have the impression that, at this conclusion to his monograph, Honey is not after all totally committed to bilectalism as most would understand it. This impression is strengthened by his penultimate paragraph in which he compares traditional shapers of education and language (the Bible, and prayer and hymn books) with contemporary influences (*Crossroads, Coronation Street*, television advertisements). I think he overstates his case here; there have always been 'contemporary' influences on culture, side by side with more enduring ones, which have aroused the concern of educators and others (Edwards, 1981). In fairness, Honey does acknowledge that we 'have to face up to the fact that important elements of the common culture which shaped our model of the educated person's language are fast being lost' [p. 186], but am I wrong in detecting a tone of regret that the *status quo* must change? It lends a special piquancy to the whole monograph to consider that Honey's underlying reason for writing may be, after all, a desire to defend traditional values. For, as to values, the arguments he criticizes throughout have, or should have, no relevance at all.

References

Abrahams, R. D. (1976) *Talking Black*. Rowley, Massachusetts: Newbury.

Bernstein, B. (1973) 'A brief account of the theory of codes'. In V. Lee (ed.) *Social Relationships and Language*. Bletchley: Open University Press.

Edwards, J. (1979) *Language and Disadvantage*. London: Edward Arnold.

— (1981) 'The reading public and the school'. In J. Edwards (ed.) *The Social Psychology of Reading*. Silver Spring, Maryland: Institute of Modern Languages.

Halliday, M. A. K. (1968) 'The users and uses of language'. In J. Fishman (ed.) *Readings in the Sociology of Language*. The Hague: Mouton.

Hymes, D. (1974) 'Speech and language: On the origins and foundations of inequality among speakers'. In E. Haugen and M. Bloomfield (eds) *Language as a Human Problem*. New York: Norton.

Keenan, E. (1974) 'Logic and language'. In E. Haugen and M. Bloomfield (eds) *Language as a Human Problem*. New York: Norton.

Kochman, T. (1972) *Rappin' and Stylin' Out: Communication in Urban Black America*. Chicago: University of Illinois Press.

Labov, W. (1973) 'The logic of nonstandard English'. In N. Keddie (ed.) *Tinker, Tailor . . . The Myth of Cultural Deprivation*. Harmondsworth: Penguin.

— (1976) *Language in the Inner City*. Philadelphia: University of Pennsylvania Press.

Philips, S. (1972) 'Acquisition of roles for appropriate speech usage'. In R. Abrahams and R. Troike (eds) *Language and Cultural Diversity in American Education*. Englewood Cliffs, NJ: Prentice-Hall.

Shuy, R. (1971) 'Sociolinguistic strategies for studying urban speech'. *Bulletin of the School of Education (Indiana University)*, **47**, 1–25.

Sutcliffe, D. (1982) *British Black English*. Oxford: Blackwell.

3.5 Sociolinguistics and Gender Divisions

J. French and P. French

Source: French, J. and French, P. (1984) 'Sociolinguistics and gender divisions'. In Acker, S. *et al.* (eds) *World Yearbook of Education 1984: Women and Education*. London: Kogan Page, pp. 52–63.

Introduction

In this chapter we present and discuss a range of research into language and gender. In the main, we shall confine our attention to work which investigates differences in men's and women's use of language and their social-interactional behaviour (Kramer, 1977).

The chapter is organized around two central themes: first, women's and men's use of prestige and low-status linguistic forms and the role of each sex in bringing about language innovations, and second, the alleged tentativeness of women in social interactions and men's dominance in mixed-sex conversations. Although we refer to studies relating to these issues collectively as 'sociolinguistic' research, this is merely a convenient cover term, for they do not share a unitary set of research assumptions and methods. As we shall be passing critical comment upon the assumptions made in some studies, it is helpful to begin with a brief statement explaining two methodologically distinct strains of sociolinguistic work.

Form-based and activity-based approaches

Undoubtedly, there are many dimensions upon which studies of socially situated language could be arrayed and contrasted. For the purposes of this chapter, however, we shall simply distinguish between form-based and activity-based approaches.

We use the term 'form-based' to denote studies which have emerged from, or are aligned with, a linguistic (as opposed to sociological) tradition of analysis. Studies of this kind take linguistic forms — grammatical constructions, words or pronunciation features — as their basic units of analysis. Samples of language are scanned for instances of particular linguistic forms, and attempts are then made to establish statistical correlations between their incidence and facets of speaker identity. By working in this way, studies have been able to show that language varies not only in accordance with the particulars of the 'local' interactive situation (the setting and purpose of the communication), but also with more 'enduring' speaker characteristics. Social class, education, occupation and, as one might expect, gender have all been established as important predictors of the form one's speech will actually take (Labov, 1972; Trudgill, 1974; Hudson, 1980).

As we shall suggest, form-based studies have yielded much useful information about women's and men's differential use of high- and low-status forms of language, and about gender as a factor in linguistic change. However, we shall also argue that there is a danger of extending this approach into areas it is ill-suited to illuminate. In particular, it would seem that it cannot provide one with reliable information about the claimed tentativeness of women in social interaction (Lakoff, 1975), or men's tendency to dominate mixed-sex talk. If understanding of these issues is to advance, the approach required is an activity-based one.

By 'activity-based' we mean an approach to the study of language in use which takes as its basic elements not linguistic forms but interactional activities. Socially situated utterances not only express referential meanings but also perform activities (Turner, 1974a; Austin, 1976). Conventional labels for these activities include 'questioning', 'promising', 'inviting', 'refusing' and so on, and considerable headway has been established within the sociological subdiscipline of conversation analysis in examining how activities from the various classes are managed and coordinated. (For explanatory introductions to this work, see Atkinson and Drew, 1979, Chapter 1; Wootton, 1981a; for overviews see Atkinson and Heritage, Introduction; 1984.) A small but growing body of work has begun to use insights provided by this tradition as a resource for investigating gender differences in interaction. Through examining who typically does what in mixed-sex talk, for example interrupting, requesting confirmation or reassurance, or giving or withholding supportive feedback, activity-based studies have made a promising beginning at answering questions of whether women are less assertive than men and how men achieve conversational dominance over women.

Before proceeding to these studies, we shall first examine the issues of gender-differential use of prestige and low-status forms, areas to which the former, form-based studies have made a substantial contribution.

Prestige and low-status forms

Most, if not all, languages are internally differentiated in terms of both grammar and sound structure. As social-psychological investigations have firmly established, certain regionally marked systems of grammar (dialects) and pronunciation (accents) carry less prestige than others, and tend to be judged negatively in comparison with regionally neutral systems (Giles et al. 1975; Giles and Powesland, 1975).

A large body of form-based sociolinguistic work has been directed towards plotting the incidence of prestige and low-status accent and dialect forms across subpopulations of language communities (Trudgill, 1974; Dittmar, 1976; Hudson, 1980). Studies which have examined the occurrence of such features against speaker gender suggest that, in general, men are most likely to use low-status forms. Some examples of findings from these types of study are represented below. (For a further indication of findings in relation to accent alone, consult Farb, 1973; Kramer, 1975; for a review which includes dialect forms see Trudgill, 1974, Chapter 4).

With regard to dialect, data from Shuy's study of Detroit English show, as one might predict, that the use of non-standard, multiple negation (for example, 'I don't want none') increases as one descends through the social class bands (U M C, L M C, U W C, L W C). However, within each class, one finds many more instances of these forms being produced by men than by women (Trudgill, 1974). Trudgill has disclosed similar trends in relation to accent, both by reference to the Detroit data and to his own work on Norwich English (1974, 1975a). In respect of the Detroit study, it is shown that some speakers use an 'r' consonant (usually termed 'post-vocalic 'r') at the ends of words such as 'car' and 'better' and before other consonants in words like 'hurt' and 'park' whilst others do not. In America, the high-status pronunciation is with the 'r' present and the low-status without the 'r' (in fact, the reverse of the situation for British English). Again, speakers belonging to the lower social groupings utilized more 'r'-absent forms than did those from the higher ones, but men across the social classes used more 'r'-absent forms than did women (see also Levine and Crockett, 1966). A similar pattern is thrown by data from Trudgill's Norwich study where, in words like 'walking' and 'speaking', women of all social classes showed a much lesser tendency than men to use the low-status pronunciation with an 'n' consonant in final position (see also Fischer, 1958). This same type of distribution by gender is also reported in more recent work on language and social networks where it is noted that, with regard to the vowel and consonant systems in Belfast speech, men use 'higher levels of the vernacular variants than women' (Milroy, 1980, p. 157). And yet further instances are provided by Shuy et al. (1967) and Wolfram (1969).

There are occasional exceptions to the tendency. For example, Labov (1972) notes that the Chicago accent is undergoing changes to its vowel system, and that these are most apparent in a low-status group: 'young working-class speakers'. Of the vowel shifts recorded in the casual speech of people in this category, though, 'it is the women in the group who show the most extreme forms' (1972, p. 302). A similar finding is reported in Labov et al. (1972) with regard to women's use of non-prestigious vowel pronunciations in New York. However, the general picture is that, as Trudgill says, 'Men's and women's speech . . . is not only different: women's speech is also (socially) "better" than men's' (1974, p. 94).

There is a good deal of evidence that women's greater linguistic 'correctness' is not only a matter of conventionalized habit, but that their speech may, in fact, be targeted towards prestige norms. When informants are faced with speech situations of increased formality (for example, having to read aloud from prepared texts or word lists), women shift their speech more sharply towards received standards than do men (Fischer, 1958; Labov, 1966; Levine and Crockett, 1966; Labov, 1972). Further, when asked to provide self-reports on pronunciation, women tend to state that they speak in a more standard fashion than they actually do, whereas men evince the opposite trend (Trudgill, 1975a).

Women's and men's different aspirations towards received standards result in a gender-differential division of responsibility for advancing linguistic innovations. In general, the situation is such that the new vernacular forms become established, in the first instance, through the speech of males. Women, on the other hand, tend to be prominent in developing new prestige forms (Anshen, 1969). (See Trudgill, 1974, pp. 98–101 for instances of this trend from American Indian languages, Norwegian, British and American English; see Labov, 1972, pp. 301–304 for some counter-instances.)

An understanding of why women should aspire to the use of high-status forms is, as yet, imperfectly developed. Trudgill, for example, has explained the situation in terms of women being 'more status-conscious than men, generally speaking' (1975a, p. 91). And their status-consciousness is, he suggests, in turn precipitated by macro-economic and social factors: 'Since they are not rated [by society] by their occupation or by their occupational success, other signals of status, including speech, are correspondingly more 'important' (1975a, 91–92). However, it is quite possible that women's greater 'correctness' has as much to do with gender-differential linguistic socialization as with a general status-consciousness. As Clarricoates (1980) remarks in an ethnographic study of a British primary school: 'There was . . . a verbal double standard, with teachers censuring girls more harshly than boys for using improper language' (p. 33). We shall return to this point in our concluding section where we consider the classroom as a forum for the acquisition of gender-differentiated linguistic and interactional practices.

The avoidance of vernacular forms which carry associations of 'roughness' is only one from a range of language features which researchers have attributed to women, and which, it is claimed, render their language behaviour 'more polite than that of boys or men' (Lakoff, 1975, p. 19). Other features said to operate to this effect are the tendency to avoid strong expletives (Jespersen, 1922, pp. 246–247; Kramer, 1975, Lakoff, 1975, p. 10) and terms of obscenity (Miller and Swift, 1977, pp. 111–122), together with 'an absence of . . . strong statement' (Lakoff, 1975, p. 19). This last claim by Lakoff, that women tend to make greater use of various 'weaker' modes of expression, has initiated a number of empirical studies of the form-based type. We shall examine the claim in some more detail below, and attempt some critical appraisal of the work which has attempted to investigate it.

Tentative expression and male assertiveness

Lakoff suggested that women's avoidance of 'strong statements' was observable in their formal features of intonation and grammar. In particular, tag questions (for example, 'isn't it?', 'aren't you?') and rising intonation were thought to be relevant.

Tag questions are claimed to attenuate or downgrade the force with which statements are expressed. Thus, the sentence with the tag attached ('Books can impart knowledge, can't they?) is said to be less definite and less forceful than its non-tagged equivalent ('Books can impart knowledge'). Lakoff proposed that the tag question 'is more apt to be used by women than men' (1975, p. 16), and that, by using it, they avoid commitment and hence potential 'conflict with the addressee' (1975, pp. 16–17). Whilst being quite clear that this was an 'impression' and that she did not have 'precise statistical evidence' relating to women's greater use of the form (1975, p. 16), the contention that women were the predominant tag users nevertheless quickly found its way into subsequent sociolinguistic statements on language and gender (Thorne and Henley, 1975a). However, in a thoroughgoing empirical study of tag questions in one (albeit limited) authentic social setting (an academic meeting), Dubois and Crouch have reported that 'men did, and women did not, use tag questions' (1975, p. 294). To the best of our knowledge, there is no evidence for the view that women and men make differential use of tags as a general feature of their language.

A second indicator of female tentativeness outlined by Lakoff was the use of rising intonation. The production of declarative sentences on rising pitch is said functionally to transform them into 'yes/no' questions ('Books can impart knowledge?'). Lakoff's suggestion was that women use this pattern of pitch in their responses to questions about matters upon which they alone can deliberate (A: 'What time will dinner be ready?' B: 'About six o'clock?). Thus, answers which one might expect to be delivered in a relatively certain or definitive way are made to sound 'as though one were seeking confirmation' (1975, p. 17).

Although there is some rather anecdotal indication in a study by Brend that women may make distinctive use of a rising 'request confirmation' contour (1975, p. 85; Key, 1972), a more recent study by Edelsky (1979) which set out directly to test Lakoff's hypothesis failed to find supportive evidence. Although Edelsky found that in interviews women did show a very slight tendency to produce a subtype of rising tone (rise–fall–rise), the functional value of this tone may have been not tentativeness but incompleteness: through its use 'the women might have been trying to facilitate the interview or continue the interaction' (Edelsky 1979, p. 28). As with tags, there is little empirical support for the view that women make greater use of rising, 'questioning' intonation than men.

Finally, a third form which has been linked with women's inclination towards 'weak' expression is the qualifier. Some types of qualifier which can operate as sentence adverbials are said to downgrade the assertiveness of statements in a way similar to tags ('Perhaps books can impart knowledge' may equal 'Books can impart knowledge, can't they?'). Unlike tags and questioning intonation, there does appear to be some evidence for a gender-differential distribution of these forms. In a study by Hartman (1976) it was found that women made greater use of qualifiers whereas men made more use of absolutes. However, we would suggest that the significance of this finding should be approached with caution in view of the points disscussed below.

Of the forms examined here it seems that, with the exception of qualifiers, there is scant evidence of gender-differential usage. One can be sure, however, that further attempts will be made (and probably are being made) to establish such usage. It is clear to us that research into this particular area of language and gender would profit from methodological reflection. The question we would pose is this: if a study were done which linked, unequivocally, the vast majority of tag questions to women, could one then conclude with any certainty that women were more tentative than men in expressing their meanings? Contrary to the reasoning informing form-based studies in this area, we think not. Our grounds for taking this view concern the disjunction which often exists between researchers' abstract, a–contextual specifications of the meanings of linguistic forms, and the meanings these forms may actually express in empirical instances of usage. It has long been recognized within certain traditions of linguistic philosophy and microsociology that there is no homological relationship between linguistic forms and meanings (Garfinkel, 1967). A given meaning (such as 'tentativeness') may be expressed through a variety of linguistic forms, and any form is capable of realizing not one but many meanings (Heritage, 1978). The actual meaning that an empirical production of a form is expressing cannot be derived from linguists' statements about what the form 'seems to mean' when considered out of context, but only by examining it against the backcloth of discourse in which it occurs (Schegloff, 1977). An inkling of how this may relate to tag questions is provided in Dubois and Crouch's (1975) study. On the basis of previous work and personal communication, they note that, in addition to 'signalling lack of confidence', tags 'can function as a request'; they can express condescension; and they can be used in an 'overbearing' way to 'forestall opposition' (p. 292). Yet a further deployment is mentioned by Wootton (1981b) who provides transcripts of interactions where they are used to solicit responses in certain types of communication breakdown. We would be surprised if this list exhausted the functions that tags are capable of fulfilling. In the light of it, though, it becomes clear that a statement of tag frequencies may mask what is happening in interactions. Speakers *might* be expressing tentativeness in using them; on the other hand, they might not. One cannot simply set up tags, or other linguistic forms, as objective indices of speaker tentativeness and then plot their incidence against speaker gender. Or, if one does, one is likely to be rewarded with unreliable information.

This becomes even more apparent when one considers that at least some aspects of women's and men's usage may operate simply to display gender identity. It has long been known that in the Koasati language, for example, women and men until quite recently used different words and constructions to refer to the same objects, events and processes (Haas, 1944). It is now emerging that there are similar (perhaps more subtle and less immediately visible) conventions operating within modern European languages. In Local's (1986) work on urban Tyneside English, for instance, it was discovered that formal patterns of intonation of the type we have been discussing were used mainly by women. Men used high-level tones as their neutral, or unmarked, contour on statements, whereas women's neutral contour was a rise. There is no functional significance attaching to this beyond the display of gender-identity, however; women's rising tones do not signify, and are not taken by their interlocutors as signifying, a confirmation-requesting intent. It is quite possible that women's frequent use of, for example, qualifiers, as found by the Hartman study, has little to do with the meanings 'hesitant' or 'tentative' (1976, p. 87), but serves simply to mark out their speech as 'female speech'. The interpretation is purely speculative, and there is nothing much to recommend it over other possibilities. This, however, is our whole point. Statements of gender-differential distributions of forms and structures in themselves tell one very little about the sorts of issues at stake here; they allow for *no more than* speculation. Whilst a form-based approach may illuminate women's and men's different orientations towards 'correct' grammar and pronunciation, it is not a suitable tool for investigating the present area. If one is to gain reliable knowledge of whether women are more tentative or less forceful interactants than men, then the place to begin is by looking at the interactional activities women and men perform with respect to one another.

There is, in fact, a small but rapidly increasing, number of activity-based studies in this area. These studies begin from the proposition that 'power and hierarchical relations are not abstract forces operating on people' and that 'power must be a human accomplishment situated in everyday interaction' (Fishman, 1978, p. 397). If, as feminist researchers have suggested, male–female relationships are hierarchically organized so that men wield the power (Spender, 1980), then one would expect power to be made manifest in asymmetries between the activities women and men perform in everyday social encounters. Drawing upon the descriptions of, for example, turn-taking systems (Sacks et al., 1974) and devices for securing speaker attention (Schegloff, 1977; Sacks, 1974) provided by conversation analysts, some researchers of gender have begun to investigate this possibility. To conclude this section we shall briefly consider their findings.

In a study of couples interacting in their homes, Fishman (1978) notes that the women, unlike the men, frequently prefaced utterances on new topics with 'attention beginnings'. These activities function to secure the interest and attention of the other party and take such forms as 'this is interesting . . .'. In performing them, Fishman suggests the women were showing that they 'cannot assume the remark itself will be seen as worthy of attention' by their male partners (1978, p. 401; see also Bernard, 1972). Similarly, once they had begun to speak, the women heavily interspersed their remarks with utterances designed to elicit evidence of listening from their partners (for example, 'y' know?), thereby showing that they were anticipating problems in being able to hold their attention. When male partners were speaking, however, females showed a strong tendency to insert unsolicited 'minimal responses' like 'yeah', 'umm', 'huh', thus giving the men constant supportive feedback on what they were saying (see also Hirschmann, 1974). In view of these observations, Fishman concludes 'there is a division of labor in conversation' whereby 'the people who do the routine maintenance work' are the women (1978, pp. 404–405).

In contrast to this, men's conversational work is seen as non-supportive. Although they used the same minimal response forms as women, they showed less inclination to insert them within the flow of women's talk. The forms 'yeah' and 'umm' tended to be produced only after the women had completed a lengthy remark, and fulfilled a different type of activity. They were used in a way that displayed 'lack of interest' and served as attempts to 'discourage interaction' (Fishman, 1978, p. 402). (A purely form-based study undoubtedly would have missed this difference.) This finding was further elaborated in a similar study by Zimmerman and West (1975) of talk between acquaintances. Here it was found that not only were men's minimal responses to the women 'retarded beyond the end of the utterance' but sometimes also delayed 'by pauses of up to 10 seconds in length' (p. 122). The latter study also showed that in single-sex interactional dyads (both female-female and male-male), interruptions 'seem to be fairly equally divided between the first and second speaker' (p. 115). However, in mixed-sex dyads, of 48 interruptions, 46 were produced by males and only 2 by females. In interpreting the findings, the authors conclude: 'we view the production of both retarded minimal responses and interruptions by male speakers interacting with females as an assertion of the right to control the topic of the conversation reminiscent of adult-child conversations where . . . the child has restricted rights to speak and to be listened to' (Zimmerman and West, 1975, p. 124).

More recent work by Edelsky (1981) on turn-taking and floor-holding in academic meetings bears out this view of men as 'directors' of mixed-sex interactions, but also provides some rather telling findings about the conditions under which interactional inequalities may be levelled. Edelsky (1981) distinguishes between two types of conversational floor. The first is 'a singly developed floor' which one speaker holds while others attend. The second type is a more 'collaborative venture where several people seemed to be operating on the same wavelength or engaging in a free-for-all' (p. 383). In singly developed floors, 'the men held forth, took longer turns though not more of them . . . dominated the construction of floor by virtue, at least, of the time they took talking' (p. 415; see also Wood, 1966; Chesler, 1971; Swacker, 1975). In collaborative floors, however, differences in male and female turn length were equalized. Further, in these situations women were found to be 'joking, arguing, directing, and soliciting responses more and men less' (Edelsky, 1981, p. 415). These findings suggest that when there is a collaborative, or supportive, aspect to the interaction, women feel able and inclined to take an equal part in the proceedings. It was this very element of interactional support that Fishman and Zimmerman and West found being denied to women both by their male acquaintances and their sexual partners.

It is clear that the results of these studies on female–male interaction are of more than purely academic interest, and bear close relevance to the formulation of social and educational policy. We shall take up this point in the concluding section of the chapter.

Conclusion

In substantive terms, two general trends have emerged from the studies of language, interaction and gender discussed here. First, available evidence overwhelmingly suggests that the forms of language women use approximate more closely than those of men to prestige norms, and second, that, in social interactions, the part played by women tends to be supportive while that of men is dominant. In discussing the studies which have produced these findings, we have devoted space to methodological criticism. An awareness of methodological issues is, we believe, extremely important in this area. Given that in many nations gender divisions in society are becoming a subject of political debate, and that the findings of academic researchers may be used to influence social policy, it is necessary that those findings arise from sound methodological footings. Indeed, it is at least partly this type of concern that has dictated the range of topics addressed here. Sociolinguistic study has the potential to illuminate areas of language and gender other than sex-differential usage and interactional behaviour. One such area concerns differences in language (oral and written) used to describe women and men. As yet, however, this field is relatively underdeveloped, with available studies relying quite heavily upon a–contextual methods of linguistic analysis (Schulz, 1975; Spender, 1980, pp. 14–19) or 'journalistic' commentary (Miller and Swift, 1977, pp. 55–70). Another area of relevance is the disparity between the language used to address women and that used to men. Again, the little available work directly on this topic tends to be form-based (Brouwer et al. 1979), and thereby suffers from the problems of interpretation outlined earlier (but see Brooks Gardner, 1980). Accepting for the present, then, the limitations of our focus, what social directions does the work on usage and interaction suggest to us?

In our thinking, the research bears obvious relevance to teachers' practices in the school classroom. We suggested earlier that differences in adult women's and men's use of 'correct' forms may be partly attributable to teachers' enforcing different linguistic standards for girls and boys. As Trudgill (1975b) has pointed out, there are very good reasons for teachers not intervening in any child's use of regional speech, but if we have a situation where some pupils are corrected whilst others are not then this clearly is in need of remediation.

With regard to male dominance in mixed-sex interaction, we have ourselves found evidence of this in British primary school classes of children as young as 10 and 11 years (French and French, 1983). In one lesson, which comprised 66 pupil turns at interaction, 50 of these were produced by boys who numbered less than half the class (see also Brophy and Good, 1970, p. 373; Galton et al., 1980, p. 66; Stanworth, 1981; Spender, 1982). What is more, a good many of these turns were not 'spontaneously' allocated to boy pupils by the teacher, but achieved through interactional techniques designed to gain the teacher's attention. Whilst the point at which these techniques is acquired is, as yet, unknown, it nevertheless seems clear that a first step towards evening out the imbalance consists in making teachers (in addition to others) aware of them. As we conclude in the original study, 'much would be gained from developing, in the context of teacher education programmes, an interaction-based approach to language and gender which sought to increase teachers' knowledge and awareness of what may be involved' (French and French, 1983, p. 12).

References

Anshen, F. (1969) Speech variation among Negroes in a small Southern community. Unpublished dissertation. New York University, New York.

Atkinson, J. M. and Drew, P. (1979) *Order in Court: The Organization of Verbal Interaction in Judicial Settings* London: Macmillan.

Atkinson, J. M. and Heritage, J. C. (1984) 'Conversation analysis'. In Atkinson and Heritage (1984).

Atkinson, J, M. and Heritage, J. C. (eds) (1984) *Structures of Social Action*. Cambridge: Cambridge University Press.

Austin, J. L. (1976) 'How to do things with words'. In Urmson and Sbisa (1976).

Bernard, J. (1972) *The Sex Game*. New York: Atheneum.

Brend, R. M. (1975) 'Male-female intonation patterns in American English'. In Thorne and Henley (1975b).

Brooks Gardner, C. (1980) 'Street remarks, address rights, and the urban female'. In Zimmerman and West (1980).

Brophy, J. E. and Good, T. L. (1970) 'Teachers' communications of differential expectations for children's classroom performance: some behavioural data'. *Journal of Educational Psychology*, **61**(5), 365–374.

Brouwer, D., Gerritsen, M. and De Haan, D. (1979) 'Speech differences between women and men: on the wrong track?' *Language in Society*, **8**, 33–50.

Chesler, P. (1971) 'Marriage and psychotherapy'. In Radical Therapist Collective (1971).

Clarricoates, K. (1980) 'the importance of being Ernest . . . Emma . . . Tom . . . Jane . . . The perception and categorisation of gender conformity and gender deviation in primary schools'. In Deem (1980).

Deem, R. (ed.) (1980) *Schooling for Women's Work*. London: Routledge and Kegan Paul.

Dittmar, N. (1976) *Socio-linguistics: A Critical Survey of Theory and Application*. London: Arnold.

Dressler, W. U. (ed.) (1977) *Current Trends in Textlinguistics*. Berlin: de Gruyter.

Dubois, B. L. and Crouch, I, (1975) 'The question of tag questions in women's speech: they don't really use more of them, do they?' *Language in Society*, **4**, 289–294.

Dubois, B. L. and Crouch, I. (eds) (1976) *The Sociology of the Language of American Women PISE Papers IV*. San Antonio, Texas: Trinity University.

Edelsky, C. (1979) 'Question intonation and sex roles'. *Language in Society*, **8**, 15–32.

Edelsky, C. (1981) 'Who's got the floor?' *Language in Society*, **10**, 383–421.

Farb, P. (1973) *Word Play: What Happens when People Talk*. New York: Knopf.

Fischer, J. L. (1958) 'Social influences on the choice of a linguistic variant'. Word, **14**, 47–56.

Fishman, P. (1978) 'Interaction: the work women do'. *Social Problems*, **25**(4), 397–406.

French, J. and French, P. (1983) Gender imbalances in the primary classroom: an interactional account. Unpublished paper, New College, Durham.

French, P. and MacLure, M. (eds) (1981) *Adult-Child Conversation*. London: Croom Helm.

Galton, M., Simon, B. and Croll, P. (1980) *Inside the Primary Classroom*. London: Routledge and Kegan Paul.

Garfinkel, H. (1967) *Studies in Ethnomethodology*. Englewood Cliffs, NJ: Prentice Hall.

Giles, H., Bouris, R. Y. and Davies, A. (1975) 'Prestige speech styles: the imposed norm and inherent value hypotheses'. In McCormack and Wurm (1975).

Giles, H. and Powesland, P. (1975) *Speech Style and Social Evaluation*. London: Academic Press.

Haas, M. R. (1944) 'Men's and women's speech in Koasati'. *Language*, **20**, 142–49.

Hartman, M. (1976) 'A descriptive study of the language of men and women born in Maine around 1900 as it reflects the Lakoff hypothesis'. In Dubois and Crouch (1976).

Heritage, J. C. (1978) 'Aspects of the flexibilities of natural language use' *Sociology*, **12**, 79–103.

Hirschmann, L. (1974) 'Analysis of supportive and assertive behaviour in conversations'. Paper delivered to meeting of Linguistic Society of America, July.

Hudson, R. A. (1980) *Socio-Linguistics*. Cambridge: Cambridge University Press.

Jespersen, O. (1922) *Language: its Nature, Development and Origin*. London: Allen and Unwin.

Johns-Lewis, C. (ed.) (1986) *Intonation and Discourse*. London: Croom Helm.

Key, M. R. (1972) 'Linguistic behaviour of male and female'. *Linguistics*, **88**, 15–31.

Kramer, C. (1975) 'Women's speech: separate but unequal'. In Thorne and Henley (1975b).

Kramer, C. (1977) 'Perceptions of female and male speech'. *Language and Speech*, **20**(2), 151–161.

Labov, W. (1966) *The Social Stratification of speech in New York City*. Washington, DC: Centre for Applied Linguistics.

Labov, W. (1972) *Sociolinguistic Patterns*. Philadelphia: University of Pennsylvania Press.

Labov, W., Yaeger, M. and Steiner, R. (1972) *A Quantitative Study of Sound Change in Progress*. Final report on National Science Foundation contract N S F-GS-3287, Philadelphia.

Lakoff, R. (1975) *Language and Woman's Place*. New York: Harper and Row.

Levine, L. and Crockett, H. J. Jnr (1966) 'Speech variation in a Piedmont community: postvocalic r.' In Lieberson (1966).

Lieberson, S. (ed.) (1966) *Explorations in Sociolinguistics*, special issue of *Sociological Inquiry*, **36**(2).

Local, J, K. (1986) 'Patterns and problems in a study of Tyneside intonation'. In Johns-Lewis (1986).

McCormack, W. C. and Wurm, S. (eds) (1975) *Language in Anthropology IV: Language in Many Ways*. The Hague: Mouton.

Miller, C, and Swift, K. (1977) *Words and Women*. London: Gollancz.

Milroy, L. (1980) *Language and Social Networks*. Oxford: Blackwell.

Radical Therapist Collective (eds) (1971) *The Radical Therapist*. New York: Ballantyne.

Sacks, H. (1974) 'On the analysability of stories by children'. In Turner (1974b).

Sacks, H. Schegloff, E. A. and Jefferson, G. (1974) 'A simplest systematics for the organisation of turn-taking for conversation'. *Language*, **50**, 696–735.

Schegloff, E. A. (1968) 'Sequencing in conversational openings'. *American Anthropologist*, **70**, 1075–1095.

Schegloff, E. A. (1977) 'On some questions and ambiguities in conversation'. In Dressler (1977).

Schulz, M (1975) 'The semantic derogation of women'. In Thorne and Henley (1975b).

Shuy, R., Wolfram, W. and Riley, W. K. (1967) *A Study of Social Dialects in Detroit*. Final report on Project 6-1347. Washington, DC: Office of Education.

Spender, D. (1980) *Man Made Language*. London: Routledge and Kegan Paul.

Spender, D. (1982) *Invisible Women: The Schooling Scandal*. London: Writers' and Readers' Co-operative Group with Chameleon Editorial Group.

Stanworth, M. (1981) *Gender and Schooling: A Study of Sexual Divisions in the Classroom*. London: Women's Research and Resources Centre.

Swacker, M. (1975) 'The sex of the speaker as a sociolinguistic variable'. In Thorne and Henley (1975b).

Thorne, B. and Henley, N. (1975a) 'Difference and dominance: an overview of language, gender, and society'. In Thorne and Henley (1975b).

Thorne, B. and Henley, N (eds) (1975b) *Language and Sex: Difference and Dominance*. Rowley, Mass.: Newbury House.

Trudgill, P. (1974) *Sociolinguistics: An Introduction*. Harmondsworth: Penguin.

Trudgill, P. (1975a) 'Sex, covert prestige, and linguistic change in the urban British English of Norwich'. In Thorne and Henley (1975b).

Trudgill, P. (1975b) *Accent, Dialect and the School*. London: Arnold.

Turner, R. (1974a) 'Words, utterances and activities'. In Turner (1974b).

Turner, R. (ed.) (1974b) *Ethnomethodology*. Harmondsworth: Penguin.

Urmson, J. O. and Sbisà, M. (eds) (1976) *How to do Things with Words* 2nd ed. Oxford: Oxford University Press.

Wolfram, W. (1969) Linguistic correlates of social stratification in the speech of Detroit Negroes. Unpublished thesis, Hartford Seminary Foundation.

Wood, M. (1966) 'The influence of sex and knowledge of communication effectiveness on speech'. *Word*, **22**, 112–37.

Wootton, A, (1981a) 'Conversation analysis'. In French and MacLure (1981).

Wootton, A. (1981b) 'Children's use of address terms'. In French and MacLure (1981).

Zimmerman, D. H. and West, C. (1975) 'Sex roles, interruptions and silences'. In Thorne and Henley (1975b).

Zimmerman, D. H. and West, C. (eds) (1980) *Language and Social Interaction*, special issue of *Sociological Inquiry*, **50**, 3–4.

SECTION IV

Literacy, its Nature and Development

Introduction

Although decades of research have provided a great deal of information about the nature of literacy and its development, there are still key issues on which researchers do not agree. One of the most interesting concerns the possible effects of becoming literate on a person's way of thinking. Thus it has been claimed that the use of certain kinds of logic, and the development of a capacity for explicit, abstract and generalized modes of communication are facilitated by (or even derived from) the acquisition of literacy. If this is so, then there are educational implications. The prominent place occupied by the teaching of literacy within our school system is additionally justified, for being illiterate must represent not only a lack of access to written information but also an impediment to the acquisition of certain sophisticated modes of thought.

The first article of this section is a reflective address by the psychologist George Miller to a 1971 conference entitled 'Language by Ear and by Eye'. In it, he asserts the social significance of literacy, historically and contemporarily, before discussing its psychological significance. In the second article, David Olson asserts that becoming literate entails the development of *metalinguistic awareness*, the ability to perceive, and talk about, language as an object. This, he argues, has profound cognitive consequences.

There are, however, those within the interdisciplinary field of literacy studies who are unhappy with the notion of literacy as an accomplishment with intrinsic qualities and which carries essential cognitive benefits. In the third article, Street argues that the 'autonomous' model of literacy employed by many researchers is basically flawed. He suggests that this model is no more than the theoretical manifestation of a particular, culturally specific form of literacy, and that claims for the cognitive benefits of literacy are not well substantiated.

In the next article, Scribner and Cole again attack an autonomous, unified conception of literacy by showing how various kinds of literacy practices have, at the most, only very specific cognitive effects. Drawing on their research with the Vai people of Liberia, they argue that the effects of 'schooling' and 'literacy' are often confused.

The final article in this section takes a very different perspective on the relationship between cognitive growth and literacy development. In it, Teale and Sulzby discuss changing views about how young children become writers and readers.

4.1 Reflections on the Conference

G. A. Miller

Source: Edited version of Miller, G. A. (1972) 'Reflections on the conference'. In Kavanagh, J. F. and Mattingly, I. G. (eds) *Language by Ear and by Eye*. Cambridge, Mass.: MIT Press, pp. 373–381.

Let me say immediately that I am not going to attempt to review or evaluate all that has been said here concerning the relations between speech and learning to read. I will select only a few of the ideas that were particularly interesting to me, and try to say why I found them so.

Before I do that, however, I want to take a few minutes of my time to stand back from our topic and to try to see it in perspective. We have, quite properly, been concerned primarily with the internal properties, structural and functional, of speaking and writing; but occasionally we have found it necessary to refer outward to the relation our topic has to broader concerns, and to the reasons, social and personal, why it is currently so important. I shall therefore take these occasional references as a precedent and an excuse for seeking some larger view — in short, a perspective.

The most obvious source of perspective, of course, is history. I find it interesting that writing did not originate as a means for encoding speech. Talking and writing seem to have evolved separately and grown together later. So far as we know, man has always had language, although the details of the evolution of this unique means of communication are lost in the vast distance of time. Writing, however, is a much more recent acquisition, perhaps 6000 years old, and alphabetic writing — which really brought speech and writing together — is probably less than 3000 years old. In terms of an evolutionary time scale, therefore, writing the spoken word was invented only a few moments ago.

It has frequently happened that the introduction of writing and the mastery of it by a substantial fraction of a society has immediately preceded profound social and political changes in that society. Indeed, the invention of writing was sufficiently important to justify, for many scholars, the claim that it signalled the birth of civilization. Goody and Watt (1963) have attempted to use ancient Greece as a case history in the study of the consequences of literacy; they make the point that the invention and relatively wide adoption of writing and reading had pervasive effects on Greek culture. Perhaps the most important in our modern view were (1) the rejection of myth and its replacement by history; and (2) the invention of logic as a formal representation of the thought involved in argumentation and rhetoric.

Behind the birth of logic and history there were, no doubt, profound changes of a social and psychological nature. The basic change was that their alphabetic writing objectified language, the product of thought, and gave it a permanence that the spoken word lacked. Writing also objectified and externalized personal memory, and the existence of written records from the past was obviously propaedeutic to historical studies. Thus, one consequence of writing was improved memory, made possible by the physical persistence of the written record.

I believe that the birth of logic, however, requires a more subjective explanation. The written proposition is a tangible representation of an act of thought. It is a physical thing, an object, and it can be reacted to as any other object can. Thus writing made it possible to react to one's own thoughts as if they were objects, so the act of thought became itself a subject for further thought. Thus extended abstraction became possible, and one of the brilliant abstractions recognized by the Greeks concerned the form of valid arguments. And so, out of writing, was logic born.

In my opinion, the more significant of these two intellectual activities was logic, which directly affected the way the mind worked. The development of history was merely a natural response to a larger and more trustworthy data base, made possible by the permanence of the written record. But something more than permanence — something related to the mind's awareness of its operations — was involved in logic.

Let me put it this way. Suppose that, by some anachronistic inversion of events, a phonographic recording device had been invented instead of writing. Suppose further that the Greeks had been clever enough to preserve the spoken word in a permanent and easily accessible form. In short, imagine the permanence had been achieved without the kind of linguistic analysis entailed by alphabetic writing.

Since no one knows what difference this would have made, everyone is free to speculate. My own speculation is that history would have developed in either case, but logic would have been much harder to achieve. Not impossible, I grant, but far more difficult. The analysis of words into sounds, and the analysis of syllogistic arguments into premises and conclusions, are, to my mind, closely akin. Writing makes language self-conscious in a way that recorded echoes probably could not.

In short, therefore, writing not only contributed permanence to the social record, but it also facilitated an awareness of one's own speech that would otherwise have been extremely unlikely. Since the question of linguistic awareness has been a central theme of this conference, I will leave the matter here: not only does writing build on those aspects of language that are accessible to our conscious attention, but writing itself makes accessible aspects of language that are probably beyond the grasp of the illiterate thinker. I shall return to this question of self-awareness later.

Next, however, I want to consider an alternative context for our topic. History gives us one perspective, but the social sciences give us another. Let me try, therefore, to put literacy in a social context. Morris Halle has eloquently reminded us of the social context of our topic, and I know of no way to improve on what he has already said and illustrated in terms of the Cherokee experience. But perhaps even that can be seen in a larger context.

It is a basic fact about the twentieth century that we are moving rapidly into an age when knowledge is becoming increasingly important and valuable. Sociologists and economists have many ways of referring to this transition, but whether one calls it the rise of postindustrial society, or the growth of the knowledge industries, or the birth of an information-based economy, or the latest stage in the Industrial Revolution, the facts are that our population is becoming increasingly urbanized, an increasing fraction of the GNP is devoted to the creation and dissemination of knowledge, and education generally is becoming an indispensible prerequisite to economic survival — education in general, and literacy in particular.

This is not the time and I am not the person to document these generalizations about the Knowledge Revolution, so I must rely on your sense of the century to supply the details. The fact is that our technological progress is creating a socioeconomic system in which the ignorant, illiterate individual is useless and barely tolerated at a level of existence we call 'welfare'. In order to escape this modern version of purgatory, a person must have enough education to contribute to our technological society. If you have been excluded from access to that education, or have valid reasons for resisting assimilation into the system, your outlook can only be described as bleak.

I will not pursue the reasons why poverty and illiteracy are so inextricably linked in our society. As a political liberal my impulse is to do everything possible — and much more is possible than has been done — to make literacy and assimilation available to everyone who desires them. Those who do not wish to be assimilated, and there are many, may still wish to be literate, and somehow we must learn to accommodate them. But the right to read is not an obligation to read, and those who refuse to read must still be allowed to eat.

My point is simply this. On the one hand, knowledge is becoming increasingly necessary for survival, and literacy is the key tool for the acquisition of that knowledge. On the other hand, the teaching of reading in our public schools — especially in the ghettoes, both urban and rural — is failing badly, and all subsequent education built on reading fails with it. That is the social context in which I must view our present topic, and the reason that our discussion merits all the energy and insight and commitment that the participants have devoted to it.

Professor Halle has said that our scientific analysis of the reading process can deal only with secondary issues, and that the real problem lies beyond our ability to remedy. Perhaps he is right, but I do not believe that that reduces our obligation to do all we can, within the limits of our technical competence, to understand what is going wrong and why. That, then, is the context of special urgency I bring with me. On the one hand, we know that literacy nurtures the growth of knowledge and analytical thinking; and on the other hand, we know that the failure of our efforts to teach reading skills universally is both a cause and a symptom of grave socioeconomic difficulties in our society.

From a distance, therefore, I can only express disappointment that our discussions have contributed so little to these larger questions. In my opinion, the most important issue we raised, chewed on, and returned to repeatedly was the issue Mattingly referred to as 'linguistic awareness' and Klima called 'accessibility'. With respect to the social problems underlying reading difficulties, we had very little to say and even less to contribute. Although we may (or may not) believe that reading materials written in the black dialect, and teachers willing to respect that dialect, would help to ease the difficulties of millions of children who are handicapped in learning to read a language they do not speak, none of the papers delivered here has attempted to consider the possible effect of dialectal variations on the relation between speaking and learning to read, to assemble and evaluate the facts relevant to this aspect of the problem. All we have is Savin's observation that one critical source of difficulty is independent of dialect.

Instead, we tended to concentrate on an analysis of the information processing that must occur when a literate reader casts his eyes over a printed text, and to a lesser extent on the development of those processing skills in a beginning reader who comes to the task with all the linguistic competence that spoken language can instil. Even that is too broad a characterization, for we have repeatedly focused on reading as a process leading to, and evaluated in terms of, comprehension and memory. In short, we have taken a much narrower view of the relation between speech and reading than a disinterested layman might have expected us to.

Lest I sound too censorious, however, let me quickly add that I believe other conferences have done even worse. In October 1968 the Division of Medical Sciences of the National Research Council held a conference whose proceedings have now been published by the National Academy of Sciences under the title *Early Experience and Visual Information Processing in Perceptual and Reading Disorders* (Young and Lindsley, 1970). A very distinguished group of scientists contributed, but the whole enterprise was, in my view, rendered worthless by virtue of a narrow presupposition that reading has something to do with vision, but nothing to do with language. Whatever else one may say about the present conference, at least we recognized that reading skills must derive ultimately from linguistic skills. That in itself represents a giant step forward.

Even so, however, I felt there was too quick a willingness to talk about *the* skill of reading, as if reading were some monolithic, well-defined process used only to suck up sentences, massage them appropriately for comprehension, and deposit the residuum in some capacious receptacle called 'long-term memory'; and as if there were only one kind of problem — *the* problem — encountered in learning to read. The word 'reading' is ordinarily used to refer to many different and only loosely related perceptual skills — we proofread one way, we memorize another way, and we comprehend still another way; then we go on to read for amusement, or translate from another language, or skim for an overview, or puzzle out a handwritten message, or search for a target, or read aloud to others, or lull ourselves to sleep, or read a label on a bottle in the medicine cabinet, or worship our gods, or sing our verses. Wittgenstein chose the concept of a game to illustrate the diversity of meanings a word can have, but he might have made the point equally well in terms of reading.

In her keynote address Gibson urged us to keep in mind that we read for a purpose, and there are almost as many different ways to read as there are purposes for reading. Moreover, different reading skills may be differently acquired, and may encounter many different forms of disability. By confining ourselves largely to the kind of reading we ourselves do most often and the kind of reading we demand most often of our students, we constantly flirted with the temptation to overgeneralize our results. The proper *caveats* were always issued, of course, but an unwary reader of these proceedings might easily conclude that we did not take them very seriously.

Since we tended to concentrate on that kind of reading, there was an important and recurring theme in the conference having to do with the apparent necessity of going through acoustic, articulatory, phonetic, phonological or abstract phonological representations of the words one is reading. No doubt most people do go through some or all of these representations when they are reading aloud or reading to understand and remember, and it may be an essential process during the learning period, but Conrad presented clear evidence from his non-articulatory deaf readers that such imagery is not indispensible. Perhaps a broader conception of what reading can be would have led to even more evidence that it is possible to disconnect the visual from the phonological system. In any event, the case for the *universal* necessity of internal speech representations during reading was not convincing, and we are left rather with the conclusion that such a route into the internal lexicon seems to be the most efficient one, but not the only conceivable one in every situation.

Many of these different forms of internal representation seemed to be intimately linked to a particular method of experimentation, and defined as much in terms of the experimental procedures used as in terms of the language user's normal preferences and aptitudes. Thus, although few of the methods used seemed to have been developed specifically to study the reading process, there was necessarily a considerable amount of discussion devoted to the differences among or convergences between different experimental methods. I am no slavish admirer of parsimony, but I must confess that when every method leads to the postulation of a new wing on the information-processing house, I begin to get a little suspicious.

Years ago the behaviourally inclined psychologists rejected introspection because every experimenter who used it seemed to find whatever process he was looking for. It would be cruelly ironic if our current methods of experimentation were to suffer a similar fate. Such rejections are only temporary, however, as the history of introspection demonstrates.

It was Mattingly, I think, who made the best case for introspection, although he did not call it that. It should be pointed out, I think, that what he called 'awareness' and what Klima called 'accessibility' are related but not identical concepts. That is to say, I can conceive of some level of linguistic processing being accessible, in the sense that special transformations, like spelling or versification, could take advantage of it, yet it might not be describable at the level of conscious awareness. I say I can conceive of such a situation logically, although I have difficulty in imagining any empirical facts that might settle the issue one way or the other.

If some level of representation more abstract than the final phonetic string is taken as the basis for an orthography, then learning to use the orthography might well make a person aware of that level even though he might not have been aware of it otherwise. Thus, what is accessible and what we can become aware of in using language are not immutable given, fixed once and for all, but can change with maturation and experience. And I have no difficulty believing that an experienced linguist can be aware of processes that even a literate person does not notice and cannot control voluntarily.

In particular, Savin's fascinating observations seem to mean that a child may use phonemes quite acceptably without being aware of them or having access to them for the purpose of alphabetic writing. But with the proper experience he should be able to become aware of them by additional processing of the syllabic perceptual unit, and so use his new awareness as a basis for reading. The fact that we have no notion how to help the child achieve this level of awareness poses a challenging problem for research.

Most of the component processes that Posner, Conrad, Crowder and Gough described, however, do not seem to be accessible to consciousness or to voluntary control. Inasmuch as these processes have been inferred from performance data and not from introspection, they represent particularly valuable additions to our knowledge of the system. But, on the other hand, inasmuch as they are not accessible to voluntary control, they cannot provide a basis for our voluntary choices of what to say and how to say it. Their functioning is only indirectly controllable by the language user, and their relevance for linguistic theory — which is, of course, based largely on one kind of introspective data — remains to be determined. This gap is sometimes discussed in terms of a difference between linguistic theories of competence and psychological models of performance, but I think it might better be considered as a gap between two different kinds of data derived from very different methods of observation.

It seems unlikely that a writing system can reflect directly the surface phonetics of speech, for this seems not to be accessible to the language user. Something more abstract is necessary, and Klima gave us several alternative levels of abstractness whose accessibility might be empirically tested. There are advantages in an abstract representation because it can accommodate itself to dialectal variations, it need not change as pronunciation evolves, and it may make the language user appreciate aspects of his language that he would otherwise overlook. But as Lotz pointed out, there are also disadvantages, since it takes longer to learn the more abstract systems, and they may be responsible for more failures to learn. This, too, is an empirical question worth investigating further. [. . .]

As I listened to all these admirable attempts to organize the experimental data in terms of an information-processing system for spoken and written language, I waited with much interest for the discussion of long-term memory, for that is surely where most of the skills and knowledge that are involved in speaking and learning to read must be lodged. I did not hear much about it, however, perhaps because it was assumed to be well understood, or perhaps because it was thought to play a relatively passive role in processing the linguistic input. Neither reason would be justifiable, of course, so I must be wrong. In any case, I must note that this obviously important psychological component of the system received little attention in our discussions. We left it with a general agreement that long-term memory must be shared by both the speaking and reading systems, and a general agreement that its organization must be inscrutably complicated — neither being a conclusion likely to surprise anybody. Long-term memory thus remains a problem for the long-term future.

In conclusion, and in spite of these largely critical reflections on what has transpired here, I intend to report to my colleagues that this was a successful conference. I consider that judgement to be less a description, however, than a prediction. The obvious interest in reading that has been expressed here by so many distinguished linguists and psychologists, plus the stimulation provided by these three days of intense interaction, seem to me very hopeful signs for the future. My critical reflections are merely intended to spur you, and to avoid fostering any complacency as to the disparity between what has been accomplished and what remains to be done. I judge the conference to have been successful because I am now far more confident that what needs doing can be done and will be done.

And so I will close by expressing my appreciation to everyone who had a hand in making it possible for us to have this stimulating and, I predict, successful conference.

References

Goody, J. and Watt, I, (1963) 'The consequences of literacy'. *Comp. Stud. in Soc. and Hist.*, **5**, 304–345.

Young, F. A. and Lindsley, D. B. (1970) *Early Experience and Visual Information Processing in Perceptual and Reading Disorders*. Washington, D C: National Academy of Sciences.

4.2 'See! Jumping!' Some Oral Language Antecedents of Literacy

D. R. Olson

Source: Olson, D. R. (1984) ' "See! Jumping!" Some Oral Language Antecedents of Literacy'. In Goelman, H., Oberg, A. A. and Smith, F. (eds) *Awakening to Literacy*. Victoria, British Columbia: University of Victoria, pp. 185–192.

Literate society, literate mind

It now is generally agreed that literacy is associated with both a distinctive form of social organization, a *literate society*, and with a distinctive form of thought and talk, a *literate mind*, although this view admits of many qualifications. The arguments for it are widely available (Goody, 1977; Olson, 1977; Eisenstein, 1979), and so I shall not examine them in detail here. Rather, the question of concern is how do we explain the development of children's literate competencies? Do we look into the mental activities of children, an essentially Piagetian undertaking, or do we look into the tutorial practices of parents, an essentially Durkheimian, Vygotskian or Brunerian undertaking? If we are tempted to do both, then precisely how are they threaded together? Psychologists tend to seek an explanation of children's literacy development in the learning activities of children. Thus, they expect changes to occur in the modes of thought and talk of children as they learn to read and write, a process that is not completed until early adulthood. In fact, this was our approach in our own research programme at the Ontario Institute for Studies in Education (O I S E). Some of the O I S E work will be discussed later in this chapter. This approach attempts to account for what an individual child is doing and learning. The focus is on the abilities, knowledge and intentions of individual children, on what is *learned*.

Sociologists and anthropologists, however, are quick to point out that literacy is not merely an individual achievement but a social one. Literacy is a part of the social order that is passed on from generation to generation through the process of socialization, particularly through literacy activities in the home and in school. Any knowledge or skill attributed to the child does not originate in the child; what the child does is simply a reflection of the transmission of this social order. From this perspective, the focus is on the role of literacy in the society and the ways in which familiarity with literacy is acquired by children — that is, on what the society, specifically parents and teachers, are doing rather than on what the individual learner is doing. In this view, the beginnings of literacy are seen primarily as cultural-historical rather than developmental. Thus, a sociological or anthropological approach to literacy development emphasizes that which is perpetuated, transmitted, passed on or *taught*, rather than what is *learned*.

The relation between individual development and social transmission is among the more challenging and pressing issues in psychology, but it takes a particularly interesting form in the discussion of the roots of language and literacy in which the relation between what is taught and what is learned is more conspicuous. Bruner (1983) has expressed the polarity well by describing as complementary the roles of the child's language acquisition device and the parents' language acquisition support system. A full account of language acquisition, he suggests, must include both the child's cognitive system for learning the language and the society's support systems for teaching that language. We may note, however, that these two systems are not fully commensurate: they involve different levels of description — the psychological and the social. One describes what is learned by the child, and the other, what is taught by the parent or teacher. Only if we assume, somewhat naively, an identity between what is learned and what is taught could we use the description of one to explain the other and so to specify the relation between the individual and the social. I suggest that the relation between what is taught and what is learned is very complex.

Nonetheless, there must be some relation between what is taught and what is learned, and it is that relation that I shall explore in regard to the antecedents of literacy. My suggestion is that the social assumptions about literacy influence what the child is taught in the course of learning his or her oral language. What the child learns from being taught these different things shall concern us later. Let us note first what it is that parents teach. Specifically, highly literate parents may teach their children a distinctive orientation to language in the very process of teaching them to talk. I propose that this orientation to language is expressed in part through a metalanguage. It is that metalanguage which differs from one part of the society to the next and which determines, at least in part, what parents teach and what children learn. In this chapter, I make and try to defend two main points. The first is that what varies from one subculture to the next is the knowledge and use of language about language, the *metalanguage*. Second, the locus at which the teaching of the adult and the learning of the child converge is the mastery and use of a common language. Let us examine these two points in regard to children's acquisition of literacy competence.

The role of metalanguage

As stated previously, literacy involves a distinctive mode of speech and thought. I must now specify what is distinctive about it. Psychologically, it is not very helpful to define literates as people who can read or sign their names or any of the other simple categorical criteria that are relevant to demographic concerns. Of greater significance is that, to a literate person, language is known as language. Literacy involves the knowledge that language exists as an artifact, has a structure, is composed of grammatical units including words and sentences, has a meaning somewhat independent of the meaning intended by the speaker, and, perhaps most importantly, that its structures may be referred to by means of a metalanguage. In short, it is the belief that language can be treated opaquely, as a structure in its own right. Derrida (1976, p. 12) puts it this way: 'Inscription alone . . . has the power to arouse speech from its slumber as sign. By enregistering speech, inscription has as its essential objective . . . the emancipation of meaning'. Elsewhere I have provided extensive if not conclusive arguments as to why that belief is tied to the existence of written artifacts. The central argument is that writing preserves surface structure, the words themselves, which can therefore be subjected to analysis, study and interpretation, none of which is encouraged by oral language (Olson, 1977).

The literate assumption, then, is that language exists as an artifact independent of the intention it is used to express in any given situation. This assumption, which I have suggested is the key to the effects of literacy, need not be expressed or learned through reading and writing. It is this fact which makes the problem of the antecedents of literacy so puzzling. According to the preceding assumption, becoming literate is only indirectly related to learning to read and write. An awareness of language may be characterized either as a prerequisite — that is, a predisposition — to literacy or as a consequence of learning to read and write. These differing premises have formed the basis of numerous studies on what is referred to somewhat unfelicitously as *metalinguistic awareness*. Whether an awareness of language constitutes a predisposition to literacy or is a consequence of literacy depends, I suggest, upon the social practices and the forms of teaching, among which the child grows up.

What, then, are some of the parental assumptions about language and literacy that may influence a child's acquisition of the belief that language is an artifact, an autonomous system. Goody (1982), in his study of the LoDagaa, a traditional African society, found that they do not treat language as a form of traditional knowledge that is taught but rather as a part of humankind's natural makeup. Unlike such activities as farming and cooking, which they believe were first taught to the LoDagaa by the gods and which they must in turn teach or pass on to the young,[1] talking, like motor development, is believed to involve simply an unfolding; therefore, it need not be taught. Conversely, if language is not considered a formal, autonomous structure, there is no need to teach it; indeed, it cannot be taught. Children can learn the language, but they cannot be taught the language as a language.

Among the LoDagaa, as in several other oral societies, there is a restricted metalanguage, which is further evidence that language is not considered an autonomous structure that may be analysed, interpreted and taught. Most conspicuously, the metalinguistic term *word* does not exist. There is a word for referrring to speech, for what was said, but it can refer to any unit of speech ranging from a single sound to an entire poem and can apply equally to the expression or the intention lying behind it. We shall return to discuss the significance of such metalinguistic terms presently.

It is not only in oral societies that language is treated as transparent to the meanings and intentions that lie behind it. Heath (1982) points out that in a working-class black community in the Carolinas, in which most adults have some degree of literacy, a similar attitude towards the teaching and learning of language exists. Heath describes how children in this community learn to talk: they are not introduced to labels for everyday objects or for pictures or words in books, nor are they given a simplified input by adults. When asked about how she taught her son to talk, one adult said, 'No use me telling him . . . He just gotta learn'. Again, the assumption is that language is not a piece of knowledge that must be taught systematically. It must be learned, but it need not be taught. To teach it is to treat language as an artifact, and to so treat it is, I suggest, central to a literate orientation to language.

Literate parents are those who, by my definition, tend to treat language as an object and who, therefore, have and use an elaborate metalanguage for referring to language. They believe that language is an object and that therefore it can be taught, somewhat systematically, to children.[2] Middle-class parents frequently introduce children to books as a means of teaching them to talk. Thus, written language is used as a means of teaching oral language. Bruner (1983) has described interactions between a mother and child around a picture book. The book provides a simple and stable environment suitable for teaching the names of objects. In these interactional formats, the adult points to a pictured object and solicits a name from the child. If the child fails to come up with it, the adult provides it. These naming games are considered paradigmatic of how some parents teach their children the language.

However, Heath's (1982) observations forestall the conclusion that these language teaching practices are universal. As we have seen in some societies and in some subcultures of our own society, the language is not taught at all; the children simply come to know it. The language teaching procedures that make up the naming game may reflect the literate middle-class assumption that language is an autonomous system or structure that must be taught to children if they are to learn to speak. This would explain the previously cited interactional formats and the simplified baby-talk register described by Snow and Ferguson (1977). Non-literate parents or less literate parents may make no such assumption and, as a consequence, may engage in no such practices.

In an extensive study of the first words uttered by a group of infants of highly educated parents, Galligan (1982) made several observations that highlight these distinctive orientations to teaching infants to talk. Several authors have noted that some parents systematically teach their children the names for objects (nouns). Galligan observed that some parents treat the language learning task even more analytically and teach their children not only nouns but verbs in a somewhat systematic fashion. It is from a transcript of such a parent's lesson that the title of this chapter is taken. While pointing to a frog jumping into a pond, a mother said, 'See! Jumping!'

What could motivate this parent to single out and attempt to teach the verb *jumping*? In the naming game, the objects usually are named by nouns; here, the action is lifted from context and explicitly taught. Presumably, it is part of the same explicit teaching program — first nouns, then verbs, then functors, and so on. The agenda is simply more striking when applied to a more abstract structure like a verb than when applied to a noun. A noun in isolation may at least seem like an elliptical demonstrative — 'this is a cat', 'this is a frog', and the like — and hence have a normal semantic context. To treat a verb in a way analogous to a noun requires a nominalization, a gerund treated like a noun: 'This is a jumping'. As a communicative sentence, it is decidedly odd. My conjecture is that the parent is not describing an event but rather teaching the verb *jump*. The resulting construction is a bit awkward, but it preserves the format of the teaching procedures that some highly literate parents use to teach nouns.

I suggest that such parents are teaching children to speak in a manner appropriated from the practice of teaching them to read. In learning to read a word-based script, words are singled out into word lists and the like which then are taught to children in the form of a recognition vocabulary. The parent in this case is proceeding on an analogous basis, teaching the child not just how to use words but also the structure of language — language as an object composed of words, nouns, verbs and so on. Thus, the parent teaches the word *jumping*.

There is other evidence that this technique is effective in acquainting children with language as an object composed of words and meanings. Children of highly literate parents have been noted to ask questions about language. One three-year-old, for example, asked his mother, 'What means "old-fashioned"?' and later 'What means "by the way"?' Like their literate parents, such children come to recognize (or believe) that language has a structure, that it consists of words, that words have a meaning, and that these structures can be discussed by use of a metalanguage (Robinson et al., 1983; Gopnik, personal communication).

Teaching and learning

In a sense, parents teach their children some nouns and verbs implicitly by using them in contexts that permit the comprehension of the utterance in which they occur. This is distinct from a parent's explicit teaching of the constituents, primarily single words, of language. Explicit teaching of words is a decontextualized form of tutoring. The parent has assumed that language is an object that has a particular structure, and he or she is systematically teaching the child that structure. The parent teaches the child words because he or she believes that language is made up of words; if the parent did not believe this literacy premise, he or she would be unable to teach the child.

This fundamental point may be seen more clearly by reflecting on the verb *teach* (Scheffler, 1960). Although the verb *teach* is used in a variety of ways, for our purposes we will consider *teach* in its role as an intentional verb. Intentional verbs mark actions done consciously and purposefully. If a child learns something from what a parent does but the parent did not intentionally attempt to influence the child, the parent cannot be said to have taught him or her. Hence, it can be said that a child learned to talk from his or her parents but that the child's parents did not teach him or her to talk.

In the intentional sense of *teach*, only those things that the adult recognizes as existing bodies of knowledge can be taught. One may teach farming, weaving or cooking because these are believed to exist as specialized bodies of knowledge. However, as Goody (1982) pointed out, language is not considered such a body of knowledge in traditional societies, and so in such societies, language cannot be taught.

As we have seen, some parents attempt to teach their children to talk, and others apparently do not, but all children do learn to talk. The analytic techniques adopted by our highly literate parents seem to be no better than those adopted by less literate parents; both are successful. Therefore, the literate assumption that language is an object, subject to analysis, learning and teaching, has nothing whatsoever to do with the acquisition of a native language. Why, then, do literate parents attempt to teach language? Although it has nothing to do with oral competence, teaching the language has everything to do with literacy. The literate parent is teaching the child an orientation to language which will not be relevant to learning to speak but which will be relevant to learning to read. The roots of literacy lie in how one learns to talk.

An explicit teaching procedure is not without risks, however. The child, in being exposed to the formal structure of language, may fail to grasp the meanings that language expresses, just as some children apparently fail to learn to read because they become confused about the functions of the visual shapes that they are learning to recognize (Smith, 1971).

Assuming a child succeeds in pairing forms with meanings and does learn to talk, it is important to know what else the child has learned through being taught language as an analysable system. The literacy premise is a misleading representation of speech but an accurate representation of print. In learning to talk in this way, the child is taking the first step towards becoming literate.

At one level of description, we may say that literate parents transmit a literate orientation in the process of teaching their children to talk. Still, such a notion of transmittal cannot adequately account for what, precisely, the child has learned in learning to talk that explains his or her ease in learning to read and write. Although correct, it is clearly inadequate to say that highly literate parents have highly literate children, a relation that is evidenced by the high correlations between literacy skill and social class (Wells, 1985). To explain this relation, we must turn from the social question 'What specifically have the parents *taught*?' and turn to the psychological question: 'What, specifically, has the child *learned*?' In other words, how is the literate orientation represented in the knowledge, beliefs and skills of the children of literate parents?

My hypothesis is that the child is learning a set of concepts for referring to language *per se*, and this set of concepts is expressed largely (if not exclusively) through the terms of the metalanguage. It is in the metalanguage that the concepts critical to literacy are carried. As Reid (1966), Downing and Leong (1982), Wells (1985), Clay (1972), and others have shown, children's knowledge of such things as words, letters, sounds, their names, and their correspondences correlates highly with their progress in learning to read: that is, children's knowledge of the metalinguistic nouns *sentence, word, letter, sound* is related to children's progress in learning to read and write. More importantly, these critical literacy concepts are part of the oral language competence of the children of more highly literate parents. Children who are taught to talk learn not only the language but also the metalanguage, and the metalanguage is relevant to learning to read a word-based script.

Nonetheless, only part of the metalanguage is represented in these structural nouns. Equally important are the set of metalinguistic verbs that have been discussed by such philosophers of language as Grice (1957), Searle (1979) and Vendler (1970). The central point of their theories is that there is a direct relation between speech acts and mental states and that these relations are made explicit in the set of speech act verbs and mental state verbs, which may be called *metalinguistic verbs* and *metacognitive verbs*, respectively. Specifically, to sincerely *assert* x, one must *believe* x; to sincerely *request* y, one must want or *desire* y; and to sincerely *promise* z, one must *intend* z. Of course, one may carry out these speech acts and entertain the corresponding mental states without knowing the metalinguistic verbs *say, ask, promise* or the metacognitive verbs *believe, desire* or *intend*, but to carry the speech acts successfully, children would have to grasp the concepts expressed by these terms, and the terms would at least be useful in the clarification of these concepts. The words are important only because they represent concepts, and it is the concepts that are critical to learning the structure of written language.

In defence of this statement, we may note that a child need not know what the word *word* means to know what a word is (this is true for other nouns as well, such as *letter, sound, sentence* and *language*), but it is the child's knowledge of the metalinguistic terms that correlates with learning to read. Presumably, this is because the words adequately represent the conceptual distinctions the child can make; the distinction is made clear by a linguistic expression.

In addition, we have some evidence from our own laboratory that children's knowledge of metalinguistic and metacognitive verbs is related to their progress in learning to read and write. First, children who become better readers use a greater variety of these terms in their free conversational speech. Examples are 'I wonder what' 'I think I know what'. Second, a test designed to determine children's competence with such verbs as *mean, intend, think, know, pretend, wonder, decide, realize, remember, doubt* and *deny* showed that knowledge of these verbs was indeed related to the child's acquisition of literacy skills (Torrance and Olson, 1985). Third, in a more careful analysis of one particular pair of these metalinguistic and metacognitive verbs, namely *say* and *mean*, we have found that children's competence is closely associated with the acquisition of literacy. For example, preliterate children are unlikely to say, 'He said x, but he meant y'. Moreover, those children who do make this distinction come from more highly literate homes in which a parent has explicitly marked the distinction with a metalinguistic verb.

Finally, there is a logical reason why knowledge of the metalanguage is related to the development of literacy. As previously stated, in some traditional societies there is no conception of language as an autonomous system or structure of knowledge that can be intentionally taught to children. The metalanguage, including a name for language, permits reference to language, and it creates entities — language, sentence, words, and the like — which, when recognized as such, may be intentionally taught to children.

Thus, to understand talk about language and to think about language or to be taught about language, the child must have access to the concepts represented in the metalanguage. Children from more literate homes learn an explicit set of concepts, represented in the metalanguage, for referring to and thinking about language and its structure, the very structure they will use in learning to read and write. Other children presumably will learn this same set of concepts and the metalanguage for representing them in the course of learning to read.

Frank Smith (personal communication) has argued that it is possible for children to learn to read and write without a metalanguage just as they learn to talk and understand without one. Whereas children can learn without a metalanguage, they cannot be *taught* without one. Teaching, in the intentional sense, requires the metalanguage, and reading and writing, more than talking, seem to depend on explicitly being taught. To this extent, learning to talk and learning to read and write are dissimilar. I do not believe a child could learn to read without knowing he or she knew how to read and still be a fluent reader. Certainly, a child could not do so and still be literate in the sense that this chapter describes.

Fowler (1981) recently has re-examined the famous Terman studies of genius (1918) with a view to determining the role that parents played in such precocity. He found two patterns — parents who explicitly taught their children and acknowledged their roles and parents who disavowed that role but who nonetheless spent 'numberless hours weekly over periods of months and years in responsive labelling, question answering, and reading to the child' (Fowler, 1981, p. 353). Fowler concludes that the patterns were equally effective in developing precocity whether the teaching was direct or indirect. For our purposes, it would be interesting to know if the indirect forms relied as heavily on the metalanguage for coordinating reference as does the explicit, direct form of teaching. My conjecture is that the metalanguage is used and acquired in both cases.

Conclusion

My conclusion about the role of the metalanguage in literacy is not significantly different from the traditional assumption that the antecedents of literacy lie in the knowledge of the language and that children from more literate homes have a larger vocabulary than those from less literate ones, both because their parents have larger vocabularies and because they are exposed to the larger vocabularies of books. It alters that view only in claiming that the important and relevant part of their vocabulary is that pertaining to the structure and meaning of language — that is, to the metalanguage — and to the mental states implicated by the metalanguage. Although the metalanguage is designed to cope with problems of referring in written texts, it is applied to oral language by literate parents and taught to their children as part of ordinary speech.

The link, then, between the structures of society and the structures of the individual are to be found in their sharing of a common language which, in this case, is the metalanguage for referring to language. It is in this common language that we may find an identity between what is taught and what is learned.

Notes

1 Edwina Taborsky (mimeo.) recently has suggested that literacy encourages not only the differentiation of language from speech, but also the differentiation of the knower from the known.

2 This is not to imply that there is only one possible set of assumptions about language and literacy that are accepted by literate parents or that there is one view of reading that these parents accept. Heath's (1982) work indicates some alternative views.

References

Bruner, J. S. (1983) *Child's Talk*. New York: Norton.

Clay, M. M. (1972) *The Early Detection of Reading Difficulties: A Diagnostic Survey*. London: Heinemann Educational Books.

Derrida, J. (1976) *Of Grammatology*. Trans. G. Spivak. Baltimore, MD: Johns Hopkins University Press.

Downing, J. and Leong, C. K. (1982) *Psychology of Reading*. Toronto: Macmillan.

Eisenstein, E. (1979) *The Printing Press as an Agent of Change*. Cambridge: Cambridge University Press.

Fowler, W. (1981) 'Case studies of cognitive precocity: the role of exogenous and endogenous stimulation in early mental development'. *Journal of Applied Developmental Psychology*, **2**, 319–367

Galligan, R. F. (1982) Individual differences in learning to speak: a study of the use of whole phrases, jargon and intonation. PhD dissertation, University of Toronto.

Goody, J. (1977) *The Domestication of the Savage Mind*. New York: Cambridge University Press.

Goody, J. (1982) 'Alternative paths to knowledge in oral and literate cultures'. In Tannen D. (ed.) *Spoken and Written Language*. Norwood, NJ: Ablex.

Grice, H. P. (1957) 'Meaning'. *Philosophical Review*, **3**, 377–388.

Heath, S. B. (1982) 'What no bedtime story means: narrative skills at home and school'. *Language in Society*, **11**, 49–76.

Olson, D. R. (1977) 'From utterance to text: the bias of language in speech and writing'. *Harvard Educational Review*, **47**, 257–281.

Robinson, E., Goelman, H. and Olson, D. R. (1983) 'Children's understanding of the relation between expressions (what was said) and intentions (what was meant)' *British Journal of Developmental Psychology*, **1**, 75–86.

Reid, J. F. (1966) 'Learning to think about reading'. *Educational Research*, **9**, 56–62.

Scheffler, I. (1960) *The Language of Education*. Springfield, Ill.: Charles C. Thomas.

Searle, J. R. (1979) 'Intentionality and the use of language'. In Margalit A. (ed.), *Meaning and Use*. Jerusalem, Israel: The Magnes Press, The Hebrew University.

Smith, F. (1971) *Understanding Reading*. New York: Holt, Rinehart and Winston; 2nd ed. 1978.

Snow, C. and Ferguson, C. (eds) (1977) *Talking to Children*. Cambridge: Cambridge University Press.

Torrance, N. and Olson D. R. (1985) 'Oral and written competencies in the early school years'. In Olson, D., Torrance, N. and Hildyard, A. (eds) *Literacy, Language and Learning*. Cambridge: Cambridge University Press.

Vendler, Z. (1970) 'Say what you think'. In Cowan, J. L. (ed.) *Studies in Thought and Language*. Tucson: University of Arizona Press.

Wells, G. (1985) 'Preschool literacy-related activities and success in school'. In Olson, D., Torrance, N. and Hildyard, A. (eds) *Literacy, Language and Learning*. Cambridge: Cambridge University Press.

4.3 The 'Autonomous' Model: Literacy and Rationality

B. Street

Source: Extracts from Street, B. (1984) 'The "autonomous" model: I literacy and rationality'. In *Literacy in Theory and Practice*. Cambridge: Cambridge University Press, pp. 19–31.

I shall attempt to establish the general outlines of what I term the 'autonomous' model of literacy by examining in detail the work of some writers who have explicitly addressed themselves to questions of literacy and its cognitive consequences. Highlighting its features in this way will, I hope, enable us to recognise them more easily when they occur in embedded form in other writers.

Angela Hildyard and David Olson have put forward a 'strong' version of the 'autonomous' model in a recent article. They begin by challenging the current opinion that all peoples share basic functions of the mind such as logical and abstract abilities. They find this view 'alarming' since 'if it is indeed the case that intellectual resources of Savage and Modern minds are essentially equivalent [then] what legitimises the extraordinary efforts and resources that go into compulsory schooling?' (Hildyard and Olson, 1978, p. 4). There are a number of sociological and political answers to this question, such as the contention that compulsory schooling serves a variety of social functions, including those of social control, transfer of dominant values, etc. In the language of some recent approaches, 'compulsory schooling' asserts the 'hegemony' of a ruling class (cf. Dale et al., 1976; Graff, 1979). I will examine such contentions below. They entail quite different assumptions about the nature of literacy than those put forward by Hildyard and Olson. *Their* answer to the question they pose is to say that education systems are to be justified on the grounds that they develop 'intellectual competence that would otherwise go largely undeveloped' (1978. p. 4). They conjecture that literacy plays a central part in this process. The qualities which they attribute to literacy thus take on the more general significance of justifying the vast expense on Western education systems. Seen in this perspective, the claims already have political and ideological significance — they are not as neutral or detached as internal presentation of the argument would appear to suggest. The 'autonomous' model is, then, constructed for a specific political purpose.

This is apparent in their claim that differences in intellectual performances of modern and traditional societies are 'sufficiently deep and of sufficient significance to warrant, at least in a literate society, the continued emphasis on schooling and the acquisition of literacy' (Hildyard and Olson, 1978, p. 5.). They attempt to justify the claim and the assumptions that underlie it, by 'advancing some conjectures and some evidence regarding the ways in which language and thought change under the impact of the specialised forms of written text' (ibid). Their central conjecture is that there are functions of language that are significantly affected by the mastery of a writing system, particularly its logical functions. Written forms, they argue, enable the user to differentiate such functions in a way less possible in oral language. They distinguish between the function of language as imparting meaning, 'making statements which can be assigned a set of truth conditions' (ibid), and its function of regulating and maintaining social or interpersonal relations between people. Most utterances, they claim, serve both functions but written forms facilitate the differentiation and separation of the functions. It thus becomes possible, through writing, to specialize language, to use it to serve a specific function rather than conflating different functions. Writing has the effect of distancing the speaker from the hearer; what is said need not be suited to the requirements of the listener because the listener is absent. Consequently the interpersonal or social functions of the language can be more or less held constant. The logical functions of language are given free rein. The invention of writing and particularly the attempt to create autonomous text has resulted in a realignment of the two primary functions of language. Oral language is always directed to a particular individual usually with some intended effect such as influencing his views, maintaining a certain relationship or controlling his actions. It can be constantly modified according to its effect and thus the social function dominates the logical. Written language, on the other hand, makes such interpersonal functions less critical; it can be conducted over time and space and is less subject to immediate feedback. It thus comes to serve the logical function rather than the interpersonal one. It develops the 'ability to operate within the boundaries of sentence meaning, on the meaning expressly represented in the sentence *per se*, and thereby to operate within the boundaries of an explicitly presented problem' (Hildyard and Olson, 1978, pp. 8–9).

It follows from these conjectures that members of literate societies have the possibility of developing logical functions, of specializing in the 'truth functions' of language, and of extracting themselves from the embeddedness of everyday social life. As Hildyard and Olson (1978) put it: 'the authority of rhetorical conditions are collapsed onto the truth conditions so that if a statement is true to the facts or to the text itself, that is sufficient condition for its being interpersonally appropriate' (p. 9). To support these conjectures they cite cross-cultural research into cognitive difference, in particular Patricia Greenfield's (1972) study of the differences between schooled and unschooled children amongst the Wolof of Senegal.

Greenfield argues that the significant differences that are revealed by her tests on schooled and unschooled groups derive from fundamental differences between oral and written language. She maintains that 'speakers of an oral language rely more on context for the communication of their verbal messages' (1972, p. 169), and this has implications for cognitive processes. Her hypothesis is 'that context-dependent speech is tied up with context-dependent thought, which in turn is the opposite of abstract thought' (ibid.). She glosses 'abstraction' in a sense close to the literal one: a separation from. Abstraction is, therefore, 'the mental separation of an element from the situation or context in which it is embedded' (ibid.). Oral speech depends on context to communicate meaning; it is therefore egocentric and takes for granted a common point of view as though no others were possible. This quality derives from the fact that oral speech involves face-to-face contact and also that oral languages are less widespread than written languages and so are shared by smaller groups. Written language is also more widespread across cultural groups, and its users do not share a common frame of reference.

She pursues the consequences of these differences for educational modes and for cognitive operations. Education in oral language is context-based and imitative. Kpelle education, for instance, is largely non-verbal, the child learning by imitation. She infers from this: 'thus, in the appropriate real-life situation he learns concrete activities, not abstract generalisations' (Greenfield, 1972, p. 170). Even where words are used, this form of education 'avoids the classificatory and analytic isolating functions which words have in Western culture' (ibid.). [. . .] Schools in 'technical societies', she continues, develop reading and writing which, unlike oral education systems, emphasize 'telling out of context rather than showing in context' (ibid.). School is isolated from life and 'the pupil must therefore acquire abstract habits of thought if he is to follow the teacher's oral lessons' (ibid. p. 171). Indeed, written language in itself entails higher levels of abstraction because 'while the spoken word stands for something, the written word stands for something that stands for something' (ibid.).

Tests on working-class black people are then cited as evidence that in oral contexts education is by demonstration and is 'totally dependent on the concrete physical situation' (ibid.). This has grave consequences for their children who 'do not learn as much from their mothers as do their middle-class counterparts' (ibid.). Moreover these children are deprived intellectually by such an upbringing: 'Thus, a context-dependent teaching style on the part of the mothers is associated with a lesser development of an ability to form conceptual and linguistic abstractions on the part of the children' (ibid., p. 172). One vital consequence was highlighted by Bernstein in his tests of working-class children in England. Much of Greenfield's paper derives from the theoretical foundations laid by Bernstein and she is surprised how closely the 'verbal deprivation' he identifies in working-class English youths corresponds to that which she found amongst the Wolof. Bernstein argued (1971) that the working-class spoke in 'restricted code' which entailed a failure 'to perceive the informational needs of the listener as being different from their own' (Greenfield, 1972, p. 172). Greenfield picks up as most pertinent to her own argument his attempt to trace 'this failure to a lack of conscious differentiation of self from others' and his prediction that this will be 'reflected in the structure of communication, as for example, in failing to make one's point of view known' (ibid.).

Greenfield's comparable studies and conclusions are related to her research into different groups of Wolof children in Senegal, namely: 'rural unschooled', 'bush schooled' and those who attended westernized schools in the cosmopolitan capital, Dakar. She provided tests for three different age groups in each set, corresponding to 6- and 7-year-olds, 8- and 9-year-olds and 11- to 13-year-olds. In tests designed to examine 'concept formation' she asked children to put together those pictures or objects in an array that were most alike, and then to explain the reasons for their choice. Unschooled children gave answers that led Greenfield to frighteningly large conclusions:

> It seemed that the unschooled Wolof children lacked Western self-consciousness; they did not distinguish between their own thought or statement about something and the thing itself. The concept of a personal point of view was also absent to a greater degree than in Western culture, for the unschooled children could group a given set of objects or pictures according to only one attribute, although there were several other possible bases for classifications. The Wolof school children, in contrast, did not differ essentially from Western children in this respect. It appeared that school was giving both urban and rural children something akin to Western self-consciousness for they could answer questions implying a personal point of view; and as they advanced in school they became increasingly capable of categorising the same stimuli according to different criteria or 'points of view'. (Greenfield, 1972, p. 173)

[. . .] Asked to select all the objects in an array that shared a particular attribute and to name the attribute, these children could provide an answer but the grammatical form revealed, according to Greenfield, inferior cognitive facility. Thus, if they said of a group of red objects simply 'red', their answer is taken to be satisfactory because 'we are not told *what* is red'. Its communication value is 'more dependent on the situational context'. Saying 'this' or 'they' 'red' is better practice because it entails use of pronouns which 'symbolise what concrete objects belong to the category'. The 'superordinate grouping' has been explained by 'linguistic predication'. 'Schooled children did this more often than unschooled and so were less context-bound' (Greenfield, 1972, p. 174).

Further refinements proposed by Greenfield include an analysis of the significance of grammatical forms for cognitive facility. In Wolof language it is possible to say either 'this is round' or 'this — round'. Greenfield found that the particular form used corresponded to the degree of what she calls 'abstractness'. 'A superordinate grouping in which it is explicitly stated that all members share a single attribute was, however, much more likely when linguistic predicates were formed as complete sentences with copula ['they are round'] than as incomplete sentences without. For a schooled child, the probability was increased threefold; for an unschooled child, it was increased sixfold' (ibid.). Similarly, schooled children were more likely to say 'they — round' than to itemize each member of the array 'this — round; this — round' etc. Greenfield takes this to be further evidence of the greater degree of abstraction being learned in schools.

She links such abstraction explicitly with the fact that schools teach literacy:

> The results led to the hypothesis that school is operating on grouping operations at least partly through the training embodied in the written language. Writing is practice in the use of linguistic contexts as independent of immediate reference. Thus the embedding of a label in a total sentence structure (complete linguistic predication) indicates that it is less tied to its situational context and more related to its linguistic context. The implications of this fact for manipulability are great; linguistic context can be turned upside down more easily than real ones. Once thought is freed from the concrete situation the way is clear for symbolic manipulation and for Piaget's stage of formal operation in which the real becomes a sub-set of the possible. (Greenfield, 1972, p. 175.)

Greenfield's appeal, here, to literacy as the source of significant cognitive differences is crucial. It demonstrates, I would argue, the ideological use to which conceptions of literacy are being put in current academic practice. The appeal to literacy as the basis for mental differences is apparent in her claim that the superior cognitive operations of schooled children amongst the Wolof were 'learnt through the training embodied in written language' (ibid.). The reference to literacy in this context is what induced Hildyard and Olson to quote Greenfield in their own work in order to support their conjectures about the consequence of literacy for such aspects of thought as 'abstractness', 'logic' and 'embeddedness'. Furthermore, its application to class differences has been recognized by many commentators, most notably in the work of Basil Bernstein (1971) on whom Greenfield leans heavily. Stubbs (1980), for instance, notes that 'Bernstein's distinction between restricted and elaborated codes' has often 'been related to distinctions between spoken and written languages respectively' [. . .] (p. 111).

This trend represents, I would argue, a shift in traditional representations of the differences in thinking between members of different cultures. Writers concerned to establish a 'great divide' between the thinking processes of different social groups have classically described them in such terms as logic/pre-logical, primitive/modern and concrete/scientific. I would argue that the introduction of literate/pre-literate as the criterion for making such a division has given the tradition a new lease of life just as it was wilting under the powerful challenge of recent work in social anthropology, linguistics and philosophy. I would maintain that claims for the cognitive consequences of literacy must take account of this challenge. They cannot simply side-step it by claiming that the appeal to literacy has altered the nature of the 'great divide' theory.

In order to sustain the argument that I am putting forward here, it is important to establish what were the major arguments levelled by anthropologists and others against the 'great divide' theory. We can then proceed to apply them to the work on literacy that we have been examining.

The major challenge has been to question the evidence on the basis of which the distinction 'logical/pre-logical' was made. Analysis has been brought forward to show that what was taken as proof of a lack of logical processes amongst 'primitive' peoples was often simply misunderstanding by ill-informed European commentators of the meaning of what was being said and done. They were ill-informed in the sense that the conceptual basis for understanding such meaning was not carefully theorized, as well as in the more obvious sense that the travellers often simply did not know the language and did not spend enough time living in a particular society. A powerful challenge to such approaches was made as long ago as the 1930s by Professor E.E. Evans-Pritchard who lived with and studied the Azande of Central Africa, a technologically simple society whom Europeans therefore tended to assume were intellectually simple as well. He argued, however, that their views on witchcraft were not, in fact irrational, illogical or 'mystical' as European conceptions commonly supposed them to be. Once one had accepted the initial premise of statements about witchcraft, the processes of thought could be shown to be the same as those entailed in scientific thought. Other writers have enlarged on these insights, comparing the mechanisms for establishing proof in scientific practice with those of the Azande for establishing the nature of witchcraft. Michael Polanyi (1965), for instance, argued that the way in which a proposition is protected, through such mechanisms as 'nucleated suppression' etc., is exactly the same in both cases. Differences in the content of thought, such as concern with witchcraft or with physics, should not blind us to similarities in the fundamental processes of thought. Robin Horton, in a widely cited article on African systems of thought (1967), likewise attempted to break down the elements of scientific thinking in order to demonstrate that so-called 'primitive' peoples such as the Azande did in fact make use of the same elements of thought, although applied to different content. He argued that it is too simplistic, and indeed ethnocentric, to dismiss such peoples as irrational and unscientific. Too often all that is at fault is the observer's understanding of what other people's statements and actions mean.

Evans-Pritchard and others have also pointed out that the divisions between scientific and non-scientific thinking as such, if they can indeed be reliably established, do not necessarily correlate with different social groups. Members of supposedly 'primitive' societies clearly engage in scientific practices, such as empirical testing of hypotheses, when they plant seed, the successful growth of which is vital for their survival. Lévi-Strauss (1966) has shown, further, that the classification of the natural world amongst South American Indian tribes is as complex and as interesting as those of the academic biologist, at an intellectual as well as utilitarian level. Conversely, in many contexts in Western 'scientific' society, it is clear that what some writers have labelled 'non-scientific' thought is as evident as in non-Western societies. This has been investigated in close detail by such social anthropologists as Edmund Leach (1954, 1976), who attempted to describe the 'expressive' and symbolic aspects of thinking in industrial and non-industrial society alike. Wedding rituals in either case are a classic example of how the statements made by participants in a particular context should not be taken literally or at face value but must be interpreted as standing for something else, rich in ambiguity and figures of speech. The extent to which it would be mistaken to take our own rituals literally provides a standard from which to assess our understanding of the rituals and statements of other cultures. Too often what has been taken as 'illogical' or 'mystical' is, in reality, pregnant with symbolic meaning which the observer has failed to appreciate through attempting to interpret it literally.

The anthropological evidence, then, suggests that there is scientific and non-scientific thought in all societies and within all individuals. Observers have simply failed to remark the scientific nature of much of the thinking of so-called 'primitive' peoples and have perhaps overstated the 'scientific' nature of thinking in their societies.

The recognition of these misunderstandings, and of the amount of dead wood that has to be cleared away before a reliable account of cognitive operations and differences can be provided, is also apparent in recent work by sociolinguists. This work complements that of the anthropologists in the sense that it uses a cross-cultural perspective to study the thinking processes of different social groups within the researcher's own society.

Labov (1973), studying Negro youths in the New York ghetto, discovered, as did anthropologists studying other cultures, that representations of cognitive 'deprivation' were founded upon misunderstanding of the real meanings of such people's statements and actions, and upon ethnocentric assumptions about the ways in which logic can be recognized. On investigation, the speech of supposedly retarded New York ghetto youths turned out to have all of the qualities generally associated with logical thought — facility with complex propositions, meaningful sequence, rule recognition, syllogistic reasoning, etc. [. . .]

One reason for the previous misrepresentation of the logical abilities of such social groups is that the tests carried out to assess such abilities were unreliable both in method and in conception. The test situation itself was often authoritarian and unfamiliar, discouraging response, and leading to bright children being labelled unresponsive and subnormal. Labov, by simply altering the test situation, such as by creating informality or having two youths to one researcher, etc., came up with far 'better' results for clever youths who had been labelled ESN (educationally subnormal) by the conventional system.

[. . .] Learning to frame written material, particularly in test conditions, is a convention of our education systems. It can be shown to have uses and it may well be advantageous for working-class children to learn it for certain purposes. Its use for examination purposes is clearly a rather restricted justification, although it may account for much of the labelling of 'failure' which the working-class child experiences. Its uses for other social purposes, however, would need to be specified and justified in relation to the context. Moreover, it is only one convention amongst many. The conventions of working-class speech also have their uses, and one could provide an argument for some of these being taught to middle-class children. Perhaps some of the middle-class verbosity found by Labov could be eradicated in this way.

What is clear from this, though, is that what we are talking about are conventions, and it is obvious that conventions derive their meaning from social contexts. What some researchers have done is to shift the significance of their findings away from such socially precise conditions, and to claim a kind of extra-social status for their own conventions by associating them with supposedly general logical qualities. Greenfield in testing Wolof children is really testing for such conventions, although she describes her results in general cognitive terms as though they represented general mental qualities.

In doing so she is reviving the 'great divide' theory that has been so discredited by social anthropologists and sociolinguists. [. . .] Where Lévy-Bruhl's (1962; cf. also Evans-Pritchard, 1970) version of the 'great divide' theory claimed differences in cognitive *capacity* between members of different cultures, those appealing to literacy simply claim differences in cognitive *development*. The suggestion is no longer that a culture has acquired such technological skills as literacy because it is intellectually superior, as earlier racist theories have argued. Rather, it is claimed that a culture is intellectually superior because it has acquired that technology.

[. . .] The 'great divide' has been re-established, by the appeal to literacy, apparently on a 'scientific' basis and apparently without the offensive appeals to inherent cultural and intellectual superiority that discredited its early phases.

If, however, we do apply anthropological and linguistic perspectives to this recent work on the consequences of literacy, as I claim we must despite its claim to protection from them, then that work in fact turns out to be as biased as that of the earlier phases. If we strip it of the insulation apparently provided by its appeal to the technology of literacy, we will expose the same ethnocentric claims and uncritical faith in the observer's own ways of thinking.

When Greenfield claims that oral speech is context-dependent, the anthropological evidence would challenge her to demonstrate what speech, whether oral or written, was not. If she is simply referring to degrees of context-dependency, then she must establish a scale on which such things can be measured. She must also show the relationships of such a scale to the claims for detachment made within particular cultural conventions. Merina orators in Madagascar, for instance, make claims for detachment similar to those of Westernized educators in Senegal (Bloch, 1975). Greenfield's scale must be capable of distinguishing such local claims from 'true' evidence of detachment. The example, however, demonstrates the conceptual problems in devising such a scale since 'detachment' and 'context-dependency' are themselves culturally loaded terms. Greenfield (1972) attempts to avoid this by claiming to test for 'abstractness'. When, however, we examine her definitions and her evidence we find that the differences she discovers in performance skills are no more than differences in explicitness, of the kind noted by Labov. She defines abstraction, for instance, as 'a separation from' or 'the mental separation of an element from the situation or context in which it is embedded' (p. 169). When she applies this to her test situations, however, she tends to interpret it in the narrow sense of explicitness rather than with reference to the higher orders of logic to which abstractness usually refers and which the general weight of her argument implies. If, in fact, we apply the higher order definition to the evidence she adduces from Wolof schoolchildren we will find that it applies to schooled and unschooled alike. When unschooled children group the members of an array according to some such criterion as 'red' or 'round', they reveal exactly the higher processes of 'abstraction' even if their language use stops short of explicitness. Indeed, Labov's work and that of other linguists argues that any user of language is of necessity involved in abstraction in its higher order sense. The simple fact of referring to something not present is already a separation from the immediate context, while the concepts and terms employed in any language involve degrees of such separation. The word 'red' separates the colour of an object from its form. The word 'round' separates form from function, etc. Furthermore, the grammatical structure and the rules it entails are, as Labov (1973) points out, 'essential parts of any logical system'(p. 45). In observing such rules, as they clearly do since otherwise they would not communicate, unschooled Wolof children are demonstrating a use of logic, and of abstraction. The differences between schooled and unschooled children that Greenfield's material suggests are at a less universal and profound level than her descriptions imply.

On the least culture-bound scale for determining cognitive operations, that of 'degree of abstractness', the anthropologist and the linguist would tend, then, to argue that all societies and social groups share common capacities. Further, most would argue that all peoples have evidenced certain basic developments of these capacities, notably with regard to language facility and abstract thought. Where differences can be found in language use and mental skills, they are more appropriately described as cultural conventions than seen as evidence for profound disjunctures in mental development between members of different groups. The differences between schooled and unschooled Wolof children are more appropriately described as differences in conventional uses of explicitness than as differences in 'abstraction'. The reasons for such different conventions must then be sought in the social context.

[. . .]

References

Bernstein, B. (1971) *Classes, Codes and Control, Vol. 1.* London: Routledge and Kegan Paul.

Bloch M. (ed.) (1975) *Language and Oratory in Traditional Societies*. London: Academic Press.

Dale, R. et al. (eds) (1976) *Schooling and Capitalism*. Milton Keynes: Open University.

Evans-Pritchard, E. E. (1937) *Witchcraft, Oracles and Magic Amongst the Azande*. Oxford: Clarendon Press.

Evans-Pritchard, E. E. (1970) 'Lévy-Bruhl's Theory of Primitive Mentality', *Journal of the Anthropological Society of Oxford*, **1**(1).

Graff, H. J. (1979) *The Literacy Myth: Literacy and Social Structure in the 19th Century City*. London: Academic Press.

Graff, H. J. (1982) *Literacy and Social Development in the West: A Reader*. Cambridge: Cambridge University Press.

Greenfield, P. (1972) 'Oral or written language: the consequences for cognitive development in Africa, U.S. and England'. *Language and Speech*, No. 15.

Hildyard, A. and Olson, D. (1978) Literacy and the Specialisation of Language. Unpublished MS, Ontario Institute for Studies in Education.

Horton, R. (1967) 'African traditional thought and Western Science. *Africa*, **37**(1 and 2).

Labov, W. (1973) 'The logic of non-standard English'. Article 3.2, this volume.

Leach, E. (1954) *Political Systems of Highland Burma*. London School of Economics Monographs No. 44. London: Athlone Press.

Leach, E. (1976) *Culture and Communication*. Cambridge: Cambridge University Press.

Lévi-Strauss, C. (1966) *The Savage Mind*. London: Weidenfeld and Nicolson.

Lévi-Strauss, C. (1968) *Structural Anthropology*. Harmondsworth: Penguin.

Lévy-Bruhl, L. (1962) *How Natives Think*. Translated by L. A. Clare, London.

Polanyi, M. (1965) *Personal Knowledge*. London: Routledge and Kegan Paul.

Stubbs, M. (1980) *Language and Literacy*. London: Routledge and Kegan Paul.

4.4 Unpackaging Literacy

S. Scribner and M. Cole

Source: edited version of Scribner, S. and Cole, M. (1981) 'Unpackaging literacy'. In Whiteman, M. F. (ed.) *Writing: The Nature, Development and Teaching of Written Communication.* Hillsdale, N. J: Lawrence Erlbaum, pp. 71–87.

One of the important services anthropology has traditionally provided other social sciences is to challenge generalizations about human nature and the social order that are derived from studies of a single society. The comparative perspective is especially valuable when the topic of inquiry concerns psychological 'consequences' of particular social practices, such as, for example, different methods of child-rearing (permissive vs. restrictive) or schooling (formal vs. non-formal) or mass communication (oral vs. literate). It is a hazardous enterprise to attempt to establish causal relationships among selected aspects of social and individual function without taking into account the totality of social practice of which they are a part. How are we to determine whether effects on psychological functioning are attributable to the particular practices selected for study, or to other practices with which they covary, or to the unique patterning of practices in the given society? When we study seemingly 'same' practices in different societal contexts, we can better tease apart the distinctive impact of such practices from other features of social life.

Here we apply one such comparative approach to questions about reading and writing practices and their intellectual impact. Our approach combines anthropological field work with experimental psychological methods in a study of 'literacy without schooling' in a West African traditional society. We hope our findings will suggest a new perspective from which to examine propositions about the intellectual and social significance of literacy whose uncertain status contributes to our educational dilemmas.

[. . .] The argument for the general intellectual importance of writing is sometimes expressed as accepted wisdom and sometimes as knowledge revealed through psychological research. At one end of the spectrum there is the simple adage that 'An individual who writes clearly thinks clearly', and at the other, conclusions purporting to rest on scientific analysis, such as the recent statement that 'the cognitive restructurings caused by reading and writing develop the higher reasoning processes involved in extended abstract thinking' (Farrell, 1977, p. 451).

This is essentially a psychological proposition and one which is increasingly moving to the forefront of discussion of the 'writing problem'. Our research speaks to several serious limitations in developing this proposition as a ground for educational and social policy decisions. [. . .]

Speculations about cognitive consequences of literacy

[. . .]

While most psychologists have been interested in the psycholinguistic aspects of reading, some have concerned themselves with these theoretical conjectures on the cognitive consequences of writing. Vygotsky (1962) considered that writing involved a different set of psychological functions from oral speech. Greenfield (1968) has suggested that written language in the schools is the basis for the development of 'context-independent abstract thought' — the distinguishing feature of school-related intellectual skills. Scribner (1968) speculated that mastery of a written language system might underlie formal scientific operations of the type Piaget has investigated. Olson (1975) argues that experience with written text may lead to a mode of thinking which derives generalizations about reality from purely linguistic, as contrasted to, empirical operations. In his view, schooling achieves importance precisely because it is an 'instrument of literacy'. 'There is a form of human competence', he states, 'uniquely associated with development of a high degree of literacy that takes years of schooling to develop' (p. 148).

[. . .] Olson, to our knowledge, has developed his case from a theoretical analysis of the kind of inferential operations that the processing of written statements 'necessarily' entails. Scribner employed the same method of procedure.

These are perfectly satisfactory *starting* points for a theory of the intellectual consequences of reading and writing but they do not warrant the status of conclusions. At a minimum, we would want evidence that the consequences claimed for literacy can be found in comparisons of literate and non-literate adults living in the same social milieu whose material and social conditions of life do not differ in any systematic way.

We not only lack evidence for theoretical speculations about the relationship between writing and thinking, but in our opinion, the model of writing which underlies most psychological theorizing is too restricted to serve as a guide for the necessary research.

Some dominant conceptions of writing

Although all disciplines connected with writing acknowledge that it has different 'functions', these are often conceived as external to the writing act itself — that is, the functions being served by writing are not seen as intrinsic to an analysis of component skills. In theory and in practice, writing is considered a unitary (although admittedly complex) phenomenon representing some given and fixed set of processes. These processes, it is assumed, can be ferreted out and analysed by the psychologist, linguist and educator without regard to their contexts of use. The call for the present conference suggests such a view. It urges that national attention, which for some years has been directed towards the 'reading process', now be turned towards an investigation of the 'writing process'. Writing, together with reading, are described as 'abilities' which it is the task of education to enhance.

The 'writing process' is typically identified with the production of written discourse of text. Non-textual uses of writing, such as the notational systems employed in mathematics and the sciences, which also require complex symbol manipulation, are excluded from the domain of writing, along with other types of graphic representation which use non-linguistic elements (diagrams, codes, maps, for example).

In practice, a prototypical form of text underlies most analyses of the writing process[1]. This is the expository text or what Britton and his colleagues (1975) characterize as 'transactional writing'. Transactional writing is described as writing in which it is taken for granted that the writer means what he says and can be challenged for its truthfulness and its logicality: '. . . it is the typical language of science and of intellectual inquiry . . . of planning, reporting, instructing, informing, advising, persuading, arguing and theorising' (Martin et al., 1976, pp. 24, 25)'.

Models of the cognitive skills involved in writing are intimately tied up with this type of text. Thus in making the claim that certain analytic and inferential operations are only possible on the basis of written text, Olson (1975) selects the analytic essay to represent the 'congealed mental labor' represented in writing. Non-literate and literate modes of thought are basically distinguished by differential experience with the production and consumption of essayist text.

The development of writing skills is commonly pictured as a course of progression towards the production of expository text. Bereiter's (1977) suggested model of writing, for example, rests on the assumption that there is a lawful sequence in the growth of writing competence and that this sequence progresses towards the production of a well-crafted story or a logical coherent discussion of a proposition. At the apex of progressively more complex structures of writing skills is epistemic writing — writing that carries the function of intellectual inquiry. (Similar views are expressed by Moffett, 1968.)

What is apparent from this somewhat simplified sketch, is that most of our notions of what writing is about, the skills it entails and generates, are almost wholly tied up with school-based writing. Centrality of the expository text and well-crafted story in models of the writing process accurately reflects the emphasis in most school curricula. A recently completed study of secondary schools in England (Martin et al., 1976) found that writing classed as transactional (see definition above) constituted the bulk of written school work, increasing from 54 per cent of children's writing in the first year to 84 per cent in the last. Since such writing skills are both the aim of pedagogy and the enabling tools which sustain many of the educational tasks of the school, their pre-eminence in current research does not seem inappropriate. But we believe that near-exclusive preoccupation with school-based writing practices has some unfortunate consequences. The assumption that logicality is in the text and the text is in school can lead to a serious underestimation of the cognitive skills involved in non-school, non-essay writing, and, reciprocally, to an overestimation of the intellectual skills that the essayist test 'necessarily' entails. This approach binds the intellectual and social significance of writing too closely to the image of the academic and the professional member of society, writ large. It tends to promote the notion that writing outside of the school is of little importance and has no significant consequences for the individual. The writing crisis presents itself as purely a pedagogical problem — a problem located in the schools to be solved in the schools through the application of research and instructional techniques. What is missing in this picture is any detailed knowledge of the role and functions of writing outside of school, the aspirations and values which sustain it, and the intellectual skills it demands and fosters. As our study of literacy among the Vai indicates, these facts are central to an evaluation of the intellectual and social significance of writing.

Three literacies among the Vai

The Vai, a Mande-speaking people of northwestern Liberia, like their neighbours, practise slash-and-burn rice farming using simple iron tools, but they have attained a special place in world history as one of the few cultures to have independently invented a phonetic writing system (Koelle, 1854; Gelb, 1952; Dalby, 1967). Remarkably, this script, a syllabary of 200 characters with a common core of 20–40, has remained in active use for a century and a half within the context of traditional rural life and in coexistence with two universalistic and institutionally powerful scripts — the Arabic and Roman alphabets. Widely available to all members of the society (though in practice confined to men), Vai script is transmitted outside of any institutional setting and without the formation of a professional teacher group.

The fact that literacy is acquired in this society without formal schooling and that literates and non-literates share common material and social conditions allows for a more direct test of the relationship between literacy and thinking than is possible in our own society. Among the Vai we could make direct comparisons of the performance on cognitive tasks of reasonably well-matched groups of literate and non-literate adults. To do so, however, required us from the outset to engage in an ethnographic enterprise not often undertaken with respect to literacy — the study of literacy as acquired and practised in the society at large. Our effort to specify exactly what it is about reading and writing that might have intellectual consequences and to characterize these consequences in observable and measurable ways forced us away from reliance on vague generalizations. We found ourselves seeking more detailed and more concrete answers to questions about *how* Vai people acquire literacy skills, *what these skills are, and what* they do with them. Increasingly we found ourselves turning to the information we had obtained about actual literacy practices to generate hypotheses about cognitive consequences.

From this work has emerged a complex picture of the wide range of activities glossed by the term 'writing' the varieties of skills these activities entail and the specificity of their cognitive consequences.

What writing 'is' among the Vai

Our information about Vai literacy practices comes from a number of sources: interviews with some 700 adult men and women, in which anyone literate in one of the scripts was questioned extensively on how he had learned the script and what uses he made of it; ethnographic studies of literacy in two rural towns;[2] observations and records of Vai script teaching sessions and Qur'anic schools; analyses of Vai script and Arabic documents as they relate to Vai social institutions (see Goody et al., 1977).

We estimate that 28 per cent of the adult male population is literate in one of the three scripts, the majority of these in the indigenous Vai script, the next largest group in Arabic and the smallest in English. There is a substantial number of literate men who read and write both Vai and Arabic and a small number of triliterates. Since each script involves a different orthography, completion of a different course of instruction and, in the cases of Arabic and English, use of a foreign language, multiliteracy is a significant accomplishment.[3]

As in other multiliterate societies, functions of literacy tend to be distributed in regularly patterned ways across the scripts, bringing more clearly into prominence their distinctive forms of social organization, and transmission and function. In a gross way, we can characterize the major divisions among the scripts in Vai life as follows: English is the official script of political and economic institutions operating on a national scale: Arabic is the script of religious practice and learning; Vai script serves the bulk of personal and public needs in the villages for information preservation and communication between individuals living in different locales.

In daily practice these distinctions are often blurred, raising a host of interesting questions about the personal and situational factors which may influence the allocation of literacy work to one or another script.

English script has least visibility and least impact in the countryside. It is learned exclusively in Western-type government and mission schools, located for the most part outside of Vai country. Students leave home to pursue their education and to win their place in the modern sector. Little is seen of English texts in the villages, but paramount chiefs and some clan chiefs retain clerks to record court matters in English, and to maintain official correspondence with administrative and political functionaries.

Arabic writing, on the other hand, is an organic part of the village life. Almost every town of any size has a Qur'anic school conducted by a learned Muslim (often the chief or other leading citizen). These are usually 'schools without walls' — groups of boys ranging in age from approximately 4 years to 24, who meet around the fire twice a day for several hours of recitation and memorization of Qur'anic verses which are written on boards that each child holds. (Qur'anic teaching in West Africa is described in Wilks, 1968.) In Islamic tradition, committing the Qur'an to memory (internalizing it in literal form) is a holy act, and the student's progress through the text is marked at fixed intervals by religious observances and feasting. Initially, learning can only proceed by 'rote memorization' since the students can neither decode the written passages nor understand the sounds they produce. But students who persevere, learn to read (that is, sing out) the text and to write out passages — still with no understanding of the language. Some few who complete the Qur'an go on to advanced study under tutorship arrangements, learning Arabic as a language and studying Islamic religious, legal and other texts. In Vai country, there are a handful of outstanding scholars with extensive Arabic libraries who teach, study and engage in textual commentary, exegesis and disputation. Thus Arabic literacy can relate individuals to text on both the 'lowest' (repetition without comprehension) and 'highest' (analysis of textual meaning) levels. Arabic script is used in a variety of 'magico-religious' practices; its secular uses include correspondence, personal journal notes and occasionally trade records. The overwhelming majority of individuals with Qur'anic training, however, do not achieve understanding of the language and their literacy activities are restricted to reading or writing out known passages of the Qur'an or frequently used prayers, a service performed for others as well as for oneself.

Approximately 90 per cent of Vai are Muslim and, accordingly, Qur'anic knowledge qualifies an individual for varied roles in the community. Becoming literate in the Arabic language means becoming integrated into a close-knit but territorially extended social network, which fuses religious ideals, fraternal self-help, trade and economic relationships with opportunities for continuing education (see Wilks, 1968).

Knowledge of Vai script might be characterized as 'literacy without education'. It is typically learned within a two-week to two-month period with the help of a friend, relative or citizen who agrees to act as teacher. Learning consists of committing the characters to memory and practice in reading, first lists of names, later personal letters written in the Vai script. Demonstration of the ability to write a letter without errors is a common terminating point for instruction. With rare exceptions, there are no teaching materials except such letters or other written material as the teacher may have in his personal possession. 'Completion of lessons' is not the endpoint of learning: there are frequent consultations between ex-student and teacher. For practised scribe as well as novice, literacy activities often take a cooperative form (e.g. A goes to B to ask about characters he can't make out) and sometimes a contentious one (e.g. A and B dispute whether a given character is correct or in error).

Vai script uses are overwhelmingly secular. It serves the two classical functions of writing: memory (preserving information over time) and communication (transmitting it over space) in both personal and public affairs, with a heavy emphasis on the personal.[4]

From an analytic point of view, focusing on component skills, it is useful to classify script functions according to whether or not writing involves the production of text or non-text materials. Non-textual uses range from very simple activities to complex record-keeping. Among the simple activities are the uses of individual written characters as labels or marking devices (e.g. marking chairs lent for a public meeting with the names of owners, identifying one's house, clarifying information displayed in technical plans and diagrams).[5] Record-keeping, most typically a list-making activity, fulfills both social cohesion and economic functions. Lists of dowry items and death feast contributions, family albums of births, deaths, marriages — all help to regulate the kinship system of reciprocal rights and obligations. Lists enlarge the scope and planful aspects of commercial transactions: these include records of yield and income from cash-crop farming, proceeds netted in marketing, artisan records of customer orders and payments received.

A mere 'listing of lists', however, fails to convey the great variation in levels, systematicity, organization and completeness displayed in records. Some are barely decipherable series of names; others orderly columns and rows of several classes of information. Some genealogies consist of single-item entries scattered throughout copy books, others of sequential statements which shade off into narrative-like texts.

The more expert Vai literates keep public records from time to time when asked to do so. These are less likely to be continuing series than single list assignments: house tax payments for the current year, work contributions to an ongoing public project such as road- or bridge-building, a population headcount and the like.

Personal correspondence is the principal textual use of the script. Letter-writing is a ubiquitous activity which has evolved certain distinctive stylistic devices, such as conventional forms of salutation and signature. It is not uncommon to see letters passed from hand to hand in one small town, and many people who are not personally literate participate in this form of exchange through the services of scribes. Since Vai society like other traditional cultures developed and still maintains an effective system of oral contact and communication by message and 'grapevine', reasons for the popularity of letter-writing are not self-evident, especially since all letters must be personally sent and hand-delivered. Protection of secrets and guarantee of delivery are among the advantages most frequently advanced in favour of letters rather than word-of-mouth communication.

For all its popularity, letter-writing is circumscribed in ways which simplify its cognitive demands: the majority of Vai literates correspond only with persons already known to them (78 per cent of literates interviewed in our sample study reported they had never written to nor received a letter from a stranger). Many factors undoubtedly contribute to this phenomenon, among which the non-standardized and often idiosyncratic versions of script characters must figure prominently, but it is significant for hypotheses about intellectual skills that written communication among the Vai draws heavily upon shared background information against which the news is exchanged.

What about other texts? The first thing to note is that all textual material is held in private; texts are rarely circulated to be read, though on occasion and under special circumstances they might be made available for copying. Thus the relationship of Vai script literates to text is primarily as producer or writer, seldom as reader of another's work. This social arrangement has several important consequences. One is that reading is not an activity involving assimilation of novel knowledge or material; another is that existing texts reflect what people choose to write about, depending on their own interests and concepts of what writing is 'for'. Many texts are of a cumulative nature — that is, they are not set pieces, but rather comprise 'journals' or 'notebooks'. Each such 'book' might contain a variety of entries, some autobiographical (personal events, dreams), others impersonal and factual (facts of town history, for example). While not read as continuous texts, such materials are often used as important source books or data records and depending on their scope and age, may serve as archives.[6]

Some texts fit recognizable (in terms of Western literacy) genres. There are histories, for example, fables, books of maxims, parables and advice. In at least one instance, we have been able to obtain a set of documents of a Muslim self-help organization which included a Vai-script written constitution and bylaws (see Goody et al., 1977). As in the case of lists, the range of skills reflected in texts is broad. 'Histories' may be a collection of what were originally notes on scattered sheets of paper, assembled under one cover with no apparent chronological or other ordering: at the other extreme they might be well-organized and fluent narrations of a clan history or ambitious accounts of the origin and migration of the Vai people as a whole. While we do not know the relationship between written and oral history and narrative, and thus cannot determine whether written works are continuous or discontinuous with respect to the oral tradition, there clearly are individual texts which bear the stamp of creative literary and intellectual work. But it must be added that texts of this nature are the exception: most histories are brief, often fragmentary and written stories rare discoveries.

There are two types of text rarely found thus far, Britton et al.'s (1975) two polar types — the poetic, concerned with exploring personal experiences and feelings, and the transactional or expository, basically concerned with examining ideas or presenting a persuasive argument.

Vai script literates are known in the community and admired for their knowledge of books. Motivations sustaining the script are not restricted to pragmatic ones; individuals will cite its utilitarian value for correspondence, records and 'secrets' but will as often speak about the importance of the 'book' for self-education and knowledge and for preserving the history and reputation of the Vai people. To be looked upon with respect and to be remembered in history are important incentives to many Vai journal-writers.

It is apparent from this quick review that Vai people have developed highly diversified uses for writing and that personal values, pride of culture, hopes of gain — a host of pragmatic, ideological and intellectual factors — sustain popular literacy. The level of literacy that obtains among the Vai must, however, on balance be considered severely restricted. Except for the few Arabic scholars or secondary school English students, literacy does not lead to learning of new knowledge nor involve individuals in new methods of inquiry. Traditional processes of production, trade and education are little affected by the written word.

Effects of literacy

Should we conclude that these restrictions disqualify indigenous Vai literacy as 'real literacy'? It clearly has social consequences for its practitioners and (we hypothesized) might have identifiable cognitive consequences as well. It seemed unlikely, however, that it would have the very general intellectual consequences which are presumed to be the result of high levels of school-based literacy.

Nonetheless, this possibility was explored as part of our major survey of Vai adults at the outset of the project. In fact, we found no evidence of marked differences in performance on logical and classificatory tasks between non-schooled literates and non-literates. Consequently, we adopted a strategy of making a functional analysis of literacy. We examined activities engaged in by those knowing each of the indigenous scripts to determine some of the component skills involved. On the basis of these analyses, we designed tasks with different content but with hypothetically similar skills to determine if prior practice in learning and use of the script enhanced performance.

Communication skills

Since letter-writing is the most common use to which Vai script is put, it is reasonable to look here for specific intellectual consequences. In the psychological literature, written communication is considered to impose cognitive demands not encountered in face-to-face oral communication. In writing, meaning is carried entirely by the text. An effective written communication requires sensitivity to the informational needs of the reader and skill in use of elaborative linguistic techniques. We believed it reasonable to suppose that Vai literates' experience in writing and receiving letters should contribute to the development of these communication skills. To test this proposition, we adapted a communication task used in developmental research (Flavell et al., 1968). With little verbal explanation, subjects were taught to play a simple board game and then were asked to explain the game without the board present to someone unfamiliar with it.

We compared a full range of literate and non-literate groups, including junior high and high school students, under several conditions of play.

Results were quite orderly. On several indices of amount of information provided in an explanation, groups consistently ranked as follows: high school students, Vai literates and non-literates. Vai literates, more often than other non-student groups, provided a general characterization of the game before launching into a detailed account of rules of play. If there is anything to the notion that what is acquired in a particular literacy is closely related to practice of *that* literacy, the differential between Vai and Arabic literates is exactly what we would expect to find: on the average, Vai literates engage in letter-writing more frequently than Arabic literates. It is interesting, too, that both Vai and Arabic letter-writing groups were superior to all non-literate groups.

Memory

We were also able to show specific consequences of Qur'anic learning. Regardless of what level of literacy they attain, all Arabic literates begin by learning to recite passages of the Qur'an by heart, and some spend many years in the process. Learning by memorization might promote efficient techniques for learning to memorize. To test this possibility, we employed a verbal learning task (Mandler and Dean, 1969) involving processes that our observations indicated matched those in Qur'anic memorization. In this task, a single item is presented on the first trial and a new item is added on each succeeding trial for a total of 16 trials and 16 items. The subject is required to recall the words in the order presented. Our comparison groups were the same as those used in the communication experiment. English students again ranked first, but in this task, Arabic literates were superior to Vai literates as well as to non-literates in both amount recalled and in preservation of serial order. If this superiority were simply the manifestation of 'better general memory abilities' on the part of Qur'anic scholars, we would expect Arabic literates to do better in *all* memory tasks, but this was not the case. When the requirement was to remember and repeat a story, Qur'anic students did no better, and no worse, than other groups. When the requirement was to remember a list of words under free recall conditions, there were no significant performance differentials. Superiority of Arabic literates was specific to the memory paradigm which shadowed the learning requirements of Qur'anic school.

Language analysis

In a third domain, we were again able to demonstrate the superiority of Vai literates. Vai script is written without word division, so that reading a text requires as a first step the analysis of separate characters followed by their integration into meaningful linguistic units. Our observations of Vai literates 'decoding' letters suggested that this process of constructing meaning was carried out by a reiterative routine of sounding our characters until they 'clicked' into meaningful units. We supposed that this experience would foster skills in auditory perception of semantically meaningful but deformed (i.e. slowed down) utterances. Materials consisted of tape recordings in which a native speaker of Vai read meaningful Vai sentences syllable by syllable at a two-second rate. The task was to listen and to repeat the sentence as well as to answer a comprehension question about it. Vai literates were better at comprehending and repeating the sentences than Arabic literates and non-literates; and Vai literates with advanced skills performed at higher levels than Vai literates with beginning skills. Comparisons of performance on repetition of sentences in which words, not syllables, were the units showed no differences among literate groups but a sizeable one between all literate and non-literate populations. The comparison of the two tasks isolates skill in syllable integration as a specific Vai script-related skill.

Taken as a group, these three sets of studies provide the strongest experimental evidence to date that activities involved in reading and writing may in fact promote specific language-processing and cognitive skills.

Implications

Our research among the Vai indicates that, even in a society whose primary productive and cultural activities continue to be based on oral communication, writing serves a wide variety of social functions. Some of the pragmatic functions we have described are by no means trivial, either in indigenous terms or in terms of the concerns in economically developed countries for the promotion of 'functional literacy' skills. Vai literates routinely carry out a variety of tasks using their script which are carried out no better (and perhaps worse) by their English-educated peers who have completed a costly 12-year course of school study. The record-keeping activities which we described briefly in earlier sections of this paper provide the communities within which the literates live with an effective means of local administration. The fact that court cases were once recorded in the script and that religious texts are often translated into Vai as a means of religious indoctrination suggest that uses of writing for institutional purposes are fully within the grasp of uneducated, but literate, Vai people.

While the bulk of activities with the Vai script may be characterized in these pragmatic terms, evidence of scholarly and literary uses, even rudimentary ones, suggest that non-schooled literates are concerned with more than the 'immediate personal gain' aspects of literacy. We could not understand in such narrowly pragmatic terms the effort of some Vai literates to write clan histories and record famous tales nor the ideological motivations and values sustaining long years of Qur'anic learning.

Of course we cannot extrapolate from Vai society to our own, but it is reasonable to suppose that there is at least as wide a range of individual aspirations and social practices capable of sustaining a variety of writing activities in our own society as among the Vai. Since our social order is so organized that access to better-paying jobs and leadership positions commonly requires writing skills, there are even more powerful economic and political incentives at work to encourage interest. It seems premature to conclude that only schools and teachers are concerned with writing and that writing would perish in this era of television if not artificially kept alive in academic settings.

An alternative possibility is that institutionalized learning programmes have thus far failed to tap the wide range of 'indigenous' interests and practices which confer significance on writing. Ethnographic studies of writing in different communities and social contexts — in religious, political and fraternal groups — might help broaden existing perspectives.

Our research also highlights the fact that the kind of writing that goes on in school has a very special status. It generates products that meet teacher demands and academic requirements but may not fulfil any other immediate instrumental ends. Is this an unavoidable feature of writing instruction?

When we look upon school-based writing within the context of popular uses of writing found among the Vai, we were also impressed by what appears to be the unique features of the expository or essay type text. In what non-schooled settings are such texts required and produced in our own society? Although developmental models of writing place such texts at the 'highest stage' of writing ability, we find it difficult to order different types of texts and writing functions to stages of development. Our evidence indicates that social organization creates the conditions for a variety of literacy activities, and that different types of text reflect different social practices. With respect to *adult* literacy, a functional approach appears more appropriate than a developmental one. The loose generalization of developmental models developed for work with children to instructional programmes with adolescents and adults is certainly questionable.

With respect to intellectual consequences, we have been able to demonstrate that literacy-without-schooling is associated with improved performance on certain cognitive tasks. This is certainly important evidence that literacy does 'count' in intellectual terms, and it is especially important in suggesting *how* it counts. The consequences of literacy that we identified are all highly specific and closely tied to actual practices with particular scripts; learning the Qur'an improved skills on a specific type of memory task, writing Vai script letters improved skills in a particular communication task. Vai literates and Arabic literates showed different patterns of skills, and neither duplicated the performance of those who had obtained literacy through attendance at Western-type English schools.

The consequences we were able to identify are constrained by the type of practices common in Vai society. We did not find, for example, that performance on classification tasks and logic problems was affected by non-school literacy. This outcome suggests that speculations that such skills are the 'inevitable outcome' of learning to use alphabetic scripts or write any kind of text are overstated. Our evidence leaves open the question of whether conceptual or logical skills are promoted by experience with expository text; in fact if our argument that specific uses promote specific skills is valid, we should expect to find certain skills related to practice in written exposition. The challenging question is how to identify these without reintroducing the confounding influence of schooling.

Perhaps the most challenging question of all is how to balance appreciation for the special skills involved in writing with an appreciation of the fact that there is no evidence that writing promotes 'general mental abilities'. We did not find superior 'memory in general' among Qur'anic students nor better language integration skills 'in general' among Vai literates. Moreover, improvements in performance that appear to be associated with literacy were thus far only observed in contrived experimental settings. Their applicability to other domains is uncertain. We do not know on the basis of any controlled observation whether more effective handling of an experimental communication task, for example, signifies greater communication skills in non-experimental situations. Are Vai literates better than Arabic literates or non-literates at communicating anything to anybody under any circumstances? We doubt that to be the case, just as we doubt that Qur'anic learning leads to superior memory of all kinds in all kinds of situations. There is nothing in our findings that would lead us to speak of cognitive consequences of literacy with the notion in mind that such consequences affect intellectual performance in all tasks to which the human mind is put. Nothing in our data would support the statement quoted earlier that reading and writing entail fundamental 'cognitive restructurings' that control intellectual performance in all domains. Quite the contrary: the very specificity of the effects suggests that they may be closely tied to performance parameters of a limited set of tasks, although as of now we have no theoretical scheme for specifying such parameters. This outcome suggests that the metaphor of a 'great divide' may not be appropriate for specifying differences among literates and non-literates under contemporary conditions.

The monolithic model of what writing is and what it leads to, described at the beginning of this paper, appears in the light of comparative data to fail to give full justice to the multiplicity of values, uses and consequences which characterize writing as social practice.

Notes

1 The narrative text is also a common prototype, but we are leaving aside for the time being approaches to creative writing which have largely been initiated and developed outside the public school system.

2 These were carried out by Michael R. Smith, an anthropologist from Cambridge University.

3 Because this phenomenon is rarely encountered in our own culture, we tend to peg our 'basic skills models' of writing very closely to the particular characteristics and structure of a single orthographic system and assumptions of pre-writing fluency in the language represented. As Fishman (1975) suggests was the case with bilingualism, studies of

multiscript-using communities might well enlarge the framework in which basic research on literacy is conducted. For accounts of other non-industrialized societies with a number of simultaneously active scripts, see Gough, 1968: Tambiah, 1968; Wilder, 1972, Schofield (1968) reminds us that between the sixteenth and nineteenth centuries in England, early instruction in reading and writing was conducted with texts in English while higher education was conducted in classical Latin.

4 Public functions of Vai script appear to be declining as English becomes mandatory for administrative and judicial matters.

5 Gelb (1952) presents an interesting argument that social origins of non-pictorial writing systems are to be found in the use of individualized symbols as brands of ownership.

6 It is reported (Scribner, field notes) that an entire Vai community in Monrovia was able to retain its right to disputed land because an elderly kinsman had recorded in his book the names of the original deed-holders.

References

Bereiter, C. (1977) Integration of skill systems in the development of textual writing competence (Mimeo.)

Brifton, J.; Burgess, T., Martin, N., McLeod, A. and Rosen, H. (1975) *The Development of Writing Abilities.* London: McMillan Edinburgh Ltd.

Dalby, D. (1967) 'A survey of the indigenous scripts of Liberia and Sierra Leone'. *African Language Studies,* **VIII**, 1–51.

Farrell, T. J. (1977) 'Literacy, the basics, and all that jazz'. *College English,* January, 443–459.

Fishman, J. A. (1975) 'The description of societal bilingualism'. In Fishman, J. A., Cooper, R. L. and Ma, R. *Bilingualism in the Barrio.* Bloomington, Indiana: Indiana University Publications, pp. 605–611.

Flavell, J. H., Botkin P. J., Fry, C. L., Wright, J. W. and Jarvis, P. E. (1968) *The Development of Role-taking and Communication Skills in Children.* New York: Wiley.

Gelb, I. J. (1952) *A Study of Writing.* Chicago: The University of Chicago Press.

Goody, J., Cole, M. and Scribner, S. (1977) 'Writing and formal operations: a case study among the Vai.' *Africa,* **47**(3).

Gough, K. (1968) 'Implications of literacy in traditional China and India'. In Goody, J. (ed.) *Literacy in Traditional Societies.* Cambridge: Cambridge University Press, pp. 69–84.

Greenfield, P. (1968) 'Oral or written language: the consequences for cognitive development in Africa and the United States'. Presented at Symposium on Cross-Cultural Cognitive Studies, Chicago, 1968.

Koelle, S. W. (1854) *Outlines of a Grammar of the Vai Language.* London: Church Missionary House.

Mandler, G. and Dean P. (1969) 'Seriation: the development of serial order in free recall'. *Journal of Experimental Psychology,* **81**, 207–215.

Martin, N., D'Arcy, P., Newton, B. and Parker, R. (1976) *Writing and Learning Across the Curriculum 11–16.* London: Ward Lock Educational.

Moffett, J. (1968) *Teaching the Universe of Discourse.* Boston: Houghton-Mifflin.

Olson, D. R. (1975) 'Review of *Toward a literate society,* John, B. Carroll and Jeanne Chall (eds)'. *Proceedings of the National Academy of Education.* **2**, 109–178.

Schofield, R. S. (1968) 'The measurement of literacy in pre-industrial England'. In Goody, J. (ed.) *Literacy in Traditional Societies.* Cambridge: Cambridge University Press, pp. 311–325.

Scribner, S. (1968) Cognitive consequences of literacy. New York: Albert Einstein College of Medicine, (Mimeo.)

Tambiah, S. J. (1968) 'Literacy in a Buddhist village in north-east Thailand'. In Goody, J.

(ed.) *Literacy in a Traditional Society*. Cambridge: Cambridge University Press, pp. 85–131.

Vygotsky, L. S. (1962) *Thought and Language*. Cambridge, Mass.: M I T Press.

Wilder, B. (1972) An examination of the phenomenon of the literacy skills of unschooled males in Laos. PhD Dissertation. Michigan State University.

Wilks, I. (1968) 'The transmission of Islamic learning in the Western Sudan'. In Goody, J. (ed.) *Literacy in Traditional Societies*. Cambridge: Cambridge Universities Press. pp. 161–197.

4.5 Emergent Literacy as a Perspective for Examining How Young Children Become Writers and Readers

W. H. Teale and E. Sulzby

Source: Extracts from Teale, W. H. and Sulzby, E. (1986) 'Introduction: Emergent literacy as a perspective for examining how young children become writers and readers'. In *Emergent Literacy: Writing and Reading*. Norwood, N. J: Ablex, pp. vii–xxv.

[. . .]

From reading readiness to emergent literacy: the challenge

For years the classroom experiences of many kindergarten and early childhood educators and results from research projects such as Durkin's (1966) have indicated that the reading readiness paradigm was theoretically and practically inappropriate. However, it has only been within the past decade that a substantial and unified challenge to the traditional approach has arisen.

The roots of this challenge can be traced to two broader trends: (a) cognitive approaches to issues of learning and development and their increasing influence on educationally related research and classroom practice, and (b) renewed interest in the first few years of life as a period of critical significance in development. These trends pointed to the importance of looking carefully at children during the early years when the foundations for all development are being laid, and to regarding children as active participants in learning — hypothesis generators and problem solvers — rather than as passive recipients of information.

The influence of these trends is nowhere more apparent than in the field of psychology of language. The year 1956 is generally regarded as marking the birth of the 'cognitive sciences' (Bruner, 1983). By 1960 the Center for Cognitive Studies had been established at Harvard, and during the 1960s and early 1970s, researchers increasingly turned their attention to the close observation of young children. They developed sophisticated research techniques, adapted from a variety of disciplinary fields and intended to shed light on the mental processes involved in learning language. In short, there formed an area of study identified as *language acquisition research* that sought to desribe the strategies employed in learning and using language.

This research found that, indeed, the child is an active hypothesis-generating language user. Eventually the child-as-hypothesis-tester description was modified towards the notion of child-as-constructor-of-language. In all, cognitive models proved to be far more successful at accounting for first-language learning than were stimulus-response models. Reasoning that reading was also a language process, people began to apply a similar theoretical/research approach in the attempt to understand early reading better. Findings from the language acquisition research (which had focused entirely on *oral* language) were used by researchers who hypothesized that oral language and written language proficiency might develop in parallel ways.

In the field of education, Marie Clay was a pioneer in examining young children's reading and writing in the light of language acquisition research. Up to this point, ages one through five were generally regarded as the period during which oral language and reading readiness were developed, with writing and reading starting for almost all children only after they entered school. Clay began her research with five-year-old entrants in New Zealand (Clay, 1967). Her main objective was to provide better descriptions of the early reading behaviours of children so that children with reading difficulties could be identified as early as possible. The five-year-olds received deliberate instruction in reading, but the method used was one which 'stressed fluency, meaning and "learning as one reads", with only slight attention to letter–sound associations and learning a basic sight vocabulary' (Clay, 1967, p. 12). This early research showed that young children could engage in important reading behaviours such as visual sensitivity to letter and word forms, appropriate directional movements, self-correction, and synchronized matching of spoken word units with written word units. Clay (1967) concluded, 'There is nothing in this research that suggests that contact with printed language forms should be withheld from any five-year-old child on the ground that he is immature' (p. 24).

This work seems to have brought Clay 'naturally' in touch with reading during the *pre*school years as well. Certainly the influence of Dolores Durkin's studies of early readers (Durkin, 1966) on Clay's work is in evidence. [. . .] The first edition of *Reading: The Patterning of Complex Behaviour* (Clay, 1972) also contained considerable reference to preschool reading experience and brought to light how Clay felt her thoughts on reading development during the early years differed from the traditional concept of reading readiness.

> . . . the transformation [to understanding the links between oral and written language] at the early reading stage takes place only in the presence of print and when the child actively seeks to discover how oral and written language are related. . . . It is the need to transform preschool skills into new ways of responding that . . . makes early reading behaviour a matter of learning and discredits the 'growth from within' concept of readiness. In this book the new entrant stage of being introduced to printed language

will be referred to as the 'early reading behaviour stage' and the terms 'preparation for reading' or 'reading readiness training' or 'prereading' will be avoided. (pp. 5–6)

Clearly, though perhaps not surprisingly for the 1970s, Clay rejected the neural ripening philosophy. However, her rejection of *prereading* and *reading readiness* indicated that although she recognized that becoming literate implies discontinuities in development because it requires the child to develop new ways of responding, there are important continuities between what she termed the child's *emergent literacy* (Clay, 1966) behaviours and those behaviours employed when the child is able to read independently.

Finally, we see another important seed in this volume that would eventually grow into a separate book (*What Did I Write?* 1975): the inclusion of some writing samples from young children and discussion of their significance for literacy development. Though the book is definitely one about reading, the attention to writing portends the general move by researchers towards focusing on the relationships between writing and reading in early literacy development.

Reading: The Patterning of Complex Behaviour (1972) was a significant volume for several reasons. First, it emphasized the importance of the early childhood period in the development of literacy. In particular, it illustrated that there was a great deal for researchers and teachers to learn by examining what children do with books and reading and writing, even though the children cannot yet read or write in the conventional sense. Finally, in this book the process of distinguishing between an emergent literacy approach to literacy development in early childhood and a reading readiness approach was in evidence.

At the same time that Clay was conducting her work, Yetta Goodman was examining the reading processes of beginning readers in the United States (Y. Goodman, 1967). Kenneth Goodman's model of the reading process (K. Goodman, 1967, 1968) was gaining widespread acceptance as a more adequate description of fluent reading than previous conceptualizations. Yetta Goodman hypothesized that the model was also appropriate for describing beginning reading. In the course of completing her doctoral dissertation research with first graders (Y. Goodman, 1967), Goodman found that even children who would be described as 'at risk' for becoming competent readers had knowlege about many aspects of reading: They knew how to handle books and they understood the directionality of written language and the function of print in a book, for example. As she said later, 'It slowly became obvious to me that children's discoveries about literacy in a literate society such as ours must begin much earlier than at school age' (Y. Goodman, 1984, p. 102). This realization and the influence of Dolores Durkin's studies of early readers (Durkin, 1966) prompted her to look at even younger children.

Thus, the early environmental print awareness studies were begun. Labels, signs and logos common to preschool children's environments were presented to the children in varying degrees of contextualization to check on their awareness of environmental print. Results from these studies indicated that the roots of the reading process are established very early in life. Furthermore, the results supported the notions that function precedes form in learning to read and that there is a 'movement from learning to read printed symbols in familiar situational contexts toward more reliance on language contexts' (Goodman and Goodman, 1979, p. 145). The print awareness work led the Goodmans to their conclusion that learning to read is natural in a literate society.

This work and subsequent research by Goodman and her students [. . .] directly contradicted many of the principles upon which the traditional reading readiness approach was based. The studies of Clay and Goodman from an educational perspective, and the work of others from the fields of psychology and linguistics inspired many researchers interested in child development and education to approach the study of the writing and reading of very young children. Hallmarks of this new approach have been its cognitive and developmental underpinnings. [. . .] The study of literacy development in early childhood has expanded to the point where in the mid-1980s we can truly say that the new perspective has become legitimized as a field attracting wide interest.

Furthermore, the conclusions emanating from the body of research cast serious doubt on the tenets outlined earlier which underlie the concept of reading readiness. Specifically, what has been learned over the past few years about literacy development in early childhood leads to the following conclusions:

1. Literacy development begins long before children start formal instruction. Children use legitimate reading and writing behaviours in the informal settings of home and community. The search for skills which predict subsequent achievement has been misguided because the onset of literacy has been misconceived.
2. *Literacy* development is the appropriate way to describe what was called *reading* readiness: the child develops as a *writer/reader*. The notion of reading preceding writing, or vice versa, is a misconception. Listening, speaking, reading and writing abilities (as aspects of language — both oral and written) develop concurrently and interrelatedly, rather than sequentially.
3 Literacy develops in real-life settings for real-life activities in order to 'get things done'. Therefore, the functions of literacy are as integral a part of learning about writing and reading during early childhood as are the forms of literacy.
4 Children are doing critical cognitive work in literacy development during the years from birth to six.
5 Children learn written language through active engagement with their world. They interact socially with adults in writing and reading situations; they explore print on their own, and they profit from modelling of literacy by significant adults, particularly their parents.
6 Although children's learning about literacy can be described in terms of generalized stages, children can pass through these stages in a variety of ways and at different ages. Any attempts to 'scope and sequence' instruction should take this developmental variation into account.

We said earlier in this article that we felt a term was needed to summarize/capture thus new paradigm for understanding early childhood reading and writing. We have decided to employ the term *emergent literacy*, to the best of our knowledge a notion first developed by Marie Clay (1966) in her doctoral dissertation research. Our choice of *emergent literacy* was made for a variety of reasons, which can be explained by examining the significance of each of the words comprising the term. Let us start with *literacy*. In research and teaching both, considerably less attention has been paid to writing than to reading (Graves, 1978), but the writing development of preschool children in particular has been neglected. However, we can now see a growing realization that in order to understand reading we must understand writing, and vice versa.

In 1970 Charles Read completed his pioneering study of young children's categorization of speech sounds as evidenced by invented spellings found in their compositions. Read's research prompted Carol Chomsky (1971) to suggest that young children should 'write first, read later' and stimulated considerable work in young children's spelling in subsequent years (see Henderson and Beers, 1980). In general, this work was concerned with sound–symbol correspondences and orthographic patterns in written language rather than with children encoding intended meanings or showing evidence of composing in their writing.

Following this period, numerous parents, researchers, and teachers produced evidence that young children do indeed write, whether it be by 'scribble', strings of letters, invented spelling, or other means of representation, some manifestations of which include drawing. In 1975 Marie Clay published *What Did I Write?*, cataloguing a series of principles evidenced in children's early writing. Subsequent years have seen more and more attention being given to children's ability to compose text (see Farr, 1984, 1985). Even the mechanics of writing have been re-examined. In addition to spelling, letter formation has been found to emerge conceptually rather than just as rote imitation (see Simmer, 1981; and note the renewed attention to Hildreth, 1932, 1936), and space as a marker for word boundaries shows evidence of being learned through a process of hypothesis-guided construction (Clay, 1975, 1979; Sulzby, 1983).

Glenda Bissex's *GNYS AT WRK: A Child Learns to Write and Read* was published in 1980. Its subtitle captures the tenor of the present times. Literacy — writing as well as reading rather than reading itself — is what is of interest. The two processes develop in coordination with each other. Bissex, for example, chose to focus on how her child treated himself as a writer. But reading is integrally involved in becoming a writer. When children write, they read their own texts and thereby monitor their production. In fact, we now have substantial evidence to indicate that there exists a dynamic relation between writing and reading, because each influences the other in the course of development (Ferreiro and Teberosky, 1982; Sulzby, 1983) and that reading comprehension is engaged in during writing (through reading one's own writing) and is not a trivial matter (Sulzby, 1983, 1985b,c).

In fact, research in early writing has helped us rethink research in early reading. Now we know that we must understand both processes if we are fully to understand written language development in the young child. [. . .]

The term *emergent* also has special significance. Let us make clear that the term is not without considerable history. '*Emergent*' has long been used in the fields of philosophy, sociology, biology and developmental psychology. Though having somewhat different connotations in each of these disciplines, it contains some core features which are elegantly suited to describe literacy in the young child. First, '*emergent*' connotes development rather than stasis; it signifies something in the process of becoming, as is implied by Mead (1932). As we have argued earlier, the first years of the child's life represent a period when legitimate reading and writing development are taking place. These behaviours and knowledges are not *pre-* anything, as the term *prereading* suggests. Nor is it accurate to regard this as stage 0(zero) in literacy development as Chall (1983) proposes in her scheme of reading stages. Such a label suggests that only at stage 1, after about 6 years of age, does initial reading, i.e. 'real' reading (or writing), begin. But as researchers have increasingly focused on literacy learning in very young children, more and more of these scholars have come to the conclusion that it is not reasonable to point to *a* time in a child's life when literacy begins. Rather, at whatever point we look, we see children *in the process of becoming* literate, as the term '*emergent*' indicates.

[. . .]

References

Bissex, G. L (1980) *GNYS AT WRK: A child learns to write and read*. Cambridge. MA: Harvard University Press.

Bruner, J. S. (1960) *The process of education*. Cambridge. MA: Harvard University Press.

Bruner, J. S. (1983) *In search of mind*. New York: Harper & Row.

Chall, J. S. (1983) Stages of reading development. New York: McGraw-Hill.

Chomsky, C. (1971) Write now, read later. *Childhood Education*, **47**, 296–299.

Clay, M. M. (1966) *Emergent reading behaviour*. Unpublished doctoral dissertation. University of Auckland, New Zealand.

Clay, M. M. (1967) 'The reading behavior of five-year-old children: A research report'. *New Zealand Journal of Educational Studies*, **2**, 11–31.

Clay, M. M. (1972) *Reading: The patterning of complete behaviour*. Auckland, New Zealand: Heinemann Educational.

Clay, M. M. (1975) *What did I write?* Auckland, New Zealand: Heinemann Educational.

Clay, M. M. (1979) *Reading: The patterning of complex behaviour* (2nd ed.). Auckland, New Zealand: Heinemann Educational.

Durkin, D. (1966) *Children who read early*. New York: Teachers College Press.

Farr, M. (1984, April) 'State of the art: Children's early writing development'. Paper presented at American Educational Research Association Annual Meeting, New Orleans, LA.

Farr, M. (Ed.) (1985) *Advances in writing research*. Vol. 1: *Children's early writing development*. Norwood, NJ: Abex.

Ferreiro, E., & Teberosky, A. (1982) *Literacy before schooling*. Exeter, NH: Heinemann Educational.

Goodman, K. S. (1967) 'Reading: A psycholinguistic guessing game'. *Journal of the Reading Specialist*, **4**, 126–135.

Goodman, K. S. (1968) *Study of children's behavior while reading orally*. (Final Report, Project No. S 425). Washington, DC: U. S. Department of Health, Education, and Welfare.

Goodman, K. S. & Goodman, Y. M. (1979) 'Learning to read is natural'. In L. B. Resnick & P. Weaver (Eds.). *Theory and practice of early reading*. Hillsdale, NJ, Erlbaum.

Goodman, Y. M. (1967) A psycholinguistic description of observed oral reading phenomena in selected young beginning readers. Unpublished doctoral dissertation. Wayne State University, Detroit.

Goodman, Y. M. (1980) 'The roots of literacy'. In M. P. Douglass (Ed.). *Claremont Reading Conference Forty-fourth Yearbook*. Claremont, CA: The Claremont Reading Conference.

Goodman, Y. M. (1984) 'The development of initial literacy'. In H. Goelman. A. Oberg. & F. Smith (Eds.). *Awakening to literacy*. Exeter, NH: Heinemann Educational.

Graves, D. H. (1978) *Balance the basics: Let them write*. A Report to the Ford Foundation. New York: Ford Foundation.

Henderson, E. H. & Beers, J. (Eds.) (1980) *Development and cognitive aspects of learning to spell*. Newark, DE: International Reading Association.

Hiebert, E. H. (1981) 'Developmental patterns and interrelationships of preschool children's print awareness'. *Reading Research Quarterly*, **16**, 236–260.

Hildreth, G. (1932) 'The success of young children in letter and number construction'. *Child Development*, **3**, 1–14.

Hildreth, G. (1936) 'Developmental sequences in name writing'. *Child Development*, **7**, 291–303.

Mathews, M. M. (1966) *Teaching to read: Historically considered*. Chicago. IL: University of Chicago Press.

Read, C. (1970) Children's perceptions of the sounds of English: Phonology from three to six. Unpublished doctoral dissertation. Harvard University, Boston, MA.

Simmer, M. L. (1981, April) 'Printing errors in kindergarten and the prediction of academic performance'. Paper presented at the Biennial Meeting of the Society for Research in Child Development, Boston, MA.

Sulzby, E. (1985a) 'Children's emergent reading of favorite storybooks: A developmental study'. *Reading Research Quarterly*, **20**, 458–481.

Sulzby, E. (1985b) 'Kindergartens as writers and readers'. In M. Farr (Ed.). *Advances in writing research, Vol. 1: Children's early writing development*. Norwood. NJ: Ablex.

Index

DATE DUE

OCT 25 2001	
DEC 1 5 2002